The EDUCATOR'S HANDBOOK for

Understanding
and Closing
Achievement
Gaps

To state-based colleagues from the Wallace Foundation who
allowed me to leave a policy fingerprint or two on the field of educational leadership.

The EDUCATOR'S HANDBOOK for

Understanding
and Closing
Achievement
Gaps

JOSEPH MURPHY

CORWIN
A SAGE Company

For information:

Corwin
A SAGE Company
2455 Teller Road
Thousand Oaks, California 91320
(800) 233–9936
Fax: (800) 417–2466
www.corwinpress.com

SAGE Ltd.
1 Oliver's Yard
55 City Road
London EC1Y 1SP
United Kingdom

SAGE India Pvt. Ltd.
B 1/I 1 Mohan Cooperative
    Industrial Area
Mathura Road, New Delhi 110 044
India

SAGE Asia-Pacific Pte. Ltd.
33 Pekin Street #02-01
Far East Square
Singapore 048763

Printed in the United States of America.

Library of Congress Cataloging-in-Publication Data

Murphy, Joseph F.
The educator's handbook for understanding and closing achievement gaps/Joseph F. Murphy.
    p. cm.
Includes bibliographical references and index.
ISBN 978-1-4129-6454-8 (cloth)
ISBN 978-1-4129-6455-5 (pbk.)
    1. Academic achievement. 2. Educational change. I. Title.

LB1062.6.M87 2010
371.2′07—dc22   2009035695

This book is printed on acid-free paper.

09   10   11   12   13   10   9   8   7   6   5   4   3   2   1

Acquisitions Editor:	Hudson Perigo
Associate Editor:	Julie McNall
Editorial Assistant:	Brett Ory
Production Editor:	Eric Garner
Copy Editor:	Gretchen Treadwell
Typesetter:	C&M Digitals (P) Ltd.
Proofreader:	Joyce Li
Indexer:	Jean Casalegno
Cover Designer:	Scott Van Atta
Graphic Designer:	Rose Storey

Contents

About the Author   vii

PART I. BACKGROUND   1

1. **Bringing Achievement Gaps Into Focus**   3
   Setting the Stage   3
   The Importance of the Problem   5
   Defining the Achievement Gap   9
   Cautions for the Voyage   10
   Conclusion   21

2. **Portraying and Tracking Achievement Gaps**   23
   Coby V. Meyers

   Tracking the Gaps   24
   Looking at the Gap Across Levels   67
   Conclusion   74

**PART II. GRINDING UP HOPE: EXPLAINING THE DEVELOPMENT
AND PERSISTENCE OF ACHIEVEMENT GAPS**   77

     Introduction   77

3. **Environmental Causes of Achievement Gaps: An Introduction**   83

4. **Environmental Causes of Achievement Gaps: Socioeconomic Status**   87
   Family Occupation and Educational Backgrounds   88
   Family Income and Wealth   91
   Conclusion   98

5. **Environmental Causes of Achievement Gaps: Family Environment**   99
   Family Structural Characteristics   101
   Family Home Environment   104
   Conclusion   121

6. **Environmental Causes of Achievement Gaps: Community,
   Racism, and Individual Differences** **123**
   Community 123
   Racism and Discrimination 127
   Individual Differences: Genetics and Ability 131
   Conclusion 134

7. **Environmental Causes of Achievement Gaps:
   Out-of-School Learning Experiences** **135**
   Education Before Kindergarten: Readiness 136
   Educational Opportunities in the Summer 140
   Conclusion 145

8. **Schooling Causes of the Achievement Gap: The Instructional Program** **147**
   Introduction 147
   Teachers and Teaching 151
   Curricular Courses of Study 164
   Conclusion 177

9. **Schooling Causes of the Achievement Gap:
   School Culture, Structure, and Support** **179**
   School Culture 180
   Structure and Support 189
   Conclusion 203

**PART III. OPENING THE DOORS OF POSSIBILITY:
STRATEGIES FOR CLOSING ACHIEVEMENT GAPS** **205**
   Introduction 205

10. **Closing Achievement Gaps: Focusing on the Social
    and Economic Environment** **209**
    Improving the Economic and Social Conditions of Low-Income Families 212
    Compensating for the Conditions of Poverty and Discrimination 214
    Conclusion 230

11. **Closing Achievement Gaps: A Focus on Schooling** **231**
    Introduction 231
    General Rules of Engagement 233
    Gap Closing Strategies 237
    Conclusion 269

References **271**

Index **287**

About the Author

Joseph Murphy is the Frank W. Mayborn Chair and associate dean at Vanderbilt's Peabody College of Education. He has also been a faculty member at the University of Illinois and The Ohio State University, where he was the William Ray Flesher Professor of Education.

In the public schools, he has served as an administrator at the school, district, and state levels, including an appointment as the executive assistant to the chief deputy superintendent of public instruction in California. His most recent appointment was as the founding president of the Ohio Principals Leadership Academy. At the university level, he has served as department chair and associate dean.

He is past vice president of the American Educational Research Association and was the founding chair of the Interstate School Leaders Licensure Consortium (ISLLC). He is coeditor of the AERA *Handbook on Educational Administration* (1999) and editor of the National Society for the Study of Education (NSSE) yearbook, *The Educational Leadership Challenge* (2002).

His work is in the area of school improvement, with special emphasis on leadership and policy. He has authored or coauthored eighteen books in this area and edited another twelve. His most recent authored volumes include *Understanding and Assessing the Charter School Movement* (2002), *Leadership for Literacy: Research-Based Practice, PreK–3* (2003), *Connecting Teacher Leadership and School Improvement* (2005), *Preparing School Leaders: Defining a Research and Action Agenda* (2006), and *Turning Around Failing Schools: Lessons From the Organizational Sciences* (2008).

One of the most perplexing questions in debates about education policy in the United States concerns the so-called race gap in student achievement scores. (Bali & Alvarez, 2003, p. 485)

The persistence of the gap and the slow rate at which it is decreasing indicate the need for a careful rethinking of the problem in order to establish effective research-based intervention strategies aimed at reducing and eventually eliminating the gap. (Norman, Ault, Bentz, & Meskimen, 2001, p. 1104)

The achievement gap is real, the achievement gap is complex, the achievement gap is stubborn; we—educators and families—must be just as stubborn and diligent in our efforts to eliminate the gap. (For, Grantham, & Whiting, 2008, p. 236)

If life chances depend so heavily on education, it is important that educational inequalities be redressed so as to equalize opportunities in a democratic society. (Levin, Belfield, Muenning, & Rouse, 2007, p. 2)

———————— ✖ ✖ ✖ ————————

Achieving success in this area helps ensure that America's democratic institutions are in the hands of an informed citizenry, that its economy has a work force that can "think for a living," and that its society is just, inclusive, humane, and reasonably harmonious. (Miller, 1995, p. 379)

———————— ✖ ✖ ✖ ————————

PART I

BACKGROUND

1

Bringing Achievement Gaps Into Focus

America is a diverse society in which educational differences have the potential to become a progressively larger source of inequality and social conflict. Many people now recognize that eliminating these differences has become a moral and pragmatic imperative. (Miller, 1995, pp. 1–2)

Beyond policy mandates, however, there is a moral mandate. A good education, one that overcomes the burdens on children of racial discrimination and poverty, is the hope of every parent in schools where too many children are failing. (Lewis, 2008, p. xi)

SETTING THE STAGE

The term "achievement gap" is used to describe differences in learning among specified groups of students (Reynolds, 2002). More specifically, it refers to differences in academic achievement between socioeconomically advantaged and white and Asian students, and their minority and socioeconomically disadvantaged peers (Symonds, 2004). It is also widely used to capture efforts to reduce these learning differentials (Bingham, 1994; North Carolina State Department of Education, 2000).

The achievement of minority students represents a long-standing issue in the field of education. Across the U.S., white students and students from wealthy, well-educated

*families have consistently outperformed students from most other ethnic back-
grounds and students from impoverished families on virtually every indicator of
academic achievement in the host of studies that have addressed this issue. The term
"achievement gap" is often used to refer to this phenomenon. (North Carolina State
Department of Education, 2000, p. 4)*

While the achievement gap represents "a long standing issue in the field of education"
(North Carolina, 2000, p. 4) and while analysts have taken notice of differences in achievement between youngsters from different races, cultures, and levels on the economic ladder for
some time (Hedges & Nowell, 1999; Meehan, Cowley, Schumacher, Hauser, & Croom, 2003),
the achievement gap problem did not begin to generate concerted attention in the United
States until the mid-1960s. Or, as Miller (1995) reports, "Substantial societal interest in identifying, understanding, and attempting to eliminate variations in educational attainment and
achievement patterns among racial/ethnic groups is a very recent phenomenon" (p. 85). In a
broad sense, the civil rights and Great Society movements directed interest to disparities in
learning opportunities and outcomes for minority and low-income youngsters. In addition,
the achievement gap problem was propelled onto the school-reform stage with the publication of important research studies conducted during these movements. Noteworthy here are
the studies of inequality by Coleman and his colleagues (1966) and by Jencks and his research
associates (1972). Also important were the development of more refined methodologies to
study achievement gaps, especially the introduction of large-scale surveys that employed
nationally representative samples (Hedges & Nowell, 1999).

More recently, especially over the last decade, the spotlight has been focused even more
directly and more brightly on achievement gaps. Indeed, it is accurate to assert that the issue
of learning disparities among groups of students has moved onto center stage in society in
general and in the education industry in particular (Hertert & Teague, 2003). As Kober (2001)
has observed, "Racial/ethnic gaps in test performance have long been observed and debated,
but recent trends in education, demographics, and the economy have made the achievement
gap a high priority issue" (p. 15).

If the first wave of attention in the 1960s and 1970s was driven by a sense that addressing
the gap problem was the right thing to do for children, the current second wave of attention is
also rooted in a sense of the necessity of action. This necessity is for the well-being of the
nation in a postindustrial economy and a twenty-first-century society. As the subsequent discussion illustrates, the costs of failure to confront the gap problem are larger and more noticeable today than they were forty years ago (Alvermann, 2005; Ferguson, 2002). Concomitantly,
the threads of accountability are much more visible in the educational tapestry today than they
were during the 1960s and 1970s (Murphy, 2006), thus pushing educators to assume ownership for problems that could have been simply attributed to others in the past.

For all of these reasons, addressing achievement gaps—which includes an understanding of the problem, an analysis of its root causes, and an investigation of potential solutions
(Miller, 1995)—has assumed an unparalleled position of concern, a heightened sense of
seriousness, and a palpable sense of urging in America at the dawn of the twenty-first century (Becker & Luthar, 2002; Bennett et al., 2007; Braun, Wang, Jenkins, & Weinbaum, 2006;
Chatterji, 2006; Ford, Grantham, & Whiting, 2008; Shannon & Bylsma, 2002). Indeed, it is
routinely suggested these days that gaps in academic achievement between minority and

majority students and higher-income and lower-income youngsters represent the most significant educational problem in the United States (Slavin & Madden, 2001; 2006) as well as "the most critical problem facing . . . continued economic development" (McGee, 2003, p. 64) in the nation in general and the major dilemma for urban education in particular (Norman, Ault, Bentz, & Meskimen, 2001). It is now at the "forefront of the debate over public education" (Symonds, 2004, p. 5).

In the balance of this introductory chapter, we undertake three assignments. We investigate the importance of achievement gaps for individuals and for society. We explore definitions of the achievement gap. We also outline important cautions readers need to carry with them as they travel through this volume in particular, and as they think about achievement gap issues generally.

THE IMPORTANCE OF THE PROBLEM

The gaps . . . are enormously costly for minorities as well as for society as a whole. (Miller, 1995, p. 83)

Racial equality is still a dream—and will remain a dream as long as blacks learn less in school than whites and Asians. (Thernstrom & Thernstrom, 2002, p. 131)

As noted above, acknowledgment of, and demands for, action on the achievement gap have grown as the consequences of the problem have come into sharper relief over the last dozen years and as the depth of the problem—its pervasiveness and resistance to change (Ford, Grantham, & Whiting, 2008)—threatens to overwhelm schools. The importance of the problem and the urgency for action are amplified by the fact that the economic, social, and political infrastructure of the nation is being transformed in ways that magnify the consequences of inequalities inherent in patterned achievement differentials by race and class. In terms of "consequences," we are discovering that the achievement gap problem imposes tremendous costs on both individuals and society at large (Becker & Luthar, 2002; McGee, 2003; Schwartz, 2001): "The persistence of achievement gaps has both immediate and long-term consequences, not only for students . . . but also for the economic and social well-being of a state" (Spradlin et al., 2005, p. 2).

Cost to Individuals

It is widely recognized that these differences in educational outcomes contribute to large disparities in life chances. Viewed solely from the perspective of employment and earnings, educationally underrepresented minorities have much less opportunity to pursue well-paying professional careers and are much more likely to hold low-wage jobs that provide few chances for advancement. (Miller, 1995, p. 1)

While it is true that eliminating the black-white test score gap would not eliminate the black-white earnings gap, the effect would surely be substantial. (Jencks & Phillips, 1998, p. 46)

According to scholars from a wide array of disciplines, "Disparities in test scores are troubling not only for the underlying educational inequalities that they suggest but also because of the link between performance on tests and outcomes later in life" (Stiefel, Schwartz, & Ellen, 2006, p. 7). The argument in play is (1) that gaps "tilt the playing field precipitously" (McGee, 2003, p. 7) and negatively for many low-income and minority students; gaps are about "opportunities that some students will have and others never will" (p. 13) and (2) "similar achievement outcomes will lead to more equitable access to future education and jobs as well as a better quality of life" (Chatterji, 2005b, p. 48).

Achievement gaps are seen as significant contributors to opportunity structure (Hedges & Nowell, 1999) and to the educational attainment, employment opportunities, and wages of individuals (Hedges & Nowell, 1999; McGee, 2003; Stiefel, Schwartz, & Ellen, 2006; Toenjes, Dworkin, Lorence, & Hill, 2002). Achievement differences reflected in gaps "hold severe consequences for life trajectories" (Seiler & Elmesky, 2007, p. 394); they "translate directly into differences in high school graduation rates . . . and in income and socioeconomic status" (Slavin & Madden, 2001, p. 4): "These differences have dire consequences once students leave school. Black and Hispanics are much less likely than whites to graduate from high school, acquire a college or advanced degree, or earn a living that places them in the middle class" (Chubb & Loveless, 2002, p. 1). According to scholars who study this area, because of the increasing importance of education in the postindustrial world (Ferguson, 1991; Kosters & Mast, 2003; Marshall & Tucker, 1992; Murnane & Levy, 1996) and because income and class are becoming "increasingly determined by educational success, the gap in achievement has shifted from being an indicator of educational inequality to being a direct cause of socioeconomic inequity" (Harris & Herrington, 2006, p. 210).

For minority and low-income students, achievement gaps are linked to increased risks of falling behind (Neuman & Celano, 2006, p. 179), and significant struggles as one moves into higher grades in the K–12 system (McGee, 2003); higher dropout rates (Balfanz & Byrnes, 2006; Land & Legters, 2002; Natriello, McDill, & Pallas, 1990); lower college attendance (Orr, 2003); higher enrollment in lower-ranked universities (Dabady, 2003; Orr, 2003), and lower college graduation rates (Slavin & Madden, 2006; U.S. Commission, 2004)—to reduced opportunities for higher education across the board (Lee, 2002).

Not unexpectedly, employment opportunities for youngsters on the wrong side of the achievement gap are truncated, leading to quite different and more limited career paths (Maruyama, 2003; McGee, 2003; Miller, 1995; Roscigno, 1998). Given the storyline of reduced career opportunities and a narrowed employment vista, it will come as no surprise to learn that low-achieving students earn less than their higher-achieving peers when they enter the workforce (Ceci & Papierno, 2005; Hedges & Nowell, 1999; Johnson & Neal, 1998; Velez, 1989): "People with higher scores tend to have higher earnings.... Disparities in reading and math achievement, as measured by test scores, explain a larger share of the differences between the races in average weekly earnings for young adult males" (Ferguson, 1991, pp. 1, 20). More troubling still, as Clotfelter, Ladd, and Vigdor (2005) document, the gap in scores today "explains a larger percentage of the income gap between the races than it did in the 1960s" (p. 377). Or, seen from a different angle, "A test score gap of a given size involves a greater cost today than was the case in the past" (Murnane & Levy, 2004, p. 402). The takeaway message here is quite clear; reducing test-score differentials is an important dimension of eliminating inequalities in earnings (Fryer & Levitt, 2004).

Costs to Society

The achievement gaps are so wide that they threaten the well-being of the state and its economy. (Gandara, Rumberger, Maxwell-Jolly, & Callahan, 2003, p. 3)

Thus, on economic grounds, anything that can be done to prevent school failure from occurring (or to remediate it quickly after the first signs appear) seems like a rational economic choice. (Ceci & Papierno, 2005, p. 150)

In addition to having a negative impact on individuals, the achievement gap also has profound implications for the larger society (Kober, 2001; Slavin & Madden, 2001). For example, analysts routinely demonstrate that "the magnitude and persistence of [achievement] disparities is rightly regarded as problematic both for our long-run economic competitiveness and the health of our democracy" (Braun, Wang, Jenkins, & Weinbaum, 2006, p. 7) and for social cohesiveness in the nation (Kober, 2001; Miller, 1995). In short, it "will help shape the future of the country" (Becker & Luthar, 2002, p. 209). According to Miller (1995):

If these disparities are allowed to continue, the United States inevitably will suffer a compromised quality of life and a lower standard of living. Social conflict will intensify. Our ability to compete in world markets will decline, our domestic economy will falter, our national security will be endangered. (p. 2)

On the other side of the ledger, closing achievement gaps, in part or whole, will have "beneficial effects on social and economic mobility" (Kosters & Mast, 2003, p. 96). Thus:

Among the most compelling reasons for seeking to eliminate these gaps as soon as possible are the following: (1) the achievement of significantly higher minority education levels is essential to the long-term productivity and competitiveness of the U.S. economy; (2) if minorities are to enjoy the full benefits of their recently won civil rights, they need formal-education-dependent knowledge and skills much closer in quantity and quality to those held by whites; and (3) the maintenance of a humane and harmonious society depends to a considerable degree on minorities' reaching educational parity with whites. (Miller, 1995, p. 4)

On one front, educational equality via a leveling of the achievement playing field is held to be a necessary factor in "the development and maintenance of a just, socially stable America" (Miller, 1995, p. 12), including reduced crime (Levin, Belfield, Muenning, & Rouse, 2007) and a drop in the social differences and conflicts that amplify racial tensions in the country (Chubb & Loveless, 2002), and as an avenue for "building strong cultural bridges between groups" (Miller, 1995, p. 380). Indeed, Jencks and Phillips (1998) contend that "reducing the black-white test score gap would probably do more to promote [racial equality] than any other strategy that commands broad political support" (p. 45).

On the economic front, analysts connect education in general and academic achievement specifically to the financial health of the nation (Hanushek & Raymond, 2005; Levin et al., 2007). They have established that achievement gaps act as a "growing impediment to U.S.

productivity performance" (Baumol, Blackman, & Wolff, as cited in Miller, 1995, p. 8; Maruyama, 2003) and that they are responsible for the "declining economic health of the United States" (Miller, 1995, p. 5). These scholars have also documented that efforts to strengthen the education of those on the wrong side of the achievement gap can be viewed "as a public investment that yields benefits in excess of investment costs" (Levin et al., 2007, p. 2).

Finally, attacking the achievement gap is important for the larger society because it is a required step in providing citizens with "the knowledge and skills necessary to exercise their legal rights effectively" (Miller, 1995, p. 10). Analysts here discern "a strong link between educational performance and the capacity of minority groups to climb all rungs of the intergenerational advancement ladder" (p. 11). They assert:

> The relatively low educational achievement and attainment levels of economically disadvantaged children and students of color are fundamentally in conflict with core principles underlying public education . . . namely, that public schools should be avenues of opportunity for children, and that children should attend schools where they all have chances of succeeding through hard work. (Maruyama, 2003, p. 655)

Context Amplifying Importance

> The demographic shift is almost certain to continue to be a powerful underlying rationale for accelerating the educational advancement of minorities for years to come. (Miller, 1995, pp. 23–24)

The answer to the following question is important for school leaders and educational policy makers alike: The achievement gap is as old as our educational system; why is it that it has only risen to the top of the reform agenda in the last dozen years? That is, as noted briefly above, "importance," "seriousness," and "urgency" are descriptors newly attached to racial and class learning gaps. What forces are in play that transformed achievement gaps into a matter of national concern? The answer can be traced, to a major extent, to the changing context in which the business of schooling exists. More specifically, economic and social forces, and movements in the larger world around education, have combined to recalibrate the value of low-achieving youngsters and to push the schooling industry to address problems that were allowed to lay fallow in the past.

Let us start with economic forces. As society has moved from a primarily industrial-based economy to a postindustrial economy, new expectations and requirements have been placed on schools (Marshall & Tucker, 1992; Murnane & Levy, 1996; 2004). Academic performance expectations have been ratcheted up across the board. Schools are being asked to help youngsters reach dramatically higher skill levels than was the case only a generation ago—something akin to a doubling of productivity. Equally important here, economic forces are pushing schools to ensure that all students, most particularly those on the wrong side of the achievement gap, reach these ambitious performance targets.

The evolution to a postindustrial, global economy has not only ushered in advanced performance expectations, it has also helped create a focus on outcomes and accountability that was largely absent for most of the twentieth century. In short, schools are being required to account for their effectiveness in ways that were not required for most of their history (Chatterji, 2005a; Stiefel, Schwartz, & Ellen, 2006). Perhaps the best example of this accountability in action are "the mandates of the federal Elementary and Secondary Education Act of 2001 (ESEA) regarding identifying and eliminating disparities in student achievement" (Shannon & Bylsma, 2002, p. 10), and the No Child Left Behind Act (Meehan et al., 2003; Rouse, Brooks-Gunn, & McLanahan, 2005). Chatterji (2005a) explains:

> The passage of the No Child Left Behind (NCLB) Act of 2001 has drawn attention to achievement differentials in diverse U.S. students, commonly referred to as the "achievement gap." By law, public schools are now held accountable for equitable achievement outcomes in subgroups of minority versus non-minority, normally achieving versus exceptional, as well as socioeconomically advantaged versus disadvantaged students (P.L. 107–110, Stat. 1425, 2002). As a consequence of such school reform legislation, disparities among children's mathematics achievement as well as factors that influence the observed differences, are now of central concern to researchers, practitioners, policy-makers, and the public alike. (p. 2)

The other upshot of the changing economy is that there is no longer a home in the economy for large numbers of students who do not perform well in school. As Miller (1995) cautions, the economic-opportunity structure for low income and minority students with limited schooling and low-level skills is bleak. And as we described above, the consequences for these youngsters are often tragic. In the new economy, the importance of education has become much more pronounced (Levin et al., 2007) and in the process, the spotlight has been directed for the first time on those groups of students who historically have not been well educated. Under the new economy and new accountability landscape, "The achievement gap has become a critical indicator of the efficacy of the educational system" (Braun et al., 2006, p. 5) for the first time.

Emerging social forces, many linked to economic factors, also are causing society and its educational institutions to underscore the significance of achievement gaps and to attend more proactively to the schooling of low-income and minority students. Most noticeable on this front is the fact that the social consequences that accompany achievement gaps become more visible (1) as the economic divide between the haves and have not widens and (2) as the social fabric of the nation is rewoven by dramatic increases in minority populations (Bempechat, 1992; Cole-Henderson, 2000; Uhlenberg & Brown, 2002). In 1970, African American and Hispanic students made up about 15 percent of the children in U.S. public schools. By 2000, they constituted 30 percent of the school-age population (Kober, 2001). By 2020, they will account for 46 percent of the school population (Miller, 1995). The result is:

> American society has a compelling interest in seeing to it that those minority groups, which have long been disadvantaged educationally, increase their academic skills rapidly enough to ensure that, as their share of the population rises, the average skill level of the population as a whole does not decline. (Miller, 1995, p. 82)

DEFINING THE ACHIEVEMENT GAP

While isolating the causes of the achievement gap is often difficult and complex work, defining the problem is rather straightforward. The achievement gap refers to patterned differences in learning and attainment outcomes between groups of students. Norm-referenced and criterion-referenced standardized test scores are the learning outcomes most commonly seen in discussions of achievement gaps. Other measures of academic performance, such as end-of-course examinations and grades, are also used to compute achievement gaps. In the domain of attainment, one often sees measures such as graduation from high school (or dropout rates), matriculation to college, and college completion. To measure gaps, students are clustered into identifiable groups—by race, ethnicity, gender, class, and special learning needs designations. The most studied achievement gap to date is between white students and African American students.

Gaps are defined in many ways in the research literature, with three predominating and with one of those dominating the narrative. The key difference between them revolves around the comparison criterion underscored and the achievement matrix employed. Infrequently used but quite useful are assessments of whether targeted students (e.g., children from low-income homes) gain more in a grade than the time spent there (Balfanz & Byrnes, 2006). Under this design, if a student gained 1.3 years in reading during the 1.0 year spent in the fourth grade, the gap would be said to be closing. The comparison criterion here is expected growth and the achievement matrix—the focus—is *value-added learning*.

While Shannon and Bylsma (2002) help explain how "the gap is usually defined in terms of the difference in academic performance on tests among identified groups, the gap can also be defined as the difference between how a group performs as compared to what is expected of it" (p. 11). Here we are "concerned not with differences in average levels but with the percent of students who do not demonstrate acceptable levels" (Hoerandner & Lemke, 2006, p. 2). Under this design, if 25 percent of African American students were expected to score in the top category (e.g., distinguished) and only 17 percent did so, it would be noted that a gap exists. The comparison criterion here is predefined proficiency, and the focus—the achievement matrix—is *level of achievement*.

Third, and by far most common, it is held that "An achievement gap exists when there is a gap in academic skills across identifiable groups of students, such as whites and blacks" (Hoerandner & Lemke, 2006, p. 3). Under this design, if low-income students scored 4.6 in mathematics at the end of fourth grade and higher-income students scored 5.4, we would say a gap exists. If at the end of the fifth grade, low-income students scored 5.8 in mathematics while higher-income students scored 6.4, we would say that the gap is closing, from .8 to .6 grade-level equivalents. Note that the distribution of scores between groups is spotlighted in this third approach (Hedges & Nowell, 1999; Shannon & Bylsma, 2002). The comparison criterion here is the growth of the other group (e.g., high-income students) and the matrix—the focus—is *equity in achievement*.

CAUTIONS FOR THE VOYAGE

One should take care not to draw conclusions about individuals from group averages or to invoke stereotypes. Many African American . . . students perform at very high levels. Indeed, the full range of achievement, from high to low, occurs in all subgroups. (Kober, 2001, p. 17)

Attempts to improve efficiency of the regular school day (e.g., lowering class size) may be beneficial, but, unless they are withheld from higher-achievement students, they may benefit all students in a way that does not close gaps. (Davison, Young, Davenport, Butterbaugh, & Davison, 2004, p. 761)

It is possible for two investigators to examine identical racial data and draw opposite conclusions about whether the status of blacks improved or deteriorated, depending on whether they focus on relative or absolute changes. (Farley, 1984, p. 13)

At first blush, strategizing about closing the achievement gap at a broad level seems fairly straightforward, a difficult task to accomplish to be sure but not an especially complex one to conceptualize. The differences in scores between group A (say low-income students) and group B (say middle-to-high income students) needs to decline, with the goal of arriving at the point where the scores between the two groups are equivalent. As we peer more deeply into the matter, however, we find that achievement gap work is a good deal more complex, more multifaceted, and more nuanced than it appears at first.

Indeed, a host of issues, beginning with decisions about the types of measures to use to chart the gap, carrying through to ways to measure and interpret scores, and ending up with questions about the effectiveness of varying gap reduction strategies belie the "straightforward" tag that just seemed so appealing. While it is not essential that educational leaders study each theme in the achievement gap narrative of caveats, it is important that they become familiar with the central cautions that need attention as the work of closing achievement gaps unfolds. In this section, we discuss the key warning signs to which leaders would do well to attend. We begin with some concerns about the measures employed to generate gap data, present some cautions about the interpretation of those data, analyze warning signs associated with efforts to close gaps, and explore concerns about outcomes of gap closing strategies.

Cautions About Understanding the Data

It is not clear from the data what policies should be pursued to mitigate the effects of group differences in the distribution of test scores. (Hedges & Nowell, 1999, p. 131)

One point worth noting at the start is that achievement gap data are enmeshed in larger sets of data on student learning. They provide one way to think about achievement. At the same time, as Kober (2001) correctly observes:

The existence of an achievement gap does not mean that student achievement is declining or that schools are getting worse. Some political leaders and analysts incorrectly point to the gap as an indicator that schools are failing. The fact is, U.S. students as a whole are performing better on key tests than they did thirty years ago, especially in mathematics. Every racial/ethnic subgroup has made gains in achievement during the past twenty-five to thirty years. (p. 10)

Concomitantly, it is instructive to place gap data in a larger historical context:

It is important to remember not only that these gaps were much larger only a few decades ago, but that our society did not begin to organize itself in a substantial way to eliminate them until the middle 1960s. That was a time when no nation in the world possessed an extensive body of research-proven strategies for modifying educational systems and practices that could quickly raise the academic achievement of students from extremely disadvantaged or undereducated segments of society to the levels of the most educationally successful groups. (Miller, 1995, pp. 12–13)

In the last section, we provided a number of ways to calculate achievement gaps. We also reported that standardized achievement tests are the overwhelming measure of choice used to portray learning differentials. While there are advantages to using standardized tests, there are disadvantages as well, limitations that "remind one that standardized test data must be interpreted with caution" (Miller, 1995, p. 46), especially when it comes to the topic of achievement gaps. Because "standardized tests themselves can give inaccurate and sometimes even misleading information about the performance of students in the academic areas that tests are supposed to measure . . . the information that standardized tests give about the academic achievement gap is not fully reliable" (Rothstein, 2004, p. 85). "Indeed, the measures of achievement that underscore the gap . . . merit skeptical scrutiny" (Norman et al., 2001, p. 1111). As we stand at the dawn of the twenty-first century:

Nearly all of our theories and explanations of the achievement gap are based on correlations, cross-sections, and/or national- or state-level comparisons many levels removed from classroom teaching and learning. As a result, many of our insights are based on mean or average levels of group performance rather than on close analysis of individual- or classroom-level achievement growth patterns. (Balfanz & Byrnes, 2006, p. 145)

In a related vein, it is instructive to note that the size of achievement gaps will vary "according to which test is used [and] which subjects, ages, and time periods are examined" (Kober, 2001, p. 17) and which company's examination is selected (Rothstein, 2004). Also, while it is not the norm in the area of state and national tests, it makes more sense for leaders to examine cohorts of students rather than simply rely on trend data (Kober, 2001). That is, the better question to ask is not how well ninth graders perform in 2010 versus how other ninth graders performed in 2005, but rather how do students entering school in a given year perform over their school career; what are the gaps for these students as first graders, fifth graders, ninth graders, and so on? Even here, it is important for educators to remember that the data show patterns, "but they give limited or no information on the reasons for the patterns" (Chatterji, 2005b, p. 62).

Cautions About Interpreting the Data

Presenting the average scores of students by broad, socially constructed racial and ethnic categorizations obscures considerable diversity within these groups. (Magnuson & Duncan, 2006, p. 367)

While the phrase "children who grow up in poverty" appears to convey a certain uniformity, this is far from the case; these children are an incredibly diverse group. (Knapp, 2001, p. 176)

If the gap were to remain because all children improved, that too would be quite acceptable. (Ferguson, 1998b, 368)

There are also important cautions that leaders need to keep front and center as they interpret achievement gap data. We examine the most important of these warnings below.

Differences Within Subgroups

One of the most critical issues is to remember that even when tests scores are disaggregated by groups (e.g., white vs. African American), these subgroup scores themselves mask differences. One part of the problem surfaces because there are often distinctive subgroups within racial and ethnic groupings. Or, as Bainbridge and Lasley (2002) note: "Each racial group is far from homogeneous in itself" (p. 425). For example, Shannon and Bylsma (2002) reveal that while the subgroup "Asian students" generally has achievement equal to or higher than white students, for some groups of Asian students (i.e., those from particular cultures and nations), there are significant achievement gaps. Miller (1995) makes the same point for Asian students using attainment data when he documents that education patterns varied dramatically within this highly diverse group. For example:

> Japanese Americans had high school and college completion rates of 82 percent and 26 percent, respectively, while the comparable rates were 31 percent and 6 percent for Laotians, 71 percent and 37 percent for Chinese, 22 percent and 3 percent for Hmong, 80 percent and 52 percent for Asian Indians, and 62 percent and 13 percent for Vietnamese. Among the Pacific Islanders, Native Hawaiians had high school and college completion rates of 69 percent and 10 percent, while the comparable rates were 47 percent and 11 percent for Melanesians and 61 percent and 7 percent for Samoans. (pp. 33–34)

Farley (1984) makes a similar point in regard to the African American population. Drawing on the scholarship of Moynihan and Wilson, he shows that there are different African American populations that correspond to economic status. And finally, Natriello and his colleagues (1990) unpack the myth of homogeneity among the Hispanic population. They reveal that there are significant "social and economic differences among the Hispanic subgroups" (p. 19), including Puerto Rican, Cuban, and Central and South American Hispanics. They maintain these differences "point to the diversity in the Hispanic population" (p. 20). The message for leaders is that differences within subgroups are lost when disaggregation stops at the currently used designations. School leaders are advised to peer more deeply into gap scores and to be more thoughtful about how they interpret gap-related data.

Second, and equally problematic, is the tendency to lump disaggregated groups together, e.g., treating African American and Hispanic children under the broader rubric of minority students (Natriello, McDill, & Pallas, 1990). Obviously, all the problems listed above arise here as well. Equally important, there is evidence that in some cases different gap-reduction strategies are more appropriate for one group than another. The lumping phenomenon negates the possibility of using this knowledge effectively.

Third, even if one were to uncover all the appropriate subgroups within the various gap classifications, the use of subgroups still masks the condition of individual students (U.S. Commission, 2004). While "almost everyone would agree that these categories are useful for discussing the needs of groups of children, they are less than precise means for characterizing the educational fate of individual children" (Natriello, McDill, & Pallas, 1990, p. 14). The "use of averages obscures considerable variation in skills within each of the racial and ethnic groups" (Magnuson & Duncan, 2006, p. 368) and within the subgroups within each classification (e.g., Puerto Rican vs. Cuban). Thus, "aggregated averages by group . . . hide important data about the performance of students" (Shannon & Bylsma, 2002, p. 14). As the U.S. Commission (2004) reminds us, "Not all Asian American students are high achievers; just as not all African American . . . students are academic underachievers" (p. 2). According to Beckford and Cooley (1993), in addition to understanding variations among groups, leaders need to pay attention to "the extensive overlap of distributions" (p. 8). There are low- and high-achieving youngsters in all groups (Beckford & Cooley, 1993; Magnuson & Duncan, 2006). Lee, Magnuson, and Duncan (2004) put the issue in concrete terms as follows:

> *Making a generalization based on the average racial achievement gaps can be misleading, as within-group variability in achievement is much greater than between-groups variability. According to the 1999 long-term trend NAEP math results, the average national Black-White gap is about 31 points, whereas the gap between high-performing (2 standard deviations above the mean) and low-performing (2 standard deviations below the mean) students of the same race (both Blacks and Whites) amount to 112 points. About 15 percent of Black students perform better than an average White student. (p. 64)*

> *The use of averages obscures considerable variation in skills within each of the racial and ethnic groups. Although the average gap in math achievement between white and black kindergartners in the ECLS-K was two-thirds of a standard deviation, nearly one-quarter of black children outscored the typical (median) white student in reading achievement. (Magnuson & Duncan, 2006, p. 367)*

The central caution on this third point is as follows: equity in learning in the achievement gap literature is defined in terms of groups rather than in terms of individuals. While this group definition of equity is critical, equally important is the reality that equity must be determined one student at a time.

Understanding Measures of Learning

A second caution in the area of data interpretation focuses on the truncated understanding of "success" found in the bulk of the achievement gap literature. As introduced above, work with achievement gaps highlights one measure of success, equity in the distribution of achievement scores and attainment levels. Because schools that "serve as equalizers may not be comforting to all [learners]" (Downey, von Hippel, & Broh, 2004, p. 633), they would do well to adopt a broader definition of success (Murphy, Hallinger, & Peterson, 1986)—one that includes "equity" but also incorporates information on achievement "levels" and "value added" to achievement (see Murphy, Hallinger, & Peterson, 1986; also Baenen, Dulaney, Yamen, & Banks, 2002; Downey, von Hippel, & Broh, 2004). In short, not all gap reductions are equal.

On the issue of achievement "level," Lee (2004) provides a critical insight when he concludes that, "no matter how much the relative achievement gap among different racial and social groups has been narrowed, some disadvantaged minority students' performance level still may not be acceptable" (p. 61). Magnuson and Duncan (2006) apply the same logic when they observe that:

Interventions can be designed to improve black (and/or white) children's relative skills and absolute levels of academic skills at differing points in the skill distribution. However, it is not immediately obvious which is more detrimental to blacks and to society in general—lower levels of achievement among black children or lower achievement of black as compared with white children. (p. 388)

On the "value added" dimension of success, the critical issue is what gains over time are attributable to the school. As we illustrate in Figure 1.1, schools sometimes: (1) are given credit for high levels of student learning for which they may not be responsible (e.g., a fourth-grade student who starts the year at 7.2 grade-level equivalents in reading and exits at 7.9 grade-level equivalents looks very strong in terms of level, but the school has not contributed much to that success, at least not in the fourth grade) and (2) are blamed for gaps not under their control (increasing gaps because of higher summer gains for white than for African American youngsters).

Figure 1.1   Equity, Level, and Value-Added Dimensions of Achievement Gaps

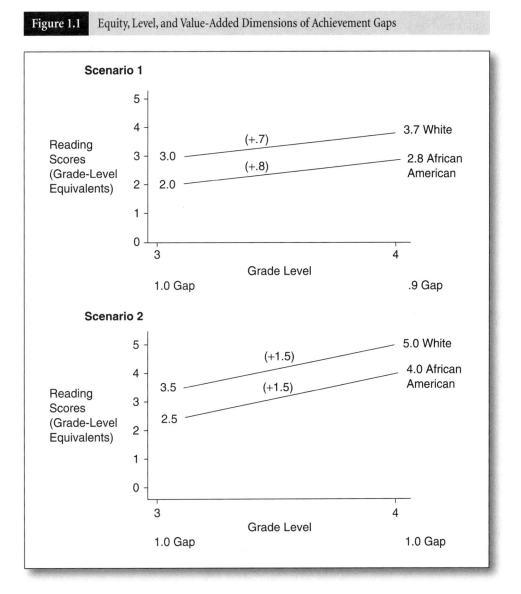

Figure 1.1 helps us see these cautions in concrete terms. In Scenario 1, we see a portrait that many working on the gap problem would consider good news. "Equity" is increasing; the gap is declining. While the achievement gap in reading was 1.0 grade levels at the start of third grade, by the start of the fourth grade, it was only .9 grade levels. However, when we factor in the "level" and "value added" dimensions of success to the analysis, we arrive at a less sanguine conclusion. While equity has been enhanced, neither growth (value added) (only eight months for African American students in Grade 3) nor the level of achievement (Grade 2, eighth month at the start of Grade 4) is acceptable. The overall storyline here is not one that should be labeled as successful.

In Scenario 2, using the traditional (i.e., "equity"-only) achievement gap frame, the assessment would not be viewed positively as the reading gap has remained unchanged from the start of Grade 3 to the beginning of Grade 4. However, when we apply "level" and "value-added" criteria, we arrive at a different conclusion. African American students gained a full year and a half in reading in Grade 3, nearly double the growth noted in each of the three previous years on average. Also, they are now reading at grade level. Even though the gap has not closed, the overall storyline in Scenario 2 is positive.

Our earlier caution was that equity needs to be assessed using more than subgroup averages. Our warning here is that using equity as the only barometer for measuring success is problematic. Equity, level, and value-added scores all need to be examined to make thoughtful judgments about school success. Our next caveat in the area of data interpretation leads into a discussion of the importance of examining both absolute and relative improvement.

Absolute vs. Relative Improvement

We argued above that the metrics employed have a good deal to do with the conclusions one reaches about the gap problem and work to confront it. Here we see that the lenses used to interpret scores are also important. The caution spotlighted is whether attention is directed to improving the absolute level or reducing the relative gap (Lee, 2004). Figure 1.2 helps us to illustrate this concern. The question in play for Figure 1.2 is as follows: Is progress being made in closing the achievement gap? Using absolute lenses, the answer is "no." At the start of fourth grade, there is a 2.0 year gap in mathematics achievement between low-income and high-income students. By the beginning of the sixth grade, the gap had increased to 3.0 years. Using relative lenses, the answer would be "yes," the gap is closing. Even though the overall gap has expanded, the rate of growth for low-income students is much higher than for high-income youngsters (125 percent vs. 88 percent). Also, while the low-income students were performing only 50 percent as well as their high-income peers at the start of the fourth grade, at the beginning of the seventh grade, they are doing 60 percent as well. (Note that using our earlier categories, that "level"[4.5] remains unacceptable for low-income youngsters but growth ["valued added"] is good, 2.5 years across the fourth and fifth grades.)

The goal, here, and in Scenario 1 as well, is not simply to provide equations to evaluate claims about whether the gap problem is being addressed effectively or not. Rather, it is to help leaders understand that appropriate metrics and lenses need to be employed in making judgments about gap reductions. We want to reinforce the conclusions by scholars who argue that policy frameworks for helping eliminate school achievement gaps should spotlight increasing achievement among low-skilled children more than reducing gaps between groups.

We also want to presage a point threaded throughout this volume. That is, that gains designed to assist African American and low-income pupils are likely to benefit all youngsters (Natriello, McDill, & Pallas, 1990) and may accelerate the growth of nontargeted youngsters more quickly than targeted students.

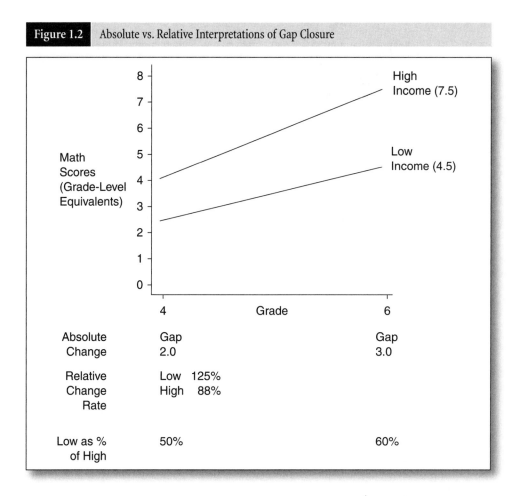

Figure 1.2   Absolute vs. Relative Interpretations of Gap Closure

Cautions About Efforts to Close Gaps

Nearly all the research on racial gaps has focused specifically on children's academic achievement. Yet other dimensions . . . may also be of consequence for school success. (Magnuson & Duncan, 2006, p. 391)

When predicting test scores, the effect of a school policy by racial group may . . . vary by race. (Bali & Alvarez, 2003, p. 488)

To reduce and ultimately close the gap, students of color will need to accelerate their achievement at a much faster rate in the future if whites continue to improve as well. (Shannon & Bylsma, 2002, p. 17)

In this section, we introduce some cautions for leaders to attend to as they undertake the work of closing achievement gaps.

Those who assume the mantle of gap closer need to be attentive to claims about the grounds of recovery actions, including the promulgation of overly simplistic strategies that it is argued will alleviate learning disparities. As Braun and colleagues (2006) conclude, there are reasons why achievement gaps have been "generally resistant to policy interventions" (p. 5). And Barton (2003), in his work on the gap problem, points out another caution that requires notice: "The current knowledge base . . . does not inspire as much confidence as desired" (p. 5). Two points in particular merit notice here. First the knowledge base on closing the achievement gap for minority students is especially thin (Miller, 1999). Second, there is a host of preestablished solutions in the general school-reform environment (e.g., school choice, comprehensive school reform) that advocates link to the achievement gap problem with very little evidence that they will impact learning differentials—solutions in search of problems, if you will. In short, understanding needs to connect to data. There is no magic elixir that will solve the achievement gap problem.

Undue Limiting of Focus

One of the most cogent critiques of the work in the area of gap closures is the nearly exclusive focus on standardized measures of achievement, and achievement often limited to the domains of language arts and mathematics. Rothstein (2004), in particular, raises warning flags first about the dangers of ignoring the many noncognitive, social skills we would like to see developed at school and, second, about the failure to measure gaps in these important areas. He and other analysts also warn against inattention to the measurement and documentation of gaps in subjects other than reading and mathematics. Finally, Rothstein (2004) reminds leaders to be cautious about relying almost exclusively on indices of accomplishment on basic skills, as opposed to more advanced and generally more valued skills. His overarching caution is against narrowness in the quest to enhance equity and quality. His concern is "that a too-exclusive focus on academic test scores may blind us to the relative benefits that Black students gain from education" (p. 103). His antidote is for balance, balance of domains (i.e., cognitive and noncognitive), subjects, and skills.

Attending to Factors That Advantage Students At Risk

If we return to the dominant understanding of closing the achievement gap as an increase in equity—or improving the rate of learning of targeted students at a faster rate than for other pupils (Davison et al., 2004; Kober, 2001), then it is apparent that closure requires actions that disproportionately advantage these students (Braun et al., 2006; Harris & Harrington, 2006; Myers, Kim, & Mandala, 2004; Spradlin et al., 2005): "Disadvantaged students cannot catch up to their initially higher scoring peers by making the same progress as those peers" (Ding & Davison, 2005, p. 94); "as long as the same level of improvement occurs, the gap will not close" (Shannon & Bylsma, 2002, p. 48). The advantaging process can occur in two ways. First, as Alexander, Entwisle, and Olson (2001) remind us, "To address the achievement gap specifically, programs will need to target disadvantaged students specifically" (pp. 176–177). Second, leaders can underscore interventions that "influence the test scores of groups differentially" (Bali & Alvarez, 2003, p. 486). That is, they can spotlight strategies that provide greater gains to targeted students. For example, the use of cooperative learning strategies and small class sizes in the early grades benefit African American students more than white students. The key warning signs for leaders are as follows: (1) raising student achievement generally and reducing the achievement gap are not the same thing; (2) if equity is the goal, focusing on reform strategies that power higher achievement for all youngsters along similar trajectories will not ameliorate the gap problem; (3) "Most school policies have a small effect on test scores, impacting all racial groups in a similar manner, without redistributing benefits across groups" (Bali & Alvarez, 2003, p. 485); and (4) different policies are required for different goals (Hanushek & Raymond, 2005).

Not All Groups Are the Same, and Students Within Specific Groups Are Not the Same

An important caution to carry as work unfolds on addressing the needs of African American and low-income youngsters is to pay attention to differences between groups and within groups (Carpenter, Ramirez, & Severn, 2006). To begin with, as we noted above, evidence suggests that some gap-solution strategies work better with one group (say Hispanic youngsters) than others (say African American students) (Bali & Alvarez, 2003; Downey, von Hippel, & Broh, 2004). That is, "school factors [may] influence the test scores of racial groups differently" (Bali & Alvarez, 2003, p. 486) and the commonly accepted assumption that factors contributing to gaps and their reductions "are the same or sufficiently similar for all minority groups" (Carpenter, Ramirez, & Severn, 2006, p. 113) may not be accurate. For example, Ferguson (1991) found that while greater teaching experience and the possession of a master's degree had a small positive impact on African American students relative to white students (i.e., helped close the African American-white achievement gap) these factors were negative for Hispanic students relative to white youngsters (i.e., increased the Hispanic-white achievement gap).

Second, there are differences within groups of students that have real implications for how schools address learning gaps (Knapp, 2001). All African American students are not the same; nor are all low-income youngsters. For example, while it is true that the average twelfth grade African American pupil performs significantly below the average white student, in the neighborhood or four years below, some African American students perform very well relative to other African Americans and relative to whites. The caution is that grouping masks individual differences, differences to which leaders need to attend.

Implementation Designs Matter

Over the last few years, we have been able to forge important principles of work that need to be followed if gap-reduction work is to be most effective. We illustrate these principles throughout the volume, especially in Part 3 where we explore solution strategies. We introduce some of them here as cautionary rules of thumb that should be added to the achievement gap toolbox at the outset of our work.

- Race is important but socioeconomic status is the critical issue; "social class matters more than race" (Rothstein, 2004, p. 52).
- There is no silver bullet that will solve the achievement gap problem; a combination of strategies is required to gain traction on the issue.
- An integrated, cohesive design that thoughtfully brings multiple strategies together is desirable; isolated actions and ad hoc work are of more limited value.
- Equity can only be achieved if the design features strategies that disproportionately advantage students on the wrong side of the achievement gap.

- The cohesive design needs to include both out-of-school factors (e.g., academically oriented summer programs in elementary school) and in-school variables (e.g., more rigorous curriculum).
- In the school part of the cohesive design, both academic (e.g., quality instruction) and environmental (e.g., clubs for African American students) factors need to be included.
- Some factors carry more weight in certain periods of a student's career (e.g., small class size is more valuable in the early grades).
- Not all factors are equal; some carry more weight than others (e.g., prekindergarten).
- Local context matters a good deal; indeed, "There is considerable evidence that different strategies … work best in different settings" (Thompson, 2002, p. 4).
- Since closing achievement gaps once they have developed is difficult work, prevention always trumps remediation in dealing with achievement gaps (Heckman, 1995); it is easier to solve the ninth-grade problem in preschool than in the ninth grade.
- Length of time in treatment is important; for many gap interventions, benefits escalate the longer the intervention unfolds (e.g., small class size, quality instruction).
- There are no short-term solutions.
- Students rarely arrive; supports often should not be withdrawn even when gaps are reduced; continued work is required to hold gains.

Cautions About Outcomes

There are trade offs. Class size reductions may mean cuts in other programs that schools now offer or might offer. (Thompson & O'Quinn, 2001, p. 11)

Since the 1970s, dropout rates have been declining faster for Blacks than for Whites.… This particular type of effect might act to increase the Black-White achievement difference on the assumption that the more precipitous decline in Black dropout rates is likely to increase the number of academically weak students in a Black sample. (Bacharach, Baumeister, & Farr, 2003, p. 116)

The literature on achievement gaps is nearly silent on two issues of great importance to educational leaders, costs and cost-benefit data and unintended consequences of interventions. School leaders and policy makers need to remember that interventions to close gaps (e.g., reducing class size at the elementary level, adding advanced placement classes in high schools) have both benefits and costs. And while it is often difficult to isolate the impact of particular interventions (Thompson, 2002), "Considerably more effort than is now the norm needs to be devoted to assessing both of these dimensions of reform efforts and trying to determine the ratio between the two, to determine where efforts are most cost effective" (Barton, 2003, p. 37). If the same gain, say a 10 percent reduction in the achievement gap between low- and high-income pupils, can be garnered from strategy A that costs one-half the amount of strategy B, absent some really strong countervailing information, it would be wise to pursue strategy A.

Leaders would also be wise to anticipate unintended as well as hoped-for outcomes of gap-reduction initiatives. The operant caution is to assume that there will be some. The policy landscape of districts and schools is pot marked with seemingly wise reform strategies that produced, in addition to benefits sought, quite unpleasant results, often of a magnitude to more than offset the benefits gained. This was the case with the famous homestead acts that opened up the Southwest plains to farmers in the early part of the twentieth century. These policies led directly to the worst natural disaster in the history of the United States, the dust bowl of the 1930s (Egan, 2006). Closer to home, many school leaders can remember when the policies of the 1960s and 1970s to provide services to at-risk youngsters and students with special needs resulted in the promulgation of "pullout" programs and the separation of at-risk students from regular students. The message is that some thought needs to be devoted to working through these potential unintended consequences before gap initiatives are undertaken. And positive, unintended consequences should not be overlooked either.

CONCLUSION

Addressing the achievement gap is both important and urgent.

(Shannon & Bylsma, 2002, p. 13)

In this chapter, we reported that achievement gaps in education have important consequences for individuals and for the nation as a whole. We observed that gaps are associated negatively with measures of educational attainment, employment opportunities, and earnings. We also noted that achievement gaps damage the economic and social fabric of society, undermine civil rights and social justice for a growing segment of the population, and destroy the principles of democracy. Because of significant economic and social shifts under way and a rising sense of national outrage, we argued that the achievement gap problem has moved to center stage in society in general, and in education specifically. A palpable sense of urgency around this issue has emerged in the last dozen years. We recorded how the new commitment is leading to new gap closing strategies.

To provide an understanding of the extent and depth of the achievement-gap problem, we spent some time exploring the definition of the problem. We then laid out a series of cautions and warning signs that require attention as we move into our discussion of the causes of the gap in Part 2, and more important, into our analysis of solutions to the gap problem in Part 3. The focus here was on helping the reader develop a deeper and more nuanced understanding of the achievement gap problem.

What should be clear at this point in our chronicle is that efforts to address the problem are much in demand: "We must commit ourselves to overcoming the substantial racial and ethnic [and class] differences in educational achievement that remain" (Haskins & Rouse, 2005, p. 1). As Shannon and Bylsma (2002) maintain, both individual and organizational analysis and reflection are called for, "followed by courageous actions to change the status quo across school systems" (p. 12) and the policy frameworks buttressing, or failing to support, the social structures that help determine educational opportunity (Rothstein, 2006; 2008).

Going forward naively, however, will do no one any good. Given what we have seen so far, it should also be clear that closing gaps will be arduous work. The gap remains and continues to bedevil change agents of all ideological and reform persuasions (Ainsworth-Darnell & Downey, 1998; Hedges & Nowell, 1998). As Neuman and Celano (2006) remind us, "Achievement differences among poor and minority children compared to their middle-class counterparts have deep roots" (p. 179). And let us not forget that some of those who are advantaged by these inequalities are likely to resist action that might disturb the current state of affairs. In addition, the obvious should not be overlooked: "With growing minority populations and an increasing percentage of students living in poverty, the threat of the achievement gap widening is very real" (Spradlin et al., 2005, p. 3). In short, "There is nothing inevitable about achieving the goal" (Haskins & Rouse, 2005, p. 6) and, "Evidence provides little hope that achievement gaps will simply disappear with the passage of time" (Magnuson & Duncan, 2006, p. 372).

Yet, there is a real sense of hope here as well. A moral ground swell has materialized around the achievement gap problem (Jencks & Phillips, 1998), one that supplements the press for action resulting from the changing economic and social conditions of a postindustrial world. Across the spectrum, we have discovered that the "Black-white tests score gap does not appear to be an inevitable fact of nature" (Jencks & Phillips, 1998, p. 44): "Academic abilities are not simply inherited aptitudes," but are subject to change "through a broad range of social and educational interventions" (Gordon, Frede, & Irvine, 2004, p. 1). We also have some fairly impressive examples of places that are tackling the problem effectively.

$$2$$

Portraying and Tracking Achievement Gaps

Coby V. Meyers

In the past few decades, many minorities have moved into the lower and middle ranks of the middle class as defined by their educational attainment and occupational and income levels. Nevertheless, an examination of the standardized test scores and grades of their children shows that collectively these youngsters are performing much less well in school than are middle-class white children. Moreover, relatively few middle-class minority students are performing at the highest academic levels in verbal or quantitative areas. Among minority groups this problem seems to be most acute for African American children. (Miller, 1995, pp. 10–11)

African Americans currently score lower than European Americans on vocabulary, reading, and math tests, as well as on tests that claim to measure scholastic aptitude and intelligence. This gap appears before children enter kindergarten, and it persists into adulthood . . . the median American black still scores below 75 percent of American whites on most standardized tests. On some tests the typical American black scores below more than 85 percent of whites. (Jencks & Phillips, 1998, p. 44)

The narrowing of the racial achievement gap during the 1970s and 1980s has been well documented (Haycock, 2001; Hedges & Nowell, 1998; 1999; Jencks & Phillips, 1998), as has its suspension and "erosion" (Chubb & Loveless, 2002, p. 2; Haycock, 2001) in the 1990s and early 2000s (Shannon & Bylsma, 2002). If the progress of the late 1960s through the early

1980s had continued at the same rate, racial achievement gaps would have disappeared (Thompson & O'Quinn, 2001). Although "past experience offers more fuel for optimism" (Kober, 2001, p. 10), "School efforts to close the gap in academic achievement between ethnic and racial minority students and white students have been largely unsuccessful to date" (Schwartz, 2001, p. 2). Today, racial and economic class achievement differences remain large in "grades, test scores, retention and dropout rates, graduation rates, identification for special education and gifted programs, extracurricular and cocurricular involvement, and discipline rates" (Mickelson, 2003, p. 1055), as well as "college attendance and completion" (Shannon & Bylsma, 2002, p. 14). Achievement "gaps are pervasive, profound and persistent" (Braun et al., 2006, p. 2).

The high correlation of race and social class complicates discussion of achievement gaps, especially considering poverty's "disproportionate rates among African Americans and Hispanics, and among English learners" (Hertert & Teague, 2003, p. 3). In our synthesis of achievement gap research, we separate race and social class whenever possible while recognizing their strong interplay, a practice commonly followed in the studies reviewed (Miller, 1995). Like Shannon and Bylsma (2002), we recognize that achievement gap can be defined in many ways but as noted in Chapter 1, focus specifically on gaps between white students and students of color (specifically, African Americans) and between students from "more affluent backgrounds and their lower-income counterparts" (p. 8). When data permit, to provide context, we also consider non-English language learners with English background students. Again, as discussed in Chapter 1, we also recognize that the use of broad categories such as race/ethnicity "masks the ranges of performance that exist among particular groups" (Bylsma, 2002, p. 8).

In this chapter, we track achievement gaps through various data sources (i.e., standardized test scores) while supplementing our findings with an exhaustive review of achievement gap literature. We follow this review with a brief portrayal of the gap from prekindergarten through college.

TRACKING THE GAPS

Overall, in terms of achievement competence in mathematics and reading, U.S. high school students today are scoring about the same as they were in the early 1970s.

> These overall trends mask significant progress made among certain groups. For instance, over the past thirty years, minority students made substantial progress toward closing the minority-nonminority test score gap in both mathematics and reading. In 1999 black students scored 13 points higher on the NAEP mathematics test and about 27 points higher in reading than black students in the early 1970s. Similarly, Latinos made large improvements in achievement. Between 1973 and 1994 Latinos gained 16 points on the NAEP mathematics test, and between 1975 and 1994 Latinos gained 11 points in reading. (Berends, Lucas, Sullivan, & Briggs, 2005, pp. 4–5)

> After at least thirty years of decline in the achievement gap [NAEP and SAT], the achievement gap began stagnating or rising in the 1990s, and it continued throughout the decade. (Harris & Herrington, 2006, p. 210)

Over the course of the twentieth century, essentially all racial/ethnic groups in the United States have experienced substantial educational advancement, as measured by increases in attainment levels. Yet some extremely large minority-majority gaps remain, and relatively little progress has been made in closing them. (Miller, 1995, pp. 43–44)

"The potential for tests to be biased has long been recognized" (Magnuson & Duncan, 2006, p. 369), and the results from any single test should be viewed with caution. However, Miller (1995) reminds us, "Some standardized tests are especially valuable because they have been designed to be administered to representative samples of students over a period of many years" (p. 45). Long-term trends in achievement tests provide evidence that white students outperform African Americans in mathematics, reading, and science (Everson, 2007), which should not be surprising when one considers that "African Americans . . . have historically been overrepresented among low-achievers and underrepresented among high-achieving students" (Miller, 1995, p. 49).

When considering achievement gap trends, Miller (1995) contends, "School-grade data are most useful as single-point assessments of academic competencies" (p. 45). Still, much of trend data must be reviewed with caution. Many assessments begin once children have already completed some education and, as we report in Chapters 3–7, achievement gaps reflect factors beyond the education students are receiving in schools (Magnuson & Duncan, 2006). Even with the concerns noted above, measuring the performance of minorities relative to the performance of their white peers "will likely continue to be based on standardized test scores for some time to come" (Hallinan, 2001, p. 63). We consider the National Assessment of Educational Progress (NAEP), other national assessments, state assessments, international assessments, advanced placement exams, and college admissions tests below.

National Assessment of Educational Progress

Discussion of student performance on a national scale is limited because the United States does not have a national test. Launched in 1970, the federally funded NAEP has served as the closest thing to such an evaluation, providing the "only uniform, representative, and continuous assessment of American students" (Spradlin et al., 2005, p. 4). According to Thernstrom and Thernstrom (2002), "Only NAEP provides a consistent instrument administered at frequent enough intervals to draw a clear picture of trends since the 1970s" (p. 132). Known as "The Nation's Report Card," NAEP provides a battery of tests in various subjects to nationally representative samples of students (Hertert & Teague, 2003). Each NAEP mathematics and reading test is scored on a 0-to-500 scale with five anchor points for each subject, describing different levels of competencies ranging from rudimentary skills to advanced skills (Miller, 1995). However, "Interpretations of the NAEP results can be confusing because there are two different NAEP assessments" (Spradlin et al., 2005, p. 10): "trend" and "main."

Long-Term Trend

The NAEP trend assessment began in 1969 and measures long-term trends in student performance. Specifically, these assessments are designed to yield scores that are comparable over time (Kober, 2001). Trend analysis is possible because NAEP uses "the exact same questions over time" (Spradlin et al., 2005, p. 10). They are administered periodically to a representative sample of students at ages 9, 13, and 17 and assess performance in mathematics, reading, and science every four to five years (Cook & Evans, 2000).

NAEP results indicate that cases of test score convergence are "driven primarily by rising black scores" (Cook & Evans, 2000, p. 730), especially in the lower end of the achievement distribution (see Hedges & Nowell, 1998; Magnuson & Duncan, 2006): "Students, especially black and Latino students, are scoring higher on mathematics and reading tests today than they were a few decades ago" (Berends et al., 2005, p. 4). Still, "These students remain much farther behind their peers in meeting basic academic achievement levels in both reading and math" (Becker & Luthar, 2002, p. 199). This is highlighted by limited progress and setbacks during the 1990s (Lee, 2002). Since 2000, most NAEP achievement gaps have remained virtually unchanged (Lee, 2006).

NAEP achievement gaps in mathematics and reading for nine-year-olds have stood in contrast to the achievement-gap patterns of thirteen- and seventeen-year-old students. Although gaps are clearly smaller now than they were in the early 1970s, there have not been clear trends for nine-year-olds since the inception of the NAEP test (see Figures 2.1 & 2.4 and Tables 2.1, 2.3, & 2.6). For example, in reading, the African American-white gap for students at age 9 has altered between closing and growing for the last seven test years. Moreover, until recently, the narrowest gap margins in mathematics and reading achievement gaps were found in years in the late 1980s and early 1990s. The 2004 long-term trends data illustrate some of the most encouraging news on the achievement gap front since the late 1980s or early 1990s. Indeed, the most recent NAEP long-term test discloses the narrowest achievement gaps for African American nine-year-old students in the thirty-plus years of NAEP existence.

At ages 13 and 17 (see Figures 2.2 & 2.3 and Tables 2.2 & 2.3), the smallest African American-white and Hispanic-white mathematics achievement gaps also occurred between 1986 and 1992. The size of the gaps has been consistent for Hispanics over at least a decade. The Hispanic-white gap for thirteen-year-olds was 22 points (.44) in 1982 and 23 (.46) points in 2004, and it never exceeded 25 (.50) points or dropped below 20 points (.40). The Hispanic-white gap for seventeen-year-olds is similar for the test years between 1992 through 2004. The African American-white mathematics gap has been more prominent, however. Since attaining the narrowest gaps in 1986 and 1990, respectively, the African American-white mathematics achievement gap for students ages 13 and 17 has risen somewhat steadily. In 2004, the African American-white gap for thirteen-year-olds was only one point greater than it was in 1986, but the upward trend in all other years indicates that the most recent score could be anomalous.

The African American-white and Hispanic-white reading achievement gaps were smallest in 1988 (1990 for seventeen-year-old Hispanics). In all four cases, the achievement gap increased in the early 1990s before declining slightly to close out the decade. Still, the "somewhat discouraging decline" (Kober, 2001, p. 22) among African American seventeen-year-olds of the 1990s has continued into the 2000s, as the gaps for both African American and Hispanic seventeen-year-olds have remained fairly constant from 1994 through 2004 (see Figure 2.6 and Table 2.6). However, the most recent NAEP results indicate a considerable closure for thirteen-year-old students with the smallest achievement gaps since 1990 (see Figure 2.5 and Table 2.3).

(Text continued on page 33)

| Figure 2.1 | NAEP Long-Term Mathematics Trends for Students Age 9 |

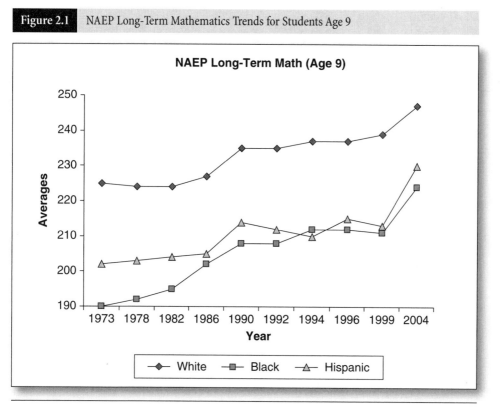

(Kober, 2001; U.S. Department of Education, 2009a)

| Table 2.1 | NAEP Long-Term Mathematics (Age 9) |

Gap Between White and Black Race/Ethnicity						
	White		Black			
	Average	Scale Score	Average	Scale Score	Difference	
2004	247.3	(0.9)	224.4	(2.1)	22.9	(2.2)
1999	238.8	(0.9)	210.9	(1.6)	27.8	(1.8)
1996	236.9	(1.0)	211.6	(1.4)	25.3	(1.8)
1994	236.8	(1.0)	212.1	(1.6)	24.7	(1.8)
1992	235.1	(0.8)	208.0	(2.0)	27.1	(2.2)
1990	235.2	(0.8)	208.4	(2.2)	26.8	(2.4)
1986	226.9	(1.1)	201.6	(1.6)	25.3	(2.0)
1982	224.0	(1.1)	194.9	(1.6)	29.0	(2.0)
1978	224.1	(0.9)	192.4	(1.1)	31.7	(1.5)

(U.S. Department of Education, 2009a)

Figure 2.2   NAEP Long-Term Mathematics Trends for Students Age 13

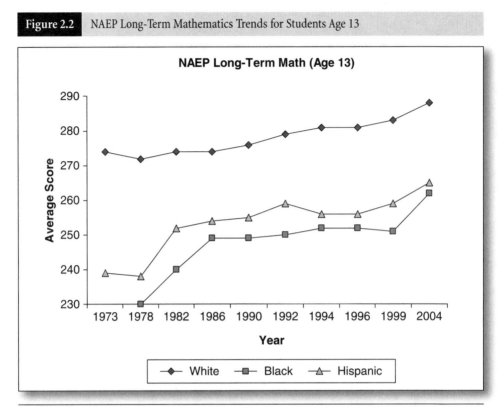

(Kober, 2001; U.S. Department of Education, 2009a)

Table 2.2   NAEP Long-Term Mathematics (Age 13)

	Gap Between White and Black Race/Ethnicity					
	White		Black			
	Average	Scale Score	Average	Scale Score	Difference	
2004	288.4	(0.9)	261.7	(1.6)	26.6	(1.8)
1999	283.1	(0.8)	251.0	(2.6)	32.2	(2.7)
1996	281.2	(0.9)	252.1	(1.3)	29.1	(1.6)
1994	280.8	(0.9)	251.5	(3.5)	29.3	(3.7)
1992	278.9	(0.9)	250.2	(1.9)	28.7	(2.1)
1990	276.3	(1.1)	249.1	(2.3)	27.2	(2.6)
1986	273.6	(1.3)	249.2	(2.3)	24.4	(2.6)
1982	274.4	(1.0)	240.4	(1.6)	34.0	(1.9)
1978	271.6	(0.8)	229.6	(1.9)	42.0	(2.1)

(U.S. Department of Education, 2009a)

Figure 2.3   NAEP Long-Term Mathematics Trends for Students Age 17

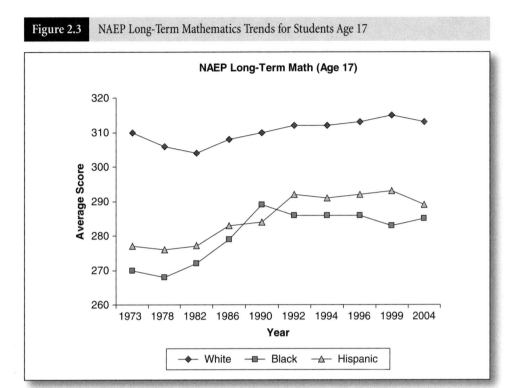

(Kober, 2001; U.S. Department of Education, 2009a)

Table 2.3   NAEP Long-Term Mathematics (Age 17)

	Gap Between White and Black Race/Ethnicity					
	White		Black			
	Average	Scale Score	Average	Scale Score	Difference	
2004	313.4	(0.7)	285.3	(1.6)	28.2	(1.8)
1999	314.8	(1.1)	283.3	(1.5)	31.5	(1.9)
1996	313.4	(1.4)	286.4	(1.7)	27.0	(2.2)
1994	312.3	(1.1)	285.5	(1.8)	26.8	(2.1)
1992	311.9	(0.8)	285.8	(2.2)	26.1	(2.4)
1990	309.5	(1.0)	288.5	(2.8)	20.9	(3.0)
1986	307.5	(1.0)	278.6	(2.1)	28.9	(2.3)
1982	303.7	(0.9)	271.8	(1.2)	31.9	(1.5)
1978	305.9	(0.9)	268.4	(1.3)	37.5	(1.6)

(U.S. Department of Education, 2009a)

| Figure 2.4 | NAEP Long-Term Reading Trends for Students Age 9 |

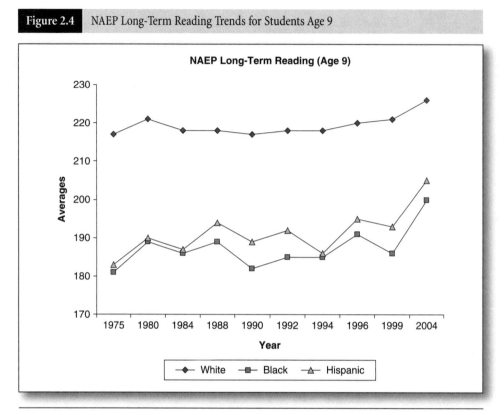

(Kober, 2001; U.S. Department of Education, 2009a)

| Table 2.4 | NAEP Long-Term Reading (Age 9) |

	Gap Between White and Black Race/Ethnicity					
	White		**Black**			
	Average	**Scale Score**	**Average**	**Scale Score**	**Difference**	
2004	226.4	(1.1)	200.4	(2.2)	26.0	(2.5)
1999	221.0	(1.6)	185.5	(2.3)	35.4	(2.8)
1996	219.6	(1.2)	190.9	(2.6)	28.8	(2.8)
1994	218.0	(1.3)	185.4	(2.3)	32.6	(2.6)
1992	217.9	(1.0)	184.5	(2.2)	33.4	(2.4)
1990	217.0	(1.3)	181.8	(2.9)	35.2	(3.2)
1988	217.7	(1.4)	188.5	(2.4)	29.2	(2.8)
1984	218.0	(0.9)	185.7	(1.3)	32.3	(1.6)
1980	221.3	(0.8)	189.3	(1.8)	32.0	(1.9)
1975	216.6	(0.7)	181.2	(1.2)	35.4	(1.4)

(U.S. Department of Education, 2009a)

Figure 2.5	NAEP Long-Term Reading Trends for Students Age 13

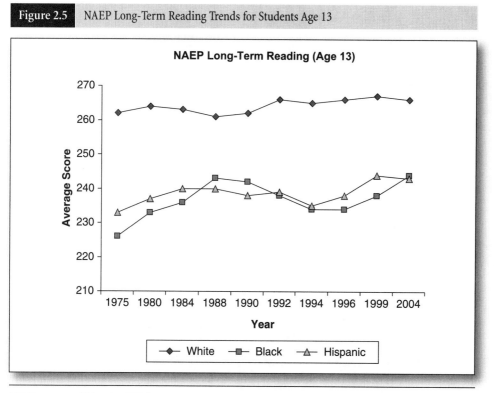

(U.S. Department of Education, 2009a)

Table 2.5	NAEP Long-Term Reading (Age 13)

Gap Between White and Black Race/Ethnicity						
	White		Black			
	Average	Scale Score	Average	Scale Score	Difference	
2004	266.0	(1.0)	244.4	(2.0)	21.6	(2.3)
1999	266.7	(1.2)	238.2	(2.4)	28.5	(2.7)
1996	265.9	(1.0)	234.0	(2.6)	31.9	(2.8)
1994	265.1	(1.1)	234.3	(2.4)	30.8	(2.7)
1992	266.4	(1.2)	237.6	(2.3)	28.8	(2.7)
1990	262.3	(0.9)	241.5	(2.2)	20.8	(2.4)
1988	261.3	(1.1)	242.9	(2.4)	18.4	(2.6)
1984	262.5	(0.6)	236.2	(1.2)	26.3	(1.3)
1980	264.4	(0.7)	232.8	(1.5)	31.6	(1.6)
1975	262.1	(0.7)	225.7	(1.2)	36.3	(1.4)

(U.S. Department of Education, 2009a)

Figure 2.6   NAEP Long-Term Reading Trends for Students Age 17

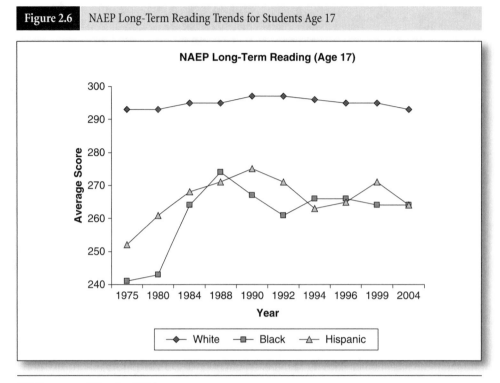

(U.S. Department of Education, 2009a)

Table 2.6   NAEP Long-Term Reading (Age 17)

	Gap Between White and Black Race/Ethnicity					
	White		Black			
	Average	Scale Score	Average	Scale Score	Difference	
2004	292.8	(1.1)	263.8	(2.7)	29.0	(2.9)
1999	294.6	(1.4)	263.9	(1.7)	30.7	(2.3)
1996	295.1	(1.2)	266.1	(2.7)	29.0	(3.0)
1994	295.7	(1.5)	266.2	(3.9)	29.6	(4.2)
1992	297.4	(1.4)	260.6	(2.1)	36.9	(2.5)
1990	296.6	(1.2)	267.3	(2.3)	29.3	(2.6)
1988	294.7	(1.2)	274.4	(2.4)	20.3	(2.7)
1984	295.3	(0.9)	263.5	(1.2)	31.8	(1.5)
1980	292.8	(0.9)	243.1	(1.8)	49.7	(2.0)
1975	293.0	(0.6)	240.6	(2.0)	52.3	(2.1)

(U.S. Department of Education, 2009a)

Interpretations of this reduction should be made with caution. Until future assessments indicate that this closure is more than a blip, it is difficult to refute Thernstrom and Thernstrom's (2002) claim that for older students, the racial gaps in reading have not been narrowing for a "dismayingly long time" (p. 133).

Comparing the percentage of student racial groups reaching NAEP anchor points has been an alternative way to consider achievement gaps. Anchor points are those minimum NAEP scores that are representative of a specified level of subject-specific sophistication. For example, as relayed by Natriello and colleagues (1990), level 150 [rudimentary] in mathematics "represents mastery of simple addition and subtraction facts, while level 200 [basic] represents beginning skills and understanding" (p. 17). Other levels, for mathematics and reading, are 250 (intermediate), 300 (adept), and 350 (advanced) (Miller, 1995; Natriello et al., 1990).

Miller (1995) reported extensively on racial achievement gaps by the percentage of students reaching NAEP achievement levels. At age 9, white students are twice as likely as African American students to score at or above the basic (200) level on reading, a considerable improvement over the 3:1 ratio originally found in 1971. The Hispanic-white gap at the basic level decreased over time, too, although not as rapidly. For both racial gaps, margins continue to widen as higher levels of attainment are considered. For example, white students are more than seven times more likely than African American students (2.2 to .3), and eleven times more likely than Hispanic students (2.2 to .2), to reach the adept (300) level.

By age 17, in reading, nearly all white, African American, and Hispanic students tested are reaching the basic level anchor point (200) with respective pass percentages of 99, 96, and 96. African American and Hispanic students have also reduced the achievement gaps at the adept level (300), as 20 percent of African Americans and 27 percent of Hispanics reach this level, in comparison to 48 percent of whites. Across the basic, intermediate, and adept levels, the racial gaps have decreased. However, sizable gaps remain at the advanced (350) level, where 8.7 percent of white students demonstrate the requisite skills, while only 1.5 percent of African American students and 2.4 percent of Hispanic students do so. In other words, it seems, the achievement gap differences by race increase by levels as students grow older.

In mathematics, results appear to be more positive when considering lower anchor points. While 87 percent of white nine-year-old students reach the basic level (200), 60 percent of African American students and 68 percent of Hispanics reach this point. Similar to the reading results, the gaps, especially the African American-white one, shrinks over time but widens as achievement levels increase. Approximately 1.5 percent of white students attain the adept level (300) in comparison to only .1 percent of African American students and .2 percent of Hispanic students. "Thus, we continue to have a crisis at the top of the math achievement distribution for African American [and Hispanic] children in the early elementary school years" (Miller, 1995, p. 55). For seventeen-year-old students, the racial gaps remain at each anchor point but are closing in all of them, including the advanced level. From 1986 to 1990, the percentage of white students scoring in at least the advanced anchor increased from 7.9 percent to 8.3 percent, while African American students increased from .2 percent to 2.0 percent and Hispanics from 1.1 percent to 1.9 percent.

Occasionally, the desire to see results inhibits a complete consideration of the data. For example, some researchers have happily pointed out that achievement gaps in long-term trends in both mathematics and reading are narrower now than they were when the NAEP assessments began in the early 1970s. Kober (2001), for example, discusses in some length the African American-white gap reductions found in mathematics and reading in the 1980s, but emphasizes the overall reduction of the gap in the approximate thirty-year existence of NAEP over the gap inflations of the immediately previous ten years. This interpretation, although accurate, seems to neglect full disclosure. Miller (1995) contends that the gap closures seen in the late 1980s and early 1990s send "mixed messages" (p. 82) because progress has not been uniform. Hertert and Teague (2003) suggest that in some more current cases, achievement gaps remain as prevalent as those found in the Coleman Report (Coleman et al., 1966).

In both mathematics and reading and at all three ages tested, the African American-white achievement gap decreased considerably in the late 1980s and into the early 1990s. Since then, the gaps have remained relatively steady or have increased slightly. The gaps between white and African American nine-year-old students have consistently been the smallest and most stable, with the gaps amongst the two older student sets larger and usually more volatile. When gap closures have occurred, they typically do so because of increased African American scores within the lowest anchors of achievement, but exceedingly large gaps remain between the proportion of white students attaining the highest levels of achievement and their African American peers. Although the 2004 NAEP results offer some hope that gaps are shrinking again, trends are not yet discernable.

Main NAEP

Since 1990, NAEP has periodically conducted a second national assessment that incorporates different test instruments and more "innovative assessment methods" than those used in the trend assessment (Kober, 2001, p. 18). The main NAEP assesses students in Grades 4, 8, and 12. In addition to math, reading, and science, the main NAEP assessments test students in civics, geography, history, writing, and the arts. Also, student performance is reported both in terms of raw scores and according to criterion-referenced performance levels—below basic, basic, proficient, and advanced (Hertert & Teague, 2003). Test results are available at both the national and state levels. Although main NAEP test instruments and performance levels are modified periodically (Kober, 2001), the assessment has gained traction as another national measure of achievement gaps.

In the assessments immediately after the initial test given in 1990, changes in African American-white and Hispanic-white test score gaps varied by grade and subject. In some cases (e.g., eighth grade African American-white gap), the differences in test scores increased considerably. In nearly every instance, however, these enlarged gaps were followed by noticeable decreases. In fact, Lubienski (2002) reports that student performance for every mathematics strand in every grade improved between 1990 and 2000, and any increased disparity in African American-white achievement was "due to the gains of white students being larger than the gains of black students, as opposed to a decrease in black students' scores" (p. 271). This progress should not be overstated. Using more longitudinally robust data, Braun and colleagues (2006) point out that main NAEP results have "remained nearly constant" (p. 4) and Lee (2006) suggests that racial and socioeconomic achievement gaps in mathematics for fourth- and eighth-grade students have "remained the same throughout the 1990–2005 period" (p. 30).

In fourth grade, the African American-white achievement gap in mathematics has been reduced by 6 points, from 32 (.64) in 1990 to 26 (.52) in 2007 (see Figure 2.7 and Table 2.7). The Hispanic-white gap, although diminishing in most years, was actually 1 point larger in 2007 than it was in 1990 (21 to 20). A similar pattern emerges when we examine the data for eighth-grade students (see Figure 2.8 and Table 2.8). The African American-white gap has closed by just two points since 1990 (33 to 31), and the Hispanic-white gap is actually two points greater (24 to 26). In other words, the narrowing of the mathematics achievement gaps, after the large inflation of them in 1992 for fourth graders and in 1992 and 1996 for eighth graders, have returned us to the starting line of nearly twenty years ago. For twelfth graders, the inverse is true (see Figure 2.9 and Table 2.9). After narrowing the achievement gaps significantly, both African American and Hispanic students scored lower comparatively over the next two examinations, culminating in gaps nearly identical to the ones in 1990.

Reading achievement gaps by race, however, are noticeably narrower in Grades 4 and 8. Grade 4 results for the African American-white and Hispanic-white gaps follow a pattern similar to those in mathematics, as achievement gaps immediately after the first assessment rose greatly (see Figure 2.10 and Table 2.10). Then, the reading achievement gap began to shrink somewhat consistently over the next fifteen years. Unlike the achievement gaps in mathematics, the fourth-grade reading gaps are noticeably smaller now (27) than they were in 1992 (32). Eighth-grade reading gaps are also smaller now (27) than they were in 1992 (29) (see Figure 2.11 and Table 2.11). Reading achievement gaps for students in eighth grade never grew inordinately in any year, and thus the narrowing of the gap has been less dramatic. The reading achievement gaps for students in Grade 12 did increase in the second year of assessment, before returning to sizes similar to those seen in the original 1992 evaluation (see Figure 2.12 and Table 2.12).

Racial gaps in mathematics and reading achievement are amplified when we examine NAEP's alternate assessment, however. For example, in 1992, NAEP mathematics contained extended-response items in addition to the regular constructed-response items typically asked. According to Klein and colleagues (1997), 49 percent of white students tested in Grade 8 provided "at least a minimal response" (p. 85) to the extended-response tasks. Only 13 percent of African American students and 16 percent of Hispanic students tested did the same. Examining NAEP from 1996, Strutchens and Silver (2000) confirm these findings. Moreover, in reading in 1992, an oral reading test was conducted. The racial achievement gaps found in the regular NAEP assessment of reading existed in the oral reading proficiency assessment as well (Klein et al., 1997).

The African American-white and Hispanic-white achievement gaps in science are also large. Klein and team (1997) report that in the 1990 NAEP assessment, white fourth-grade students outscored their African American peers by 37 points (.74), and their Hispanic peers by 30 points (.60). The sizes of the gaps across all grades are similar, and they appear to be holding steady or closing only slightly.

In addition to race, student socioeconomic status (SES) is another way to compare student achievement. Because African American and Hispanic students are overrepresented in low-income categories, it is sometimes difficult to "untangle matters of race/ethnicity and

(Text continued on page 42)

Figure 2.7   NAEP Main Mathematics Trends for Students Grade 4

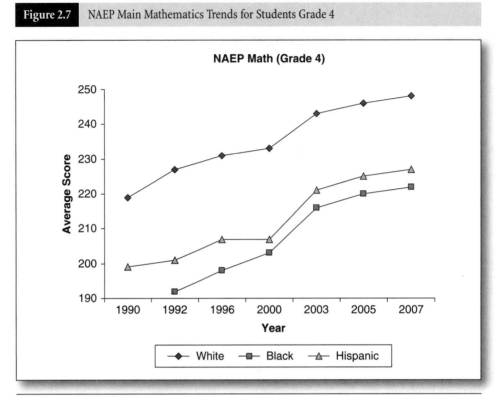

(U.S. Department of Education, 2009b)

Table 2.7   NAEP Main Mathematics (Grade 4)

Gap Between White and Black (Race/ethnicity used in NAEP reports after 2001)						
	White		Black			
	Average	Scale Score	Average	Scale Score	Difference	
2007	248.1	(0.2)	222.2	(0.3)	25.9	(0.4)
2005	246.1	(0.1)	219.8	(0.3)	26.2	(0.3)
2003	243.4	(0.2)	216.1	(0.4)	27.3	(0.4)
2000	234.4	(0.8)	203.4	(1.2)	31.0	(1.5)
1996	232.1	(1.0)	197.8	(1.6)	34.2	(1.8)
1992	227.3	(0.8)	192.8	(1.4)	34.5	(1.6)
1990	219.8	(1.0)	187.5	(1.8)	32.3	(2.0)

(U.S. Department of Education, 2009b)

Figure 2.8   NAEP Main Mathematics Trends for Students Grade 8

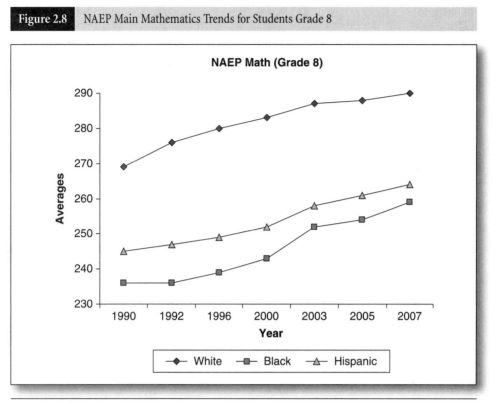

(U.S. Department of Education, 2009b)

Table 2.8   NAEP Main Mathematics (Grade 8)

Gap Between White and Black (Race/ethnicity used in NAEP reports after 2001)						
	White		Black			
	Average	Scale Score	Average	Scale Score	Difference	
2007	291.3	(0.3)	259.5	(0.4)	31.7	(0.5)
2005	288.7	(0.2)	254.8	(0.4)	33.9	(0.4)
2003	287.7	(0.3)	252.2	(0.5)	35.5	(0.6)
2000	283.9	(0.8)	244.1	(1.2)	39.7	(1.5)
1996	280.7	(1.1)	239.8	(1.9)	40.9	(2.2)
1992	276.8	(1.0)	237.0	(1.3)	39.8	(1.7)
1990	269.6	(1.3)	236.8	(2.7)	32.9	(3.0)

(U.S. Department of Education, 2009b)

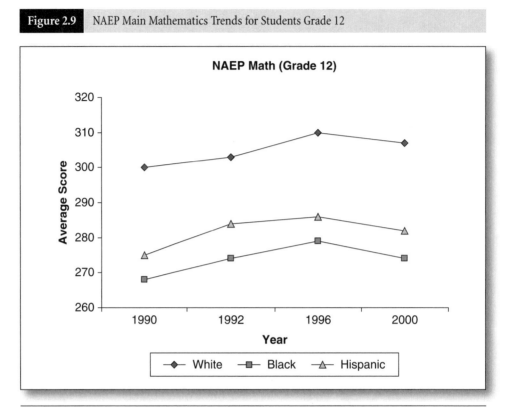

Figure 2.9   NAEP Main Mathematics Trends for Students Grade 12

(U.S. Department of Education, 2009b)

Table 2.9   NAEP Main Mathematics (Grade 12)

Gap Between White and Black (Race/ethnicity used in NAEP reports after 2001)						
	White		Black			
	Average	Scale Score	Average	Scale Score	Difference	
2000	307.6	(1.0)	274.5	(2.0)	33.1	(2.2)
1996	310.8	(1.0)	279.9	(2.2)	30.9	(2.4)
1992	305.2	(0.9)	275.1	(1.8)	30.1	(2.0)
1990	299.9	(1.2)	267.9	(2.0)	32.0	(2.3)

(U.S. Department of Education, 2009b)

Figure 2.10   NAEP Main Reading Trends for Students Grade 4

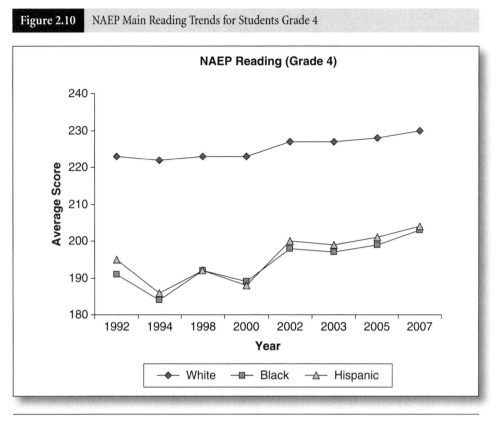

(U.S. Department of Education, 2009b)

Table 2.10   NAEP Main Reading (Grade 4)

Gap Between White and Black (Race/ethnicity used in NAEP reports after 2001)						
	White		Black			
	Average	Scale Score	Average	Scale Score	Difference	
2007	230.5	(0.2)	203.4	(0.4)	27.1	(0.5)
2005	228.9	(0.2)	199.8	(0.3)	29.1	(0.4)
2003	228.6	(0.2)	197.9	(0.4)	30.6	(0.5)
2002	228.6	(0.3)	198.8	(0.5)	29.8	(0.6)
2000	224.3	(1.1)	190.2	(1.8)	34.1	(2.1)
1998	224.7	(1.0)	192.9	(1.9)	31.8	(2.2)
1994	223.5	(1.3)	185.3	(1.8)	38.2	(2.2)
1992	224.3	(1.2)	192.0	(1.7)	32.3	(2.1)

(U.S. Department of Education, 2009b)

Figure 2.11   NAEP Main Reading Trends for Students Grade 8

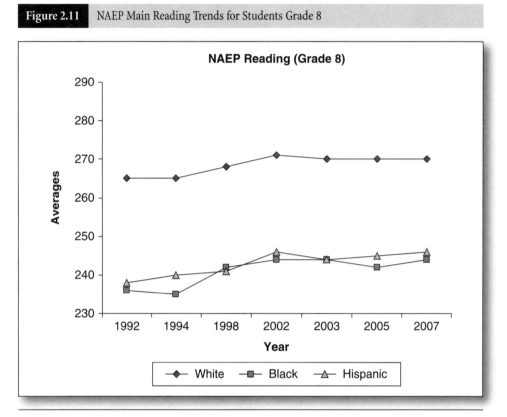

(U.S. Department of Education, 2009b)

Table 2.11   NAEP Main Reading (Grade 8)

	White		Black			
Gap Between White and Black (Race/ethnicity used in NAEP reports after 2001)						
	Average	Scale Score	Average	Scale Score	Difference	
2007	272.0	(0.2)	244.7	(0.4)	27.3	(0.4)
2005	271.0	(0.2)	243.0	(0.4)	28.0	(0.5)
2003	272.3	(0.2)	244.5	(0.5)	27.8	(0.5)
2002	272.5	(0.4)	245.5	(0.7)	27.0	(0.9)
1998	270.2	(0.9)	244.0	(1.2)	26.2	(1.5)
1994	266.6	(1.0)	236.1	(1.8)	30.5	(2.1)
1992	267.0	(1.1)	237.4	(1.7)	29.6	(2.0)

(U.S. Department of Education, 2009b)

Figure 2.12   NAEP Main Reading Trends for Students Grade 12

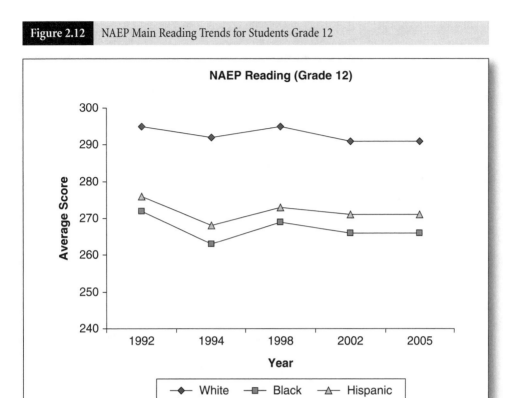

(U.S. Department of Education, 2009b)

Table 2.12   NAEP Main Reading (Grade 12)

Gap Between White and Black (Race/ethnicity used in NAEP reports after 2001)						
	White		Black			
	Average	Scale Score	Average	Scale Score	Difference	
2005	292.7	(0.7)	266.7	(1.2)	26.0	(1.4)
2002	292.3	(0.7)	267.5	(1.3)	24.9	(1.5)
1998	296.5	(0.7)	269.4	(1.4)	27.1	(1.6)
1994	293.4	(0.7)	264.8	(1.6)	28.6	(1.8)
1992	297.4	(0.6)	273.2	(1.4)	24.3	(1.5)

(U.S. Department of Education, 2009b)

economic condition in . . . NAEP findings" (Strutchens & Silver, 2000, p. 51). Still, students in all three assessed grades who were eligible for free or reduced-price lunch "are more than twice as likely as their ineligible peers to score below basic levels in reading and mathematics achievement" (Land & Legters, 2002, p. 5). Mathematics test scores gaps by SES (based on student eligibility for free and reduced-price lunch) for students in Grades 4 and 8 (NAEP does not currently provide SES information in mathematics or reading for Grade 12) fluctuate little. For example, as pointed out by Lee (2006), the poor/nonpoor gap was 26.6 (.53) in 1996 and 26.7 (.53) in 2005. Gap size fluctuation has occurred more often in reading, but after six assessments for fourth-grade students and five assessments for eighth grade students, SES reading gaps have not changed much. In the three years of science assessment, SES gaps have decreased by three points in Grades 4 and 12 and increased by one point in Grade 8. Interesting to note, the SES gap is consistently smaller than the African American-white gap in mathematics but not the Hispanic-white gap. In addition, the SES gap is consistently smaller than both the African American-white gap and the Hispanic-white gap in reading and science.

When considered by the percentage of students attaining the various anchor levels of performance, NAEP results by grade on the main assessment are not very different than those found by age on the trends assessment. Overall, "The percentage of students who reach the Proficient and Advanced levels (the two highest levels) on the main NAEP assessment is smaller for African Americans and Hispanics than it is for whites" (Kober, 2001, p. 23; see also Camara & Schmidt, 1999). Miller (1995) reports on the racial gaps in mathematics for the 1990 NAEP assessment. According to his findings, approximately 80 percent of white fourth-grade students scored at least basic, but only about 40 percent of African American students and 50 percent of Hispanic students did so. Nearly 100 percent of twelfth-grade students of all three races reached the basic level, but racial gaps became clearer as achievement levels increased. Just over 50 percent of white students were at least adept in comparison to 16 percent of African American students and 25 percent of Hispanic students. If mathematics achievement results are considered conversely, we see that in 1996, "24 percent, 26 percent, and 21 percent of white fourth, eighth, and twelfth graders, respectively, scored below basic levels . . . compared to 68 percent, 72 percent, and 62 percent of black students and 59 percent, 61 percent, and 50 percent of Hispanic students" (Land & Legters, 2002, p. 7; see also Lee, 2004).

Similar achievement differences exist in other NAEP subject assessments. Kober (2001) reports that on the 1996 NAEP science assessment, about 4 percent of African American twelfth graders and 6 percent of Hispanic twelfth graders scored at the proficient level, compared with 24 percent of white twelfth graders. On the 1998 NAEP writing assessment, 8 percent of African American and 10 percent of Hispanic fourth-grade students scored at the proficient level, compared with 27 percent of white students (Kober, 2001).

Achievement gap differences are also noticeable by poverty measures. "In 1998, [NAEP] tests found that over twice as many students eligible for free- or reduced-price lunches scored below basic proficiency levels in reading achievement than their peers (fourth grade, 58 percent vs. 27 percent; eighth grade, 44 percent vs. 19 percent; twelfth grade, 43 percent vs. 20 percent)" (Maruyama, 2003, p. 656). Hertert and Teague (2003) report similar results for Grades 4 and 8 in mathematics and science. Furthermore, they note, "The percent of poor students scoring at or above the 'proficient' level tends to be about one-third that of higher-income students across all subjects and . . . grade levels" (p. 7). These disparities are even more striking when examining results of twelfth graders (Camara & Schmidt, 1999).

Although the National Center for Education Statistics (NCES) points out that the main NAEP is not as reliable as the long-term trend NAEP, some findings from the main NAEP appear robust. The most substantial decreases in gaps for both reading and mathematics have occurred at the fourth-grade level, but even these gap reductions appear modest overall. The fourth-grade reading gap has been reduced by about 16 percent over fifteen years, while the mathematics gap has been reduced by about 19 percent over seventeen years. These are clearly positive steps, but the gaps remain very large in the fourth grade and even larger in other assessed grades. Moreover, the fluctuations in gap sizes make trends difficult to identify, although recent results mostly indicate a slow but steady decline in African American-white gaps. Perhaps more troubling is that the remaining achievement level differences "are even more evident when newer types of tasks are considered, such as the extended constructed-response tasks" (Strutchens & Silver, 2000, p. 51).

Other National Measures

A small number of other national assessments of student achievement have been developed over the last twenty years. Occasionally, some of these assessments are considered in tandem with NAEP data to provide fuller achievement gap portraits (e.g., Berends et al., 2005; Hedges & Nowell, 1998; 1999; Miller, 1995). Studies of these assessments generally show ranges of large (typically 0.5–1.1 standard deviations in magnitude) African American-white and socioeconomic achievement gaps at all grades: Camara and Schmidt (1999) suggest .50–1.10 standard deviations while Berends and his colleagues (2005) focus on race and provide an equally large but narrower range of .75–.90. We turn now to two of the most analyzed "other" national assessments—the Early Childhood Longitudinal Study and National Education Longitudinal Study—before considering studies that combine these and other national assessments.

Early Childhood Longitudinal Study, Kindergarten Class of 1998–99

Probably the "nation's most comprehensive assessment of school readiness" (Duncan & Magnuson, 2005, p. 36), the Early Childhood Longitudinal Study, Kindergarten Class of 1998–99 (ECLS-K) is a longitudinal study of a nationally representative sample, following students who entered kindergarten in the 1998–99 academic year through their eighth-grade year. Information was collected from the students, their families, their teachers, and their schools in the fall and spring of kindergarten (1998–99), the fall and spring of first grade (1999–2000), and the spring of third grade (2002), fifth grade (2004), and eighth grade (2007). ECLS-K is the first national collection of longitudinal student data following kindergarteners into middle school.

African American children had "lower overall reading achievement scores than other ethnic groups [in the third grade], even when their background differences were controlled"

(Chatterji, 2006, p. 492), and they made smaller gains in both subjects than did students in any other racial category (Rathbun & West, 2004). From the start of kindergarten through the end of third grade, "Black children demonstrated gains that were about 6 to 7 points lower in reading and 8 to 9 points lower in mathematics than White, Hispanic and Asian/Pacific Islander children" (p. 14).

At the end of fifth grade, white students had higher mathematics, reading, and science scores than African American and Hispanic students, and Hispanic children obtained higher scores than African Americans did in all three subjects. Between the start of kindergarten and the end of fifth grade, ECLS-K mathematics and reading achievement gaps increased steadily. For both the African American-white and Hispanic-white achievement gaps, differences are generally larger for mathematics than for reading. The largest African American-white differences are found in mathematics while the Hispanic-white differences are largest in reading (Lee & Burkam, 2002). These patterns also hold in specific content area. For example, "In third grade about half of White . . . children were proficient in understanding place value, compared with 35 percent of Hispanic children and 20 percent of Black children" (Rathbun & West, 2004, p. 21). Across ECLS-K (and other assessments), "Black students are not only losing ground relative to whites, but even more so relative to Hispanics" (Fryer & Levitt, 2004, p. 455).

Consistent with the racial achievement gaps noted above, children with one or more family risk factors (including living below the federal poverty level) demonstrated lower achievement scores than children with no family risk factors. In addition, as the number of family risk factors increased, "Children tended to gain less in both subject areas than children with fewer family risk factors" (Rathbun & West, 2004, p. v) even when gender and ethnicity were controlled (Chatterji, 2006).

National Education Longitudinal Study of 1988

The National Education Longitudinal Study of 1988 (NELS: 88) is a longitudinal study of a nationally representative sample of eighth-grade students first surveyed in the spring of 1988. A sample of these respondents was resurveyed through follow-ups in 1990, 1992, 1994, and 2000. Achievement tests in mathematics, reading, science, and social studies were administered for the three in-school waves conducted between 1988 and 1992, placing the students at Grades 8, 10, and 12.

The poorest students most frequently scored at the bottom. Almost half of the eighth graders in the NELS: 88 study who were from families with incomes of less than $15,000 per year scored in the bottom quartile (Miller, 1995). This trend is consistent within ethnic categories, too (Camara & Schmidt, 1999): "More specifically, each racial/ethnic group's standardized test scores tend to go up with increases in social class and down with decreases in social class" (p. 159). Moreover, a higher poverty concentration at the school level depresses student achievement even further.

Roscigno (1998) analyzed many characteristics on student achievement by race, supplementing NEL: 88 data with Common Core Data and limiting his results to public schools. He reports mean African American-white achievement differences for tenth graders in 1990 to be about 8 points in mathematics and 6 points in reading. After controlling for familial and school organizational factors, he found a mathematics achievement difference of 3.8 points, statistically significant at the rigorous .001 level. A similar finding developed in reading, where the achievement gap remained statistically significant at 3.5 points after controlling for the same factors. In a follow-up study, Roscigno (1999) conducted similar statistical analyses on the composite African American-white difference, where a statistically significant difference of 4.4 points was discovered. Moreover, he found that increased local poverty levels, which are often prevalent in minority neighborhoods, increased the overall achievement differences between white and African American students.

Combining Assessments

Hedges and Nowell (1998; 1999) used the following national assessments to obtain evidence on the African American-white gap chronologically: Equality of Educational Opportunity (EEO), National Longitudinal Study of the High School Class of 1972 (NLS: 72), High School and Beyond (HSB), National Longitudinal Study of Youth (NLSY), NELS: 88, and NAEP. Adjusting for social class, family structure, and communal differences, the researchers consistently found sizable African American-white assessment score differences nearing and occasionally topping one standard deviation. (As an example of how large a difference this is, a one standard deviation in SAT scores is approximately 100 points.) It is important to note, however, that they found statistical evidence of the gap closing, although such positive trends have since halted and/or reversed.

Berends and his colleagues (2005) also examined multiple national assessments, including the NLS: 72, HSB, NELS, and NAEP. Specifically, they analyzed trends in mathematics achievement differences among racial-ethnic groups over time. Like Hedges and Nowell (1998; 1999), Berends and team concluded that significant progress has been made in closing the mathematic achievement gaps as follows:

> The black-white difference was over a standard deviation in 1972, and this gap narrowed by about 20 percent by 1992.... In 1972, the [Hispanic]-white gap in mathematics was nearly 9/10ths of a standard deviation, but by 1992 the gap narrowed by about one-third, to 6/10ths of a standard deviation. (p. 71)

Even with that progress, the gaps clearly remained substantial, and as noted, the convergence of both the African American-white and Hispanic-white achievement gaps have stopped and/or reversed.

Analyses of other national assessments generally mirror NAEP findings. Studies such as Hedges and Nowell (1998; 1999) and Berends et al. (2005) underscore the reductions of the achievement gaps, but the data that they consider do not extend beyond the mid-1990s. More recent consideration of the achievement gaps in national assessments also reveals that the African American-white and Hispanic-white gaps have leveled off or are increasing. Some research indicates that these large differences are the product of class differences and other external factors, but some of the best evidence shows that race alone is a critical factor. The large overlap between minority status and economic disadvantage only exacerbates the achievement differences that span national assessments.

State-Level Assessments

"The increased focus on high academic standards for all students has brought a heightened awareness of the disparities in student achievement as measured on various statewide assessments" (Shannon & Bylsma, 2002, p. 8). State-assessment results, like national ones, consistently show that "certain groups of children repeatedly score far below children in other groups" (Hertert & Teague, 2003, p. 5).

High-stakes state assessments were becoming increasingly widespread even before the legislation of No Child Left Behind in 2001, but NCLB necessitated state-level testing and gap tracking nationwide. As a consequence, a multitude of state-level data has emerged in the last fifteen years. States vary in the ways they test students and frame results, but, overall, the achievement gap differences mirror national trends (Shannon & Bylsma, 2002). We highlight only a sliver of it here.

Spradlin and associates (2005) report detailed results for Grades 3, 6, 8, and 10 of the Indiana Statewide Testing for Educational Progress-Plus (ISTEP+). From the 1998–99 school year to the 2004–05 school year, the African American-white achievement gap, based on passing rates, shrunk in both Grades 3 and 6, by 6 and 2 percentage points, respectively. The African American-white trends for Grades 8 and 10 narrowed only slightly, however, and the gaps appear to remain "quite alarming" (p. 4) at 35 and 38 points, respectively. Indeed, "Grade 10 gaps are most disconcerting across all comparison categories" (p. 24).

White student performance typically far exceeds the scores of African American and Hispanic students in Washington, too (Shannon & Bylsma, 2002). The Washington Assessment of Student Learning (WASL) includes multiple-choice and open-ended questions. Open-ended questions require students to explain their answers in narrative form or show their work. While white students performed better than African American students on multiple-choice items, they "scored *much* better on open-ended items" (p. 15). Racial achievement gaps were large in all grades (4, 7, and 10) and subjects (mathematics, reading, and writing) tested. The gaps were largest in Grade 10, where the percentage of white students meeting the WASL pass standard was 64.6 percent in reading, 41.9 percent in mathematics, and 59.6 percent in writing. These pass rates were approximately 28, 29, and 26 percentage points higher than for African Americans.

A quick scan across states usually reveals similar racial gap results. The following are just a few examples:

- African American-white mathematics and reading gaps for Minnesota eighth graders were approximately 20 points each in 1996 (Myers, Kim, & Mandala, 2004).
- The pass rate gaps for non-Chicago elementary school students taking the Illinois Standards Achievement Test (ISAT) were sizable, with approximately 86 percent of white students passing in comparison to 60 percent of African American students (Hoerandner & Lemke, 2006).
- On the Prairie State Achievement Examination (PSAE) conducted throughout Illinois, the percentage of minority students meeting state standards is already poor in elementary school in reading and mathematics before dropping "precipitously" in eleventh grade, where only 20 percent of African Americans meet state standards (McGee, 2003).
- Williamson's (2005) inspection of northwestern states (Alaska, Idaho, Montana, and Oregon; grades reported on varied considerably by state) showed white students reaching proficiency at 13 to 35 percentage point clips more than African Americans and Hispanics.

- Chatterji (2005b found that clear progress toward closing African American-white and Hispanic-white achievement gaps in Florida is only evident in fourth-grade reading.
- According to Bankston and Caldas (1998), on the Louisiana Graduation Exit Examination, African American students performed "markedly poorer" (p. 718) than white students.

In addition to standardized tests, some states conduct alternative assessments at the end of the academic year. For example, students taking California's High School Exit Exam (CAH-SEE) also showed patterns of differential achievement based on ethnicity (Hertert & Teague, 2003). White students passed the mathematics section of the exam at rates more than twice as high as those for African American students. The difference in the English language arts section was about one-and-a-half times.

North Carolina gives end-of-grade tests to students in Grades 3 through 8. When all grades are combined, approximately 92 percent of white students passed both the reading and mathematics tests in the spring of 2001 in comparison to 58 percent of African American students (Baenen et al., 2002). Moreover, with results similar to those found in California, passing scores for white students were "considerably higher" (p. 30) than those of African American and Hispanic students on the North Carolina Competency Test, a requirement for high school graduation.

In Texas, however, Toenjes and colleagues (2002) found increasing passing rates for all ethnicities and closing African American-white gaps in mathematics and reading from 1994 to 1999 on the Texas Assessment of Academic Skills (TAAS). These results included adjusted mean scores (scores after other social factors have been statistically accounted for). Fuller and Johnson (2001) confirm these results, pointing out that all racial groups improved reading and mathematics scores substantially from 1994 through 2000, with scores for African Americans increasing more rapidly than those for whites. They contend that these results "suggest that the performance gap between white students and students of color has diminished" (p. 263), though ceiling effects are not considered.

As with the racial gaps, there has not been any "dramatic and widespread shrinking . . . of the achievement gap between more and less advantaged students" (Balfanz & Byrnes, 2006, p. 144). Analyzing achievement data from the California Standards Test (CST), Hertert and Teague (2003) report that percent of poor students scoring "below basic" or worse is about twice as high in mathematics and English language arts across all grades tested than it is for students from higher-income families. Moreover, "The percent of poor students scoring at or above 'proficient' tends to be about one-third that of higher-income students" (p. 8).

In Illinois, based on McGee's (2003) study focused on the Prairie State Achievement Examination (PSAE), achievement differences between poor students and their peers are striking:

It is a gap that exists statewide at third grade where 40 percent of students from low-income families meet state standards compared to 75 percent of their peers. It is a gap which persists to the extent that in grade eleven a mere 20 percent of low-income students meet high school mathematics standards compared to 65 percent of their classmates from middle- and high-income families. (p. 7)

Results of a second assessment in Illinois—the Illinois Standards Achievement Test (ISAT)—confirm these differences (Hoerandner & Lemke, 2006). In fact, such assessment score differences based on socioeconomic status can be seen throughout the United States (Campbell & Ramey, 1995; Fuller & Johnson, 2001; Myers, Kim, & Mandala, 2004).

Although less common, some state-level, race-based achievement gap research has been conducted using NAEP. For example, Braun and colleagues (2006) compared NAEP African American-white gap trends of eighth-grade mathematics achievement in ten states. They report that of the ten states, Kentucky had the smallest achievement gap in 1992 (23 points) and 2000 (22 points) while the largest achievement gaps were found in New York in 1992 (47 points) and Michigan in 2000 (44 points). Lee (2006) found substantial variations in the initial status of the African American-white gap (e.g., the fourth-grade African American-white math gap in West Virginia was 15 points in 1992 compared to 42 points in Michigan), but "most states made little or no progress in narrowing the gap" (p. 39). In a similar vein, Balfanz and Byrnes (2006) report, "In nearly all of the nation's states there is a 30 to 50 percentage-point difference between white students and the largest minority group in the percentage of students scoring at the basic level on the eighth-grade [NAEP] exam" (p. 144).

Spradlin and colleagues (2005) report on NAEP achievement in Indiana in some detail. For students in Grade 4, African American-white gaps have decreased in mathematics from 1992 to 2003. Those gaps, measured by percentage of students reaching basic levels, shrunk from 44 percentage points to 33 percentage points, and from 24 percentage points to 18 percentage points, respectively. In reading, however, it appears that the "most appropriate conclusion is that the gaps between the ethnic groups . . . are relatively stable" (p. 13). Similar achievement gaps exist by race in Grade 8 and by SES in Grades 4 and 8.

With few exceptions, state results more concretely highlight the lessons from the national assessments. State assessments, exit exams, and other measures confirm what has already been presented: minority and poor students continue to achieve well below the levels of their white and nonpoor peers. There is little evidence that achievement gaps are shrinking in any region of the country.

International Assessments

The Program for International Student Assessment (PISA) is an international assessment that measures the performance of fifteen-year-olds in reading literacy, mathematics literacy, and science literacy every three years. Although all three subjects are assessed, one subject is considered the major subject area for each testing period—reading in 2000, mathematics in 2003, and science in 2006. Although the United States generally outscores non-Organisation for Economic Co-operation and Development (OECD) nations, the American mean performance is less than the OECD mean. Even though the mean was lower than the OECD average, American scores in all three subjects are not significantly different than other nations near the mean (Braum et al., 2006).

In 2001, the U.S. Department of Education (2001b) reported on PISA 2000 results. The United States' combined reading literacy mean was 504, 4 points above the international mean, ranking fifteenth out of the twenty-seven participating OECD countries. This is the only emphasized subject in the three years of PISA in which the American mean was above the international average. Results disaggregated by race/ethnicity reveal a stark contrast in

American scores: white students averaged 538 points (.38 standard deviations above the overall mean), African American students 445 points (.55 standard deviations below the overall mean), and Hispanic students 449 points (.51 standard deviations below the overall mean). If taken in the context of OECD-participating nations, white American fifteen-year-olds would have placed second out of twenty-seven nations, whereas Hispanic-Americans and/or African Americans would have placed twenty-fifth.

As reported by Lemke and team (2004), in 2003, the United States' combined mathematics literacy mean was 483, 17 points below the international mean, ranking twenty-fourth out of the twenty-nine participating OECD countries. Results disaggregated by race/ethnicity reveal a stark contrast in American scores here as well: white students averaged 512 points (.12 above), African American students 417 points (.83 below), and Hispanic students 443 points (.57 below). If taken in the context of OECD-participating nations, white American fifteen-year-olds would have placed thirteenth out of twenty-nine nations, Hispanic Americans would have placed twenty-seventh, and African Americans would have placed next to last (twenty-eighth).

As reported by Baldi and his colleagues (2007), in 2006, the United States' combined science literacy mean was 489, 11 points below the international mean and ranking twenty-first out of the thirty participating OECD countries. The following are the results disaggregated by race/ethnicity: white students averaged 523 points (.23 above), African American students 409 points (.91 below), and Hispanic students 439 points (.61 below). If taken in the context of OECD-participating nations, white American fifteen-year-olds would have placed seventh out of thirty nations, Hispanic Americans would have placed twenty-eighth, and African Americans would have placed last (thirtieth).

Advanced Placement

Similar racial gap results have been found consistently in the College Board's Advanced Placement Program (AP), a program in which high school students take college-level courses in high school and take AP exams in them. Scores range from 1.0 to 5.0 with a 3.0 or better being a passing score. Minority students are heavily underrepresented among students who are tested. Moreover, those minority students who do take AP exams "are much less likely than white . . . students to perform well enough on the exams to receive college credit or advanced placement" (Miller, 1999, p. 8), i.e., earn a score of 3 or higher. We consider racial achievement gaps on four AP exams: Calculus AB, Calculus BC, English Language and Composition, and English Literature and Composition.

Both calculus classes are a year in length and develop students' understanding of the concepts of calculus, emphasizing a "multi-representational approach . . . with concepts, results, and problems being expressed graphically, numerically, analytically, and verbally" (College Board, 2009a, p. 6). Calculus BC is an extension of Calculus AB. Over the last decade, the achievement gaps for each Calculus AP exam are similar. Results by ethnic group for Calculus AB and BC are reported in Figures 2.13 and 2.14.

African American-white gaps are larger than Hispanic-white ones, and they have grown consistently. (The term Hispanic is disaggregated into multiple, smaller groups. The results used for our AP comparisons are those of Puerto Rican students. They have consistently been the highest-scoring subgroup of Hispanic students on AP exams, and their trends, overall, are representative of all other Hispanic subgroups.) In 1997, the African American-white gap was

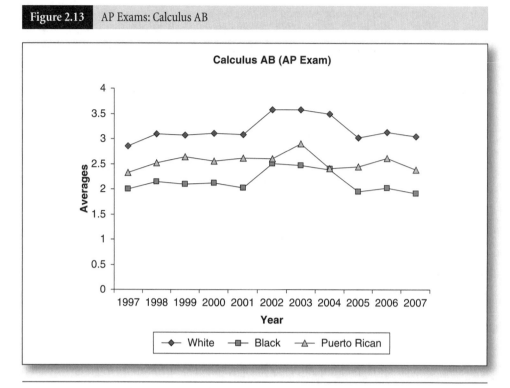

Figure 2.13 AP Exams: Calculus AB

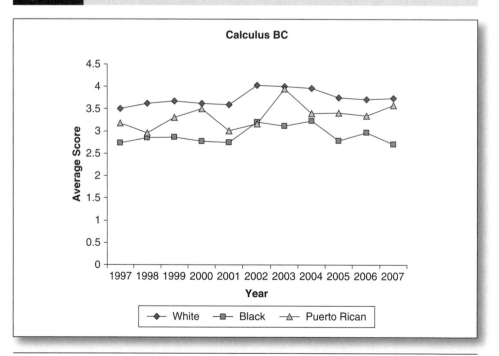

Figure 2.14 AP Exams: Calculus BC

.85 on the AB exam and .76 on the BC exam. In 2007, these gaps had grown to 1.14 and 1.03, more than a 20 percent difference in assessment score by race. The Hispanic-white gaps, on the other hand, were smaller in 1997 (.52 and .32) and have shown no real trends. Thus, a larger AB gap and a smaller BC gap in 2007 do not appear to be reliable indicators of significant Hispanic-white change.

The AP English Language and Composition exam is intended to assess students' "ability to read complex texts with understanding and to write prose of sufficient richness and complexity to communicate effectively with mature readers" (College Board, 2009b, p. 8). The English Literature exam, on the other hand, is intended to assess students' ability to read and critically analyze imaginative literature. Results by ethnic groups on the English Language and English Literature exams are reported in Figures 2.15 and 2.16.

In English Language, white students scored 3.05 in 1997 and 3.04 in 2007. English Literature scores decreased over time for all three racial subgroups, most notably for white students. Although the .78 African American-white gap and the .37 Hispanic-white gap found in 2007 are the smallest gaps in the entire period, achievement gap decreases were sporadic over the ten-year period.

College Entrance Exams

Many colleges and universities require students to take college entrance exams in order to assess each student's ability to perform college-level work. The SAT and ACT are the two major college exams. Acceptance of these exams varies by institution, but, overall, they appear to be "better suited than the NAEP [or other large-scale data sets] for examining trends in the

| Figure 2.15 | AP Exams: English Language |

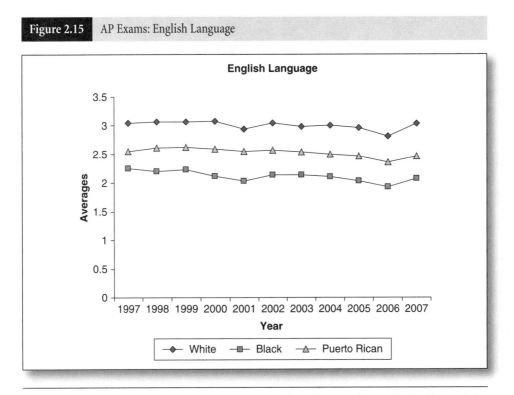

| Figure 2.16 | AP Exams: English Literature |

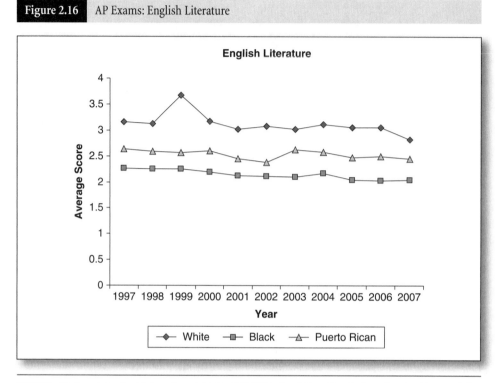

SOURCE: AP Report to the Nation. Copyright © 1997-2007, the College Board. Reproduced with permission. www.collegeboard.com.

proportions of different racial/ethnic groups that are well prepared for higher education" (Miller, 1995, p. 59). Since the SAT and ACT exams are "not designed to be representative of the population and [are] affected by changes in the composition of test takers" (Krueger & Whitmore, 2002, p. 13), results are difficult to interpret.

SAT

"The 1970s saw large numbers of blacks and Hispanics seeking college admission and scoring approximately a standard deviation behind whites on the SAT" (Chubb & Loveless, 2002, p. 2). In his consideration of the SAT as part of his achievement gap research, Miller (1995) reports that there is a positive side to the minority advancement story. Specifically, the overall gap in SAT scores between African Americans and whites "fell from 258 points (2.35) in 1976 to 196 points in 1992, a 24 percent reduction" (p. 3). In addition, improved minority scores appear to be even more impressive considering the large increase of minority SAT test takers over the last twenty years. Still, since the early 1990s, minority gaps on SAT assessments have remained relatively stable (Kober, 2001; Krueger & Whitmore, 2002) or have grown wider (Everson, 2007). These findings appear similar to NAEP results presented above (Miller, 1999). Moreover, the percentage of non-Asian minority students who score at least a 600 level (the high-scorer threshold) have remained "far below" (Miller, 1995, p. 62) that of white (and Asian) students.

SAT scores in critical reading have remained fairly stable over time for white, African American, and Hispanic students (see Figure 2.17). From 1987 through 2007, critical reading scores for each ethnic group increased slightly, by 3, 5, and 2 points, respectively. So, the decrease in the African American-white gap and increase in the Hispanic-white gap are minimal and statistically insignificant. Overall, the African American-white gap (94 points/.85) and the Hispanic-white gap (69 points/.63) over this period remain considerable.

| **Figure 2.17** | SAT Critical Reading/Verbal |

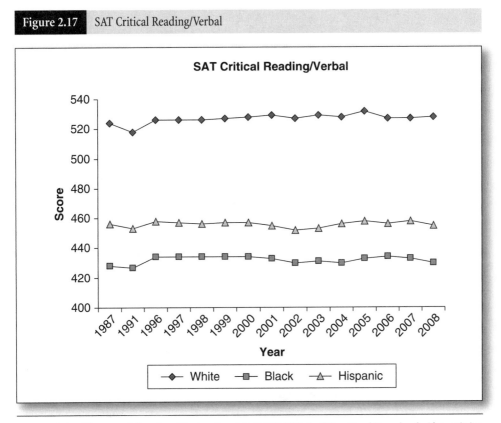

SOURCE: National Report on College-Bound Seniors. Copyright © 1996-2008, the College Board. Reproduced with permission. www.collegeboard.com.

SAT mathematics scores, however, have risen consistently over time for all three ethnic groups (see Figure 2.18). In 1987, the African American mean was 411 and the Hispanic mean was 454. By 2007, these mean scores had risen to 429 and 463. However, during this same span, white math scores increased more, from 514 in 1987 to 534 in 2007. Therefore, the African American-white gap changed minimally (2 points) and the Hispanic-white gap increased substantially (21 points). Still, the 71 points (.65) separating Hispanic and white students remain significantly smaller than the 105 points (.95) separating African American and white students in SAT mathematics scores.

| Figure 2.18 | SAT Mathematics |

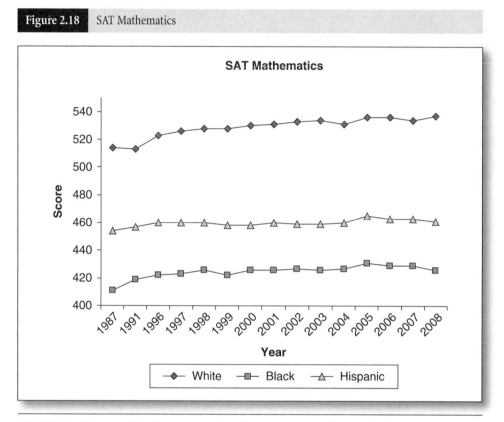

SOURCE: National Report on College-Bound Seniors. Copyright © 1996-2008, the College Board. Reproduced with permission. www.collegeboard.com.

SAT achievement increases linearly as the level of family income increases. This is consistent across subjects (critical reading, mathematics, and, most recently, writing). In 2006, for example, students whose parents earned more than $100,000 scored over 100 points higher in each subject than students whose parents earned less than $10,000. Results for 2006 are reported in Figure 2.18. "These data suggest that test takers with high-income parents tend to be well prepared for college while the opposite tends to be true for those with low-income parents" (Miller, 1995, p. 131). Similar disparities by income levels exist for prior years and across $10,000 increments (Spradlin et al., 2005).

ACT

The ACT is composed of four subject assessments: English, mathematics, reading, and science. Data from 1997 through 2007 indicate two consistent trends across three of the four subject assessments: (1) scores of white students are increasing slightly, and (2) scores of African American and Hispanics students are decreasing slightly. In fact, science is the only subject in which white students' scores are also decreasing, but even there, those scores are not declining as quickly as those of minority students. Over the last decade, the African American-white and Hispanic-white achievement gaps in all four ACT subject assessments have increased. Consequently, minority achievement gaps by composite ACT mean scores (ranging from 1–36) have increased considerably (see Figure 2.19). Since ACT changed its test significantly in 1989, African American-white and Hispanic-white gaps have increased steadily. These gaps have grown from 4.3 points (.91) and 2.4 points (.51) in 1990 to 5.1 points (1.09) and 3.4 points (.72) in 2007, as shown in Figure 2.19. The size of these gaps and the size of the increases of the gaps are especially large when one recalls that the highest attainable ACT score is 36 points.

Figure 2.19   ACT Composite

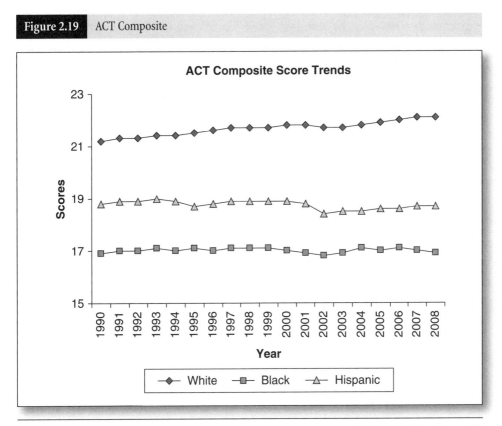

SOURCE: ACT, ACT National Scores, 1997-2008, Composite Scores. http://www.act.org/news/data.html; R. Phelps, Director, ACT Policy Research, personal communication, October 8, 2008.

Other Measures

Despite a dramatic increase in black students' enrollment and graduation, the gap between black and white educational attainment persists. College enrollment rates for white high school graduates increased from 50 percent in the early 1970s to about 60 percent in the mid-1980s and have fluctuated between 60 and 65 percent since then, compared to only 50 percent for blacks. In 1995, whites were more than twice as likely as their black peers to have earned a bachelor's degree, with about 32 percent of whites graduating from college compared to 15 percent of blacks. (Hallinan, 2001, p. 64)

"While there has been increasing focus placed on the ethnic and racial score gaps in tests over the past few years, there has been substantially less attention paid to performance on other educational measures" (Camara & Schmidt, 1999, p. 5). These measures are less about snapshots of levels of achievement and potential, but more about student persistence. Next, we examine gaps in grades; high school graduation rates and dropout rates; and collegiate measures, including matriculation, completion, and advanced degree attainment.

Grades

"The data available for [grades] analysis are much more limited in quality and quantity than are standardized test scores because there is no information analogous to the NAEP [and other large-scale exams]" (Miller, 1995, p. 70). However, "Admission officers report that the greatest weight (i.e., 40 percent) is placed on high school grades for making admission decisions" (Camara & Schmidt, 1999, p. 5). Traditional measures like grades also show a substantial under-representation of minority students among top students (Miller, 1999; Shannon & Bylsma, 2002).

Test takers of the 1990 SAT—already considered above-average students academically across ethnic groups—illustrate the preceding point; 31 percent of whites and 13 percent of African Americans reported maintaining at least an A- grade point average (Miller, 1995). Conversely, 30 percent of African Americans and 16 percent of whites maintained a C (70–79) average. "Predictably, differences in grade patterns were associated with differences in high school class rank patterns" (p. 73), with 22 percent of whites and 12 percent of African Americans ranking in the top tenth of their classes. More recent analysis shows similar trends. Of the college-bound seniors who took the SAT in 1997, over 40 percent of white students reported having an A average in high school in 1997, "compared to less than 20 percent of African-Americans students" (Camara & Schmidt, 1999, p. 5), disparities that exist when mean high school grades and class rank are examined.

In addition to grade point averages, minority students and students from disadvantaged backgrounds are more likely to repeat grades and/or courses, especially African American students (Hallinan, 2001; Mickelson, 2003). Failure rates for minority and low-income students are "unacceptably high" (Burns, Keyes, & Kusimo, 2005, p. 5). "Among the sons of parents who dropped out of high school and are living in poverty, retention rates by age fifteen reach 50 percent" (Entwisle, Alexander, & Olson, 2000, p. 11) compared to 20 percent for sons in an "average" household. The difference in retention by SES is evident as early as kindergarten (Burkam et al., 2004).

High School Completion Rates

Even without full consensus on a high school graduation standard, there is a general agreement on two facts. First, graduation rates are low in absolute terms. On-time public high school graduation rates are approximately 66 percent–70 percent, meaning that at least three out of ten students do not graduate through the regular school system within the conventional time allotted. Second, graduation rates vary by gender and race. On-time public high school graduation rates for black males are as low as 43 percent. This compares to . . . 71 percent for white males. (Levin et al., 2007, p. 3)

"Significant differences also persist in the rates at which different groups of students complete high school" (Haycock, 2001, p. 7). Figure 2.20 presents data on changes in the percentages of twenty-five- to twenty-nine-year-old whites, African Americans, and Hispanics who completed high school with a diploma, as well as those who completed high school through equivalency programs. During the approximately thirty-five years of data reported, the percentage of white and African American high school completers increased consistently, while the percentage of Hispanic high school completers has fluctuated. Still, all groups had significantly more high school completers in 2006 than they did in the early 1970s.

| Figure 2.20 | High School Educational Attainment |

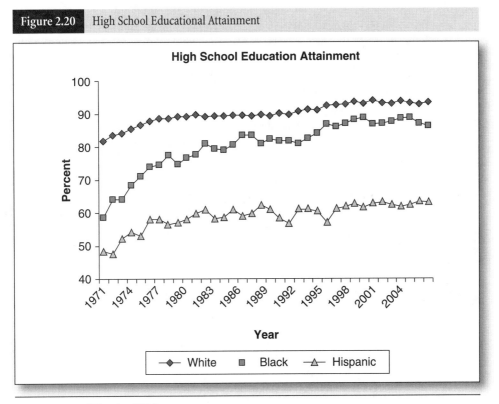

(U.S. Department of Education, 2009a)

In 1971, about 82 percent of whites completed high school in comparison to about 59 percent of African Americans and 48 percent of Hispanics—gaps of approximately 23 percentage points and 34 percentage points, respectively. Considered another way, about eight out of ten whites, six out of ten African Americans, and five out of ten Hispanics completed high school. However, "There have been encouraging increases in the number of African Americans completing high school or its equivalence in recent years" (Steele, 1997, p. 614), including a "great deal of progress" (Miller, 1999, p. 6) in the 1980s and 1990s. In 2004, the gap was smallest at 4.5 percentage points. It increased the two following years to 7.1 percentage points in 2006. In more nuanced analysis, Rothstein (2004) argues since only about 50 percent of African American students get regular diplomas versus about 75 percent of white students, the "important aspect of the black-white gap seems to be getting worse, not better" (p. 109). Shannon and Bylsma's (2002) study of achievement in Washington state seems to support this, as they show that in the 2001 cohort, about 74 percent of white students graduated on time, while only 61 percent of African Americans and 54 percent of Hispanics did.

High School Dropout Rates

Almost 40 [percent of North Carolina] students who enter the ninth grade fail to grad-uate on time four years later, and the rates for minority and economically disadvan-taged students are considerably worse. If we completely eliminate the achievement gap for students who stay in school and do not sharply reduce the dropout rate, a large gap will remain between the life chances for white and minority children. (Thompson, 2002, p. 24)

According to Lee (2002), "Any analysis of the racial and ethnic achievement gap for high school students needs to consider dropout rates" (p. 10). There are two common ways to con-sider achievement gaps by high school dropout rates. Figure 2.21 presents data on "status" dropout rates, the percentage of sixteen- to twenty-four-year-olds not enrolled in high school who lack a high school credential. Here we see that dropout rates for white and African American students have declined consistently since the 1970s. Cook and Evans (2000) report that the African American-white dropout gap fell by nearly 60 percent from the early 1970s to the late 1980s. The African American-white dropout gap was over 13 percentage points in the late 1960s and decreased most years, narrowing to 4.2 percentage points in 1990. Since then, the African American-white dropout gap has fluctuated. Most recently, in 2006, the gap was 4.9 per-centage points. When examining data from 2000, Maruyama (2003) found that the percentage of dropouts, especially for African Americans and Hispanics, increased greatly. For example, dropout rates for African American students increased from 6.1 percent to 13.1 percent.

| Figure 2.21 | Status Dropout Rates by Race |

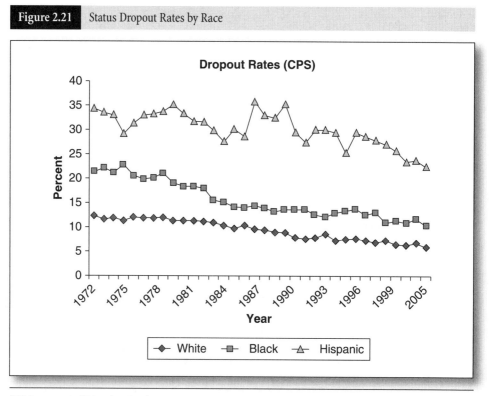

(U.S. Department of Education, 2009a)

Figure 2.22 presents data on "event" dropout rates, the percentage of high school students who left high school between the beginning of one academic year and the beginning of the next without earning a high school diploma or its equivalent. From this perspective, dropout rates for all three groups have decreased consistently since 1972, when the rates were 5.3 percent for whites, 9.5 percent for African Americans, and 11.2 percent for Hispanics. Thus, the African American-white dropout gap was 4.2 percentage points and the Hispanic-white dropout gap was 5.9 percentage points. Twice in the 1990s, the African American-white dropout gap narrowed to 1.3 percentage points, but the gap increased four of the five years from 2001 through 2005, where the gap (4.5 percentage points) was the largest it had been since 1981. "The pattern for the black-white dropout gap varies closely with that of the black-white achievement gap" (Lee, 2002, p. 10).

Figure 2.22	Event Dropout Rates by Race

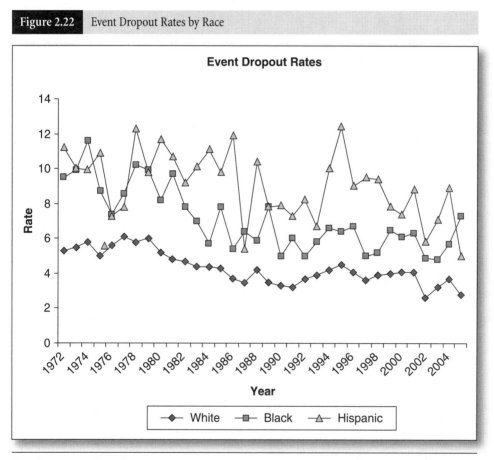

(U.S. Department of Education, 2009a)

Students from lower economic backgrounds have also been more likely to drop out historically (Bempechat & Ginsburg, 1989), and "The devastating effects that conditions of economic and social adversity within families can have on the educational outcomes of youth are well-documented" (DuBois, 2001, p. 133). For example, Figure 2.23 provides status dropout rates by SES quartile. In 1975, students from the lowest economic quartile were more than five times as likely to drop out of school as students from the highest economic quartile. Although these dropout gaps have closed over time, in 2005, students from the lowest economic quartile were still more than four times as likely to drop out.

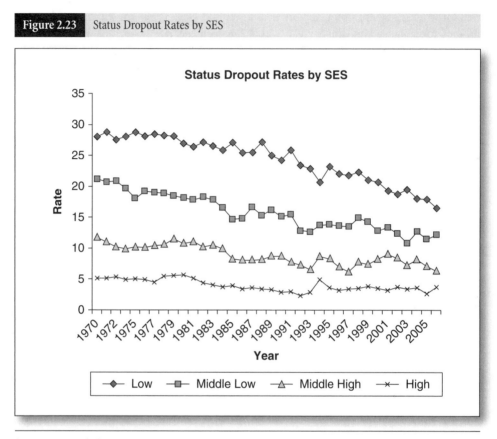

Figure 2.23   Status Dropout Rates by SES

(U.S. Department of Education, 2009a)

Figure 2.24 provides a similar picture for event dropout rates. The percentage of students by socioeconomic class not continuing high school the following year was 15.7 percent, 6 percent, and 2.6 percent for students from low-, middle-, and high-income households in 1975. In 2005, those rates had fallen to 8.9 percent, 3.8 percent, and 1.5 percent, respectively, leaving a low-/high-income dropout gap of 7.4 percentage points and a middle-/high-income dropout gap of 2.3 percentage points. Citing the U.S. Department of Education, Scales and colleagues (2006) note, "Students from lower income families drop out of school at double the rate of middle-income students and six times the rate of students in the upper 20 [percent] of income"(p. 40). Children who lived in poverty for at least one year are 6 percent less likely to graduate from high school than those not raised in poverty (Entwisle, Alexander, & Olson, 2000). Even after taking race and ethnic differences into account, "Students whose parents are poorly educated and in low-status jobs were about seven times more likely to drop out by tenth grade, compared to those whose parents are educated professionals" (Gamoran, 2000, p. 99).

| Figure 2.24 | Event Dropout Rate by SES |

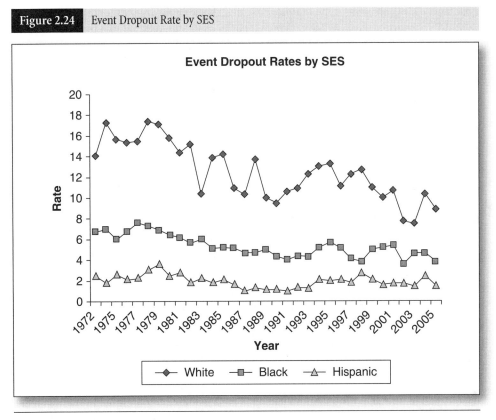

(U.S. Department of Education, 2009a)

Collegiate Measures

Sewell and Hauser (1976) found that in the U.S., high-SES children are 2.5 times more likely than low-SES children to continue education beyond high school, 4 times more likely to enter college, 6 times more likely to complete college, and 9 times more likely to receive some graduate or professional training. (Baker & Stevenson, 1986, p. 156)

"As we have seen, African Americans and Latinos continue to be significantly underrepresented among high school graduates who are academically very well prepared for college" (Miller, 1995, p. 79). And, "Minority-majority attainment gaps continue to be especially large at the higher education level" (Miller, 1995, p. 34). We consider college matriculation, college completion, and advanced degree attainment in turn.

College Matriculation

A report released by the U.S. Department of Education (2001a) claims that "the evidence on recent trends in college attendance and completion by blacks is more mixed than the evidence on recent trends in high school completion" (p. 5). However, most evidence points to African American students being "significantly underrepresented in university degree programs" (Bingham, 1994, p. 6). Put more bluntly, "Black students who complete high school are less likely than white students to enroll in and to complete college" (Hallinan, 2001, p. 52).

In an analysis of four samples of students collected between the late 1970s and the early 1990s, the U.S. Department of Education (2001a) found an evident African American-white college attendance gap across samples, ranging from 4 to 10 percentage points. Haycock (2001) reports that approximately 76 percent of white high school graduates go directly to college, compared to 71 percent of African American graduates. Interestingly, even when college enrollment increases substantially, as it did in Indiana's public four-year universities from 1999 until 2004, the demographic characteristics of the students remain relatively consistent (Spradlin et al., 2005). These figures are even less encouraging when one considers college readiness. For example, "White students completing all courses required for University of California and/or California State University entrance in 2000–01 was about twice as high as for African American and Hispanic students" (Hertert & Teague, 2003, p. 4).

College enrollment rates of recent high school completers are presented in Figure 2.25. Data from 1972 show relatively small African American-white and Hispanic-white college enrollment gaps (5.1 percentage points and 4.7 percentage points). Into the early 1980s, the Hispanic-white college enrollment gap decreased, and in many years, the percentage of recent Hispanic high school completers was greater than that of recent white high school completers. However, the percentage of whites enrolling in college has increased steadily over the last thirty-five years, whereas the percentage of African Americans and Hispanics enrolling in college varied until recently when modest advances have occurred (Steele, 1997).

Figure 2.25   College Matriculation by Race

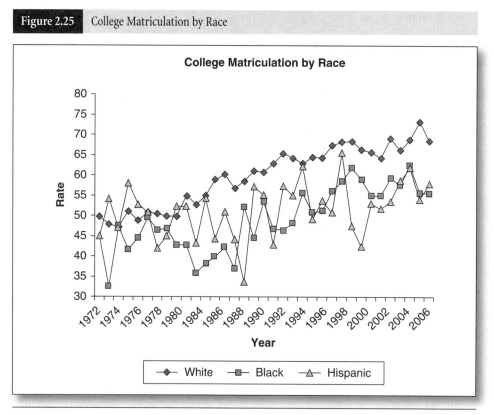

(U.S. Department of Education, 2009a)

Both African Americans and Hispanics have had periods when they closed the college matriculation gap significantly, but such gains have not been sustained. Since 1990, the African American-white college enrollment gap has ranged between from 6.3 percentage points and 19 percentage points. For Hispanics, the gap has ranged between 0.7 percentage points and 24 percentage points. However, college matriculation data from 2006 appear to be fairly representative of both gaps over the last twenty years, with the African American-white gap being measured at 13 percentage points and the Hispanic-white one at 10.6 percentage points. However, with such a large proportion of Hispanics (and African Americans) not completing high school, the percentage of high school completers enrolling in college can be misleading (Padron, Waxman, & Rivera, 2002).

According to the U.S. Department of Education (2001a), in each of the four samples studied, African American students were more likely than white students to attend college when achievement and/or parent SES were similar. Maruyama (2003) contends that there is a relation between race/ethnicity and income that should be considered:

- Success rates for each ethnic group improve as socioeconomic levels increase.
- Differences in African American-white attainment are minimal at socioeconomic levels greater than $25,000. Overall, attainment rates are substantially different, however, in large part because a larger proportion of African Americans students come from families earning less than $25,000 yearly.
- Overall, Hispanics have the lowest attainment rates regardless of socioeconomic status, although at incomes below $25,000, they resemble African Americans.

College Completion

The high college dropout rates of minority students is another regular feature of achievement gap discussions. For example, 62 percent of African Americans enrolled in college do not finish college within six years, compared with a national dropout rate of 41 percent (Steele, 1997; Steele & Aronson, 1995; Steele & Aronson, 1998). According to Haycock (2001), African Americans are only about half as likely as whites to earn a college degree. In the U.S. Department of Education (2001a) study of four samples of students, "The magnitude of the overall black-white gap in college completion ranged about 13 percentage points in the 1979 sample to about 19 percentage points in the other three samples" (p. 26). Even when we reduce the measure of college completion to *two* or more years of college, significant African American-white and Hispanic-white gaps remain (Miller, 1995).

The percentage of twenty-five- to twenty-nine-year-olds by race with a bachelor's degree or higher is shown in Figure 2.26. From 1971–2007, the percentage of whites who attained a bachelor's degree nearly doubled (18.9 to 35.5). In the same period, the percentage of African Americans attaining a bachelor's degree nearly tripled (6.7 to 19.5), while Hispanics more than doubled (5.1 to 11.6). Still, the college completion gaps increased—the African American-white gap by 3.8 percentage points and the Hispanic-white gap by more than 10 percentage points. Both African American-white and Hispanic-white gaps remained stable from the early 1970s to the early 1990s, when gap sizes began to increase. Although both gaps have narrowed recently, they remain larger than the gaps of the early 1990s and considerably larger than the gaps of the 1970s.

Figure 2.26   College Completion by Race

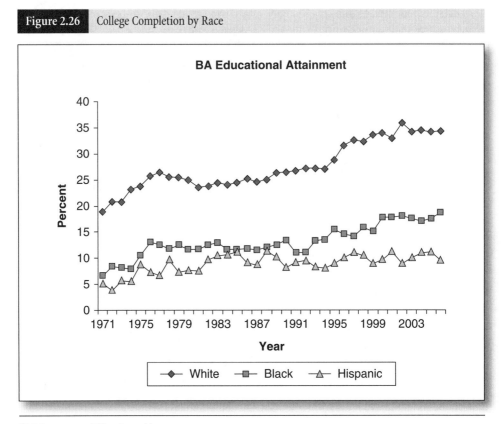

(U.S. Department of Education, n.d.)

Advanced Degree Attainment

Figures 2.27 and 2.28 highlight data from 1976–2005 on total graduate and professional fall enrollments in degree-granting institutions. In 1980, whites constituted about 82 percent, African Americans 6 percent, and Hispanics 2 percent of the total graduate student fall enrollment. By 2005, the percentage of students enrolled in graduate programs who were white had dropped to 65 percent, while the percentage of African Americans nearly doubled to 11 percent, and the percentage of Hispanics tripled to 6 percent. Still, while the gap is closing, the percentage of African Americans and Hispanics enrolled in graduate school did not meet population percentages. Professional enrollments are even more unbalanced, as whites make up 71 percent, African Americans 8 percent, and Hispanics 5 percent. For both graduates and professionals, however, African Americans and Hispanics have been enrolling at slowly but steadily increasing rates, thus reducing gaps in enrollment.

The story is even less positive when we consider the percentage of master's degrees and doctoral degrees conferred by race/ethnicity (see Figures 2.29 and 2.30). Although the percentage of African Americans and Hispanics attaining advanced degrees has increased consistently while the percentage of whites attaining advanced degrees has decreased (i.e., the gap is closing), we still find that the breakdown of the percentage of students attaining master's degrees in 2006 is as follows: approximately 66 percent white, 10 percent African American, and 6 percent Hispanic.

Figure 2.27   Graduate Enrollment by Race

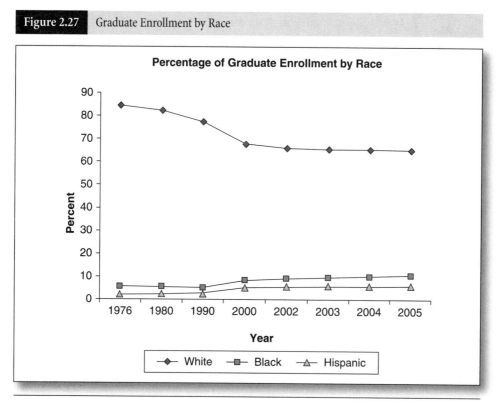

(U.S. Department of Education, 2009a)

Figure 2.28   Professional Enrollment by Race

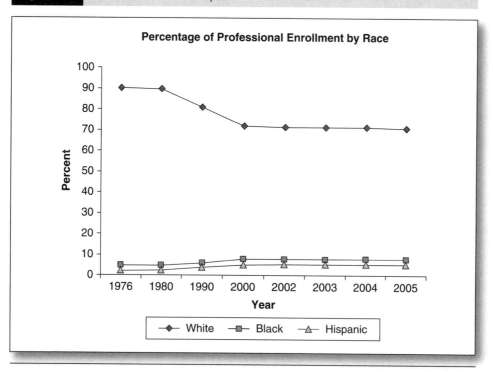

(U.S. Department of Education, 2009a)

Figure 2.29   Master's Degrees Conferred by Race

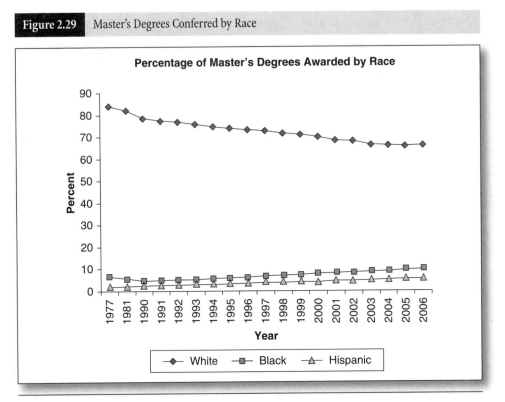

(U.S. Department of Education, 2009a)

Figure 2.30   Doctoral Degrees Conferred by Race

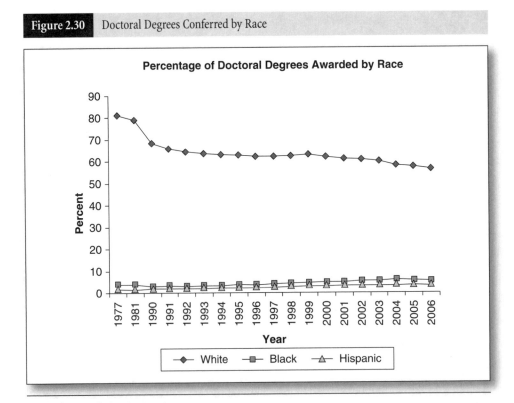

(U.S. Department of Education, 2009a)

For doctoral degrees awarded in 2006, 56 percent went to whites, 6 percent went to African Americans, and 3 percent went to Hispanics. Here again, although the African American-white gap is being reduced (from 77 percentage points in 1977 to 51 percentage points in 2006), there is much room for improvement. As the level of degree increases, the percentage of African Americans and Hispanics with degrees conferred decreases at a faster rate than does the percentage of whites with degrees conferred.

Miller (1995) presents three alternative ways to consider race differentials by advanced degrees conferred. First, examining data from 1979 and 1989, he shows that when nonresidents are withheld from the calculations, the African American-white and Hispanic-white gaps are even larger than the ones provided above. Second, analyzing the highest level of postsecondary attainment by race for the 1980 high school senior cohort in the spring of 1986, he notes that whites are four and a half times more likely than African Americans and nine times as likely as Hispanics to attain graduate and/or professional degrees. Third, reviewing data from 1964–1989, he reports that whites ages 25 to 29 are two to three times as likely as African Americans and Hispanics in the same age range to complete five or more years of college. Perhaps most telling, "In 2001, universities in the United States awarded nearly 2,000 doctoral degrees to graduates in fields such as astronomy, environmental science, petroleum engineering, and plant genetics; African Americans received none of these" (Seiler & Elmesky, 2007, p. 392).

LOOKING AT THE GAP ACROSS LEVELS

All else equal, white students who start elementary school with test scores at the population mean can be expected to finish high school with test scores that are still at the mean. Black students who start elementary school with "true" test scores at the population mean can be expected to finish high school with math scores that lie 0.34 standard deviations below the mean and reading scores that lie 0.39 standard deviations below the mean. These gaps are equivalent to a decline of about 35 or 40 SAT points. (Phillips, Crouse, & Ralph, 1998b, p. 253)

Significant achievement gaps between different populations of students exist at all levels of education and appear to increase from lower to higher grades. By the end of Grade 4, low socioeconomic and minority students lag behind their peers by two years, and this gap widens to three years by Grade 8. By high school, the average African American and Hispanic senior is four years behind. The gap persists into higher education, where there is a great disparity when comparing college attendance rates for African American and Hispanic high school graduates to those of white students. (Spradlin et al., 2005, p. 1)

[Seventeen]-year-olds should score 300 or more on the NAEP reading and mathematics tests in order to meet the New Basic Skills, the minimum skills people now need to get a middle-class job. If we accept level 300 as the minimally adequate level of achievement for high school graduates, Black and Hispanic students did make significant progress toward that goal over the last two decades. Nevertheless, the progress almost stalled during the 1990s, and the gap of Blacks and Hispanics in basic knowledge and skills still remains very large. As of 1999, 27 [percent] of Black and 38 [percent] of Hispanic

17-year-olds performed at or above Level 300 in mathematics. The corresponding figure for their White peers was 70 [percent]. (Lee, 2004, p. 61)

"One of the most controversial empirical questions has been whether the gap widen[s] as children age" (Phillips et al., 1998b, p. 229). "Research has shown that the gap in test scores between blacks and whites widens as children progress through school" (Orr, 2003, p. 286), but findings are usually presented discontinuously and only segments of the achievement gap are illustrated. In this section, we provide a portrait of the achievement gap, highlighting the research from prekindergarten through college. We note at the start that the research landscape varies considerably by assessment type and level, statistical methodology, and presentation.

PreK Education

"Although the achievement gap is normally seen as a problem affecting school-age children, in fact the gap first opens during the preschool years" (Haskins & Rouse, 2005, p. 1). "As previous research has documented, black, Hispanic, and low-SES children enter kindergarten with math and reading skills substantially lower, on average, than their white and middle-class counterparts" (Reardon, 2003, p. 17). Entwisle and Alexander (1992) contend that, at least in pre-math skills, socioeconomic differences represent most of this difference. Nonetheless, "Well over half of the black-white reading gap at each grade can be explained by black-white differences in initial skills" (Phillips et al., 1998b, p. 248).

Brooks-Gunn and colleagues (2003) underscore highly statistically significant differences by race at age three on multiple tests. An assessment of children entering Head Start indicates that the program's children, who are disproportionately minority and poor, "already fall well short . . . in vocabulary, early reading, letter recognition, and early math by ages three and four" (Haskins & Rouse, 2005, p. 2). Head Start and similar programs are designed to counteract some of this academic imbalance, but for Hispanics, the likelihood of even attending early childhood programs is significantly less than that of whites and African Americans (Padron, Waxman, & Rivera, 2002).

In a similar vein, Jencks and Phillips (1998), using National Longitudinal Survey of Youth Child Data, found about 85 percent of African American three- and four-year-olds scored lower on a vocabulary test than the average white child did, and African American students typically scored in the twentieth percentile. As perhaps a more pointed illustration, Magnuson and Duncan (2006) discuss a Farkas and Beron (2004) study in which the researchers determined the average age at which African American and white children correctly identified forty words on a test. "For whites, this happened two months after the children's fourth birthdays. For blacks, it was a full year later" (Magnuson & Duncan, 2006, pp. 368–369).

Collectively, these findings demonstrate that "substantial differences in black-white [and Hispanic-white] readiness for kindergarten" (Rock & Stenner, 2005, p. 19) exist. "Much and perhaps most of the gap appears to be present by school entry" (Magnuson & Duncan, 2006, p. 370).

Elementary School

The National Center for Education Statistics, using Early Childhood Longitudinal Study data, "shows that minority children enter kindergarten with a skills gap that widens on more sophisticated skills during the kindergarten year" (Lewis, 2008, pp. 2–3). However, the math and reading gaps between Hispanic students who pass oral language assessments at the start of kindergarten and their white peers are present at the start of kindergarten and do not change, in general, nearly as much as do the African American-white gaps from kindergarten through first grade (Reardon, 2003), and occasionally decline in math over time. Still, significant differences in reading and mathematics performance by race are apparent by kindergarten, even when background factors *and* entry-level reading skills are controlled (Reardon, 2003). Brooks-Gunn and team (2003) demonstrate this for first graders by analyzing various assessments of five-year-olds and finding consistent differences in scores by race. "Prospects data suggests that black-white learning rates differ most sharply in elementary school" (Reardon, 2003, p. 5). "For example, the vocabulary of black children in first grade is about half that of white first graders" (Rock & Stenner, 2005, p. 19).

Even when students' scores at the beginning of first grade were controlled and corrected for measurement error, African Americans' reading scores at the end of the second grade trailed that of whites' by about 0.29 standard deviations (Phillips et al., 1998b). They find similar results for fifth graders whose scores were controlled for as third graders. Noting her own work and that of others, Chatterji (2006) reports that African Americans remain behind in reading performance in elementary school and "make smaller gains in reading than other ethnic groups through third grade" (p. 503). Therefore, studies do "show modest growth in racial achievement gaps during the early school years" (Magnuson & Duncan, 2006, p. 370) in reading and mathematics. Similar results are found in vocabulary assessments.

Rathbun and West (2004) provide an example of this, using ECLS-K data to track fall 1998 first-time kindergartners through the spring 2002. They confirm that student race does have predictive value, and that African American and Hispanic students score slightly, but significantly, less than white students over this time. In addition, they report that family risk factors play a role in growing achievement gaps independent of race. "For each risk factor, children's gains in reading decreased by about 4 points and their mathematics gains decreased by about 2 points" (p. 14). The additive nature of risk factors to achievement gaps is important to consider since minorities are more likely to be exposed to them. Differences in mathematics (and reading) scores by race/ethnicity and/or family risk factors are pervasive across testing subject subcomponents. For example, when compared to white third graders, a considerably smaller percentage of African American third graders "were proficient in multiplication and division, place value, and rate and measurement (20, 23, and 11 percent fewer, respectively)" (Rathbun & West, 2004, p. 22).

Miller (1995) considers the variation between students attending low-, medium-, and high-poverty schools in the percentages of both poor and nonpoor students who scored in the bottom quartile on the achievement tests used in the Sustaining Effects Study on elementary school students in the mid- to late-1970s, and extends this to High School and Beyond conducted in the early 1980s. He underscores the importance of collective poverty, pointing out, "A nonpoor student in a high-poverty school was more likely to be in the bottom quartile than a poor student in a low-poverty school" (p. 134). According to his data, this is true for Grades 1 through 6. Moreover, he finds that, for all participating grades, "The achievement gap [between low-poverty and high-poverty schools] grew substantially during the school year and continued to grow rapidly over the summer" (p. 136). Differences in achievement at the intersection of race and SES appear to be consistent at all grade levels. In Illinois elementary schools, only 4.5 percent of high-poverty elementary schools had an average of two-thirds of their students meeting state standards over a three-year period. Over 70 percent of other elementary schools did meet the standards (McGee, 2003). In addition, as we show in Chapter 7, achievement gaps by SES appear to grow substantially during out-of-school periods (Reardon, 2003).

Spradlin and associates (2005) report that Indiana African American and Hispanic Grade 4 students are still much more likely than white students to have "Below Basic" NAEP scores, a trend that appears pervasive nationwide. Analyzing 2000 NAEP data, Lee (2004) affirms that African American students in Grade 4 are about three times more likely to be performing below the Basic proficiency level in mathematics than are white students. In reading, 38 percent of white fourth-grade students scored at the proficient level or above while only 9 percent of African American students did so (Meehan et al., 2003). Also with NAEP data, Lubienski (2002) shows that "the *lowest* SES white students consistently scored equal to or higher (often significantly so) than the *highest* SES black students" (p. 276).

Although considered much less frequently, gaps in science achievement are also sizable. Reporting on 1999 NAEP trend assessments, Kober (2001) states, "In science at age 9, the black-white score gap is 41 points, or a rough difference of almost *four* [italics added] grade levels. The Hispanic-white gap is 34 points, or roughly equivalent to *more than three* [italics added] grade levels" (p. 23).

Zimmer and Buddin (2005) contend that in California, "Language problems are much more prevalent in elementary schools than in secondary schools" (p. 10), with over 60 percent of Hispanic elementary students in Los Angeles being classified as English learners. In Grade 5, "Current and former English learners are reading at the same level as English-only students between Grades 3 and 4, a gap of about 1.5 years" (Rumberger & Gandara, 2004, p. 2035; see also Gandara et al., 2003).

Middle School

Thernstrom and Thernstrom (2002) note that if there were no racial gap at all, African American mean scores on assessments such as NAEP would consistently be at the fiftieth percentile. However, for thirteen-year-old NAEP reading test takers, African American students ranked in the fifteenth percentile—"a dismal showing" (p. 133). "Initially similar blacks also learn fewer reading skills than whites during middle school and high school, but the differences are smaller than during elementary school" (Phillips et al., 1998b, p. 248). Language challenges remain substantial for many students. Gandara and colleagues (2003) inform that by Grade 8, "English learners are reading at the same level as English only students in Grade 6, a gap of about 2 years" (p. 7).

Meehan and colleagues (2003) report a 40-point African American-white achievement gap in eighth-grade mathematics on the NAEP assessment, with 34 percent of white students scoring at or above the proficient level while only 5 percent of African Americans did so. On the 2003 main NAEP assessment, "The mean scale score . . . for black students (252) falls at the 13th percentile of the distribution of scale scores for white students . . ., which is an indication of the small overlap of the two distributions" (Braun et al., 2006, p. 4). All racial differences appear to cut across SES levels in middle school, too (Lubienski, 2002).

"In science, the average scores of black and Hispanic students at age 13 were lower than the average score of white students at age 9" (Kober, 2001, p. 23). By Grade 8, "Current and former English learners are reading at the same level as English-only students in Grade 6, a gap of about two years" (Rumberger & Gandara, 2004, p. 2035).

Examining National Education Longitudinal Study of 1988 data, Miller (1995) underscores the importance of the intersection between race and socioeconomic status for eighth-grade achievement. First, he reports that 17 percent of white students in the bottom SES quartile failed to show basic reading skills in comparison to 26 percent of Hispanic students and 30 percent of African American students. Second, he informs that 40 percent of white students in the top SES quartile were proficient in advanced mathematics in comparison to 25 percent of Hispanic students and 21 percent of African American students. In a similar vein, Myers, Kim, and Mandala (2004), reporting on Minnesota state assessments, find:

> *African Americans are 4.5 times twice as likely to be found in the bottom-ranked math schools as they are to be found in the eighth grade population, and are twice as likely to be found in the lowest ranked reading schools as in the general population of eighth graders. (p. 85)*

The racial achievement gaps most often researched and discussed center on multiple-choice assessments, which might not capture the magnitude of racial achievement differences. Strutchens and Silver (2000) analyzed the African American-white achievement gap of eighth graders' performance on the 1996 NAEP assessment, specifically focusing on extended constructed-response tasks that require more complex thought to complete. Although about 70 percent of African American students in the sample performed as well as white students on multiple-choice items, less than 20 percent performed as well on the extended constructed-response tasks.

High School

Analyses by Phillips et al. (1998b) "imply that high schools do not make the black-white math gap worse" (p. 248), but there is no indication that high schools help to close the gap, either. As we discuss in Chapter 11, high school variation in academic intensity is often aligned by school-level SES. Low-SES schools are less likely to offer advanced work and more likely to have minimal graduation requirements (Camara & Schmidt, 1999). Miller (1995) conveys that an increased duration of poverty sometimes leads to lower levels of achievement. In Illinois, "Just 6.25 [percent] of high poverty high schools have half the students meeting PSAE standards compared to 73.6 [percent] of the other high schools" (McGee, 2003, p. 12). "At the end of 4 years of high school, students in low-SES high schools have lower achievement levels, on average, than students in high-SES high schools had before they started high school" (Rumberger & Palardy, 2005, p. 2017). That is, twelfth grade low-income student achievement is the same as the average performance of an eighth grade middle-class student (Shannon & Bylsma, 2002).

"Among students completing one or more AP examinations in 1997, 71 percent of the students were white . . . compared to Hispanic and African-American students who comprised 8 percent and 5 percent of the cohort, respectively" (p. 6). Minorities tend to have less access to advanced courses when attending the same school than other groups (Murphy & Hallinger, 1989; Murphy, Hull, & Walker, 1987; Oakes, 1985). "Tracking has a strong and consistent impact on the rigor and intensity of courses completed in high school" (Camara & Schmidt, 1999, p. 7).

In the three samples studied by the U.S. Department of Education (2001a), African American-white gaps in high school/GED completion ranged from 2 percentage points to 9 percentage points, although rates of completion were similar when achievement levels were comparable.

In the 2002 NAEP, "16 percent of black and 22 percent of Hispanic twelfth-grade students displayed 'solid academic performance' in reading, as against 42 percent of their white class-mates" (Rouse, Brooks-Gunn, & McLanahan, 2005, p. 5). Considering mean scores and per-centiles, Thernstrom and Thernstrom (2002) report that the mean reading score for African American seventeen-year-olds reached only the fourteenth percentile overall. Examining 1999 NAEP data, Krueger and Whitmore (2002) find that African American seventeen-year-olds "scored at the 13th percentile of the distribution of white students on the math exam and at the 22nd percentile on the reading exam" (p. 11). "To frame the gap another way, the average 1999 reading score of black students at age 17 was about the same as that of white students at age 13" (Kober, 2001, p. 23; Slavin & Madden, 2001). As Hallinan (2001) states, this is "a sig-nificant lag in the achievement of black students" (p. 51). By the time African American and Hispanic students graduate from high school, "They will have the same skill level in reading as a white student in Grade 8" (Spradlin et al., 2005, p. 3).

Analyzing multiple assessments and controlling for multiple factors, Phillips et al. (1998b) find that in math, the African American-white gap "widens by about . . . 0.18 stan-dard deviations between the first and twelfth grades, the reading gap remains relatively con-stant, and the vocabulary gap widens by about 0.23 standard deviations. None of these linear trends differs reliably between cross-sectional and longitudinal surveys" (p. 236). Considering NAEP trend results, Chubb and Loveless (2002) suggest that African American and Hispanic students appear to be roughly four years behind white students on average by age 17. Lubienski (2002) presents another way to understand the severity of racial gaps through NAEP 2000 main results. She states:

> *The eighth-grade white students scored a significant 8 points higher than twelfth-grade black students. The NAEP scale is designed to make these cross-grade compar-isons. These data imply that, on average, black students complete high school with less mathematical knowledge than white eighth graders possess. (p. 276)*

Haycock (2001) reports the following as an illustration of how serious the reading and math achievement gaps appear to be at the end of high school:

- Only one in fifty Hispanics and one in one hundred African American seventeen-year-olds can read and gain information from specialized text—such as the science section in the newspaper (compared to about one in twelve whites).
- Less than one-quarter of Hispanics and one-fifth of African Americans can read the complicated but less specialized text that more than half of white students can read.
- About one in thirty Hispanics and one in one hundred African Americans can com-fortably do multistep problem solving and elementary algebra, compared to about one in ten white students.
- Only three in ten African American and four in ten Hispanic seventeen-year-olds have mastered the usage and computation of fractions. (p. 7)

Moreover, white high school seniors appear to be about ten times more likely than African American high school seniors to "score in the top 5 percent of the national distribution on a test of academic skills" (Hallinan, 2001, p. 51).

Thernstrom and Thernstrom (2002) maintain that no statistically significant progress has been made in science recently. "In 1999 as in 1977, more than half of all black students were as ignorant of science as whites in the bottom tenth of the distribution" (p. 136). Bempechat and Ginsburg (1989) report that the average science proficiency of African Americans and Hispanics is four years behind that of white students, and "Among seventeen-year-olds, 15 percent of black and Hispanics were able to analyze scientific procedures and data, compared to 50 percent of their white peers" (p. 13).

African American seventeen-year-olds have vocabularies roughly comparable to those of white thirteen-year-olds (Phillips et al., 1998b). For English learners, vocabulary differences appear to be even greater. By Grade 11, "Current and former English learners are reading at the same level as English-only students between Grades 6 and 7, a gap of about 4.5 years. This is especially striking given that many of the poorest scoring English learners have already dropped out of school by the eleventh grade" (Rumberger & Gandara, 2004, p. 2035). Hakuta (2002) reports that 28 percent of English learners pass the California High School Exit Exam compared to 74 percent for white, primarily English-only students. "Only 64 [percent] of Hispanic kindergartners graduate from high school" (Waxman, Padron, & Garcia, 2007, p. 132).

In some of the analyses presented here, when student characteristics are held constant statistically, actual differences in achievement might actually be greater in "real life" when these characteristics come into play (Rumberger & Palardy, 2005). The data consistently "imply that a black student who enters school with the same test scores as a comparable white students will be likely to have lower test scores than the white student at the time he or she leaves the twelfth grade" (Orr, 2003, p. 286). Moreover, Phillips et al. (1998b) point out:

> *About half of the total black-white math and reading gap at the end of high school can be attributed to the fact that blacks start school with fewer skills than whites. The other half can be attributed to the fact that blacks learn less than whites who enter school with similar initial skills." (p. 232)*

More specifically:

> *Calculations imply that 56 percent of the math gap and 43 percent of the reading gap can be attributed to the fact that blacks start school with fewer skills than whites. It follows that 44 percent of the math gap and 57 percent of the reading gap is unrelated to racial differences in initial skills. (p. 254)*

Still, according to Rumberger and Palardy (2005), "Most of the variability in student achievement overall, as opposed to achievement growth during high school, is associated with students (and their families and communities), not the schools they attend" (p. 2023). Evidence from IQ testing seems to confirm this conclusion. At all IQ levels, racial and class-level differences emerge (Gordon, 1976), appearing as early as age 2 (Duncan & Brooks-Gunn, 2001). According to Brooks-Gunn, Klebanov, and Duncan (1996), by early elementary school, the African American-white difference in mean score is greater than one standard deviation (more than 15 points). Citing the work of Loehlin, Lindzey, and Spuhler (1975) and Gordon (1984), Phillips et al. (1998b) point out that differences in IQ scores remain fairly stable throughout the school years and/or constant with age, mostly exonerating schools.

Postsecondary Education

Few minorities have had scores on the NAEP that are "consistent with being very well prepared academically for the most selective colleges and universities" (Miller, 1999, p. 6). For example, on the 1998 NAEP reading test, only one-quarter of Hispanic twelfth graders had scores at the "proficient" level, and only between two and three percent reached the "advanced" level, whereas, "Nearly half of the whites reached or exceeded the Proficient level and 7 percent reached the Advanced level" (p. 6). Miller (1995) helps us understand this further:

> These scoring patterns mean that African-American, Latino, and Native American twelfth graders collectively constituted only about one in ten of the students who scored at the Advanced level on each of the three tests, even though they made up about one-third of the age group. In fact, they made up only about one-tenth of those who scored at the Proficient level on the NAEP math and science tests. (p. 7)

These achievement differences appear to be highly correlated with college preparedness. "The percent of . . . white students scoring at or about 1000 on the year 2000 SAT for college admission was at least three times higher than for the African American and Hispanic students who took the test" (Hertert & Teague, 2003, pp. 8–9).

Similar to the trends observed throughout K–12 education, students with high-income parents "tend to be well prepared for college while the opposite tends to be true for those with low-income parents" (Miller, 1995, p. 131).

With lower high school completion rates and assessment scores, not surprisingly, fewer minority students than white students enroll in college. According to Waxman, Padron, and Garcia (2007), "22 percent [of Hispanics] enroll in college; of that 22 [percent], only 10 [percent] complete four years of college" (p. 132). The college dropout rate for African American students is also high, as 62 percent of African American college students do not finish college within six years, compared with a national dropout rate of 41 percent (Steele, 1997). "And there is evidence of lower grade performance among those who do graduate of, on average, two thirds of a letter grade lower than those of other graduating students" (p. 615).

CONCLUSION

The hope stemming from racial and economic achievement gap closures of the late 1980s and early 1990s has dimmed considerably in recent years. The preponderance of evidence indicates that achievement gaps have either halted or reversed over the last decade. This appears to be true at all ages and grade levels. Moreover, the African American-white achievement gap extends well beyond urban settings, as indicated by state (and district) assessment results. Despite the contentions of some scholars, much of the research literature also indicates that racial achievement differences persist even after economic, parenting, and other factors are controlled. Perhaps most discouraging, the minority gains on assessments that do exist might not be completely representative. Instead, mean gains for African American students typically point to increases for the lowest-achieving students only, as indicated by further racial separation in the highest ends of achievement. Indeed, even the improved scores of the lowest-achieving African American students are met with consternation when one considers that more challenging tasks or changed or new assessments show even greater achievement disparities.

Still, there are some important positives to note. First, dropout rates by race continue to narrow, overall. Second, in the same vein, college matriculation rates for minorities have grown consistently, as have rates of degrees conferred. Finally, the most recent NAEP results also reveal a narrowing of the African American-white achievement gap, especially at the lower age groups and grade levels. These results are not substantive enough to be considered a trend, yet, but there is reason for optimism.

PART II

GRINDING UP HOPE

Explaining the Development
and Persistence of Achievement Gaps

The virus of calamity

—Timothy Eagan

INTRODUCTION

*Getting a better understanding of the causes of the test score gap is of great importance.
(Fryer & Levitt, 2004, p. 447)*

*There has been a bitter controversy over whether the sources of poor educational per-
formance of the disadvantaged lie in family background or the school program.
(Natriello, McDill, & Pallas, 1990, p. 16)*

*Clearly "race gaps" in student achievement scores exist; what scholars debate are the
causes of significant racial differences in student scores. (Bali & Alvarez, 2003, p. 485)*

In the first chapter, we established that each of the three parts of this book is intended to
examine a critical aspect of the achievement gap problem. In Part I (Chapters 1 and 2), our
goal was to help readers develop an understanding of the importance and scope of achievement and attainment gaps. In Part II (Chapters 3–9), we investigate the reasons learning differentials emerge and why those gaps persist. Recall that our focus is on gaps between African

American and white students, and between high- and low-SES youngsters. In the last section of the book, Part III, we turn the spotlight on research-grounded strategies for eliminating achievement gaps. As Miller (1995) clearly asserts, this final objective is dependent upon the middle aim: "Effective strategies for eliminating these gaps as quickly as possible are unlikely to be identified unless we have a clear understanding of both their origins and why they persist" (p. 83). The good news here is that while there is still much to learn (Reardon, 2003), since the mid-1960s, "Substantial effort has been devoted to understanding what variables account for the gap" (Fryer & Levitt, 2004, p. 448) and we now have "an extensive body of research document[ing] the multiple factors associated with the achievement gap" (Hertert & Teague, 2003, p. 4). Indeed, we now know "far more . . . about the nature of the achievement gap—its causes and consequences—than about how to fix it" (Chubb & Loveless, 2002, p. 2).

Gap analysts frame up answers to the cause question in various ways (Goldsmith, 2004). Some develop causal algorithms, capturing and weighting important variables in the process. Some social scientists employ categorical approaches to conditions linked to achievement gaps. For example, Brooks-Gunn, Klebanov, and Liaw (1995) discuss five broad areas: biological, social, economic, family structure, and maternal characteristics (p. 257). Roscigno (1998) outlines causes around four lines of research: family background, family structure, peer group influences, and the institution of education (p. 1034). Ford, Grantham, and Whiting (2008) use three broad domains to explore causes of achievement gaps: social variables, family variables, and school variables. Some within this tradition also craft taxonomies and tables. Here, for example, the lists of "risk factors" associated with the achievement gap by Brooks-Gunn and her colleagues (1995) and Stevenson, Chen, and Uttal (1990) are illustrative. Brooks-Gunn, Klebanov, and Liaw (1995) list the following risk factors: very low birth weight, poor neonatal health, unemployment, low maternal education, low maternal PPVT-R, high depression, high stressful life events, low social support, teenage motherhood, father absence, high family density, and categorical child-rearing views. Others add poverty and lower job status to the list.

Still other scholars cast answers to the cause questions in theoretical terms, for example, ecosystem theories or theories of capital development. In particular, Coleman (as cited in DuBois, 2001) was a pioneer in exploring achievement gaps using "capital" lenses. He suggests that gaps can be traced to three forms of capital made available to youngsters:

> . . . financial capital (income to buy food, clothes, etc.), human capital (nonmaterial resources from parents such as the ability to help youth with school work), and social capital (people with whom youth share their household—such as parents or other adult caretakers—who can, for example, advocate for their needs in school and other settings). (p. 135)

More recently, Lareau (2002) has continued the tradition of employing a capital framework to explain the achievement gap. Stinson (2006), in turn, employs various theoretical frames to explore reasons for the African American-white achievement gap, including these five in the domain of deficiency discourse: cultural deprivation theory, culture conflict theory, institutional deficiency theory, educational equality theory, and heredity theory (p. 483).

In addition, scholars "offer a long list of potential explanations for test score gaps" (Stiefel, Schwartz, & Ellen, 2006, p. 9). Nearly all reviewers highlight two broad clusters of explanations for achievement gaps: a family and society category and a school cluster (Carpenter, Ramirez,

& Severn, 2006; Downey, von Hippel, & Broh, 2004; Lee, 2004); that is, they "tease out the extent to which variability in achievement is accounted for by a child's background versus particular schooling factors" (Chatterji, 2006, p. 492): "The home environment and effects of experiences in schools are debated as individual or complicit culprits" (Hughes, 2003, p. 313). And within that two-part framework, the literature "tend[s] to reflect either a 'cultural' perspective that views behavior as the result of the beliefs and values of the individual, family, or group, or a 'structural' perspective that views behavior as the product of environmental factors outside the individual" (Hertert & Teague, 2003, p. 9). The following analysts all represent the environment-school perspective on the causes of achievement gaps:

The two most widely cited explanations of the achievement gap are lower socioeconomic status and worse schools. (Phillips, Crouse, & Ralph, 1998, p. 254)

No simple or clear explanation exists for why there are racial/ethnic achievement gaps. Analysts have identified numerous in-school and out-of-school factors that may explain or contribute to these gaps. (Kober, 2001, p. 26)

In seeking to explain why poor children do worse academically than children from middle-class and wealthy families, analysts have focused on two major topics: differences in schools and differences in home environments. (Entwisle, Alexander, & Olson, 2000, p. 9)

Gaps in school achievement . . . have deep roots—deep in out of school experiences and deep in the structures of schools. (Barton, 2003, p. 36)

General and race-specific achievement are a function of both family/peer attributes and more structural educational processes. (Roscigno, 1998, p. 1042)

Attempts to explain the achievement gap and proposals for narrowing it can be broadly categorized as either focusing on factors external to schools or factors that are school-based. (Hertert & Teague, 2003, p. 9)

Families and school both play significant roles in the development of achievement gaps, independently or through patterns of family-school interaction processes. (Reardon, 2003, p. 2)

We will find significant disparities in performance between race groups overall, some of which are explained by differences in student characteristics, such as poverty, and some of which are explained by differences in schools. (Stiefel, Schwartz, & Ellen, 2006, p. 9)

There have been two explanations offered in the literature. One explanation centers on the students and their families . . . while the other explanation looks at school-level factors. (Bali & Alvarez, 2003, pp. 485–486)

A myriad of factors have been analyzed by researchers over the years to determine the causes of the differences in test scores between white students and students of color and between students from affluent and poor families. These factors are often categorized into two broad areas: factors outside the sphere of influence of schools . . . and factors that can be influenced by the system. (Shannon & Bylsma, 2002, p. 20)

Analysts have expanded this two-part framework in important ways as well. Ferguson (1991) adds innate ability and community to the school-family framework (see also Brooks-Gunn, Klebanov, & Duncan, 1996; and Klein et al., 1997). Phillips, Crouse, and Ralph (1998) add "genes, peers, and other factors" to the storyline. Clotfelter, Ladd, and Vigdor (2005) include cultural and psychological factors and neighborhood and community factors to the causal equation. And Hedges and Nowell (1999) view "discrimination against blacks as a stigmatized group" (p. 113) as another significant cause of achievement gaps.

In Figure II.1, we provide a comprehensive picture of the causes of the achievement gap between high- and low-SES youngsters and African American and white students. The picture was developed by examining the various ways scholars frame the gap issue, as well as the assortment of reasons they employ to explain achievement gaps. We observe that achievement gaps can be attributed to conditions and actions within five large clusters of variables: (1) social and economic context, (2) racial context, (3) family and community context, (4) individual and peer context, and (5) K–12 educational context. As we will see shortly, each context category comprises of a number of interconnected elements. For example, the social and economic context is a composite of critical indices such as education, occupation, income and wealth, and accumulated advantages. In general, the K–12 educational context cluster attends to school-based explanations for achievement gaps. The other clusters primarily address nonschool causes of achievement gaps.

The central point here is that regardless of origin, "Minority students and poor students disproportionately face conditions that are hinderous to achieving at levels reached by majority students" (Barton, 2000, p. 36). Also, "they are much less likely to receive the structural and attitudinal supports" (Gordon, 1976, p. 10) to be successful on a par with more advantaged peers. As a consequence, as we reported in great detail in Chapter 2, "Low income students and students of color underperform at all educational levels" (Maruyama, 2003, p. 655).

While we subsequently delve into these issues more fully, a number of points merit attention in this introduction, relevant to our analysis of the causes of achievement gaps. In the first chapter, we reported that no single intervention will solve the achievement gap problem, that an integrated set of social and school-based responses is required. In parallel fashion, we observe here that there is no single cause of the gap: "Inequality is a multidimensional problem" (Heckman, 1995, p. 1093). Rather, there is "a complex web of contributing factors" (Williamson, 2005, p. 5). "Numerous factors work together" (Spradlin et al., 2005, p. 2) and many variables "interact in complex ways to influence school performance" (Strutchens & Silver, 2000, p. 46). Or, in the words of Hertert and Teague (2003), "The achievement gap results from complex and confounding interrelationships among many different variables" (p. 9). Lee (2002) also reminds us that "the sheer number of factors reflects the complexity of studying racial and ethnic achievement gaps" (p. 6). We also need to acknowledge, "The distinction between school-and education-relevant family resources is somewhat artificial" (Miller, 1995, p. 287). Elements in each sector are linked (Brooks-Gunn, Klebanov, & Liaw,

Figure II.1   Causes of the Achievement Gap

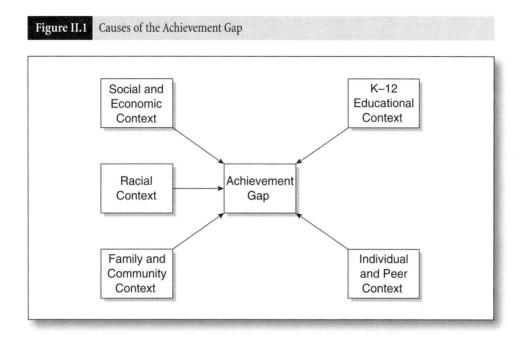

1995; Hughes, 2003; Roscigno, 2000) and "The influence of family and school are hard to separate" (Entwisle & Alexander, 1992, p. 73).

It is also instructive to remind ourselves that attributions of cause for the achievement gap have different and sometimes compelling implications for reform work. Or, as Knapp (2001) nicely encapsulates the issue, "These explanations vary in their political and value loading" (p. 179). For example, "Looking outside school will give excuses to the schools. And . . . a focus entirely on the schools will cause neglect of matters important to children's well-being and learning, and of expecting more of schools than is within their capability" (Barton, 2003, p. 36). Returning to Knapp (2001):

> *Each explanation for inequality . . . subsumes, either explicitly or implicitly, a 'theory of the problem' which locates the main sources of inequality and implies one or more "theories of intervention," which suggest how the problem can be addressed by educators and others. (p. 179)*

Finally, while some analysts maintain that "it is difficult to determine whether disadvantaged children experience lower achievement because of school or non-school influences" (Downey, von Hippel, & Broh, 2004, p. 615), the weight of the empirical evidence finds that while both social/family and school factors are implicated in the achievement gap problem—that gaps in achievement result from "deficiencies that originate outside schools and problems that are caused partially by the schooling experience itself" (Hughes, 2003, p. 298)—social/family factors dominate the narrative (Rothstein, 2004). That is, social/family factors explain more of the gaps (Grissmer, Flanagan, & Williamson, 1998; Hanushek & Raymond, 2005; Lee & Bowen, 2006; Shannon & Bylsma, 2002). Achievement gaps can be traced primarily to economic, political, social, and cultural capital issues (Hall, 2001; Stiefel, Schwartz,

& Ellen, 2006). Indeed, in the decades since publication of the Coleman Report, "Researchers have consistently found that social-class factors are powerful predictors of the academic performance patterns of groups of students, while school factors are relatively weak predictors" (Miller, 1995, p.119): "Scholarly efforts over four decades have consistently confirmed Coleman's core finding; no analyst has been able to attribute less than two-thirds of the variation in achievement among schools to the family characteristics of their students" (Rothstein, 2004, p. 14).

School factors are implicated more for failing to close achievement gaps than for causing them in the first place. "[A] single-minded emphasis on schools is misplaced since differences in elementary schools do not create the achievement gap between rich and poor children: virtually the entire gap reflects differences in home environments" (Entwisle, Alexander, & Olson, 2000, p. 9). Rothstein (2004) exemplifies this as follows:

> *Schools have demonstrated limited ability to affect differences in the rate at which children from different social classes progress. Children from higher social classes come to school with more skills and are more prepared to learn than children from lower classes. All children learn in school, but those from lower classes, on average, do not learn so much faster that they can close the achievement gap. (p. 15)*

Building on these points, we conduct our analysis of the reasons why gaps develop and persist over time. We first divide causes into those beyond or external to schools and those that can be linked to school practices. In Chapters 3–7, we sort external causes into the following bins: socioeconomic variables, family conditions, community/neighborhood dynamics, individual elements, racial discrimination, and out-of-school learning experiences. In Chapters 8 and 9, we cluster school explanations for the development and persistence of achievement gaps into the following categories: instructional programs, school culture, and structure and support.

3

Environmental Causes of Achievement Gaps

An Introduction

Disadvantaged social origins anticipate disadvantaged social destinations. (Alexander, Entwisle, & Olson, 2001, p. 173)

The primary source of inequality lies in children's disparate non-school environments. (Downey, von Hippel, & Broh, 2004, p. 632)

Most estimates of education production functions find that conditions in home and community environments outside of the school are important determinants of schooling outcomes. (Ferguson, 1991, p. 10)

One major finding has been that much of the differences can be attributed to black-white differences in family background characteristics, such as socioeconomic status (SES) and family size or composition. (Orr, 2003, p. 281)

Our starting point from Part I is that "social and ethnic inequality in educational attainment constitutes a troublesome and enduring aspect of schooling in the U.S." (Raudenbush, Fotiu, & Cheong, 1998, p. 253). Point number two, which is the focus of Chapters 3–7, is that a sizable portion of these differences in attainment can be traced to non-school conditions, conditions that we label environmental factors: "Research has found that factors outside the classroom—such as economic, family, and personal characteristics—have a strong influence on achievement" (Shannon & Bylsma, 2002, p. 9). Indeed, these factors explain more of achievement gaps than do school-based factors (Miller, 1995; Rothstein, 2004).

For example, Lee and Burkam (2002) find "Almost half of the racial/ethnic gaps in achievement is explained by taking children's social class into account" (p. 81). And Fuchs and Reklis (as cited in U.S. Department of Education, 2001a) conclude, "Child and household characteristics explain much more of the black-white difference in test scores than can be explained by school characteristics" (p. 8). The corollary is that an exclusive focus on schools in explaining achievement gaps is inappropriate (Rothstein, 2004): "To ignore the aspects of students' lives outside the school walls that contribute to achievement gaps would be irresponsible and ineffectual if the goal is to understand the problem fully and strive to ameliorate it" (Reynolds, 2002, p. 11). For low-SES youngsters and for students of color, then, "The problems of inequality of access to many environmental supports that undergird proacademic behavior in schools . . . are critical factors" (Bennett et al., 2007, p. 260).

Environmental interpretations of achievement gaps are generally grouped into categories such as SES and conditions in the home and community, "including income and resources, home environment, parental employment and marital status, language use, parent-child interactions (including parental cognitive instruction), parental warmth and discipline, and parental mental health" (Reardon, 2003, p. 8). More directly, these "economic and family factors have been viewed as causing low achievement among students of color and poverty" (Shannon & Bylsma, 2002, p. 20): "The major single explanation for racial gaps between whites and blacks . . . is SES. The second most important explanatory step is in-home activities" (Lee & Burkam, 2002, p. 59). Thus, on one front, we learn that SES is "a strong predictor of student achievement" (Berends et al., 2005, p. 25), that "student's academic achievement is strongly related to the socioeconomic status of the student's parents" (Baker & Stevenson, 1986, p. 156)—"economic level is the key influence" (Entwisle & Alexander, 1992, p. 77). On the second front, we discover, Differences in test scores between racial/ethnic groups [are] the result of environmental factors heavily associated with variations in the family and community resources necessary for school success in American society" (Miller, 1995, p. 190).

The consequence of these differences in economic and family conditions is that low-SES and African American children "grow up in environments much less favorable for developing intellectually in ways that are valued in the mainstream of our society" (Miller, 1995, p. 192; Gordon, 1976). On the issue of race, Fryer and Levitt (2004) report, "Black children are growing up under circumstances likely to be less conducive to academic achievement than white children" (p. 451). On the issue of social class, Miller (1995) "confirms that most high-SES students receive several times more resources than most low-SES students and that most of the resource gap is due to variations in family rather than school resources" (p. 339). The result is: (1) "Children who come from disadvantaged families tend to have lower achievement than do those who come from more advantaged families" (Orr, 2003, p. 295) and (2) "Children from lower social classes and from many racial and ethnic minorities, even in the best schools, will achieve less, on average, than middle-class children" (Rothstein, 2004, p. 14): "Even the best resourced school under existing arrangements is usually not able to compensate fully for a substantial shortfall on the family side—which means that a child from such a family is not likely to be educated well" (Miller, 1995, p. 87).

The reason for this, which we unpack in detail in the next four chapters, is twofold. First, economic and social advantages are directly related to resources available to families for undertaking their role in the education of their children: "Different academic performance patterns of children from different social classes are due in large measure to differences in their access to family resources . . . relevant to education" (Miller, 1995, p. 298). As we will discover shortly, scholars in this area often frame the translation of economic and social advantages and disadvantages connected to achievement gaps in terms of capital formation. They confirm that "children from poor families typically have much less human, social, health, financial, and polity capital available to them than children from middle-class families" (Miller, 1995, p. 116). These various capitals mediate between socioeconomic status and student achievement. Second, despite its central place in the achievement gap narrative, schooling occupies only a small portion of the life of young people. Conversely, "Children spend the majority of time outside of school" (Downey, von Hippel, & Broh, 2004, p. 615)— something in the neighborhood of 85 percent of their waking hours by the time a child is eighteen.

In the next four chapters, we investigate these environmental (nonschool) causes of the achievement gap more thoroughly. We begin in Chapter 4 with an analysis of socioeconomic status. In Chapter 5, we examine family and community context. In Chapter 6, we explore sociocultural and individual explanations for patterned achievement differentials by social class and race. In Chapter 7, we investigate the importance of various out-of-school learning opportunities.

4

Environmental Causes of Achievement Gaps

Socioeconomic Status

Most of the racial test score gap probably results from social class factors. (Rothstein, 2004, p. 56)

A handful of SES-related measures accounts for nearly all of the black-white difference in math and reading test scores. (Magnuson & Duncan, 2006, p. 383)

The substantial variations among groups of students in income and parent education available to them are strongly correlated with the large variations in academic performance among these groups. (Miller, 1995, p. 310)

One of the most robust findings in the social science literature concerns the linkage between social class and student achievement (Hedges & Nowell, 1998). While not explaining all of the differential (Duncan & Magnuson, 2005), measures of socioeconomic status account for a "substantial portion" (Miller, 1995, p. 141) of the achievement gap between white and African American youngsters and between high- and low-SES children (Chatterji, 2006; Lee & Burkam, 2002; Phillips et al., 1998a; Williams, 2003), something in the area of 40 to 50 percent (Miller, 1995).

A social class is defined by Miller (1995) as a "group of individuals who receive somewhat similar amounts of benefits in a society" (p. 12). The concept is used interchangeably with the term *socioeconomic status* (Biddle, 2001), which, in turn, is defined by Magnuson and Duncan (2006) as "one's access to economic and social resources and the social positioning, privileges, and prestige that derive from these resources" (p. 372). While "sociologists have long disagreed about how to measure social class" (Chin & Phillips, 2004, p. 188), most analysts unpack the concept into a handful of "fairly general" (Miller, 1995, p.121) components or elements (Hughes, 2003). Caldras and Bankston (1997) review three key elements of SES: family income status, family educational backgrounds, and family occupational backgrounds (see also Alexander, Entwisle, & Olson, 2001; Burkam et al., 2004; Chatterji, 2006; Downey, von Hippel, & Broh, 2004; Fryer & Levitt, 2002; Lee & Burkam, 2002; and Miller, 1995). In their research, Chin and Phillips (2004) provide an example of how these elements combine to define specific social classes:

> We defined middle class families as those in which at least one parent had a four-year college degree or was in a professional or managerial occupation. We defined working-class families as those that had incomes above the poverty threshold but in which neither parent had a four-year degree or was in a professional or managerial occupation. Poor families were those that reported incomes below the poverty threshold, regardless of their education or occupation. (p. 188)

An assortment of scholars helps us discern connections between social class and student achievement, especially the learning differentials that are the focus of this volume. Heyns (1978) asserts that David and Havighurst (as cited in Heyns) have provided perhaps the most eloquent statement of this connection: "The pivotal meaning of social class to students of human development is that it defines and systematizes different learning environments for children of different classes" (p. 195). Or, as DuBois (2001) asserts, "Multiple aspects of family socioeconomic disadvantage [or advantage] have been indicated to represent distinct and hence potentially cumulative sources of influence on academic achievement" (p. 162). As we stress throughout this chapter, the concept of social class is important because it has significant implications for the formation of family resources (Roscigno, 1999). Biddle (2001) illustrates this conclusion:

> Low levels of parental education will generate educational disadvantage because those parents are less able to help their children with classroom content. In contrast, parents with low-status jobs may not have the "social connections" needed if their children are to cope with educators in schools and other high-status persons. And financial impoverishment generates deficits in all sorts of physical, emotional, educational, and health-related resources needed to support children in schools. (p. 7)

We turn now to a more detailed analysis of the dimensions of SES—family occupation and educational background, and family income and wealth.

FAMILY OCCUPATION AND EDUCATIONAL BACKGROUNDS

> Differences in standardized test scores among racial/ethnic groups were most strongly correlated with variations in home background, particularly as measured by socioeconomic-status-related characteristics, such as the education levels and occupations of the parents. (Miller, 1995, p. 85)

Educational and occupational status have a more important influence on achievement per se, than whether or not an individual qualifies for the federal free/reduced-price lunch program. (Caldras & Bankston, 1997, p. 281)

On the occupational front, researchers confirm, "The masses of Black children are disproportionately located in families that suffer the turmoil of unemployment . . . and low-paying occupational positions" (Hale-Benson, 1990, p. 203). Theses researchers document that white parents are more likely to be employed (Stevenson, Chen, & Uttal, 1990) and "to be employed in more prestigious occupations" (Orr, 2003, p. 290). Equally important, they draw the connection between parental occupational status and lower student achievement for minority and low-income youngsters (Ainsworth-Darnell & Downey, 1998; DuBois, 2001; Rothstein, 2004). These analysts explain how the occupational status of the parents can influence, either positively or negatively, the "extent to which youth develop self-views and attitudes that are conducive to success in schools" (DuBois, 2001, p. 162). Specifically, they demonstrate how parents' occupations affect academic performance, especially when "formal education is not of clear relevance," as this "may tend to communicate standards and expectations for academic performance to their children that are relatively less challenging and ambitious in comparison to those conveyed by other parents (DuBois, 2001, p. 140).

Directing the spotlight to the educational dimension of social class reveals two important dynamics. First, there is a strong link between parental level of education and student academic performance (Brooks-Gunn, Klebanov, & Duncan, 1996; Ferguson, 1991; Fuchs & Reklis, 1994; Roscigno, 2000; Zill & West, 2001).

- Among those indicators of family disadvantage investigated in the present research, parental educational background emerged as having particularly strong and consistent linkages with academic achievement. (DuBois, 2001, p. 161)
- The external factor, parent education, had the strongest effect on test scores. (Shannon & Bylsma, 2002, p. 22)
- There are substantial differences in test scores attained by students from different social classes as measured by parental education level. (Miller, 1995, p. 30)
- The education level of parents has a direct or even predictive effect on a child's academic performance. (Uhlenberg & Brown, 2002, p. 498)
- Professionals have known for years that the best predictor of a child's success in school is the education level of the parents, particularly the mother. (Bainbridge & Lasley, 2002, p. 424)
- Children of highly educated mothers do better in school and stay in school longer. (Nartiello, McDill, & Pallas, 1990, p. 24)
- Children with highly educated parents routinely score higher on cognitive and academic tests than do children of parents with less education. (Duncan & Magnuson, 2004, p. 41)

Conversely, Stevenson and associates (1990) find, "Children of poorly educated mothers . . . [do] less well in mathematics than [do] children whose mothers [have] higher levels of education" (p. 520). For example, Miller (1995) reveals that 48 percent of the parents of children in the lowest quartile on the 1988 National Education Longitudinal Study (NELS) study had a high school degree or less. Only 13 percent of parents in the highest quartile were so characterized.

On the flip side, 51 percent of parents of students in the top quartile had college (23 percent) or graduate (28 percent) degrees, while only 11 percent of parents in the lowest quartile had college (7 percent) or graduate (4 percent) degrees. Magnuson and Duncan (2006) suggest that an additional year of parental education is worth about 0.15 standard deviations in children's test scores (p. 377).

In summary, "Children who do well on achievement tests tend to have mothers who [are] well educated" (Luster & McAdoo, 1994, p. 1085) and, "Children with less educated parents . . . are likely to experience some academic deprivation" (Lee, Brooks-Gunn, Shnur, & Liaw, 1990, p. 504). The impact of parental education has been reported in mathematics (Hughes, 2003), reading (Natriello, McDill, & Pallas, 1990), adolescent outcomes (Brooks-Gunn, Klebanov, & Duncan, 1996), and school retention (Natriello, McDill, & Pallas, 1990).

We know not only that "parents' education is a critical variable in children's achievement" (Kober, 2001, p. 28) but also that educational experiences are not equitably distributed in the United States Minority and low-income youngsters are more likely to have parents with lower levels of education (Camara & Schmidt, 1999; Miller, 1995; Spradlin et al., 2005). According to Natriello and associates (1990), in the 1980s, about 30 percent of African American mothers but only 13 percent of white mothers were high school dropouts (see also Grissmer, Flanagan, & Williamson, 1998). By the turn of the century, the ratio of African American-to-white dropouts for mothers had increased, from 2.3 to 2.6, even though the absolute numbers had declined, to 7 percent for white mothers and 18 percent for African American mothers (Duncan & Magnuson, 2005). Again, looking at the turn of the century as a base point, we see that "the following percentages of six-to-eighteen-year-olds' parents had less than a high school education: 19.6 percent of mothers and 14.6 percent of fathers of Black children . . . and 6.9 percent of mothers and 8.1% of fathers of White children" (Land & Legters, 2002, p. 10).

On the other end of the educational continuum, African Americans complete college at lower levels than whites—in 2000, 16.5 percent for African American men and 26.1 percent for white males (Brooks-Gunn et al., 2003). The comparable numbers for women are 9 percent and 28 percent (Magnuson & Duncan, 2006). Overall, African American and white mothers have 12.8 and 13.8 years of education respectively. For fathers, the analog numbers are 13.2 and 14.4 (Stevenson, Chin, & Uttal, 1990).

Three additional themes can be gleaned from the educational attainment data. First, educational attainment levels are rising across the board. High school completion rates, in particular, are increasing. Thus, according to scholars such as Rothstein (2004) and Land and Legters (2002), the percentage of African American children characterized as "at risk according to this indicator should continue to decline" (Land & Legters, 2002, p. 10).

Second, while the data are not completely clear on the issue, it appears that having some college education or completing college is especially important in the educational attainment chronicle (Ferguson, 1991). Or, as Roscigno (1998) captures it, "Advantages associated with parental education are even more pronounced for those whose parents hold at least a college degree" (p. 1043). And here, as we documented earlier, we find that progress by African American parents is less pronounced than it is in the area of high school completion (Ferguson, 1991).

Third, we are learning that measures of educational attainment are somewhat gross indicators of opportunity. They mask a good deal of information that is likely important in explaining race and social-class learning differentials among children. To begin with, as Miller (1995) first observed, measures of educational levels reached reveal nothing about content and performance. They are silent on issues such as grades in subjects and test scores, and about how much academic knowledge parents accumulate as they earn degrees. And, Miller reminds us, "There may be substantial differences in developed academic capacities between individuals and groups with similar educational attainment levels" (p. 314). He further explains that it is the accumulation of these capacities, not degrees, that provide parents with the wherewithal to better help their children succeed in school: "It is reasonable to assume that these differences [in accumulated capacities] are associated with human-capital gaps among parents from the several racial/ethnic groups, including parents who have similar attainment and degree levels" (p. 161). He continues his analysis by documenting an important finding for those who believe that closing the attainment gap may be a sufficient objective in the struggle to close achievement gaps for children: "Available data suggest that, at each attainment level, minority parents on average have less well developed formal-education-derived knowledge and skills (human capital) than their white counterparts" (p. 338).

Gross measures of educational attainment also convey no information about the quality of the schools parents attended or about the quality of the school experience (Magnuson & Duncan, 2006; Phillips et al., 1998a). Typical measures provide no information on the curricular content and/or on major areas of concentration (Miller, 1995). And, as Miller cautions:

> There can be enormous variation in this area . . . to the extent that [some] fields provide greater human-capital development opportunities of certain kinds (for example, in math and science) than other fields, one might expect differences in college majors to be associated with human-capital gaps among parents from different racial/ethnic groups, even when these parents have the same educational attainment/degree level. (p. 161)

We conclude our analysis here with a bit of foreshadowing of material in Part 3 of the book, where we provide solutions to narrow achievement gaps. Pointedly, even in light of the caveats from Miller just discussed, improving social class conditions of African American students "—such as parents' occupational status [and] educational attainments—correspond to significant convergence in black-white test scores" (Berends et al., 2005, p. 72). In the case of educational attainment, this appears to occur because "parent educational level may be linked directly to a wide variety of conditions and processes in the home environment that are implicated in the achievement outcomes of youth" (DuBois, 2001, p. 161). It is also the case because better-educated parents tend to "have more knowledge of their children's schooling, have more social contact with school personnel, and are better managers of their children's academic careers" (Natriello, McDill, & Pallas, 1990, p. 24).

FAMILY INCOME AND WEALTH

> In short, logic and evidence both suggest that when America tolerates a massive, uniquely high level of childhood poverty, it also imposes unfair educational disadvantages on many of its citizens. (Biddle, 2001, pp. 8–9)

A major commonly accepted reason that black children are educationally disadvantaged is because they are more likely to live in households with incomes below the poverty line. In fact, economic status and educational achievement are significantly linked. (Natriello, McDill, & Pallas, 1990, p. 21)

Much of these test score gaps are explained by racial and ethnic differences in poverty rates. (Stiefel, Schwartz, & Ellen, 2006, p. 26)

As the gap in wealth between children increases, so will the gap in test scores. (Orr, 2003, p. 292)

No single variable has received more attention in the achievement gap literature than income, or, more accurately, poverty. Research documents that income inequality and poverty are rampant in American society and that African American children disproportionately find themselves living in low-income homes. Studies also consistently "document a strong association between poverty and students' academic success" (Hertert & Teague, 2003, p. 1). Finally, social scientists provide useful insights about the pathways between low-income status and learning differentials. We explore each of these aspects of the achievement gap below.

Extent of Poverty

There is abundant data on the nature and depth of poverty in the United States. We know, most critically, that poverty is a defining pattern in the tapestry of American society. Biddle (2001) confirms that the gap between the rich and the poor in the U.S. is larger than in most of the Western world. He reveals that in the early 1990s, about 17 percent of Americans were living in conditions of poverty. In contrast, in over half of the OECD nations, less than 5 percent of residents were poor, and only one country exceeded the 17 percent rate in the United States. Using a more appropriate and fairer measure than the fiscal poverty line used in official government documents, a threshold of "income needed to assure minimal stability," Rothstein (2006, p. 2) argues that fully 50 percent of African Americans and 20 percent of whites have inadequate incomes—are poor in the real sense of the word. Research also informs us that the income gap between citizens in the middle and those in the bottom has been expanding over the last half century (Duncan & Brooks-Gunn, 2001; Rothstein, 2006). Biddle (2001) states:

More importantly for our purposes in this volume, we discover that poverty is disproportionately associated with childhood. Indeed, "[The] rate of poverty among children [in the U.S.] is far higher than in other advanced nations" (Payne & Biddle, 1999, p. 7). The data from 2003, for example, "indicate that 20 percent of children under age eighteen live in families with income below the poverty line. What this means is that at least one-fifth of all children who come through the schoolhouse door in America today are likely to be experiencing poverty-associated problems such as substandard housing, an inadequate diet, threadbare or hand-me-down clothes, lack of health insurance, chronic dental or health problems, deprivation and violence in their communities, little or no funds for school supplies, and whose overburdened parents subsist on welfare or work long hours at miserably paid jobs. These facts pose enormous problems for America's schools. (p. 5)

Taking a longitudinal perspective, Miller (1995) and Duncan and Brooks-Gunn (2001) provide even more troubling data. They document that at some period during childhood, nearly four in five African American students and one in five white students are touched by poverty. Consistent with the general patterns discussed, Duncan and Brooks-Gunn (2001) furnish evidence that (1) poverty rates for children are higher than they were a quarter century ago and (2) are "1.5 to 4 times as high as the poverty rates in Canada and Western Europe" (p. 49).

Given the analysis to this point, it will come as no surprise to learn that poverty in general, and childhood poverty in particular, are much more prevalent in the African American population (Karoly, Kilburn, & Cannon, 2005; Duncan & Aber, 1997; Stevenson, Chen, & Uttal, 1990). At the dawn of the twenty-first century, fully one-third of all African American Americans and 46 percent of African American children fell below the official poverty line (Roscigno, 2000, p. 268). The rate of poverty for African American youngsters is three to four times that for white youngsters (Bempechat & Ginsburg, 1989; Shannon & Bylsma, 2002). "Data from the nationally representative Panel Study on Income Dynamics (PSID) estimated that over a six-year period, 66.4 percent of Black and 25.8 percent of White children's families lived below the poverty line in at least one of the six years" (Brooks-Gunn et al., 2003, p. 239). Clearly, as Miler (1995) affirms, "Poverty is an extremely important problem for children, especially minority children" (p. 109).

While it is not a topic that we need to explore in detail, it is useful to mention some of the formulas scholars and policy makers employ to determine poverty status. Historically, percent of families receiving Aid for Dependent Children can be seen in the literature (Bali & Alvarez, 2003). Eligibility for, or participation in, the Women, Infant, and Children (WIC) program is also used (Fryer & Levitt, 2004). Poverty level is sometimes computed from real estate values of the student's home address (Ingersoll, Seamman, & Eckerling, 1989). In addition, the federal government has established official poverty thresholds for families of various sizes (Lee & Burkam, 2002). For school-aged children, receiving free or reduced-lunch support is often employed as a proxy for poverty status (Baenen, Dulaney, Yamen, & Banks, 2002; Biddle, 1997). Analysts also often calculate income averages across years on these various indices to arrive at more accurate measures of poverty (Turley, 2003).

Key Dimensions of Poverty

Over the last two decades, social scientists have also uncovered dimensions of poverty that exacerbate its impact. To begin with, they confirm that the timing of poverty, *the period of childhood* when poverty is experienced, is important. In short, there are "differential effects of income according to the childhood stage in which it is received" (Duncan & Brooks-Gunn, 2000, p. 189). In this regard, Duncan and Brooks-Gunn (2001) conclude, "Family economic conditions in early and middle childhood appear to be far more important for shaping ability and achievement than do economic conditions during adolescence" (p. 58). Turning specifically to poverty, analysts explain that "because young children may be more susceptible to negative effects of poverty than older children," (Magnuson & Duncan, 2006, p. 376) low-income status "has been shown to be particularly detrimental in early childhood" (Karoly, Kilburn, & Cannon, 2005, p. 7). And, spotlighting student learning, "Research suggests that economic deprivation is most harmful to a child's chances for achievement when it occurs early in the child's life" (Duncan & Brooks-Gunn, 2000, p. 194).

Investigations also affirm that it is crucial to consider the *length of time* that youngsters are in poverty status (Bempechat & Ginsburg, 1989; Miller, 1995; Rothstein, 2004). The authors of these studies document, in general, that longer periods in poverty status are more detrimental than shorter periods. They confirm, more specifically, "Long-term poverty is associated with less academic success" (Miller, 1995, p. 308). They also show that African American children are "more likely to be poor for longer periods of time" (Brooks-Gunn et al., 2003, p. 240). For example, Brooks-Gunn and colleagues (2003) report that only "5.6 percent of white children were poor for five or more years over a six-year period in contrast to 33.6 percent of black children" (p. 240). In an earlier report employing the same five-year band, Miller (1995) presented quite similar findings—5 percent of white students versus 46 percent of African American children. Finally, analysts document that the "persistence of poverty is important" (Duncan & Brooks-Gunn, 2000, p. 189) in the learning algorithm. Duncan & Brooks-Gunn (2000) illustrate:

> *For example, controlling for other family demographic conditions, being poor in all of the first four years of life is associated with about a nine-point difference in Wechsler Preschool and Primary Scale of Intelligence (WPSSI) IQ test scores at age 5, compared with not being poor in those years. In contrast, being poor for some of those years but not all of the time was associated with about a four-point difference, compared with not being poor. (p. 189)*

In short, "Children from [these] permanently poor black families will have more obstacles to learning" (Rothstein, 2004, p. 47).

In addition to timing and duration, *depth* of poverty has been surfaced as an important marker on the achievement gap landscape. Researchers find that children who come from truly impoverished homes do less well than youngsters from families only slightly below the poverty-line threshold. Importantly, analysts draw strong negative linkages between deep poverty and student learning and achievement (Duncan & Brooks-Gunn, 2001). They also show that deep poverty haunts African American families more aggressively than white families (Magnuson & Duncan, 2006). On a positive note, as we will see in Chapter 10, researchers reveal that the impact of increased income on achievement is larger "for families at the lower end of the income distribution" (Magnuson & Duncan, 2006, p. 375).

Finally, *concentration* is an important dimension of poverty, what Biddle (1997) calls a "collective environment of poverty" (p. 12). As was true with the other three elements, higher concentrations of poverty are linked to reduced learning outcomes and increases in achievement gaps (Bempechat & Ginsburg, 1989; Myers, Kim, & Mandala, 2004). Here again, the data confirm, "Poor blacks are much more likely to be living in high poverty concentration neighborhoods than are poor whites" (Natriello, McDill, & Pallas, 1990, p. 15). African Americans "are more likely to live in segregated communities which often include high rates of poverty" (Brooks-Gunn et al., 2003, p. 240). As Entwisle and associates (2000) maintain, "[These] poor neighborhoods accentuate the disadvantage of poverty" (p. 18). They create a "more extreme form of poverty than is typically experienced by poor whites" (Miller, 1995, p. 131). Concentration of poverty in schools is also important because, as Land and Legters (2002) acknowledge, "Concentration of students living in poverty within schools is negatively related to academic achievement, even after accounting for individual-level variables, including family income" (p. 13). Not surprisingly, "High poverty schools are disproportionately black" (Miller, 1995, p. 133).

Poverty and Educational Outcomes

In a variety of ways over the last forty years, researchers have drawn strong associations between poverty and school achievement. That is, they have implicated poverty in the achievement gap problem: "[A] common explanation for the test score gap is that black parents are poorer than white parents" (Phillips et al., 1998a, p. 115). While the question of "whether family income and poverty are causal determinants of children's achievement" continues to be debated (Magnuson & Duncan, 2006, p. 375), and while scholars concur that poverty "by no means determines a child's academic success" (Hertert & Teague, 2003, p. 7), and "that differences in family income contribute to the achievement gap but do not entirely explain it" (Kober, 2001, p. 5), there is nearly universal agreement that poverty and student achievement are strongly associated (Burkam et al., 2004; Halpern-Felsher et al., 1997; Karoly, Kilburn, & Cannon, 2005).

Analysts conclude, "Large differences in economic resources may go a long way to explaining racial achievement gaps" (Magnuson & Duncan, 2006, p. 374). They find that existing "data document a strong association between poverty and students' academic success" (Hertert & Teague, 2003, p. 1), that "poverty has substantial and negative effects on education" (Biddle, 2001, p. 8), and that "the influence of higher poverty levels is consistently negative on achievement" (Chatterji, 2005a, p. 23). Johnson, Howley, and Howley (2002) argue, "The strongest and most prevalent threat to normal academic achievement for individuals is poverty" (p. 7). This conclusion is consistently reinforced by researchers tracking learning differentials of youngsters in the United States:

> *Poverty is the single best explanation research has found for why children differ in ways that affect school performance, both before they enter school and once they are enrolled. (Hertert & Teague, 2003, p. 9)*

> *Poverty . . . is the most consistently associated indicator of poor academic achievement and school failure. (Land & Legters, 2002, pp. 4–5)*

> *The Washington School Research Center found that the strongest predictor of student performance on the WASL and ITBS could be explained directly by family income status. (Shannon & Bylsma, 2002, p. 21)*

> *The net effect for poverty remains huge. (Biddle, 1997, p. 12)*

More specifically, investigators routinely report, "Enrollment in free-lunch programs corresponds to lower scores" (Bali & Alvarez, 2003, p. 494), and "School lunch program [is] negatively associated with student achievement" (Lee & Bowen, 2006, p. 206). Indeed, "Subsidized lunch eligibility [is] consistently the best predictor of achievement among demographic variables" (Maruyama, 2003, p. 673).

A variety of estimates on the impact of poverty on educational outcomes can be culled from the research literature. Smith, Duncan, and colleagues report that poverty explained, "about 0.30 standard deviations of the gap in achievement scores between poor and nonpoor children . . . enough to explain a substantial share of the racial gap in achievement" (as cited in Duncan & Magnuson, 2005, p. 40). In their work, Abbott and Joireman document, "Across a variety of grade levels, instruments (WASL, ITBS) and subscales . . . low income explains the bulk of the variance in academic achievement (12–29 percent) when compared to ethnicity (0.6 percent)" (as cited in Shannon & Bylsma, 2002, p. 21). Also, Hughes (2003) provides this analysis: "Given that a student is on reduced lunch, there is a 71 percent probability that he or she will have a low mathematics score. . . . Given that a student is on free lunch, there is an 82 percent probability that he or she will have a low mathematics score" (p. 308). In the area of holding power, scholars consistently observe a connection between poverty and dropouts (Biddle, 2001; Brooks-Gunn, Klebanov, & Duncan, 1996; Valez, 1989). Duncan and Brooks-Gunn (2000) quantify this association, documenting, "The risk of poor relative to nonpoor children is 2.0 times higher for high school dropout" (p. 188).

The Pathway From Poverty to Achievement Gaps

Most scholars hold that while poverty is strongly implicated in the achievement gap problem, it is not the direct cause of learning gaps. Rather, "Poverty sets the conditions for the gap" (Hertert & Teague, 2003, p. 9) and "Understanding how poverty impacts students' lives and learning . . . [remains] an important challenge" (Williamson, 2005, p. 26): "We need to learn more about possible pathways to understand more completely the effects of poverty on children and to identify leverage points amenable to policy intervention" (Duncan & Brooks-Gunn, 2000, p. 190). This is a topic to which we return in considerable detail in Chapter 10. Here, we simply report that poverty creates the problems that in turn are more tightly linked to low student achievement. That is, poverty is mediated by a variety of intervening variables; "It is the concomitants related to poverty and not poverty itself that takes such a toll on children's cognitive processes" (Neuman & Celano, 2006, pp. 179–180). For example, "Many children living in poverty . . . are exposed to certain risk factors that are thought to contribute to poor student performance" (Hertert & Teague, 2003, p. 9). We also know that students who carry the burden of multiple risk factors (e.g., residing in a poor neighborhood, living in an unstable family) are less likely to perform well in school, and that poor families are "more likely to have multiple risk factors, compared to families who [are] not poor" (Brooks-Gunn, Klebanov, & Frong-Liaw, 1995, p. 259).

Scholars who investigate the association between poverty and poor achievement scores highlight a variety of potential pathways. Neuman and Celano (2006) focus on material and physical resources. Duncan and Brooks-Gunn (2000) underscore "the home environment, quality of child care, perceived economic pressure, parental mental health, parent-child relationships, and neighborhood residence" (p. 190). At the core of all this pathway analysis "through which income may influence children" (p. 190) is the understanding that "children from higher income families may benefit from a range of positive developmental contexts which lower income children do not experience" (Magnuson & Duncan, 2006, p. 375) and that "in myriad ways poverty can constrain a family's ability to provide the type of care, environment, and experiences children need to grow and develop in the same ways at the same rate as their more affluent peers" (Hertert & Teague, 2003, p. 10).

One well-ingrained theme in the literature about linkages between income and achievement is, "Better-off families have more resources to buy things that help children learn"

(Entwisle, Alexander, & Olson, 2000, p. 12): "Because financial capital can often be readily converted into other forms of education-relevant capital, it is an especially valuable resource" (Miller, 1995, p. 90). On the upside, Duncan and Magnuson (2005) report:

> Financial resources can enable parents to secure access to good parental health care and nutrition; rich learning environments, both in the home and through child care settings and other opportunities outside the home; a safe and stimulating neighborhood; and, for older children, good schools and a college education. (pp. 39–40)

On the downside, "Limitations in financial resources may serve to restrict opportunities for educational experiences in and out of the home that are important in providing a foundation for a positive academic self-concept" (DuBois, 2001, pp. 139–140). The reality, then, is that "children from economically affluent families have an extremely important advantage over children from economically impoverished families. . . . Most educationally advantaged students receive several times more education-relevant resources than most educationally disadvantaged students" (Miller, 1995, pp. 90, 94).

Another linkage leitmotif underscores the impact of income on the texture of the home environment, especially the formation of social capital (Duncan & Brooks-Gunn, 2001). The spotlight here, as we will see in the next chapter, is almost always on the experiences in which families engage that can support or hinder academic achievement of children (Magnuson & Duncan, 2006)—the adequacy of parenting and the quality of the home environment in which children reside (Brooks-Gunn, Klebanov, & Frong-Liaw, 1995; Brooks-Gunn et al., 1997). The core argument is "that social capital in the form of home environment conducive to parental investments in their children's learning" (Myers, Kim, & Mandala, 2004, p. 83) can significantly advantage achievement by nonpoor students.

A Note on Wealth

While researchers devote only a small fraction of the attention they pay to income to wealth, with some small differences, it appears that the picture on this aspect of SES mirrors the portrait we painted above. The major difference is that research on the impact of wealth on student learning in general and the achievement gap in particular is quite limited (Orr, 2003; Rothstein, 2004). Treatment of the critical contextual issues we introduced above (e.g., concentration of wealth) is conspicuous by its absence.

Turning to the similarity side of the ledger, we find first, "Differences in wealth between parents of different social classes are also likely to be important determinants of student achievement" (Rothstein, 2004, p. 3) and also, "Wealth is not only a determinant of achievement in general but can help to explain the gap in black-white tests scores" (Orr, 2003, p. 282). However, Magnuson and Duncan (2006) suggest that the data are less than firm on this conclusion. More nuanced analysis reveals that the type of asset in the wealth portfolio is important. Specifically, "Wealth in income-producing assets has a significant effect on achievement, whereas net worth of non-income producing assets does not play an important role in a child's achievement" (p. 298).

Second, we discover that wealth, like income, is not equitably distributed (Wilson, 1998): "Blacks have less wealth than do whites, regardless of income, education, and occupation"

(Orr, 2003, p. 281). African American families have only about one-fifth of the wealth held by white families (Orr, 2003). Painfully, Orr (2003) reveals that progress on wealth equalization lags far behind progress on reducing inequalities in income.

Finally, scholars concur that the pathways between wealth and student achievement parallel the pathways between income and student learning outcomes. Here, as there, effects are mediated by bridging variables such as parenting practices and consumption patterns that rest between wealth and academic success. As with income, wealth can be converted into social and cultural capital that advantages richer children while disadvantaging poorer ones (Bol & Berry, 2005). Indeed, Orr (2003) asserts, "The effect of wealth on achievement is explained mainly by the effect of wealth on the amount of cultural capital to which a child is exposed" (pp. 297–298), a process in which "economic capital is converted into other forms of capital" (Bol & Berry, 2005, p. 35).

Income and Wealth and Race

As we discussed in Chapter 1, the focus in this volume is on achievement gaps between high- and low-income students and between white and African American youngsters. Throughout the book, we will see how these two constructs—income and race—intertwine and nest within each other. Our objective here is to take the initial step in that explanatory work. We maintain that the data on the achievement gap reveal this cardinal principle: while race is important, social class is critical. That is, while there is some independent impact of race on learning outcomes, in large part race is mediated by income (poverty) (Chatterji, 2006; Roscigno, 2000): "The net effects of child poverty are substantial and largely independent of those of race" (Payne & Biddle, 1999, p. 11): "The relationship between ethnicity and academic achievement appears to be mostly indirect: ethnicity is related to low income, which in turn is related to academic achievement" (Abbott & Joireman, as cited in Shannon & Bylsma, 2002, p. 22).

CONCLUSION

In this chapter, we examined the role of SES in explaining achievement gaps between African American and white youngsters and high-income and low-income children. We reported on the three key dimensions of SES: occupational status, educational level, and income. We found that students of color and poor students are much more likely than their more advantaged peers to have parents with jobs marked by less occupational status, with less education, and with less income and wealth. We also reported that there are strong associations between these conditions and low levels of student achievement.

We turn now to the role that home environment plays in the creation and maintenance of achievement gaps.

5

Environmental Causes of Achievement Gaps

Family Environment

Proximal environments, particularly family and childrearing environments, are the critical link between a family's SES and a child's well being. (Magnuson & Duncan, 2006, p. 372)

The most authoritative and influential research on factors influencing children's achievement points to the overriding importance of long-term family characteristics. (Kosters & Mast, 2003, p. 97)

The point is that Black-White test score gaps may very well be due to the striking disparities in living conditions. (Brooks-Gunn et al., 2003, p. 240)

In the introduction to Part II, we disclosed, "The source of the [achievement gap] problem may rest with the school and/or the family and the community in which the child is reared" (Natriello, McDill, & Pallas, 1990, p. 13). In this chapter, we continue our analysis of conditions enveloping children, specifically focusing on the family environment. Our starting assumption is that examination of educational opportunities for different groups requires looking at inequalities at home as well as in schools, that in addition "to the conditions found in society and in schools . . . family attributes may impact student learning" (Shannon & Bylsma, 2002, p. 33). Or, as Luster and McAdoo (1994) remind us, "The contribution of the family to success among African American children needs examination given that the home is the major ecological setting for children" (p. 1080).

What should become clearer as we proceed through the analysis is that, in many ways, family context is the bridging variable between the economic environment and student achievement: "Family environment may mediate the role socioeconomic factors play in youth achievement" (Darity, Castellino, Tyson, Cobb, & McMillen, 2001, p. 18). Social class heavily shapes (but does not determine) family structure and home and community environments (Myers, Kim, & Mandala, 2004; Spradlin et al., 2005). The family is the "pathway by which social class influences learning" (Rothstein, 2004, p. 14). The impact of "family income on student achievement is often indirect" (Miller, 1995, p. 312). As reported earlier, this pathway to learning—family context—works through the ability of families to use economic and social resources to create health, cultural, and social capital for their children (Caldas & Bankston, 1997; Knapp, 2001; Velez, 1989). We learn here, not surprisingly given our previous treatment of SES, that "there are enormous variations in human capital among parents of . . . children from the different racial/ethnic groups" (Miller, 1995, p. 166).

What will also become clear "is that the disadvantages low-income students face in the home are greater than the ones that these same students face at school" (Downey, von Hippel, & Broh, 2004, p. 632): "Existing achievement gaps are not caused by schools; they are caused by powerful family risk factors that impact children" (Armor, 2008, p. 323). Indeed, as an assortment of researchers have concluded, "The influence of family characteristics on children's achievement may be so important that their influence on achievement is difficult to offset with any remedial programs" (Kosters & Mast, 2003, p. 97), and "Economic, educational, and cultural characteristics of families have powerful effects on learning, effects that even great schools cannot obliterate, on average" (Rothstein, 2004, p. 17). As we will observe later, "Family effects on children [also] overshadow neighborhood effects" (Chase-Lansdale, Gordon, Brooks-Gunn, & Klebanov, 1997, p. 115; Halpern-Felsher et al., 1997). The corollary, of course, is "that families should be viewed as the key agents in promoting positive develop-ment in children" (Brooks-Gunn et al., 1997, p. 281) and that any comprehensive attack on achievement gaps should highlight strategies to strengthen family environments and the cap-ital parents have to nurture school success for their children (see Chapter 10).

Finally, we will report, "Differences in family dynamics and the logic of childrearing across social classes have long-term consequences" (Lareau, 2002, p. 774) for the development and learning of children (Caldas & Bankston, 1999). While they do not fully explain learning differentials (Bol & Berry, 2005), they occupy considerable space in the achievement gap causal portrait (Berends et al., 2005), explaining between one-third and two-thirds of gaps in reading and mathematics (Phillips et al., 1998a; Roscigno, 1998).

In the balance of this section, we divide family context into two primary components for analysis: family structural characteristics and family home environment. Family structural characteristics include various background variables, generally family arrangements that are linked to student learning in general and to "the relatively lower average achievement of black students" (U.S. Department of Education, 2001a, p. 8) in particular. Indeed, as Roscigno (2000) reminds us, "In general inequalities in family background have a great deal of explana-tory power when it comes to making sense of contemporary racial variations in achievement" (p. 277). As we soon relate, these structural characteristics (e.g., family composition, home language, employment status of parents) are especially important in the early years of child-hood (Roscigno, 2000) and as risk factors in this domain accumulate achievement gaps increase (Rathburn & West, 2004).

Family home environment is generally defined in terms of the resources parents make available for their children and the activities they engage in with those children. From a growing body of scientific studies, we know that there are "substantial differences between the home environment of poor and middle-class families" (Entwisle, Alexander, & Olson, 2000, p. 9). Researchers here substantiate that African American youngsters are often "growing up under circumstances likely to be less conducive to academic achievement than White children" (Fryer & Levitt, 2004, p. 12). Miller (1995) explains:

> To the degree that some groups in America have fewer education-relevant family/ community resources of all kinds than other groups, this "generic" social capital problem can be expected to make it even harder for educationally disadvantaged groups to reach substantially higher levels of academic achievement. (p. 100)

Research also reveals that these "family resources and parenting behaviors have powerful effects on children's performance" (Reardon, 2003, p. 1): "The adverse effects of inadequate home environments . . . include a slower rate of cognitive development and lower levels of school achievement" (Entwisle, Alexander, & Olson, 2000, p. 10).

FAMILY STRUCTURAL CHARACTERISTICS

> Social scientists continue to look to differences in the family structures of blacks and whites for explanations for black students' low performance in school. (Hallinan, 2001, p. 54)

> Disadvantages in family structure are important as well, particularly for African-American children, over half of whom live with only one of their biological parents. (Roscigno, 2000, p. 268)

> Family structural differences across racial groups are likewise important, having implications for parental time, supervision, and socialization. (Roscigno, 1999, p. 159)

For over forty years, researchers have been highlighting "the influence of family background on academic achievement" (Hallinan, 2001, p. 54). They have also been documenting significant variations in family structure between high- and low-SES students and between white and African American students (Duncan & Magnuson, 2005). Collectively, these scholars delineate six structural conditions of families that impact student learning in general and learning differentials in particular: family size, early teen motherhood, maternal employment, family composition, residence, and mobility.

Family Size, Teen Motherhood, and Maternal Employment

To begin with, analysts confirm that African American families, on average, are generally larger than white families (Hallinan, 2001; Roscigno, 2000). They also establish a "clear pattern for *family size* by SES: less-advantaged children have more siblings. . . . As children's family SES increases, the proportion of children with three or more siblings declines"(Lee & Burkam, 2002, p. 32). Sociologists also find that the number of children in the family "consistently distinguish[es] between the most successful and least successful students" (Luster & McAdoo, 1994, p. 1088) on various measures of achievement. According to Roscigno (1998), "The influence of siblings on achievement is negative and statistically significant" (p. 1048), and increasing the number of siblings depresses academic achievement (1998; 2000). Phillips and her colleagues (1998a) ascertain that household size is also an important variable in the achievement gap equation. And, Luster and McAdoo (1994) report that families of academically advanced African American youngsters have "relatively small numbers of children" (p. 1085).

Early childbearing is negatively linked to student achievement as well (Luster & McAdoo, 1994). As was the case for household size, this risk condition marks black households and low-SES families more than white households and high-SES families (Duncan & Magnuson, 2005). We return to this topic in our proceeding discussion of family health.

Maternal employment is a third structural element that is linked to academic performance and achievement gaps. As Milne and associates (1986) report, while "the effect of mother's employment varies by students' age, race, and family structure and by the amount of time mothers work, the significant effects of mother's employment are primarily negative" (p. 138). They also acknowledge the complexity of studies in this area, revealing that maternal employment in low-SES homes and homes with young African American children can be positive, especially employment that helps offset the harmful effects of poverty. At the same time, they disclose, "The effects of mother's employment on the achievement of all groups of high school students are negative" (p. 135). They hypothesize that the negative effects of mother's employment may be "cumulative over the child's lifetime" (p. 135).

Family Composition

No aspect of family structure has received more attention than family composition, the presence or absence of parents in the home. According to Roscigno (1998), "parent structural form" is measured as single-parent family, with the two-parent family as the comparison. Investigators establish that single-parent families in the U.S. are increasing for all children, but even more so for minority youngsters (Bempechat & Ginsburg, 1989; Hallinan, 2001; Miller, 1995). Researchers also consistently reveal, "Family structure differences across racial groups are large" (Duncan & Magnuson, 2005, p. 43); "The proportion of young children living in single-parent households . . . is much higher for socially disadvantaged children" (Lee & Burkam, 2002, pp. 31–32), and "Lower-income children have less stable families" (Scales et al., 2006, p. 40). Indeed, Natriello and associates (1990) ascertain, "Family structure is closely linked to poverty" (p. 23). Lee and Burkam (2002) also reveal, "The relationship between SES and single-parent family structure is strong and close to linear—that is, as SES goes up, the proportion of young children in single–parent homes goes down" (p. 32). More concretely, Burkam and his colleagues (2004) show that while about 60 percent of low-SES children reside in single-parent homes, only about 12 percent of high-SES students do so (p. 15). Barton (2003) in turn discloses, "26 percent of female heads of households were living in poverty in 2001, compared with 5 percent of married couples—a rate over five times as high" (p. 34).

Researchers highlight similar trends when they turn the spotlight from social class to race. They affirm, "Family structure is correlated with racial origin" (Natriello, McDill, &

Pallas, 1990, p. 24; Land & Legters, 2002). They disclose that intact families are increasingly an anomaly in the African American community (Bankston & Caldas, 1998; Barton, 2003). For example, Stevenson, Chen, and Uttal (1990) report that the biological father is present in only 39 percent of African American families while the biological father is present in 86 percent of white families (p. 510). Barton's (2003) analysis shows that while only 25 percent of white children are not living with two parents, fully 62 percent of African American children do not enjoy an intact family environment. Examining data on young children, Magnuson and Duncan (2006) ascertain that 15 percent of white kindergarten children live in single-parent households whereas 50 percent of African American children do (p. 378). Equally important, analysts expose the fact that African American youngsters "spend more of their childhood in one-parent families than white children"—59 percent and 31 percent, respectively (Milne, Myers, Rosenthal &Ginsburg, 1986, p. 126).

Scholars who study family composition maintain, "On average, children raised by single parents have lower social and academic well-being than children of intact marriages" (Duncan & Magnuson, 2005, p. 43). They hold that "two-parent vs. one-parent family configuration is . . . a factor explaining differences in the achievement of African-American and white children" (Entwisle & Alexander, 1992, p. 81), that children from single-parent homes "are at risk for poorer achievement as compared with children from intact families" (Magnuson & Duncan, 2006, pp. 378–379): "Children living in single-parent families have been found to score lower on standardized tests and receive lower grades in school and to be more likely to drop out of high school" (Natriello, McDill, & Pallas, 1990, p. 23). Milne and colleagues (1986), for example, suggest, "The maximum effects on achievement of number of parents can be as high as 0.25 standard deviation, or about 9 percentile points" (p. 137). Youngsters from single-parent homes also drop out of school at almost twice the rate as children from intact families (Hallinan, 2001; Natriello, McDill, & Pallas, 1990). Researchers conclude, in particular, "Female headship . . . is a statistically significant predictor of test scores for all grades up to and including ninth" (Ferguson, 1991, p. 11) and that this condition "shows a strong negative association with academic achievement" (Bankston & Caldas, 1998, p. 721). And, "The lack of a mother in the home is an even more important disadvantaging characteristic" (Natriello, McDill, & Pallas, 1990, p. 23):

> *Children who reported that their father did not live in their home scored more than half a standard deviation lower in 1986 [NAEP] reading proficiency than children with a father present. Children in homes where their mother was not present performed even worse; such third graders scored more than seven-tenths of a standard deviation lower than children with a mother present. When these shortfalls are expressed in grade equivalents, our best guess is that third-grade children in homes lacking at least one parent were at least a year behind in reading proficiency when compared to other third graders living with both parents. (p. 23)*

Researchers also remind us that the essential issue here is the association between family structure and income. More concretely, "Although most children from non-intact families fare worse than children growing up in intact families, studies suggest that parent and family characteristics (e.g., educational attainment and income), rather than family structure *per se*, account for much but not all of the gap" (Magnuson & Duncan, 2006, p. 379). Or, as Barton

(2003) captures it, "Research has pointed out that much of the (large) difference in achievement between children from two-parent and one-parent families is due to the effects of the lower incomes of one-parent families" (p. 34): "Thus the negative effects on achievement of living in a one-parent family are almost entirely mediated by other variables, particularly by income" (Milne et al., 1986, p. 132; also Orr, 2003). Single-parent families confront a host of challenges that intact families do not, "stresses imposed by economic diversity" (DuBois, 2001, p. 139) that can produce real risks to the development and learning of children (DuBois, 2001; Duncan & Magnuson, 2005).

Residence and Mobility

Researchers maintain that additional risk factors are linked to family housing patterns. Luster and McAdoo (1994) assert that urban *residence* is a risk factor in the educational achievement algorithm. Lee and Burkam (2002) extend this analysis, finding that residing in either a large city or a rural area puts youngsters more at risk of limited academic success than does living in a suburb. They also affirm that the residency risk factor is more prevalent among low-SES and African American families. For example, they document that nearly 30 percent of African American students live in large cities, compared to only 8.2 percent of white students (p. 33). They also show, "As SES goes up the proportion of children living in either larger cities or rural areas goes down" (p. 34).

Investigators arrive at similar conclusions about family *mobility* (Velez, 1989). They document that mobility is more prevalent among poor and minority families (Gandara, Rumberger, Maxwell-Jolly, & Callahan, 2003; Shannon & Bylsma, 2002). They also reveal that "student mobility is an important cause of low student achievement" (Rothstein, 2004, p. 3) and that youngsters who experience high residential mobility score lower "than their less mobile peers" (Lee & Burkam, 2002, p. 52). Also, "Moving is a family change . . . that has a well-documented adverse effect on children" (Grissmer, Flanagan, & Williamson, 1998, p. 2000) and their learning. More directly to the topic of this volume, Rothstein (2004) informs us, "An achievement gap between stable and mobile or poorly housed pupils is inevitable, on average, even though some mobile children overcome their hardships and some stable children fail to take advantage of their opportunities" (p. 47). He suggests that roughly 14 percent of the African American-white test score gap and 7 percent of the SES test score gap can be traced to differences in residential mobility (p. 46).

FAMILY HOME ENVIRONMENT

The role of families in the achievement process is ubiquitous; few educational outcomes can be unequivocally disassociated from parental influences. (Heyns, 1978, p. 195)

Parenting practices and the quality of the child's home environment have large effects on a child's test scores. (Uhlenberg & Brown, 2002, pp. 497–498)

About one half of the effect of family income on tests of cognitive ability is mediated by the home environment. (Duncan & Brooks-Gunn, 2000, p. 193)

In addition to the structural variables just reviewed, there is considerable evidence (1) that there are distinct variations in home environment by race and class status; (2) that these differences are best viewed in terms of parenting practices; (3) that these differences in family home environment influence achievement and can foster the development (or closing) of achievement gaps, i.e., are a "prime factor in school failure" (Padron, Waxman, & Rivera, 2002, p. 69); and (4) that the explanatory variable in the gap equation is resources, or rather the ability to secure resources. Or, as Neuman and Celano (2006) corral the theme, there are "striking differences in material resources and the quality of the home environment . . . [that] account for the social stratification of knowledge and achievement that we see evidenced in the gap between low-income and middle-to-higher-income children" (p. 180).

On the first issue, variations in home environment, Jencks and associates (1972) establish the foundation when they note, "Unless a society completely eliminates ties between parents and children, inequality among parents guarantees some degree of inequality in opportunities available to children" (p. 4). Additional research reveals that transmitted "cultural tendencies . . . may vary by social class and race" (Roscigno, 1998, p. 1038), that race and social structure shape the lives of children, especially the parenting they receive (Lareau, 2002). More directly, we learn that the home "developmental contexts of the average black and white children are vastly different in contemporary America" (Duncan & Abert, 1997, p. 77). And, it is the SES factors we examined in Chapter 4—parents' economic resources, occupational status, and educational backgrounds—that appear to be most salient in getting middle-class parents to act in one way and working-class and poor parents to act in different ways (Lareau, 2002). Of all the SES variables we discussed in Chapter 4, poverty has an especially negative impact on the home-environment conditions that promote academic and social learning (Brooks-Gunn, Klebanov, & Liaw, 1995): "The academic achievement gap by family SES traces substantially to unequal learning opportunities in children's home environments" (Alexander, Entwisle, & Olson, 2001, p. 168) and unequal learning opportunities trace substantially to income. Biddle (1997) illustrates further:

> *Poor children are uniquely handicapped for education because of their poverty. The homes of poor children provide little access to the books, writing materials, computers, and other supports for education that are normally present in middle-class or affluent homes in America. Impoverished students are also distracted by chronic pain and disease, have poorer nourishment, tend to live in communities that are afflicted by physical decay, serious crime, gangs, and drugs; and must face problems in their personal lives because their parents or older siblings have left home, died, been incarcerated, or, lead seriously disturbed lives. All of this means that poor children have a much harder time in school than their more affluent peers. (p. 11)*

On the second issue, parenting practices, we know from assorted studies that "there are ethnic and racial differences in parenting behaviors" (Brooks-Gunn & Markman, 2005, p. 140). We also know that children's experiences that help explain achievement gaps are mediated by these parenting practices (Magnuson, Meyers, Ruhme, & Waldfogel, 2004). There is "evidence that conditions of chronic poverty are strongly associated with parent-child interaction patterns unconducive to academic success" (Miller, 1995, p. 286); extreme poverty is hindering the ability of some minority families to support their children's academic and social development. Given the strong association between poverty and race, it will come as no surprise to discover that African American mothers generally have lower scores on measures of parenting than do white mothers (Brooks-Gunn & Magnuson, 2005). Concomitantly, we learn, even given the risk factors associated with low-SES status, "What a family does is more important than what a family has" (Peng, Wright, & Hill, 1995, p. 62).

On the third front, family home environment and student achievement, the "literature delineates the myriad ways that family resources and behavior affect child outcomes" (Farkas, 2003, p. 1122) and the ways differences in the home environment deprive poor and minority youngsters of the experiences needed to be successful in school. To be sure, "Differences in family resources and parenting behaviors have been shown to account for a considerable portion of race/ethnic differences in cognitive development in early childhood" (Reardon, 2003, p. 1); that is, "Differences in parenting account for a portion of the racial gap in school readiness" (Brooks-Gunn & Magnuson, 2005, p. 150; Jencks & Phillips, 1998). Duncan and Brooks-Gunn (2000) explain:

> *Several studies have found that differences in the home learning environments of higher- and lower-income children account for up to half of the effect of income on the cognitive development of preschool children and between one-quarter and one-third of the effect of income on the achievement scores of elementary school children. (p. 190)*

Finally, on the critical importance of resources, there is abundant data to support the conclusion that resources provide the context for, or heavily shape, parental behaviors and, "The families' ability to invest in their children's education is limited by their economic, social, and human capital resources" (Schmid, 2001, p. 75). Some children, according to Miller (1995), enjoy "very large home-based resource advantages that are likely to enable them to be much more successful academically than other youngsters" (p. 281). Some of these resources are tangible; others are nonmonetary parental resources (Chin & Phillips, 2004). And we find, on average, it is minority and low-SES families who lack these resources (Raudenbush, Fotiu, & Cheong, 1998), thus influencing parents to behave in ways that do not promote the academic success of their children (DuBois, 2001).

The general storyline here is twofold. To begin with, the SES variables that we investigated in Chapter 4 influence student learning indirectly, and they are mediated by home environment (Brooks-Gunn & Markman, 2005; Ferguson, 1991; Scarr & Weinberg, 1976). Poverty impacts family capacities and family processes, and diminished family capacities in turn impact student learning: "Poverty has an impact on family processes that affect child outcomes" (Luster & McAdoo, 1994, p. 1081). Similarly, "The effects of parents' educational level on children's academic achievement [is] mediated through the effect of this variable on parent involvement activities" (Lee & Bowen, 2006, p. 206): "A family's low socioeconomic and educational status translate directly into fewer learning opportunities and/or less support for math-related activities in the home" (Entwisle & Alexander, 1992, p. 72). We know, also, that "family resources [can] amplify families' vulnerability" (Jarrett, 1997, p. 64). Second, these intermediate variables—measures of home environment—are strongly correlated with student learning outcomes, explaining about 40 percent of school achievement gaps for young children (Magnuson et al., 2004). In the balance of this section, we examine the two components of "family home environment" in detail: home resources and parenting practices.

Home Resources

On one level, we know that economic conditions can influence children directly through the resources that "economic conditions afford, and indirectly by causing parental distress and consequently impaired parenting" (Darity et al., 2001, p. 18). More specifically, we know that "poverty affects children through its impact on the family's ability to invest in resources related to children's development" (Neuman & Celano, 2006, p. 180). In his landmark volume on the achievement gap, Miller (1995) documents the extremely large differences in education-relevant family resources by race and social class, as well as the dominance of family resources vis-à-vis school resources for the promotion of student social and academic learning. Here our focus is on the materials those resources can supply to children.

Researchers find that resources in terms of learning materials, where "materials refer to the cognitively and linguistically stimulating materials provided" (Brooks-Gunn & Markman, 2005, p. 142), are a key dimension of family home environment. They confirm that better learning outcomes are "associated with having more family resources and learning opportunities in the home" (Klein et al., 1997, p. 84), and that "household capital . . . strongly influences educational achievement controlling for other socioeconomic attributes" (Roscigno, 1998, p. 1043). They also document that the presence of these materials in homes varies by race and social class (Klein et al., 1997). For example, in their studies, Brooks-Gunn and Markman (2005) discover, "Black families have fewer reading materials in their homes [and] few educationally relevant materials of other types" (p. 150), a finding replicated by Chin and Phillips (2004), Peng, Wright, and Hill (1995), and Orr (2003). They also report, "The extensiveness of materials in the home is associated with family income" (p. 142), an outcome that holds for communities as well as families (Neuman & Celano, 2006). In general, researchers acknowledge, "Families facing economic restraints are limited in the quality and types of learning experiences they can provide for their children" (Magnuson et al., 2004, p. 177), and "Reduced financial resources may limit families' ability to provide educational materials" (Lee & Bowen, 2006, p. 199). Poverty and low parental educational levels, two of our three measures of SES, "restrict cognitive development through a paucity of stimulating home resources" (Burkam et al., 2004, p. 4).

Books in the home are an especially relevant educational material, a variable that, by itself, "seems to serve as a useful proxy for capturing the conduciveness of the home environment to academic success" (Fryer & Levitt, 2002, p. 14; Uhlenberg & Brown, 2002). Fryer and Levitt (2002) substantiate that the number of books in the home "is strongly positively associated with kindergarten test scores on both math and reading" (p. 14). Klein and colleagues (1997) reveal similar associations to mathematics and science scores in school. Here again, we observe important variations by race and class (Lara-Cinisomo, Pebley, Vaiana, & Maggio, 2004; Peng, Wright, & Hill, 1995). Lee and Burkam (2002) observe that white youngsters own more than twice as many books as their African American peers and that high-SES youngsters own roughly three times as many books as their low-SES peers (pp. 38–39).

More recent research affirms that in addition to number of books, computer ownership is a "proxy for a more educationally rich home environment" (Lee & Burkam, 2002, p. 83). Investigations reveal that after controlling for social background and family demographics, "The strongest link with achievement . . . is the presence or absence of a computer in the home" (p. 83), and that "the presence of a home computer is equally important for reading and mathematics" (p. 56). And, as with reading material, analysts uncover an association between computer ownership and race and social class (Chin & Phillips, 2004; Peng, Wright, & Hill,

1995). For example, Lee and Burkam (2002) found that there was a computer in the homes of 85 percent of the high-SES children and only 20 percent of the homes of low-SES youngsters. Uhlenberg and Brown (2002), citing the work of Novack and Hoffman, report that while 73 percent of white students have a computer in the home, only 32 percent of African Americans students do.

One conclusion here is that "poverty is clearly linked with a less supportive literacy environment" (Lara-Cinisomo et al., 2004, p. 10) at home for children. The same condition holds for race; i.e., African American youngsters, on average, experience less supportive learning environments. A second conclusion is that these differentials in home resources contribute to the achievement gaps that show up in school.

Parenting Practices

Child rearing practices represent cultural differences that exert a major influence on the learning of black and white students at school, including their performance on cognitive tests. (Wilson, 1998, p. 505)

Growing up in a poor household influences parents' behavior quite negatively. (Brooks-Gunn, Klebanov, & Liaw, 1995, p. 254)

Setting the Stage

If material resources are important for learning in general, and for explaining gaps in achievement in particular, parenting practices are critical. As Miller (1995) reminds us, this is the case because "parents are not only their children's first teachers but also their teachers for a much longer period of time than any other individuals" (p. 269). Citing the scholarship of Egbert, Miller (1995) reports that children spend fully 90 percent of their waking hours up to age 9, and 20 percent of their waking hours from age 9–18 outside school (p. 321). This places parents in an essential place in the childhood learning algorithm. In terms of an introduction, here is what we know. First, "Parents take different approaches to parenting and learning at home" (Kober, 2001, p. 29). Chen and Phillips (2004) show:

Scholarly research on the causes of these differences has yielded two competing theories: that differences in child-rearing practices stem from (1) parents' disparate values and expectations for their children or from (2) parents' unequal material resources (including the time and energy needed to focus on children). (p. 185)

Second, there are differences in these childrearing practices by race to some extent and by social class to a larger extent (Bempechat, 1992; Lareau, 2002). Parenting practices "cannot be understood independent of the context in which they occur" (Jarrett, 1997, p. 64). For example, "Parents with little formal education and parents with a great deal of formal education tend to use significantly different education-relevant parenting practices" (Miller, 1995, p. 362). And, as noted in the quotes to open this section, variations in childrearing practices are often linked to cultural and racial differences in families (Wilson, 1998). In addition, Lareau (2002) observes that social class creates "distinctive parenting styles" (p. 748). Specifically, she maintains that "middle-class parents conform to a logic of childrearing" she labels "concerted cultivation," while working-class and poor parents conform to a logic of parenting she labels "accomplishment of natural growth" (p. 748).

Third, these patterns of parenting practices matter, for they play "a critical role in child development and well being as well as performance in school" (Barton, 2003, p. 34). They "have an influence on how children learn [and] at what rate they learn" (Rothstein, 2004, p. 24). In short, "Differences in parenting styles . . . contribute to differences between children in school and cognitive development" (Miller, 1995, p. 270): "High student achievement is implicated by how parents influence the basic intellectual development of their children and how parents influence the development of attitudes and motives that are essential for school learning" (Bempechat, as cited in Hughes, 2003, p. 304). Additionally, parenting practices are directly linked to achievement gaps in schools (Phillips et al., 1998b). Indeed, "Parenting differences can explain as much as one half of the racial and ethnic differences in school readiness" (Rouse, Brooks-Gunn, & McLanahan, 2005, p. 10).

Fourth, some parenting "practices are more effective than others" (Kober, 2001, p. 29). In particular, "A substantial body of research suggests that the authoritative parenting style is more likely than others to promote academic success among children" (Miller, 1995, p. 271). Building on the work of Maccoby and Martin, Miller describes authoritative parenting as follows:

> *Authoritative parents tend to make high demands of their children and to exercise a great deal of control over their behavior. Authoritative parents set clear standards for their children and expect them to behave maturely; consistently enforce the standards and rules they have established; encourage the children to be independent and to develop their individual attributes; use a conversational style with their children characterized by open give-and-take; and make it clear that both children and parents have rights. (p. 271)*

He defines the three "other" styles as well: authoritarian, indulgent, and indifferent.

> *Authoritarian parents place high demands on their children, are determined to control their children's behavior, and tend to rely on their power as parents to get the children to comply with their wishes. At the same time, they tend to be relatively unresponsive to the wishes and needs the children express.*

> *Indulgent parents tend to place few demands on their children and make little effort to control the youngsters' behavior. They are inclined to be highly accepting of what the children say and do and tend not to punish their children for misbehavior.*

> *Indifferent parents tend to demonstrate a limited commitment to their role and responsibilities as parents. In general, they seem interested in minimizing the work they put into parenting and the interactions they have with their children. They tend to make few demands of their children and are less likely to be responsive to their wants and needs. (pp. 270–271)*

Fifth, while we reported above that parenting practices in general vary by race and social class, here we acknowledge that effectiveness in patterns of parenting practices also vary by social class and race.

Scholars have produced an assortment of frameworks to conceptualize the dimensions of childrearing, designs from which we forge the architecture for the balance of this section. Brooks-Gunn and colleagues (1995), in their research on young children and their families, explore three dimensions of parenting: the provision of developmentally appropriate, stimulating learning environments, warmth, and the physical environment (p. 252). In another line of her work, she and Markman (2005) partition parenting activities into seven behavioral categories: nurturance, discipline, teaching, language, monitoring, management, and materials (p. 140). Barton (2003) lists the following parental supports for learning in the home: "parental expectations for academic achievement, reading to young children, access to quiet study space, attention to physical and health needs, amount of TV watching, and parent availability" (p. 6). Magnuson and Duncan (2006), in turn, examine these parenting patterns: "holding higher expectations for their children, providing more stimulating learning materials and activities, engaging in higher quality instruction, using more varied and complex language and speech patterns, as well as becoming involved in and supportive of their children's learning" (p. 377). Lareau (2002) discusses four dimensions of childrearing: organization of daily life, language use, social connections, and interventions in institutions (p. 749). Jarrett (1997) also examines four bundles of parenting actions: family protection strategies, child-monitoring strategies, parent resource seeking strategies, and in-home learning strategies. And Phillips, Brooks-Gunn, and associates (1998a) sort parenting activities into six bins:

> *learning experiences outside the home (trips to museums, visits to friends, trips to the grocery store), literary experiences within the home (child has more than ten books; mother reads to child, family member reads newspaper, family receives magazine), cognitively stimulating activities within the home (materials that improve learning of skills such as recognition of letters, numbers, colors, shapes, sizes) punishment (whether child was spanked during the home visit; maternal disciplinary style), maternal warmth (mother kissed, caressed, or hugged the child during the visit; mother praised the child's accomplishments during the visit), and the physical environment (whether the home is reasonably clean and uncluttered; whether the child's play environment is safe). (pp. 126–127)*

Building on all of these designs, we collapse parenting activities into two broad domains, with specific actions clustered in each: providing a stimulating home environment and linking to the external environment.

Providing a Stimulating Home Environment

In general, the literature confirms the importance of a stimulating home environment to child well-being and to social and academic learning (Bainbridge & Lasley, 2002; Brooks-Gunn et al., 2003; Neuman & Celano, 2006), with "the flavor of the day-to-day interactions and psychic investments that parents make" (Entwisle, Alexander, & Olson, 2000, p. 13) being the critical issue. To start, researchers document that as SES declines and family structure risk factors increase, home learning environments become less stimulating (Brooks-Gunn, Klebanov, & Liaw, 1995). Or, in the obverse, "The quality of the home environment when parents have higher-level jobs is better off than that of homes where parents have lower-level jobs" (Entwisle, Alexander, & Olson, 2000, p. 13). Especially important here is family income.

Poor families, on average, have less stimulating home environments than do middle-class families (Magnuson et al., 2004; Miller, 1995). Also, because of the tight link between income and race, African American families, in general, provide less robust home learning environments (Kober, 2001), and they provide "fewer learning experiences in the home" (Brooks-Gunn, Klebanov, & Duncan, 1996, p. 400).

These same analysts also draw the link between "supportive home environment and higher scores on achievement tests" (Luster & McAdoo, 1994, p. 1085), confirming that to a considerable extent, the "associations between economic disadvantage and young children's lower academic performance are explained by lower quality home learning environments" (Chatterji, 2006, p. 490). They affirm, "The home environment is often a stronger predictor of cognitive and school readiness than is maternal education" (Brooks-Gunn et al., 2003, p. 240). In particular, they implicate "home environment differences in the provision of stimulating learning experiences [in] the Black-White test score gap" (p. 240). Subsequently, we examine patterns of parenting practices that define stimulating home environments, drawing from the preceding frameworks.

"Recognizing that different nurturing processes that take place [in families] have tremendous impact on a child's ability to learn" (Bainbridge & Lasley, 2002, p. 426), one key aspect of parenting is providing *nurturance* to support children at home. In this area, scholars generally highlight the issue of parental (generally maternal) warmth and the various parenting practices that bring (or fail to bring) warmth to the home. They also establish that warmth is related to positive social and academic development. They reveal that a greater number of risk factors and poverty in particular are "associated with less maternal warmth" (Brooks-Gunn, Klebanov, & Liaw, 1995, p. 265). And, they document that, after controlling for the effects of poverty, African American mothers exhibit fewer of the parenting practices defining warmth (Brooks-Gunn, Klebanov, & Liaw, 1995; Brooks-Gunn et al., 2003).

Relatedly, researchers identify *time* spent interacting with one's children as an important element of home environment that is associated with achievement (Milne et al., 1986). They corroborate that "little interaction with the child . . . [has] a negative impact on a child's developing capacity to learn" (Hertert & Teague, 2003, p. 10). They also substantiate that variations in parental time invested in children "have social class dimensions" (Miller, 1995, p. 267). Analysts link less interaction time and the home structural variable of family composition, documenting that interaction time is less in one-parent families (Milne et al., 1986). They maintain:

> *High-SES parents are often in a position to invest more time in their children than are low-SES parents because they can afford to have the mother spend full time at home rather than hold a job. Similarly, mothers with a great deal of formal education may be able to invest more time in each of their children because they tend to have fewer children than mothers with little formal education. (Miller, 1995, p. 267)*

Parental practices that foster healthy *physical environments* for children are correlated with higher SES. Poverty, in turn, is associated with parental actions leading to diminished physical environments (Brooks-Gunn, Klebanov, & Liaw, 1995).

Parental *discipline* practices—"responses to child behaviors that they consider appropriate or inappropriate" (Brooks-Gunn & Markman, 2005, p. 141)—also predict the development and achievement of youngsters. As with most of the dimensions of parenting actions, patterns of disciplinary practices, on average, vary by social class and race. On the SES linkage, Rothstein (2004) reviews research that shows that low-SES parents are more likely to punish their children than are higher-SES parents (see also Baker & Stevenson, 1986). On the race linkage, "Black mothers are somewhat more likely to spank their children than are white mothers. White mothers are more likely to use reasoning as a discipline technique" (Brooks-Gunn & Markman, 2005, p. 149). And again, consistent with everything related previously, parenting disciplinary practices seen in higher-SES homes are linked to social development and academic achievement of children.

A fifth component of a stimulating home environment addresses parental actions related to managing a child's time, "scheduling events, completing scheduled events, and the rhythms of the household" (Brooks-Gunn & Markman, 2005, p. 143). One important aspect of *time management* is regulating the amount of television that children watch (Uhlenberg & Brown, 2002), an activity with negative linkages to academic performance. Here again we see patterns by race and social class. On the race front, African American kindergarten children spend 17.9 hours per week watching television versus 13.2 for white youngsters (Lee & Burkam, 2002, p. 36). In fourth grade, Barton (2003) finds that while 13 percent of white children watch six or more hours of television a day, fully 42 percent of African American youngsters watch that much television (p. 32). Turning to social class, children of parents from higher-SES homes (where high SES is defined in terms of education) watch less television than their peers in lower-SES families (Barton, 2003; Lareau, 2002; Lee & Burkam, 2002). Lareau (2002) elaborates:

> In addition to these activities, television provided a major source of leisure entertainment. All children in the study spent at least some free time watching TV, but there were differences in when, what, and how much they watched. Most middle-class parents we interviewed characterized television as actually or potentially harmful to children; many stressed that they preferred their children to read for entertainment. Middle-class parents often had rules about the amount of time children could spend watching television. These concerns did not surface in interviews with working-class and poor parents. (p. 763)

A second, more general, aspect of time management is exercising control over the free time children have, how much free time youngsters have, and how they use the free time. Here, the evidence suggests that parents in middle-class homes manage the time of their children more proactively than parents in poor and working-class homes (Lareau, 2002). Indeed, as Miller (1999) communicates, "Many well-educated parents draw on their skills to provide an informal 'preschool' at home for their children that offers valuable intellectual and social preparation for succeeding in the early elementary grades" (p. 15).

Reading to children is another and especially powerful dimension of providing a high-quality home environment. Or, as Hertert and Teague (2003) remark, one common proxy for the quality of the home environment is the amount of time that parents spend reading to children. This seems to be important because reading to children fosters language acquisition, broadens vocabulary, and promotes the learning of other literacy skills (Barton, 2003; Hertert & Teague, 2003). These skills, in turn, are essential for later success in school, especially in reading comprehension. And, once again, analysts uncover social class and racial differences in parenting practices related to family reading (Lara-Cinisomo et al., 2004): "Black and Hispanic children are read to considerably less than White children, giving them a relative handicap in school achievement. Also, children in poverty are read to less than children who are not in poverty" (Barton, 2003, p. 30). Higher-SES parents (more education) "read to their young children more consistently" (Rothstein, 2004, p. 19): "Most parents with college degrees read to their children daily before the children begin kindergarten; few children whose parents have only a high school diploma or less benefit from daily reading" (p. 19).

From 40–55 percent of mothers report reading to their toddler every day. Black mothers are about two-thirds as likely as white mothers to do so . . . racial differences in frequency of reading exist in population-based as well as low-income samples. (Brooks-Gunn & Markman, 2005, p. 150)

Considerably higher proportions of white children's parents report reading often to their children compared to black children's parents (86.6 percent vs. 67.5 percent). . . . The link between reading often to children and SES is also linear, with more high-SES than low-SES parents reporting reading to their children 3–6 times a week (93.9 percent as compared to 62.6 percent). (Lee & Burkam, 2002, p. 42)

In a national survey, twice as many high-income parents reported reading daily to their young children as did low-income parents, according to a 2002 report by the Educational Testing Service (ETS). (Hertert & Teague, 2003, p. 10)

Thus, we see here, as we have throughout this section on parenting behaviors, that African American youngsters and children from working-class and poor homes often are disadvantaged in their quest for academic success.

Finally, we move to *language use* between parents and their children, the dimension of home environment that has received the greatest attention in the research literature. We know to start, as was the case with adults reading to children, language use is correlated with "children's cognitive, social, and emotional skills" (Rouse, Brooks-Gunn, & McLanahan, 2005, p. 10), and early language use in the home "leads to the development of skills necessary for the use of linguistic symbols" (Natriello, McDill, & Pallas, 1990, p. 6): "Differential language learning opportunities in economically disadvantaged households may have lasting consequences for children's language development" (Magnuson et al., 2004, p. 117). Indeed, the findings on language use "partially explain the origins of the pervasive relationship between family background and later school success" (Davison et al., 2004 p. 753). Without rich language use in the early years, children are at risk of underperformance in school (Hertert & Teague, 2003).

Scholarship here also informs us that there are significant differences in "the ways in which lower- and middle-class parents foster their children's cognitive skills" (Bempechat & Ginsburg, 1989, p. 10) and considerable variation in the ways they use language with their youngsters. In this vein, scholars reveal that the quantity of language varies by class. In their hallmark study, for example, Hart and Risley, cited by Downey and colleagues (2004), found, "Children on welfare had 616 words per hour directed to them, compared to 1,251 for children of the working class and 2,153 for children of professionals" (p. 615). Using this work, they calculate, "By the beginning of kindergarten at age five-and-a-half, the average child in a professional family has had 61 million words directed their way, compared to 36 million for working-class and only 18 million for welfare children" (p. 615). Brooks-Gunn & Markman (2005) discuss language acquisition and SES as follows:

> *Transcriptions of naturally occurring mother-child conversations suggest that children's exposure to language and conversation varies widely across social class groups, as demonstrated in a sample of forty-two children from three different social class groupings. As such differences accumulate over the first years of life, the children in families with a high socioeconomic background have engaged in literally thousands more conversations than children from lower socioeconomic backgrounds. Even when they begin speaking (around their first birthday) higher SES children have larger vocabularies than the children from middle and low SES families. By their second birthday, the children in the middle SES group have pulled away from those in the low SES group. And these differences accelerate over time. So by age three, vocabularies of the children in the low SES group are half the size of those in the high SES group and two-thirds the size of those in the middle SES group. Given the racial composition of the SES groups in this study (the majority of black families were in the low SES group), black-white differences were equally large. (p. 150)*

Analysts also unearth differences in the speech cultures of parents, that is, how language is used. These differences are linked, at least partially, with race and social class. As Brooks-Gunn and Markman (2005) illustrate:

> *The educated middle- to upper-middle class "speech culture" provides more language, more varied language, more language topics, more questions, and more conversations, all of which are linked with large vocabularies in toddlers and preschoolers. (p. 150)*

On the other hand, according to Lareau (2002):

> *Life in the working class and poor families flows smoothly without extended verbal discussions. The amount of talking varies, but overall, it is considerably less than occurs in the middle-class home. (p. 758)*

Professional parents speak to their children using more words, more multi-clause sentences, and more past and future verb tenses, and they ask more questions. Conversely, in the lower-income families, the utterances addressed to children are both fewer in quantity and less rich in nouns, modifiers, verbs, past-tense verbs, and clauses (Downey, von Hippel, & Broh, 2004). Middle-class speech culture is also defined by "conversation that promotes reasoning and negotiation" (Lareau, 2002, p. 756), while according to Rothstein (2004), "Lower-class parents are more likely to instruct children by giving directions without extended discussion" (p. 25). Thus lower-class parents are less likely, on average, to engage their children in conversations (Rothstein, 2004). Higher-SES parents, on the other hand, "cultivate conversations by asking children questions or by drawing them out" (Lareau, 2002, p. 758): "In working-class and poor homes, most parents did not focus on developing their children's opinions, judgments, and observations, vocabulary, [or] critical thinking skills" (pp. 763–764).

Linking to the External Environment

Social scientists observe that differences by race and social class in terms of supportive home environments are mirrored by variations in the ways parents link their children with actors outside the home—with the external environment. In general, "Working-class and low-income parents see a limited role for themselves, while upper middle-class families believe they are central to making connections" (Lewis, 2008, p. 14) for their children. For example, Wilson and Wacquant (as cited in Miller, 1995) report, "Not only do residents of extreme-poverty areas have fewer social ties, but also that they tend to have ties of lesser social worth" (p. 117). As we will see, Lareau's research is especially illuminating on the issue of "class differences in the context of children's social relations" (p. 764), relations that for young children are almost always brokered by parents. We examine two key dimensions of social connections, use of community resources and parent management of the school careers of their children.

Patronizing Community Resources. Analysts routinely hold that "low educational attainment may limit [lower SES] parents' familiarity with educational resources available in the community" (Lee & Bowen, 2006, p. 199). So too, as Entwisle and associates (2000) and Rothstein (2004) maintain, does the diminished resource base found in lower-income homes, both in terms of financial resources to purchase supports and the free time to link children to many organized activities. Poor and working-class parents "have less access to learning activities in the neighborhood" (Kober, 2001, p. 11) and they take advantage of the ones that do exist less frequently than higher-SES parents. On the other hand, scholars document that higher-SES families disproportionately patronize community resources for their children. They are much more likely than poor and working-class parents to connect their children to the library (Burkam et al., 2004; Lara-Cinisomo et al., 2004). They take more trips (Entwisle, Alexander, & Olson, 2000) and visit museums more often (Peng, Wright, & Hill, 1995). They are also more likely than less affluent parents to ensure that the programs in which their children participate "outside of school are consistent with the school's academic program" (Miller, 1995, p. 268).

Whereas, in general, the life of poor and working-class children is more unstructured, more emergent, and more under the direction of the children themselves, the life of children in higher-SES families is likely to be "defined by a series of deadlines and schedules interwoven with a series of activities that are organized and controlled by adults" (Lareau, 2002, p. 753). In short, "The rhythms of family life differ by social class. Working-class and poor children spen[d] most of their free time in informal play; middle-class children [take] part in many adult-organized activities designed to develop their individual talents and interests" (p. 760). Relatedly, higher-SES parents, in general, more closely monitor the activities of their children (Bennett et al., 2007; Brooks-Gunn & Markman, 2005). And, while "learning activities inside the home are more likely to mediate the link between income and child achievement than are those outside the home" (Duncan & Brooks-Gunn, 2000, p. 190), these external learning opportunities still play an important role in explaining learning differentials between children.

Managing the School Careers of Children. We understand that the way that parents manage a child's schooling "can have substantial effects on educational achievement" (Baker &

Stevenson, 1986, p. 157). We also know that there are patterned variations in the ways parents from different social classes manage the school careers of their children. The first link in the career management chain is *parental expectations* for children's school performance and for the actions of the school in relation to youngsters (Hughes, 2003; Lee & Bowen, 2006). Entwisle, Alexander, and Olson (2000) hold that "parent's expectations relate directly to the level of schooling children are likely to achieve" (p. 15) and that "parents' expectations for children's school performance before they start school [is] of about the same importance in predicting cognitive growth as family socioeconomic status" (p. 20). They conclude, "For every indicator of school achievement, whether dropout, retention, or test scores, the research shows parents' expectations to be among the strongest predictors, and stronger by far than children's own expectations" (p. 14).

In a similar vein, Rothstein (2004) finds that better measures of performance can be traced to the aspirations of parents and the pressure parents place on their children for success. Or, as Lee and Bowen (2006) maintain, "Economically disadvantaged parents are less optimistic about their children's education" (p. 211). Rothstein (2004) also discloses that white and higher-SES parents are more likely to hold expectations that are aligned with school expectations. Research confirms:

> *Parents of youth from disadvantaged backgrounds may be more susceptible to developing and subsequently communicating to their children negative views of schools and the opportunities that they are capable of providing. (DuBois, 2001, p. 10)*

Middle- and upper-class parents, however, are more likely to reinforce positive expectations (Hughes, 2003; Rothstein, 2004): "Middle-class youth are more likely to be punished by their parents for poor grades, or rewarded for good ones, and black parents are less likely to reinforce high expectations than are white parents at a similar income level" (Rothstein, 2004, p. 30).

In addition, investigators find that middle- and upper-class parents often assume a *positive stance* in relation to their child's school, directly involving themselves in a range of school-based decisions about their child. On the other hand, "poor parents, oftentimes because of the presence of institutional barriers that can make it substantially more difficult for parents with less extensive and successful educational backgrounds to advocate effectively for their children's needs as learners in the school setting" (DuBois, 2001, p. 161), often absent themselves as advocates for their children. Parents from poor and working-class homes "who themselves often struggled in school tend to defer to the school, relying on the professional authority of the institution to do what needs to be done" (Alexander, Entwisle, & Bedinger, 1994, p. 284). They often have "little or no involvement in their children's schools" (Bempechat, as cited in Hughes, 2003, p. 305). Rothstein (2004) provides a nuanced portrait of this issue of parental proactiveness and returns us to the topic at the heart of the volume, the achievement gap:

> *Middle-class parents are more confident about challenging administrators and more likely to have support from other parents with similar concerns or with expertise to share. No matter how attentive school administrators are to individual children, youngsters whose parents intervene will have an edge; on average, which children get this edge is*

predictable by parents' social class. This difference also adds to the gap in academic and achievement between lower- and middle-class children. (p. 31)

Parents in higher-SES families are much more likely to consider themselves as partners in the education process, considering it a "mutual concern between home and school" (Bempechat & Ginsburg, 1989, p. 11). On the other hand, "lower-class parents believe that their child's education is very much the responsibility of the teacher and the school. Thus, they initiate interactions with teachers and attend school events much less frequently than [do] middle class parents" (p. 11): "Overall, the working-class and poor adults had much more distance or separation from the school than their middle-class counterparts" (Lareau, 2002, p. 769). Baker and Stevenson (1986) detail this as follows:

Mothers with more education have more knowledge of their child's schooling. For example, they are more likely to be able to name their child's teachers, identify their child's best and worst subjects, and offer an overall evaluation of their child's performance, and they are more likely to have seen their child's last report card. These mothers are also more likely to have had contact with the school: i.e., they are more likely to have met with their child's teachers and to have attended parent-teacher conferences and school events. . . . If their child was performing poorly or had a school-related problem, they were more likely to know about the problem and to know the school personnel to contact. (p. 161)

Miller (1995) adds a third chapter to the parental management of a child's school career story. He reveals that high-SES/well-educated parents not only have more time to spend with their children, they *use* more of that *time for educational purposes* and they "are more likely to ensure that their children spend a great deal of their time on school-relevant activities" (p. 285). In particular, he notes that highly educated parents "tend to use teaching strategies consistent with those used by the school, while this is much less commonly the case for parents with little formal education" (p. 286).

Research also substantiates that relative to low-SES parents, high-SES parents more aggressively monitor children's work in school and their schoolwork at home. They monitor academic progress and needs in school closely (Hughes, 2003; Velez, 1989). They are more "attuned to the flow of relevant feedback from school to home" (Alexander, Entwisle, & Bedinger, 1994, p. 295) and are more prone "to initiate contact with the school in response to their child's academic difficulties" (Bempechat & Ginsburg, 1989, p. 11). They are more careful monitors of homework. Unlike "lower-class parents who report feeling reluctant to help their children for fear that they might mislead them academically" (pp. 11–12) or because of "cultural barriers, personal experiences that discourage them from having contacts, and discriminatory practices by the school" (Lewis, 2008, p. 14; Lareau, 2002), higher-SES parents are more confident in their ability to assist with the education of their children in the home. They are more likely than peers from working-class homes to allocate time and space for homework and to ask about homework (Baker & Stevenson, 1986). More important, in general, they monitor homework more effectively, as explained by Rothstein (2004):

Parents from different social classes supervise homework differently. Consistent with overall patterns of language use, middle-class parents—particularly those whose own occupational habits require problem solving—are more likely to assist children by pos-ing questions that decompose problems and that help children figure out the correct answers. Lower-class parents are more likely to guide their children with direct instruc-tions. Children from both strata may go to school with the correct answers to home-work problems, but middle-class children will have gained more in intellectual power from the exercise than do lower-class children. (p. 27)

For our purpose here, we remind the reader that "help with homework and a place to study in the home are associated with school achievement" (Learning Point Associates, 2004, p. 24).

High-SES parents are also more likely than poor parents to make *sacrifices* for their children's education, especially in how they use their own free time (Hughes, 2003). As Lareau (2002) corroborates, parents in high-SES homes are more likely to tailor their leisure time to the activities of their children than are working-class parents.

Health Conditions

Many social and economic manifestations of social class also have important implica-tions for learning. Health differences are among them. (Rothstein, 2004, p. 3)

Children with a biological risk factor in the face of poverty . . . have been considered to be at double jeopardy. (Brooks-Gunn, Klebanov, & Liaw, 1995, p. 253)

One might expect substantial differences in poverty rates (especially long-term rates) to lead to differences in access to health care, which would have serious consequences for many children. (Miller, 1995, p. 308)

In Chapter 4, we examined the topic of SES and its impact on learning. In this chapter, we are exploring the influence of family context on learning. Health issues reside at the intersec-tion of SES and family. On the one hand, they are rooted in the prevailing economic and social seedbed. On the other hand, they can be traced to various actions in families, especially by mothers. As with nearly everything we have investigated to this point, two themes dominate the research on health conditions. First, parents and children from low-SES families score more poorly on almost every measure of health than parents and children from high-SES families. Second, these negative indices of well-being are linked to lower rates of social and academic learning and are implicated in the achievement gap problem (Currie, 2005): "The United States has a large number of children with health problems severe enough to under-mine their prospects for academic success—and these children are disproportionately members of racial/ethnic minority groups (Miller, 1995, p. 90).

On the dimension of health capital, Rothstein (2004) confirms, "Lower-class children, on average, have poorer vision than middle-class children. . . . They have poorer oral hygiene, more lead poisoning, more asthma, poorer nutrition, less adequate pediatric care, more expo-sure to smoke, and a host of other problems" (p. 3). Research reveals that poor children are much more likely to be victims of a host of health problems and, "Because they make up a dis-proportionate share of the poor, minority children are much more likely than white children to be affected with these conditions" (Miller, 1995, p. 139). These are conditions that nega-tively impact student achievement, described by Currie (2005) as follows:

Poor children are more likely than better-off children to suffer from a wide array of chronic health problems, particularly severe conditions, such as mental retardation, heart problems, poor hearing, and digestive disorders. Chronic conditions affect school readiness in various ways. First, illness may simply crowd out other activities with doctor visits and treatment. Second, children with chronic conditions may experience more stress, fatigue, or pain that can interfere with cognitive development. Third, drugs used to treat some illnesses may have unanticipated effects. Fourth, illness may alter relations between children, parents, and others in a way harmful to the child's development. Fifth, illnesses directly affect the ability to learn, by altering body chemistry. (p. 121)

Poor and African American children are subject to an assortment of conditions associated with birth that negatively influence their well-being. African American expectant mothers are more than two times as likely as their white counterparts to receive no prenatal care or care only in the last trimester (Hertert & Teague, 2003). Children from low-SES families are also more likely to have mothers who smoke and drink alcohol. According to Rothstein (2004), these health differences by race and social class are quite substantial. He reveals, "During pregnancy one-fifth of high school dropouts smoke . . . thirteen times more than for college graduates" (p. 43). For alcohol consumption, he provides parallel findings, reporting, "Fetal alcohol syndrome . . . is ten times more frequent for low-income black than for middle-class white children" (p. 42). Finally, researchers document the negative relationship between teen parenthood and health (Barton, 2003; Reichman, 2005; Rouse, Brooks-Gunn, & McLanahan (2005). They also reveal that the teen birth rate for African Americans is nearly twice that for whites.

Low birth weight (LBW; 5.5 pounds or less [Reichman, 2005, p. 92]) is implicated in many health-related problems for children, and teen mothers are more likely than any other age group to deliver LBW babies (Reichman, 2005). Overall, 13 percent of African American children are LBW babies; the rate for whites is 7 percent (Barton, 2003, p. 25). Women of low SES are also "at risk for delivery of low birth weight babies" (Reichman, 2005, p. 100). Overall, "Most troubling from the perspective of eventual childhood outcomes, mothers of LBW children are more likely to be socially and economically disadvantaged than mothers of normal birth weight children" (Brooks-Gunn, Klebanov, & Liaw, 1995, p. 253).

Researchers substantiate that "disabilities arising from very low birth weight can seriously impair cognitive development" (Rouse, Brooks-Gunn, & McLanahan, 2005, p. 9). Because LBW can elevate "the risk for many long-term health conditions and developmental disabilities that can impair school readiness" (Reichman, 2005, p. 92), low birth weight children are often at risk of school failure (Chase-Lansdale et al., 1997): "Low birth weight can lead to severe problems ranging from mortality to learning problems" (Barton, 2003, p. 24). LBW children "may have low IQs throughout their lives" (Natriello, McDill, & Pallas, 1990, p. 48). In short, "LBW children are more likely than normal birth weight children to experience a variety of cognitive neurological, language, and emotional delays as well as decrements in school functioning" (Brooks-Gunn, Klebanov, & Liaw, 1995, p. 253).

African American youngsters and children from low-income families are more likely than their more advantaged peers to reside in homes with adults who "are likely to be less healthy, both emotionally and physically" (Duncan & Brooks-Gunn, 2000, p. 190). This, in turn, can produce stress which can have an adverse impact on the healthy development of children (Rouse, Brooks-Gunn, & McLanahan, 2005). Also, these youngsters are less likely to be covered by health insurance (Hertert & Teague, 2003; Rothstein, 2004). For example, Rothstein shows that "20 percent of poor children are without consistent health insurance, compared to 12 percent of all children; 13 percent of black children are without insurance, compared to 8 percent of white children" (p. 41). Miller (1995) reminds us what these numbers mean: poor and African American youngsters "are less likely to receive regular health care . . . and lack of routine health care is associated with other common medial problems . . . [that] can lead to missed days of school and low academic achievement" (p. 140).

Some of these medical problems are detailed by Rothstein (2004). He documents that poor and minority children are more likely to suffer from vision problems, hearing problems, and oral health problems, each of which individually explains a very small amount of the African American-white achievement gap (see also Currie, 2005). He reveals that African American and low-income children are more likely than their peers to suffer from iron deficiency anemia and deficiencies of other vitamins and minerals. Because of the environment in which they live, poor youngsters and minority children have higher exposure to lead and other environmental hazards (Currie, 2005; Rothstein, 2004). Indeed, children living in poverty are "three times more likely to have high levels of lead in their blood than are non-poor children" (Barton, 2003, p. 26). Rothstein (2004) and others affirm:

> Lower-class children are more likely to contract asthma—the asthma rate is substantially higher for urban than for rural children, for children whose families are on welfare than for non-welfare families, for children from single-parent than from two-parent families, and for poor than for non-poor families. (p. 40)

Also, Currie (2005) documents that asthma is more a property of African American than white youngsters. She goes on to reveal that asthma is strongly associated with various behavioral problems in school—problems that in turn predict lower academic achievement:

> Asthmatic children in grades one to twelve were absent from school an average of 7.6 days a year as against 2.5 days for well children. Nine percent of the asthmatic children (5 percent of the well children) had learning disabilities; 18 percent (15 percent of the well children) repeated a grade. (p. 123)

Finally, a variety of investigators underscore the issue of poor nutrition among children living in poverty, a condition that "can cause problems academically" (Spradlin et al., 2005, p. 2) and one that "also directly contributes to the achievement gap between lower- and middle-class children" (Rothstein, 2004, p. 44). We know that female-headed households are more at risk of "having limited or uncertain access to adequate and safe food" (Hertert & Teague, 2003, p. 10) than are other family groupings. We also know that "Black households . . . have two to three times the food insecurity and hunger than do white households" (Barton, 2003, p. 28). And while hunger marks 13 percent of families living in poverty, it touches only 1 percent of families at 85 percent or more above the poverty line (Barton, 2003).

We close this section on health with a note on our second theme, the linkage between poor health and unhealthy living conditions and academic performance. The literature here leads us to two conclusions. Because "the mean test scores of blacks and whites are driven by children who do not have any health conditions," Currie (2005) asserts, "any given health condition would have to have quite a large effect (or a very different prevalence for blacks and whites) before it could have much effect on mean differences in test scores" (p. 121). Thus, any specific health problem probably only explains a very small part of racial and social class achievement gaps. However, "Summed over all health conditions, health differentials could well explain a sizeable portion of the racial gap" (Currie, 2005, p. 132) in school readiness, as much as 25 percent (p. 133). According to Rothstein (2004):

> *Each of these differences in health—in vision, hearing, oral health, lead exposure, asthma, use of alcohol, smoking, birth weight, and nutrition—when considered separately has only a tiny influence on the academic achievement gap. But together, they add up to a cumulative disadvantage for lower-class children than can't help but depress average performance. (p. 45)*

CONCLUSION

In this chapter, we examined the influence of the family on student development and achievement. We explored family structural characteristics and family home environment. We continue our analysis of the external causes of achievement gaps in Chapters 6 and 7.

6

Environmental Causes of the Achievement Gap

Community, Racism, and Individual Differences

In Chapter 4, we investigated the connections between SES and student performance. In Chapter 5, we reviewed the critical role of the family in the student achievement equation. Here, we continue our examination of nonschool factors on the development and achievement of youngsters. We explore three variables that scholars conclude influence student learning and that are implicated in the achievement gap problem: community, racism, and individual differences.

COMMUNITY

> *Living in limited opportunity locales has consequences for family background attributes shown . . . to be conducive to educational success. (Roscigno, 2000, p. 266)*

> *Surrounding neighborhood and community conditions of disadvantage can compound those evident at the household level. (DuBois, 2001, p. 167)*

Neighborhood environments do not support healthy development for many young children. (Karoly, Kilburn, & Cannon, 2005, p. 7)

Setting the Stage

Entwisle and associates (2000) remind us of what we sometimes forget: "Families, of course, live in neighborhoods" (p. 17) and that these neighborhoods likely impact the development of children as well as their academic performance. Neighborhoods, in addition to families, are a potential pathway by which income influences child development (Duncan & Brooks-Gunn, 2000; Farkas, 2003). The underlying logic is that while social capital exists within the family, it also exists outside the family in the community. Thus, "Neighborhoods shape children's development in many ways" (Duncan & Magnuson, 2005, p. 44). They interact with and amplify the effects of family context.

We begin our analysis of the ways communities shape child development and student learning with three caveats. First, there is still some contention over the definition of community. For example, some perspectives feature geographical dimensions, while other broader conceptualizations include social aspects as well (Jarrett, 1997). Second, in comparison to SES and family, there is limited research on community effects on children (Chase-Lansdale et al., 1997; Wilson, 1998). Third, even when there are findings, the conclusions that can be drawn are less firm than with SES and family. For example, even "the importance of neighborhood income for children's cognitive development is still uncertain" (Phillips et al., 1998a, p. 130), with some analysts suggesting that neighborhood poverty can impact "child development independent of family poverty" (Duncan & Brooks-Gunn, 2000, p. 190; also Entwisle, Alexander, & Olson, 2000) and others holding that this might not be the case.

One essential line of work in the area of community attends to "measures of neighborhood characteristics" (Chase-Lansdale, 1997, p. 83). Social scientists highlight ten broad dimensions of neighborhoods: affluence, impoverishment, male joblessness, concentration of families, number of persons per occupied unit, diversity in ethnicity, age and gender segregation, safety, residential instability, and concentration of poverty (Chase-Lansdale, 1997; Duncan & Aber, 1997). They rely primarily on "neighborhood measures that can be gleaned from the data collected in the decennial census" (Duncan & Brooks-Gunn, 2001, p. 65). It is suggested that these structural factors can "have differential effects on a range of community processes which in turn affect child and adolescent outcomes" (Duncan & Aber, 1997, p. 69).

In their work, some researchers highlight single measures of community (e.g., male joblessness). Others craft compound indices that aggregate multiple measures (Duncan & Aber, 1997). For example, on the latter front, Ricketts and Sawhill (cited in Duncan & Aber, 1997) developed a concept called "underclass neighborhoods" that includes four of our broad dimensions of community.

Analysts also consistently uncover important differentials on all of these characteristics by race, with African American families consistently found to have less favorable scores. For example, on the poverty measure Duncan and Aber (1997) unearth a marked disparity of poverty by ethnicity. They explain:

More than 60 percent of whites, but only 6 percent of blacks live in neighborhoods with few (that is, less than 10 percent) poor neighbors. Using neighborhood poverty rates in excess of 40 percent to define "ghetto" neighborhoods, the incidence of ghetto poverty among blacks is dramatically higher than for whites. . . . Nearly half of the blacks, but less than 10 percent of whites, who escape poverty at the family level encounter it (in rates in excess of 20 percent) in their neighborhoods. The majority of white children, but less than 5 percent of black children, escape both family- and neighborhood-level poverty. (pp. 76–77)

Relative to whites, black adolescents grow up in neighborhoods with three times as many neighbors who are poor (22.8 percent versus 7.5 percent) and only half as many families with incomes above thirty thousand dollars (12.5 percent versus 28.2 percent). The typical black child has 58.9 percent black neighbors, as compared with only 4.4 percent for the typical white child. (p. 74)

Influence Pathways

Drawing on research from sociology and economics, important theoretical work has been forged to help us discern the pathways between measures of community/neighborhood and student learning. Chase-Lansdale and colleagues (1997), for example, posit that "direct neighborhood effects on young children will be first seen through the mechanisms of neighborhood resources and collective socialization" (p. 81). Jencks and Mayer (as cited in Turley, 2003) describe three influence pathways: (1) peers (contagion), (2) adults (collective socialization), and (3) community institutions (p. 63). Duncan and Aber (1997) construct influence linkages "from economic, sociological, and developmental theories of neighborhood effects" (p. 74). Jarrett (1997), in his summary of the literature, gleans five translation mechanisms—neighborhood resource, contagion, competition, collective socialization, and relative deprivation—by which communities are believed to influence "cognitive, economic, and social outcomes" (p. 48) for families and children. Kober (2001) clusters "community factors that affect children's opportunities to learn" into two bins: "learning resources and institutions [and] . . . environmental factors that impede learning" (p. 29). Magnuson and Duncan (2006), in turn, describe four negative pathways of "neighborhood influence [on] children" (p. 380): stress, lack of social organization, few institutional resources, and exposure to environmental toxins.

On the resource dimension, "Neighborhood resource theory holds that the quality of local resources available for families and their children affects developmental outcomes" (Jarrett, 1997, p. 61). Analysts maintain that low-income and African American children are disadvantaged because their communities have fewer institutional and other social resources, such as libraries and parks (Lara-Cinisomo et al., 2004; Brooks-Gunn et al., 1997; Chase-Lansdale et al., 1997). Jarrett (1997) details this as follows:

Neighborhoods with an extensive array of good, accessible services, such as parks, libraries, and child-care facilities, provide more extrafamilial experiences, which in turn are associated with better cognitive and behavioral outcomes. Conversely, neighborhoods lacking good, accessible services restrict extrafamilial experiences, which in turn are associated with poorer cognitive and behavioral outcomes. (p. 61)

We visit the contagion (peer) influence pathway in numerous places throughout this volume, especially in our analysis of how race impacts student learning later in this chapter, and in our analysis of schooling influences on achievement in Chapter 9. Here we simply report that communities can exercise influence on the friendships youngsters form, or their peer groups (Miller, 1995; Turley, 2003), and these groups in turn help shape academic press and subsequent performance. As we will see in detail subsequently, in some of these peer groups, there is considerable pressure toward underperformance in school, a dynamic that exacerbates the achievement gap problem.

The logic of collective socialization, in turn, posits that "neighborhood socialization is an important pathway by which neighborhood income affects children's outcomes" (Turley, 2003, p. 70). The theory has been nicely encoded by Jarrett (1997):

> *According to collective socialization theory, impoverished neighborhoods with more unemployed adults and single-parent households provide role models that eschew conventional emphases on school achievement, work skills, family organization, future orientations, and self-efficacy. In contrast, affluent neighborhoods with more working adults and two-parent families provide stronger normative support and conventional role models for school achievement, work skills, family patterns, future orientations, and self-efficacy. In both settings, albeit with different outcomes, local adults are major influences on the lives of parents and their children. In impoverished neighborhoods, parents receive little communal support for child rearing. To the contrary, the presence of adults who are involved in unconventional lifestyles and behaviors poses physical and moral risks to children's development. In affluent neighborhoods, parents receive multiple sources of support for child rearing. The presence of cooperating adults who are involved in conventional lifestyles and behaviors reinforces conventional paths for child development. (p. 62)*

Particular salience in the theoretical literature is allotted to the variable of joblessness among males in the neighborhood (Brooks-Gunn et al., 1997; Halpern-Felsher et al., 1997), and the belief "that the plight of the inner-city underclass stems from a weakening of basic social institutions attributable to prolonged joblessness in inner-city neighborhoods" (Natriello, McDill, & Pallas, 1999, p. 14). So, too, the concepts of "social isolation" and "social disorganization" are underscored (Chase-Lansdale et al., 1997; Halpern-Felsher et al., 1997), as is the larger construct of diminished social capital (Spradlin et al., 2005). According to Rothstein (2004), the resultant "social class differences in role modeling also make a social class achievement gap almost inevitable" (p. 29).

To close the loop between community and learning, we note first that community, through these various pathways, is expected to influence schooling. For example, children who live "in a high poverty zone are likely to attend schools with high concentrations of disadvantaged children" (Miller, 1995, p. 313). Thus neighborhood has a good deal to do with "the degree of class/race segregation at the school level" (Roscigno, 2000, p. 267). Also, there is evidence that the "neighborhoods surrounding America's diverse schools affect the quality of [those] schools by shaping both input and process factors" (Caldas & Bankston, 1999, p. 91).

In early chapters, we revealed that there are quite strong effects of SES and family home environment on measures of student learning, and these two bundles of variables account for something in the neighborhood of 50 to 75 percent of achievement scores; additionally, and they are heavily implicated in the formation of learning gaps between low- and high-income youngsters and between African American and white children. Here we record our second loop-closing note. The evidence to date suggests that the direct community impact on youngsters is much smaller (Halpern-Felsher et al., 1997; Jarrett, 1997), claiming, "The associations between neighborhood characteristics and children's outcomes are quite modest" (Magnuson & Duncan, 2006, p. 380; see also Chase-Lansdale et al., 1997, p. 115; Turly, 2003, p. 69)—"that the effect of neighborhood environments is less important than that of family and school environments" (Brooks-Gunn et al., 1997, p. 282). For example, Duncan and Magnuson (2005) conclude that neighborhood characteristics explain only a small part of the differential in student learning, "no more than 5 percent" (p. 44). The effects that are seen tend to be most visible in the early years of childhood and the late adolescent years (Brooks-Gunn et al., 1997). What the research on community seems to be finding is, "Many influences of the neighborhood may operate through effects on the family context" (Chase-Lansdale et al., 1997, p. 80). That is, community influences are heavily mediated by families.

RACISM AND DISCRIMINATION

There is reason to believe that historic and contemporary racism continues to take a toll on the academic development and performance of African American youngsters. (Miller, 1995, p. 195)

Racism and the devalued position of blacks in our society cannot be ignored as a primary contributing factor to black underachievement. (Irvine, 1990, p. 4)

Race has a significant negative effect on achievement. Black children tend to score lower on standardized achievement tests than do white children, even after parental income, education, occupation, and wealth are taken into account. (Orr, 2003, p. 298)

Although the conventional wisdom is that racial differences in student performance can be explained by school poverty, rejecting this wisdom invites an alternative and often more disturbing explanation—there is a race effect, or an unexplained portion of the racial gap in test scores that cannot be attributed to racial differences in characteristics of students, schools, neighborhoods, or home environment. (Myers, Kim, & Mandala, 2004, p. 82)

There is a considerable body of scholarship that confirms that racism, in addition to the explanations for learning differentials already examined, helps explain the underachievement of African American youngsters in general, and also explains part of the achievement gap between white and African Americans in particular. Scholars posit that segregation and other forms of "discrimination have caused many aspects of blacks' environment to be inferior to that of whites" (Dickens, 2005, p. 64), a theme with deep historical roots (Caldas & Bankston, 1997; Irvine, 1990; Norman, Ault, Bentz, & Meskimen, 2001). Consequently, opportunity structures for African Americans are much more limited than for whites (Spradlin et al., 2005), a condition that hinders African American youngsters' quest for school success (Roscigno, 2000). In addition, researchers document that some African American responses to marginalization can weaken connections to schooling and reduce the work effort required for higher academic achievement, and "Aspects of the black culture contribute to the gap" (Rothstein, 2004, p. 56). The logic here is that racial discrimination, both directly and indirectly, "contributes to the continued underachievement of those who are discriminated against" (Gordon, Frede, & Irvine, 2004, p. 2) and, "Sociocultural factors are clearly implicated in the establishment and maintenance of the achievement gap" (Norman et al., 2004, p. 1105).

We begin here at the end of the logic chain, that is, with student achievement. While some analysts suggest that race explanations for achievement gaps can be explained by examining SES and family factors, other scholars substantiate, "Controlling for all other individual variables, African American students' academic achievement is likely to be depressed relative to their white counterparts" (Caldas & Bankston, 1997, p. 277): "Race/ethnicity is—in many ways—the most recalcitrant and entrenched descriptor of achievement gaps. Even after controlling for families' educational backgrounds or socioeconomic status, gaps among racial/ethnic groups persist" (Symonds, 2004, p. 7; see also Myers, Kim, & Mandala, 2004). The rationale is that race has an independent effect on student achievement; that is, there is an "independent negative effect for race" (Caldas & Bankston, 1997, p. 281). The latter position seems empirically defensible. While controls for socioeconomic status and family background reduce racial gaps in student test scores (Fryer & Levitt, 2004; Myers, Kim, & Mandala, 2004), they do not eliminate them (Bol & Berry, 2005). Miller (1995) asserts that the variations in achievement cannot be merely attributed to race and social class, stating, "There are also large within-social class differences in academic achievement patterns among groups. At each social class level, whites tend to do much better academically than blacks" (p. 338). And, according to Camara and Schmid (1999), "At every income level, African Americans are less likely to excel in high school grades and class rank than other students" (p. 13). Also, significant "differences exist among racial groups having similar levels of parent education" (p. 8). The summary here has been penned nicely by Miller (1995) in his cardinal volume on achievement gaps: "Historical and contemporary racial prejudice evidently undermines the academic achievement of many minority students from all social classes" (p. 298).

Discrimination

Past discrimination may account for present racial differences. (Farley, 1984, p. 13)

One of the primary barriers to black students' achievement is racism. (Irvine, 1990, p. 89)

It does not take much of a stretch of the imagination to connect the relatively poor academic showing by African American students in the 1990s to the historical legacy of grossly inadequate, unjust educational policies and practices of the relatively recent past. (Caldas & Bankston, 1997, pp. 280–281)

A central theme of this chapter is, "The achievement gap that persists for Black students may be attributable . . . to the disadvantaged position that Blacks occupy in U.S. society" (Norman et al., 2001, p. 1105). Here we focus on the place of racism in creating that disadvantaged position. While this is not the appropriate venue to undertake a comprehensive treatment of racial prejudice and discrimination in the United States, its place in the achievement gap equation demands that we outline its central dimensions.

To start, we are aware that there are long "traditions of discrimination" (Biddle, 2001, p. 2) against African American people in the United States, "that the negative stereotypes whites hold of blacks have been enduring" (Miller, 1995, p. 221). We also understand that these traditions have been institutionally sanctioned: "Throughout most of its history, the United States has been a nation in which nonwhite minorities were the victims of a government-sanctioned and government-enforced system of racial stratification that relegated them to subordinate positions relative to the white majority" (Miller, 1995, p. 172). We know that the long history and legacy of discrimination hinders relatively responsive change efforts even when discriminatory practices are dismantled (Kober, 2001; Mickelson, 2003). For example, Rothstein (2004) observes:

> *Even if discrimination were suddenly to end completely, . . . community expectations that academic prowess will be unrewarded, based on 150 years of reality, would not disappear overnight. The culture of many black families is one where anticipation of mistreatment remains prevalent. (pp. 35–36).*

In a similar vein, Miller (1995) reminds us:

> *Although the nation's historical caste system has been largely dismantled and its legal foundations swept away, the negative stereotypes that were used by whites to justify the system live on with sufficient vigor to weaken the contemporary societal response to the pressing problems of poverty, unemployment, and under-education; that these problems are in many respects legacies of that system seems to be been forgotten. (p. 221)*

Finally, we know that these elements of discrimination are "consequential" (p. 221).

From a deep literature in this area, we understand that these racial divisions "reproduce oppression" (Knapp, 2001, p. 184) and "can present formidable polity capital problems to some or all of the population" (Miller, 1995, p. 242). The result of these patterns "of institutionalized racial/ethnic discrimination" (Miller, 1995, p. 377) is that African Americans confront what Miller (1995) calls a "negative economic and educational opportunity structure" (p. 275). African Americans have been systematically "excluded from the political, economic, and social mainstream" (p. 173): "The negative consequence of slavery, segregation, racism, and discrimination have inflicted" (Stinson, 200, p. 482) serious injustices on the African American community, injustices that in turn influence the shape and texture of America's schools (Brooks-Gunn, Klebanov, & Duncan, 1996; Michelson, 2003) and the academic performance of African American youngsters (Miller, 1995).

Discrimination has been linked to the development of a "labor market that has not historically rewarded black workers for their education" (Rothstein, 2004, p. 4). Likewise, it is connected to the erection of "formidable barriers to entry into many segments of the job market" (Miller, 1995, p. 103). Not surprisingly, these traditions of discrimination suggest to many African Americans that "hard work in schools is irrelevant and that academic endeavors will have little economic payoff" (Becker & Luthar, 2002, p. 198). Discrimination has meant patterns of residential segregation that are the norm for large numbers of African American children (Miller, 1999). Overall, discrimination "pervaded the political, economic, and social realms and kept most minorities permanently on the bottom rungs of society, regardless of their talents and abilities" (Miller, 1995, p. 172).

Finally, "Contemporary racial/ethnic prejudice contributes to the academic motivation and achievement problems of minorities" (Miller, 1995, p. 221). Scholars find, for example, "that racist white attitudes and prejudices weaken the self-esteem of blacks. . . . This racism delegitimates the aspirations of blacks, lowers their self confidence, [and] deprives them of social support" (Hallinan, 2001, p. 56; see also Shannon & Bylsma, 2002). Segregation and discrimination "take a toll on the academic performance of many minority students" (Miller, 1999, p. 16). They help contribute to the achievement gap by "undermining preparation for school" (Steele & Aronson, 1995, p. 798). They help ensure that children who are likely to be the least successful in school "are disproportionately likely to confront problems of prejudice" (Miller, 1995, p. 248; see also Phillips et al., 1998a).

African American Response to Racial Discrimination

Prejudice and discrimination also can erode minority academic performance by contributing to an alienation from the mainstream. (Miller, 1999, p. 16)

One possible contributor to the achievement gap is pressures and messages within the urban Black community that schools and teachers are not to be trusted. (Uhlenberg & Brown, 2002, p. 495)

And beyond socioeconomic structure, there are cultural patterns within these groups or in the relation between these groups and the larger society that may also frustrate their identification with school or some part of it. (Steele, 1997, p. 616)

We have just reported that racial prejudice and discrimination have created a climate of injustice that has significantly limited the educational opportunities that African Americans have had for success. We also traced the impact of racism on the motivation and achievement of African American children. More recent research also allows us to see that the ways in which African Americans respond to prejudice can exacerbate achievement gaps. That is, "Prejudice and discrimination influence not only the academic motivation and performance of minority students through the creation or maintenance of a negative economic opportunity structure" (Miller, 1995, p. 222), but also by the ways they encourage African Americans to respond to injustices and subsequent truncated opportunity structures.

Response to racism theories takes a number of forms in the scholarly literature. Building from research on "how the values and expectations of students' cultural backgrounds . . . influence student attitudes about schooling and thus academic success" (Hertert & Teague, 2003, p. 13), researchers confirm that in the face of racism African Americans sometimes develop cultural practices—values and norms—that are less conducive to school success than those found in mainstream white homes (Biddle, 2001; Hallinan, 2001; Michelson, 2003). These analysts suggest that part of the failure of African Americans is "due to blacks' own negative self-defeating attitudes" (Hallinan, 2001, p. 55). For example, African American culture often does not view poor performance in school as a setback to future plans (Hertert & Teague, 2003).

A second response to institutional racism is to avoid engagement with schools. According to Howard and Hammond (as cited in Miller, 1995), this "avoidance is rooted in the fears and self-doubt engendered by a major legacy of American racism" (p. 201). A third response is to internalize inferiority, thus undermining school success (Shannon & Bylsma, 2002).

Finally, a growing body of research posits that in the face of racism, African Americans sometimes "develop definitions of themselves that [are] oppositional to the majority culture" (Miller, 1995, p. 206). That is, they sometimes create expectations and norms that run counter to the majority white culture of schooling (Ainsworth-Darnell & Downey, 1998; Rothstein, 2004). Here, we see that African Americans "resist assimilation [and] adopt attitudes of resistance" (Ford, Grantham, & Whiting, 2008, p. 222; see also Jencks & Phillips, 1998). In some cases, African Americans "may be unable or unwilling to separate their attitudes and behaviors from other symbols of assimilation to the dominant white majority and hence may view success in school as 'selling out' to the dominant culture" (Schmid, 2001, p. 76). Overall then, according to response theorists, disillusionment of African Americans in the face of perceived truncated educational and occupational opportunities encourages them to inhibit identification with the school (Steele, 1992; 1997; 1998) and to disengage from learning activities (Hallinan, 2001).

While we examine the issue of peer impacts on learning gaps in detail in Chapter 9, it is important to acknowledge that scholars assert that peer pressure is often the vehicle through which oppositional culture materializes in schools (Cook & Ludwig, 1998; Shannon & Bylsma, 2002). In particular, researchers maintain that some African American students "condemn academic success as a rejection of their cultural identity" (Cook & Ludwig, 1998, p. 375): "One major reason that black students do poorly in school is that they experience inordinate ambivalence and affective dissonance in regard to academic effort and success" (Fordham & Ogbu, as cited in Cook & Ludwig, 1998, p. 376). As a consequence, a devaluing of schooling (Shannon & Bylsma, 2002) and "an anti-academic orientation" (Miller, 1995, p. 276) can develop "among many disadvantaged youngsters" (p. 276). In its extreme form, it is argued, "The history of discrimination in the United States has led African-American adolescents to . . . associate academic success with acting white" (Cook & Ludwig, 1998, p. 377). This response, of course, results in damped down school effort and commitment, at least for some students; undermines success in school; and contributes to the achievement gap between African American and white students.

INDIVIDUAL DIFFERENCES: GENETICS AND ABILITY

Many experts think that genetic differences are at least partially to blame for existing black-white differences in academic achievement. (Ferguson, 1998, p. 282)

Other scholarship asserts that Black students' lower academic achievement is natural and genetically inscribed. (Stinson, 2006, p. 483)

The available evidence shows that traditional explanations for the black-white test score gap do not work very well. If genes play any role, it is probably quite small. (Jencks & Phillips, 1998, p. 50)

While there are controversies about whether differences in academic achievement between racial groups as measured by standardized tests are due in part to differences in ability, no one has found genetic evidence indicating that one racial group has less innate intellectual ability than others. (Lee, 2004, p. 56)

While discussions of racial explanations for achievement gaps are controversial, they pale in comparison to analyses of the role of genetics in accounting for learning differentials between African American and white children (Phillips et al., 1998a). And, it is this issue that occupies us here. The essence of the storyline on heredity, or "individualistic explanations," for achievement gaps has been nicely summarized by Duncan and Magnuson (2005):

Many behavioral geneticists . . . put forth a different logic. They argue that genetic endowments of ability are key determinants of test scores, and children reared in more affluent families score higher on achievement tests in part because of genetic endowments passed on from one generation to the next. (p. 39)

Or, as Dickens (2005) captures it, some suggest "that there is a single ability that differs among people, that it is subject to genetic influence, and that it explains much of the correlation across tests" (p. 60). More specifically, the focus here is on inherited IQ and a kind of "biological determinism" (Hallinan, 2001, p. 53). This "biogenic" (Wilson, 1998, p. 503) logic asserts that some children are born with more or less nonmalleable amounts of intelligence—intelligence that has much to do with student achievement in schools in general and achievement gaps in particular. Thus, it is held, "Genetic differences of racial/ethnic minority and lower socioeconomic backgrounds explains why they [minority and low-SES children] do poorly in schools" (Villegas & Lucas, 2002, p. 39; Stinson, 2006). There is a lack of agreement here about the linkages between the patterns of racism and discrimination we discussed previously and intelligence. Some scholars are quick to note that if there are differences in intelligence between African Americans and whites, they are "attributable to blacks' history of slavery, segregation, and limited opportunities" (Irvine, 1990, p. 3), rather than to genetics.

More simply stated, the core proposition in this line of explanation, as summarized by Rothstein (2004), is "that the black-white achievement gap result[s], in part, from genetic difference between the races" (p. 52). While earlier explanations maintained that school and later economic success are associated with family structure, home environment, and SES, the argument in the literature here is "that a single, primarily inherited, dimension of human intelligence predicts the underachievement of blacks" (Hallinan, 2001, p. 53).

The devastating conclusion here is that differences between the races, including achievement gap differentials, resulting from inherent abilities are fixed and "therefore immutable to policies and programs" (Neuman & Celano, 2006, p. 197), and "that relatively little can be done to improve the academic performance of black children whose parents have had little formal education and low incomes" (Miller, 1995, p. 189). The end result, summarized by Villegas and Lucas (2002), is clear: "Investments in education . . . are not likely to close the achievement gap between students of color and white students in any appreciable way" (p. 39).

As noted, analyses of genetic explanations for achievement gaps are emotionally laden and highly controversial (Uhlenberg & Brown, 2002). On one side of the issue, analysts uncover support for the genetic rationale, at least as a partial explanation for achievement gaps in schools. Indeed, Biddle (2001) reports, "Various small groups of scholars—such as sociobiologists and evolutionary psychologists—continue to express enthusiasm for the notion that group differences in human behavior are inherited" (p. 10). Evidence for individualistic differences in learning, and for resulting gaps in achievement, has also been provided by some scholars of note. For example, Jensen (reviewed in Miller, 1995) asserts, "The best available evidence support[s] the conclusion that, on average, variations in intelligence among individuals [are] 80 percent due to variations in genetic makeup and 20 percent due to variations in environment" (p. 188). Later scholarship by Hernstein and Murray (reviewed in Heckman, 1995) maintains "that 40–80 percent of the variance of IQ measured around population means is attributable to biological genetic influences" (pp. 1095–1096). And Scarr and Weinberg (1983), based on studies of adopted children, conclude that 40–70 percent of IQ variance may be due to genetic differences.

Not unexpectedly, an array of scholars has taken issue with these biological-determinant explanations for learning differences among children (Haskins & Rouse, 2005; Rouse, Brooks-Gunn, & McLanahan, 2005; Wilson, 1998). According to Shannon and Bylsma (2002), these researchers have helped "dispel the myth of genetic and biological differences" (p. 22) and have "discredited the putative scientific basis for biological determinist explanations for racial differences in academic performance" (Mickelson, 2003, p. 1058). Much of this later analysis provides critical reviews of the genetically determined learning research. Based on these critiques, researchers conclude, that "there is no reasonable basis" (Rothstein, 2004, p. 7) for attributing differences in academic ability to genes and that "it is unlikely that the black-white gap has a large genetic component" (Dickens, 2005, p. 64): "that innate and genetic factors are not the reason for the achievement gap" (Kober, 2001, p. 17). In sum, as Jencks and Phillips conclude, "Despite endless speculation, no one has found genetic evidence indicating that blacks have less innate intellectual ability than whites" (p. 44). Almost all studies "suggest genetic equality between the races or very small genetic differences favoring one race or the other" (Nisbett, 1998, p. 96): "The evidence thus indicates that if there are genetically determined IQ differences between the races, they are too small to show up with any regularity in studies covering a wide range of populations and using a wide range of methodologies" (p. 101).

More generally, researchers confirm "that racial differences in test performance are mostly, perhaps entirely, environmental" (Bainbridge & Lasley, 2002, p. 423): "There is now considerable empirical evidence that variations in environmental circumstances, not differences in innate intellectual potential, account for the large differences in average IQ scores between blacks and whites" (Miller, 1995, p. 198). Indeed, as Phillips and colleagues (1998a), affirm, "It is possible to account for at least two-thirds of the black-white test score gap without having to appeal to environmental mysteries or genetic differences between blacks and whites" (p. 109).

We close this section with an important reminder. That is, individual influences on learning, and subsequently on achievement gaps, are not confined to intelligence and ability. There may be other environmentally shaped yet individually determined reasons why certain youngsters perform less well in schools than their peers (Scarr, 1983). Motivation is one of these elements (Uhlenberg & Brown, 2002) that may play out differently based on race and class. So too are aspirations and personal habits (Shannon & Bylsma, 2002). For example, African Americans, on average, have lower educational aspirations than whites (Shannon & Bylsma, 2002). The theme here is twofold. First, "Children play an important role in their own development" (Chin & Phillips, 2004, p. 204). Second, "children's agency" (p. 187) maybe patterned to some extent by race and class. We return to these nonability, individual impacts on learning in Chapter 9.

CONCLUSION

In this chapter, we added three more variables to the learning gap algorithm: community, racism and discrimination, and individual differences (genetics and ability). We found that of the three, racism and discrimination is the most impactful factor. We turn now to the last chapter of the environmental (nonschool) causal narrative, out-of-school learning experiences.

7

Environmental Causes of Achievement Gaps

Out-of-School Learning Experiences

The descriptive comparisons ... seem to implicate out-of-school learning differences as driving the achievement gap across social lines. (Alexander, Entwisle, & Olson, 2001, p. 173)

So far, we have investigated an array of nonschool factors that help explain achievement gaps between African American and white children and between youngsters from low- and high-income families. Using capital formation and ecosystem models, we have seen how conditions in the larger society, including the immediate community, place some youngsters at risk. We also reported that most of these forces are mediated by actions within families. We examined the role that heredity and individual motivation plays in generating achievement gaps. Here, we explore the final nonschool (external) causal element in the achievement gap algorithm, disadvantages associated with out-of-school learning opportunities. We attend to formal learning opportunities before the start of kindergarten, as well as summer learning experiences once students begin their school careers.

While, for analytic reasons, we treat these out-of-school learning opportunities as a separate chapter in the gap storyline, it is important to affirm that these experiences are heavily impacted by the causes we have explored in Chapters 3–6. That is, less-than-helpful conditions in the larger society (e.g., poverty, racism) and the family (e.g., low levels of parental education) often create an environment in which African American and low-income children are less well educated outside the formal system of schooling than their white and more advantaged peers (Harris & Herrington, 2006; Magnuson & Duncan, 2006; Rouse, Brooks-Gunn, & McLanahan, 2005). Indeed, a considerable body of research concludes that societal and "family circumstances cause low-income African American children to begin schooling at a disadvantage by comparison with White and middle class children" (Farkas, 2003, p. 1121). These same circumstances are in play during the summers after children begin school as well (Alexander, Entwisle, & Olson, 2001; Alexander, Olson, & Entwisle, 2007).

EDUCATION BEFORE KINDERGARTEN: READINESS

Differences in black-white achievement may also be attributable to differences in school preparedness. (United States Department of Education, 2001a, p. 8)

The out-of-school context necessarily explains the lag in achievement levels of low-income and minority youth over the preschool period. (Alexander, Entwisle, & Olson, 2001, p. 171)

Sizable racial and ethnic gaps already exist by the time children enter kindergarten. (Rouse, Brooks-Gunn, & McLanahan, 2005, p. 5)

Disparities between black and white schools cannot explain why black children enter preschool with smaller vocabularies than white children. This fact must reflect differences between black and white children's experiences before they enter school. (Jenkins & Phillips, 1998, p. 50)

We know from a large body of literature across diverse fields that "out-of-school factors affect students prior to their entering kindergarten" (Shannon & Bylsma, 2002, p. 21). This same research confirms that one of the major causes of achievement gaps that show up in schools is the fact that there is already a significant gap in the achievement of many low-income and African American students when they enter kindergarten (Armor, 2008; Bennett et al., 2007; Everson, 2007; McGee, 2003). Indeed, there is an impressive body of research that reveals, "At-risk children start with lower scores on cognitive assessments in kindergarten" (Chatterji, 2006, p. 491). Because "minority students are generally less likely to be ready for school" (Klein et al., 1997, p. 84), there are "alarming gaps" (Magnuson & Duncan, 2006, p. 365) in the readiness scores of blacks and whites (Fryer & Levitt, 2004; Zill & West, 2001). That is, "By the time of school entry, the black-white test score gap has already grown to about half of its ultimate size" (Thompson & O'Quinn, 2001, p. 8). Or, rephrased by starting at the end point, "Half of the achievement gap between blacks and whites at the end of the twelfth grade is attributable to achievement differences between students when they start school" (Le, Kirby, Barney, Setodji, & Gershwin, 2006, p. 1). And, what is true for students of color holds for students from low-income homes as well: "Low-SES children . . . arrive at school with achievement levels far below their middle-class counterparts" (Reardon, 2003, p. 27).

Dimensions of Readiness

Over the last few decades, social scientists have "voluminously documented" (Farkas, 2003, p. 1121) the dimensions and the scope of the school readiness gap in America. On the dimension issue, analysts "have used a range of tests to measure different dimensions of the skills and behaviors—word comprehension, reading, math, the ability to sit still—that make a child 'ready' to enter school" (Rock & Stenner, 2005, p. 16). They discuss patterned variations in the academic, social, and emotional realms of development (Hertert & Teague, 2003; Le et al., 2006; Rouse, Brooks-Gunn, & McLanahan, 2005) and significant differentials on factors that contribute to placing children at risk for failure (Zill & West, 2001).

On the academic front, we learn, "The average Black child arrives at kindergarten with fewer academic skills than the average White child" (Ferguson, 2003, p. 483; see also Baenen et al., 2002). More specifically, "The average black child starts elementary school with substantially weaker math, reading, and vocabulary skills than the average white child" (Phillips et al., 1998b, pp. 256–257). As depicted by Rouse, Brooks-Gunn, & McLanahan (2005):

A variety of standardized tests show substantial racial and ethnic disparities at the time children enter school. Estimates of the gap in school readiness range from slightly less than half a standard deviation to slightly more than 1 standard deviation. (p. 8)

In mathematics, low-income children, in general, enter kindergarten with fewer skills than their white counterparts (Burkam et al., 2004). In their investigations, Magnuson and Duncan (2006) report, "Black students scored about two-thirds of a standard deviation below whites . . . on skills such as recognizing numbers and geometric shapes, counting, and recognizing patterns" (p. 366). A study by the United States Department of Education (as cited in Kober, 2001) concluded that African American children "start out behind on early math skills such as recognizing numbers and shapes, understanding the relative order of objects, and solving simple addition and subtraction problems" (p. 24). Overall, Lee and Burkam (2002) report that at kindergarten entry, children from low-SES families score 60 percent lower in mathematics than youngsters from higher-SES groups.

Turning to language, researchers document that African American youngsters and children from low-income families, in general, enter kindergarten with "lower literacy skills" (Le et al., 2006, p. 1)—with less well-developed oral language, with fewer prereading skills, and with more limited vocabularies (Farkas, 2003; Hart & Risley, 1995). Mayer (as cited in Entwisle, Alexander, & Olson, 2000) reports that low-income preschool-age children "score considerably lower than affluent children on vocabulary knowledge, a difference that amounts to about nine months of cognitive growth for an average child" (p. 11). Hart and Risley (1995) confirm this finding, documenting huge differences in the vocabularies of preschool-aged children from different social classes, with low-income children on the disadvantaged side of the table. Thus, according to Phillips et al. (1998b), African American children start school approximately one year behind white students in the area of vocabulary.

Another study by the U.S. Department of Education (as cited in Shannon & Bylsma, 2002) found that while 71 percent of white children enter kindergarten able to recognize letters, only 57 percent of African American children do so (p. 21). On "skills such as recognizing letters and associating letters with sounds at the beginning of words . . . Black students scored just under half a standard deviation lower" (Magnuson & Duncan, 2006, p. 366).

Magnuson and Duncan (2006) conclude from their investigations that at the point of school entry, African American students score about one-half of a standard deviation lower in reading than their white peers. Lee and Burkam, in turn, report that children from low-income families entering kindergarten score more than 50 percent lower in reading than youngsters from high-income families.

Zill and West (2001) make important contributions on the readiness front by linking risk factors with preparation for kindergarten; these risk factors disproportionately characterize children from low-income and minority homes. They report that 47 percent of students with two or more risk factors score in the bottom quartile on state tests in reading. On the other hand, only 16 percent of students with no risk factors cluster in the bottom quartile. At the other end of the continuum, they show that while 33 percent of children with no risk factors score in the top quartile, only 9 percent of youngsters with two or more risk factors do so (p. 20).

In terms of specific reading and mathematics skills that kindergartners with risk factors do or do not have when entering school, the ECLS-K results showed the following:

- Less than half of multiple risk children were at the first proficiency level in reading. Forty-four percent of them could identify letters of the alphabet, compared with 57 percent of children in the single risk group and 75 percent of those in the no risk group.
- Children from families with multiple risk factors were roughly one-third as likely to be able to associate letters with sounds at the ends of words as children from families with none of the four risk factors. Children from families with one risk factor were half as likely to do so. Twenty-two percent of the no risk group, 11 percent of the single risk group, and 6 percent of the multiple risk group were at this third proficiency level in reading.
- Although a large majority (87 percent) of the kindergartners with multiple risk factors were at the first proficiency level in mathematics, less than half were at the second level. Thirty-eight percent of the multiple risk group could count beyond ten or make judgments of relative length, compared with 48 percent of the single risk group and 68 percent of the no risk group. (p. 21)

Zill and West (2001) also document the connections between risk factors and noncognitive aspects of school readiness. They confirm that there is a "negative relationship between risk factors and children's health, social development, and behavior" (p. 23), all conditions that in turn influence learning.

We close here by presaging the central themes of Chapter 10, in which we explore solutions to the "readiness problem." First, as Phillips et al. (1998b) note, research in this area suggests "that we could eliminate at least half, and probably more, of the black-white score gap at the end of the twelfth grade by eliminating the differences that exist before children enter first grade" (p. 257). Second, as Rothstein (2004) asserts:

Deficits like these cannot be made up by schools alone, no matter how high the teachers' expectations. For all children to achieve the same goals, those from the lower class would have to enter school with verbal fluency similar to that of middle-class children. (p. 28)

And third, from Levin and associates (2007), "Children from educationally and economically disadvantaged populations are less prepared to start school. They are unlikely to catch up without major educational interventions on their behalf" (p. 2).

Pathways of Readiness

Analysts discuss two avenues by which school readiness skills are developed, that is, pathways that explain the variability in the readiness skills just examined (Chatterji, 2006): parental care and center care (Magnuson & Waldfogel, 2005). Throughout Part II and especially in Chapter 5, we have explored how parents, in formal and informal ways, influence readiness for school, for better or for worse. We documented that parenting practices in low-income and African American families, on average, do not provide as strong a readiness foundation as do parenting practices in more affluent homes. We will not repeat that analysis here. We move forward by examining what is known about the second pathway, "the quality of care young children receive outside the home" (Duncan & Brooks-Gunn, 2000, p. 190).

An obvious starting point is to remind ourselves that center care can influence school readiness. Equally important, "Differences in early school achievement are in part attributable to differences in preschool experiences" (Maruyama, 2003, p. 656). High-quality center care has been shown to contribute to academic and social learning outcomes throughout schooling (Duncan & Brooks-Gunn, 2000; Magnuson & Waldfogel, 2005).

We also know that "African-American children [are] less likely to be enrolled in preprimary education relative to whites" (Chatterji, 2006, p. 491): "Not only are children from economically disadvantaged families less likely to experience stimulating learning opportunities in their home environments, they are also less likely to be enrolled in early education programs and center-based child care" (Magnuson, Meyers, Ruhme, & Waldfogel, 2004, p. 118). While nearly 50 percent of white children participate in center-based care, only about 33 percent of African American children do so (Lee & Burkam, 2002). Findings pinpoint SES as an even more revealing factor in center-based care. "As children's SES goes up, so does the proportion of them with center-based care experience. The proportion of high-SES children with center-based care is over three times as large as low-SES children (65.0 percent vs. 20.1 percent)" (Lee & Burkam, 2002, p. 36). Similarly, Maruyama (2003) reports:

> [There are] marked differences in the preschool experiences of students coming from families where the parents are poor. Over half of the three-year olds and three quarters of the four-year olds in families making over $50,000 attended center-based preschool programs, while a quarter of three-year olds and half of four-year olds from families making less than $10,000 attended such programs. (p. 656)

Finally, research informs us that many center-based programs do not receive high marks for quality and that African American and low-income youngsters are over represented in these lower-quality programs (Kober, 2001; Magnuson & Waldfogel, 2005): "Black children receive lower-quality care than white children, both within centers and across other types of care" (Magnuson & Waldfogel, 2005, p. 182).

Importance

We close this section on early out-of-school learning opportunities with two critical reminders. First, "It is clear that the years prior to kindergarten entry represent a foundational period for ensuring children's eventual success in school and beyond" (Karoly, Kilburn, & Cannon, 2005, p. 1) and, "Prior learning influences future achievement" (Bainbridge & Lasley, 2002, p. 429). As Le and associates (2006) affirm, the skills and knowledge that children bring to kindergarten are "predictive of later achievement" (p. 1): "Preschool verbal ability . . . is predictive of literacy scores as much as fifteen years later, even after controlling for the effects of educational, social, and economic well-being" (Chase-Lansdale et al., 1997, p.88). The implications of the foundational period are described further by Rouse, Brooks-Gunn, and McLanahan (2005):

> Children who score poorly on tests of cognitive skills during their preschool years are likely to do less well in elementary and high school than their higher-performing preschool peers and are more likely to become teen parents, engage in criminal activities, and suffer from depression. Ultimately, these children attain less education and are more likely to be unemployed in adulthood. (p. 6)

Second, disparities in readiness, fueled in part by differences in center care, are quite significant. They account for much, about 50 percent, of achievement gaps that are visible at the end of the twelfth grade.

EDUCATIONAL OPPORTUNITIES
IN THE SUMMER

> During the summer, relatively advantaged students learn at a faster rate than do less privileged pupils. (Heyns, 1978, p. 187)

> It has become increasingly apparent that the time period over the summer, when students are typically out of school, has important implications for understanding these gaps. (Borman & Dowling, 2006, p. 45)

> A sizable portion of the academic achievement gap that emerges between middle class and poor children by the end of the primary grades develops when school is not in session—that is, in the summer months. (Miller, 1995, p. 35)

> Summer learning differences during the foundational early grades help explain achievement-dependent outcome differences across social lines in the upper grades, including the transition out of high school and, for some, into college. (Alexander, Olson, & Entwisle, 2007, p. 168)

We just saw that learning opportunities during the early years, both at home and in formal care centers, explain a good deal of why African American and low-income youngsters do less well in school than their white and more affluent peers. Here, we extend the out-of-school learning narrative, chronicling how learning opportunities during the summer months, once children begin school, help account for achievement differentials by social class and race, i.e., are implicated in the achievement gap problem. The summer effect is "defined as the differences in activities and opportunities typically available to Black and White students over the summer" (Uhlenberg & Brown, 2002, p. 498). Indeed, summer provides a time when it is possible to sort out the effects of schooling and families on student learning (Heyns, 1978). In conjunction with data on the school year, it "approximates a natural experiment that affords leverage for isolating the distinctive role of schooling to children's cognitive development" (Alexander, Olson, & Entwisle, 2007, p. 167).

Summer Differentials in Learning by Social Class

It is mainly when school is not in session that consistent losses occur for poorer students. (Entwisle & Alexander, 1992, p. 82)

Although not without dissension (Fryer & Levitt, 2002) and controversy, there is an expanding body of scholarship that concludes that a sizable portion of achievement gaps can be traced to "seasonal patters in learning" (Entwisle, Alexander, & Olson, 2000, p. 16). More specifically, "Over the past few decades, sociologists of education have found that over summer vacation children from poor and working-class backgrounds lose ground relative to their middle class counterparts" (Chin & Phillips, 2004, p. 206), and, "A large portion of the differences in achievement levels between middle-class and poor students (and, therefore, between majority and minority students) is the product of different summer learning (or learning-loss) rates" (Miller, 1995, p. 136).

Burkam and associates (2004) capture this phenomenon in one form when they confirm, "Children from higher-SES families learn more over the summer months than do their less-advantaged counterparts" (p. 18). Alternatively, from the other side of the continuum, "When schools are closed for summer vacation the achievement scores of children from disadvantaged families either stay the same or slip back a little" (Entwisle, Alexander, & Olson, 2000, p. 15; see also Chin & Phillips, 2004). Indeed, almost all the research in this area uncovers a strong connection between learning gains in the summer and SES (Alexander, Olson, & Entwisle, 2007; Entwisle & Alexander, 1992). Thus, as was the case with learning opportunities before kindergarten, in the "summer-effects-studies" a strong case has been compiled in support of the importance of out-of-school conditions to learning in general, and to the development of achievement gaps in particular (Alexander, Entwisle, & Olson, 2001; Downey, von Hippel, & Broh, 2004; Heyns, 1978), leading to the conclusion that "socioeconomic inequities are heightened by the summer break" (Alexander, Entwisle, & Olson, 2001, pp. 173–174): "Results show that students learn at much more equal rates when school is in session than when it is not" (Downey, von Hippel, & Broh, 2004, p. 624). Research also suggests, "The effect of SES on children's summer learning is not linear; rather, the differences are concentrated mainly in the highest and lowest quintiles of the SES distribution—either very advantaged or very disadvantaged children" (Burkam et al., 2004, p. 25).

Specific measurements of these summer gains and losses for students from different social classes have been provided by a number of researchers. So too have assessments of the place of summer effects in the overall achievement gap algorithm. For example, Alexander and colleagues (2001) report:

> In the verbal area, lower SES youth essentially tread water, some summers gaining a few points, some summers losing a few, while in the quantitative domain losses predominate and are especially large over the first two summers. This means that lower SES children generally start the new school year about where they had been the previous spring or even behind their spring levels of performance.
>
> Upper SES children's scores, on the other hand, improve over the summer months in both domains, which means that they begin the new school year ahead of where they had been the previous spring. And the summer differences comparing lower and upper SES youth are large. This is easiest to see when the year-by-year differences are summed across the years. These totals favor children from upper SES households by sizable margins, with the differences large enough to account for almost the entire CAT gap increase that emerges over the first 5 years of the panel's schooling. (p. 177)

According to these researchers, a significant portion of the achievement gap that is not linked to readiness (ages 0–5) traces to summer learning over the elementary years (Alexander, Olson, & Entwisle, 2007). In one of their studies, the Alexander team found:

> Between the fall and spring of the first year [grade one], children from families of low socioeconomic status in the Baltimore sample gained 57 points in reading and 49 points in math, and their counterparts from families of high socioeconomic status gained almost exactly the same number of points (61 points in reading and 45 points in math). In the summer, however, while children from families of high socioeconomic status gained 15 points in reading and 9 points in math, the children from families of low socioeconomic status lost ground. For example, in the summer after first grade, they lost 4 points in reading and 5 points in math. (Entwisle, Alexander, & Olson, 2000, p. 16)

Their conclusion: "The increasing gap in test scores between children from families of high and low socioeconomic status over the elementary-school period thus accrued entirely from the differential gains they made when school was closed: that is, during the summer months" (p. 16).

Borman and Dowling (2006) provide a nice treatment of summer learning differentials using grade-level equivalents. Reviewing the work of Cooper and colleagues, they note:

> Whereas middle-class children's test scores show slight gains during the summer months, low-SES children's scores show declines of more than two months of grade-level equivalency. As a result, low-SES children's reading skill levels fall approximately three months behind those of their middle-class peers—a difference equivalent to about a third of the typical amount of learning that takes place during a regular school year. (p. 25)

Miller (1995), in turn, reveals that about 60 percent of the gap (32 of the 56-point differential) in reading scores at the end of Grade 3 occur while the students are not in school: "About 15 points emerge prior to the first grade, about 14 during the summer between the first and second grades, and about 3 points in the summer between the second and third grades" (p. 136). And finally, Alexander, Olson, and Entwisle (2007) report a 116 point difference in Grade 9 achievement between high- and low-SES students, "more than half of which (76.5 points) traces to summer learning differences carried forward from elementary school" (p. 172).

Explaining Learning Differentials

Social scientists have also devoted substantial energy to uncovering the causes for these summer-learning differentials. About half of the explanation can be traced to the finding that children from low-SES homes are more school dependent than are youngsters from high-SES families (Alexander, Entwisle, & Olson, 2001). Or, as Heyns (1978) notes, "For less privileged children, the impact of schools is more determinate" (p. 188). The other half of the explanation is found in the research that shows that students from low-SES homes, on average, have less rich, less academically focused summer experiences than their more advantaged peers (Borman & Dowling, 2006; Chin & Phillips, 2004; Rothstein, 2004). Entwisle and colleagues (2000) from their extensive research in this area, have developed the "faucet theory" to help understand summer learning differentials by social class. According to this theory:

> When school [is] in session, the resource faucet [is] turned on for all children and all gain equally; when school is not in session, the school resource faucet [is] turned off. In summers, poor families [can] not make up for the resources the school ha[s] been providing and so their children's achievement plateau[s]. Middle-class families [can] make up for the school's resources to a considerable extent and so their children's growth continue[s], though at a slower pace than during the school year. (p. 17)

This finding should come as no surprise given the conclusion we reached above about the effects of home on the slower rate of achievement for children from low-income families before they begin kindergarten (ages 0–5). It would be shocking if the "disparate home and neighborhood environments" (Downey, von Hippel, & Broh, 2004, p. 616) we discussed above were not linked to learning in the elementary years as well (ages 6–12).

The first link in the faucet theory, and a central theme in the "readiness" research, is that higher-SES families have more resources to devote to providing educational learning opportunities for their youngsters in the summer (Rothstein, 2004). Indeed, Chin and Phillips (2004) "suggest that social-class differences in parents' values and expectations are less important determinants of high-quality summer experiences than are social-class differences in parents' resources" (p. 185). From a different angle, Entwisle and Alexander (1992) capture the theme here as follows: "It is not race or family status that controls summer gains—it is economic status" (p. 82), again pointing us to "the critical nature of home resources when school is closed" (p. 79) and to "the importance of money in enabling parents to purchase better learning environments for their children" (Duncan & Brooks-Gunn, 2001, p. 59): "In the summers . . . the out-of-school resources available to [poor children] are not sufficient to support their achievement" (Alexander, Entwisle, & Olson, 2001, p. 183).

For higher-SES families, available resources are often converted into family and neighborhood activities that reinforce school actions and values (Fryer & Levitt, 2002; Reardon, 2003). For families that lack resources, this is often not possible. Chin and Phillips (2004) report that while working-class and poor parents were able to patch together experiences that somewhat mirrored those of middle-class parents, "None of the working-class or poor children . . . experienced entire summers as active or varied as the middle class children's" (p. 195). They explain further:

> Relative to the working-class and poor parents, the middle-class parents tended to be more successful in constructing highly stimulating summers for their children because they tended to have greater financial resources, more-flexible jobs, and more knowledge about how to match particular activities to their children's skills and interests. (p. 204)

During summer months, higher-SES children are more likely to experience a variety of activities that exacerbate achievement gaps (Rothstein, 2004). They are more likely "to have varied and often highly organized summer experiences" (Chin & Phillips, 2004, p. 193). For example, "[These] children are more likely to attend camp, take family vacations that expose them to new and different environments, go to zoos and museums, or take sports, dance, or music lessons" (Rothstein, 2004, p. 58). On the other hand, in the summer, low-SES children have significantly less participation in "dance and music activities, team and individual sports, swimming lessons, and Scouting during the summer months than do middle-SES children, whereas high-SES children have significantly more involvement than do middle-SES children in all these activities (except Scouting)" (Burkam et al., 2004, p. 16). The result is not surprising: "large social-class differences in children's activities" (Chin & Phillips, 2004, p. 204).

Rothstein (2004) also finds that resources committed to summer learning translate into more reading for middle-class youngsters vis-à-vis children from poor homes. This conclusion is reinforced by Burkam and associates (2004) who find, "Medium-high SES children experience similar levels of summer literacy activities, but low-SES children experience fewer (.3 SDs below the mean) and high-SES children experience more (.2 SDs above the mean)" (p. 16). Finally, resources translate into materials for use in the summer, such as computers. In this regard, Burkam and team (2004) report:

> Over half of low-SES children (56 percent) do not have a home computer and do not have access to another computer for educational use during the summer, compared to only 11 percent of the high-SES children. Conversely, only 14 percent of the low-SES children own a home computer and use it for educational purposes, compared to nearly two thirds of the high-SES children. (pp. 16, 18)

Overall, these social-class differences in summer learning opportunities help "produce both a 'talent-development gap' and a 'cultural exposure gap' which, if exacerbated each summer contribute to disparities" (Chin & Phillips, 2004, p. 206) in academic and social learning and to the formation and hardening of achievement gaps between high- and low-SES youngsters.

CONCLUSION

In the opening chapters of Part II, we investigated causes external to schooling that help explain gaps in achievement between white and African American youngsters and between higher- and lower-income children. Our overall conclusion is that a considerable portion of the differentials in learning among these groups of young people can be traced to these external forces. We crafted a model that highlights six external contributions to achievement gaps in the United States: (1) social and economic conditions, (2) family context, (3) community influence, (4) racism and discrimination, (5) genetic and other individual differences, and (6) out-of-school learning experiences. We concluded based on the work of Phillips, Crouse, and Ralph (1998b) and other scholars in this area that about half of the achievement gap found at the end of the twelfth grade appears before students even start kindergarten. And, we reported that this readiness gap can be traced primarily to social-economic environments that envelop families and to conditions in the home. We argued that the family is an especially critical variable in the achievement gap equation because it is the family that is often forced to address the harmful social and economic forces that touch children. That is, families mediate the impact of socioeconomic context. We also found that out-of-school learning opportunities, both in the period before children start school (ages 0–5) and in the summers after they begin their formal education, explain an important portion of the achievement gap between more and less advantaged youngsters.

Collectively, these external forces dwarf school contributions to achievement gaps. This conclusion tells us that concerted efforts to address these environmental forces must be a central part of any effort to reduce learning differentials between African American and white children, and youngsters from high-income and low-income families. We turn to that agenda in Chapter 10. Before we do so, however, in the next two chapters, we take up the contribution of schools to the achievement gap problem.

8

Schooling Causes of the Achievement Gap

The Instructional Program

We believe that schools account for little of the variation in young children's achievement because when they are open they furnish sufficient resources for poorer children to learn just as much as other children. (Entwisle, Alexander, & Olson, 2000, p. 22)

These findings are consistent with—but not definitive proof of—the argument that systematic differences in school quality for blacks and whites may explain the divergence in test scores. (Fryer & Levitt, 2004, p. 457)

INTRODUCTION

A Snapshot on Cause

When it comes to inequality by socioeconomic status, schools are more a part of the solution than part of the problem. (Downey, von Hippel, & Broh, 2004, p. 616)

A second set of explanations, arising in sharp contrast to the first, looks at the other side of the coin: if the learner or the learner's family are not the principal reasons for

147

school failure, then the school and schooling must be responsible. In short, the problem lies not with the learner's deficits but rather with what has been called "educational deficit. (Knapp, 2001, p. 181)

In Chapters 8 and 9, we turn to the place of schooling in the achievement gap narrative. As the quotes above indicate, the topic is considerably more complex and contested than is generally acknowledged. In one camp are those who place all of the responsibility for gaps on educators. As Rothstein (2006) observes, these analysts "conclude that the achievement gap is the fault of 'failing schools' because it makes no sense that it could be otherwise" (p. 1). According to Biddle (1997): "Is it only possible to blame the school when the impoverished student does not do well? Indeed, not only is this possible but this type of blaming provides yet another popular explanation for education 'failure' in today's America" (p. 15). In a distant camp are analysts who exonerate schools, placing almost all the blame for low achievement for African American and poorer students on society and families (see Knapp, 2001; Natriello, McDill, & Pallas, 1990; and Stinson, 2006, for descriptions). Before we begin our analysis of the role of specific dimensions of schooling (e.g., the curricular program) in the achievement gap equation, we revisit the larger question of the role of schooling in causing patterned learning differentials by race and class among youngsters.

The bulk of high-quality research concludes that schools "do not create achievement gaps" (Gamoran, 2000, p. 95), and "They promote the same rate of learning for students of all backgrounds during the school year" (p. 98). Indeed, some of the most important research in this area holds that schools actually "accelerate and equalize learning" (Downey, von Hippel, & Broh, 2004, p. 623), thus "temper[ing] socioeconomic inequality" (p. 624): "In addition to increasing *average* learning rates, schools reduce *inequality* in learning rates"(p. 621). Thus, Downey and team (2004) find:

For students in a typical school, the non-school environment encourages advantaged children to pull ahead, but the school environment helps disadvantaged children to catch up. This suggests that although advantaged student bodies pull away all year round, they would pull away faster if it weren't for schools. (p. 623)

The logic here posits that "formal schooling may ameliorate achievement gaps produced by family differences, since school curricula are likely to be considerably more standardized than are families 'curricula'" (Reardon, 2003, p. 2; see also Entwisle, Alexander, & Olson, 2000; Fryer & Levitt, 2002).

However, other researchers from the "schools not causing achievement gaps" are less sanguine on the issue of acceleration of achievement for disadvantaged children specifically and equity in general. While they concur that the locus of responsibility for achievement gaps is situated primarily in societal and family environments, they also maintain that schools "contribute in significant ways to minority achievement gaps" (Clotfelter, Ladd, & Vigdor, 2005, p. 378). They argue rather that schools serve as "an essentially neutral learning environment passively allowing sharp inequality in home circumstances to translate into similar inequalities in learning outcomes" (Raudenbush, Fotiu, & Cheong, 1998, p. 254). They maintain that schools "do not prevent them [achievement gaps] from occurring nor do they prevent them from widening during the summer" (Gamoran, 2000, p. 95).

Other research, however, attributes much more of the responsibility for gap problems to schools (Bacharach, Baumeister, & Farr, 2003; Chatterji, 2005b; Land & Legters, 2002), holding that schools play an important role in "exacerbating inequalities" (Downey, von Hippel, & Broh, 2004, p. 613). Thus, "[A] second perspective on the plight of disadvantaged students suggests that much of the difficulty they experience is connected to schooling" (Natriello, McDill, & Pallas, 1990, pp. 6–7). While not unmindful that often times this logic "fails to acknowledge limits on the school's capacity to shape or influence children's lives nor . . . take full account of the many constraints that confront . . . the system itself" (Knapp, 2001, pp. 181–182), analysts here conclude that "differences in schools explain some of the racial tests score gaps" (Stiefel, Schwartz, & Ellen, 2006, p. 17). They argue that poor achievement on the part of low-income and African American students "reflect[s] inadequacies of . . . schools" (Payne & Biddle, 1999, p. 7), "that Black children perform less well academically than white children because Black children's schooling opportunities and experiences are not equal" (Stinson, 2006, p. 485), and that "differences in school quality may be an important part of the gap explanation" (Fryer & Levitt, 2004, p. 447)—"that schools shape inequality by providing varying opportunities within schools" (Downey, von Hippel, & Broh, 2004, p. 165). What is suggested here is that "the influence of families and peer groups is partially mediated by educational processes, that the institution of education, as it currently stands, at least partially reproduces the inequalities with which children walk into school" (Roscigno, 1998, p. 1051): "Schools themselves have deeply embedded practices that provide different educational experiences for children of color and poor children" (Shannon & Bylsma, 2002, p. 33). Analysts who subscribe to "this view often cite data showing that black children are less than one year behind whites in second or third grade but have fallen three or four years behind by twelfth grade" (Phillips et al., 1998b, p. 230).

This line of reasoning seems to have more validity for race than for social class (Chatterji, 2005b; 2006; Rathburn & West, 2004). Downey, von Hippel, and Broh (2004) assert:

> *Although schools tend to reduce socioeconomic inequality, the story for racial/ ethnic inequality is not so heartening. Our results suggest that schools increase the reading gap between black and white children. The black disadvantage is .15 points per month during kindergarten and .19 months per month during first grade, but during summer blacks have a (nonsignificant) advantage of .13 points per months. The school-year gap is .29 points per month less favorable to blacks, suggesting that schools exacerbate black-white inequality. (p. 624)*

Or, as Phillips et al. (1998b) report:

> *Even when black and white children have the same prior scores, the same measured socioeconomic status, and attend the same schools, black children still gain on average about 0.02 standard deviations less in math, 0.06 standard deviations less in reading, and 0.05 standard deviations less in vocabulary each year." (p. 256)*

What conclusion can we draw about the role of schooling in the causal chapter of the achievement gap narrative? First, in general, schools do not cause achievement gaps. Most of the gaps that appear can be traced to factors in the larger environment in which schools are nested.

Second, schooling can have substantial effects on student learning. More specifically, "Schools have the power to attenuate the influence of socioeconomic status on achievement and thereby reduce the direct dependence of outcomes on family background" (Heyns, 1978, p. 187).

Third, schools have not been as effective as they could be in narrowing achievement gaps by race and social class. Since the "school's task is . . . to close gaps that have already emerged by the time students enter kindergarten" (Ding & Davison, 2005, pp. 83–84), failure to do so in effect "partially reproduces the inequalities that children walk into school with" (Roscigno, 1999, p. 180). Gamoran (2000) nicely sums up the situation here as follows: Even if schools are not the cause of inequality, they are often a barrier to eliminating it "because they prevent inequality from being addressed" (p. 96).

Fourth, "While not assuming that [climate-and] instruction-related variables are the only, or even the primary, cause of Black-White achievement gaps, it is important to give attention to the area[s] that educators are best positioned to address" (Lubienski, 2002, p. 273; see also Irvine, 1990). Schools "need to look at themselves" (Hughes, 2003, p. 313). In addition, on the task of narrowing gaps, it is clear that "school practices and policies may be more amenable to modifications" (Hallinan, 2001, p. 56) than are family and societal factors.

School Contributions to the Problem: A General Note

Educational systems have institutionalized differences in programs and opportunities for students that exacerbate the achievement gap. (Shannon & Bylsma, 2002, p. 29)

Roscigno (1998) informs us, "The institution of education shapes achievement through the stratifying and segregating of students, through the placement of expectations, and through the allocation of resources" (p. 1051). And, it is here that we find the pathway by which schools contribute to or fail to offset patterned learning differentials by race and social class. On the general front, "American public schools [do] not provide equitable and excellent education for all children" (Shannon & Bylsma, 2002, p. 33). There are "pointed differences in resources and quality between schools" (Stiefel, Schwartz, & Ellen, 2006, p. 10; see also Lee & Burkam, 2002). Specifically, students of different social classes and races often "experience dramatically different learning environments" (Stiefel, Schwartz, & Ellen, 2006, p. 19), "receive dramatically different learning opportunities" (Darling-Hammond & Post, 2000, p. 127), and are exposed to "dramatically different learning experiences" (Raudenbush, Fotiu, & Cheong, 1998, p. 254): "Given that blacks and whites have little overlap in the schools they attend, differences in school quality are plausible explanations for why black students are losing ground" (Fryer & Levitt, 2004, p. 456).

As we explore in considerable detail here and in the following chapter, poor and minority youngsters often have "unequal access to key educational resources" (Darling-Hammond & Post, 2000, p. 128). African American and low-income students are often underserved in the schools they attend (Hughes, 2003; Norman et al., 2001). According to Knapp:

A pattern of profound inequality pervades the school system: on average, where students from low-income backgrounds are concentrated, the investment of resources and the quality of educational learning opportunities are substantially lower than in schools that service more affluent, mainstream children. (p. 177)

As Haycock (2001) asserts, "We take the students who have less to begin with and then systematically give them less in school" (p. 8). Analysts regularly confirm "that low-income and minority students encounter less opportunity to learn, inadequate instruction and support, and lower expectations from their schools and teachers" (Shannon & Bylsma, 2002, p. 9). According to Klein et al. (1997):

> *In addition, minority students are more likely than Whites to attend schools with the following characteristics that are associated with lower performance: poor school climate, less qualified teachers, low curriculum requirements, less press for achievement, and more "low-track" programs. (p. 84)*

Thus, Shannon and Bylsma (2002) conclude:

> *The education that minority and low income students receive is generally characterized by lower quality teaching, lower expectations for performance and behavior, limited access to challenging and rigorous coursework, and insufficient instructional resources such as reasonable class sizes, up-to-date instructional materials, and clean and safe buildings. (p. 29)*

And, as Barton (2003) reminds us, "Differences in such key components of schooling go along with differences in achievement among different student populations, at least when average achievement is compared" (p. 36).

TEACHERS AND TEACHING

> *Teachers are significant others in their students' lives; as significant others, they affect the achievement and self-concept of their students, particularly black students. (Irvine, 1990, p. 49)*

> *A growing body of research suggests that schools do make a difference, and a substantial portion of that difference is attributable to teachers. (Darling-Hammond & Post, 2000, p.128)*

> *Of those school factors subject to some control by educators and policy-makers, variations in the characteristics of teachers were most correlated with group differences in test scores. (Miller, 1995, p. 85)*

> *Nothing affects the achievement of low-income and/or minority children as much as the quality of the teaching they receive. (Lewis, 2008, p. 20)*

A growing body of research is helping us discern conditions of schooling that are associated with student learning. We are also discovering, on a consistent basis, that one key variable—teacher quality—occupies considerable space in the performance narrative (Ferguson, 1998a; 1998b; Villegas & Lucas, 2002): "Differences in the effectiveness of teachers [comprise] the most important variable accounting for change in academic growth from year to year, far more important than class size, class grouping, or student's prior achievement levels" (Hughes, 2003, p. 299). "Teachers clearly matter" (Clotfelter, Ladd, & Vigdor, 2005, p. 378) and we are developing a fairly deep understanding of the elements of teacher quality. We are also learning a good deal about what Brookover (1985) referred to as the pattern of ineffectiveness in teaching African American and low-income children. In this section, we examine two dimensions of teaching that are associated with achievement gaps in schools: teacher qualifications and teaching practices.

Teacher Qualifications

Access to competent teachers is one of the most inequitably distributed resources between disadvantaged students and their more affluent counterparts. (Becker & Luthar, 2002, p. 202)

Research also shows that low-income and minority students are disproportionately taught by underqualified teachers. (Borman & Kimball, 2005, p. 4)

Minority and low-income students in urban settings are most likely to find themselves in classrooms staffed by inadequately prepared, inexperienced, and ill-qualified teachers. (Darling-Hammond & Post, 2000, p. 136)

Most strikingly, black students attend schools with significantly less experienced and qualified teachers as compared to the schools attended by their white and Asian counterparts. (Stiefel, Schwartz, & Ellen, 2006, p. 14)

One of the most important lines of research in the achievement gap literature focuses on "distributional equity" (Bali & Alvarez, 2003, p. 487) in the assignment of qualified teachers to students from different races, ethnicities, and social classes. The issue here is about "the distribution of assignment of teachers" (Thompson, 2002, p. 16) to youngsters in schools (Clotfelter, Ladd, & Vigdor, 2004; Rumberger & Gandara, 2004). The findings are highly consistent. "On virtually every measure, teacher qualifications vary by the status of the children they serve" (Darling-Hammond & Post, 2000, p. 138): "The poorest, least prepared minority children systematically are assigned to the least prepared instructors in the poorest quality schools" (Mickelson, 2003, p. 1073); "Schools with particularly disadvantaged students are likely to have less-educated and less-experienced teachers" (Hertert & Teague, 2003, p. 19), that is, "the least qualified teachers" (Scales et al., 2006, p. 40; Jerald, 2002). Youngsters in schools with heavy concentrations "of minority students and low-income populations have fewer qualified teachers than schools that have large white populations" (Bol & Berry, 2005, p. 33). More forceful versions of this narrative maintain that these youngsters are routinely exposed to "underqualified" (Uhlenberg & Brown, 2002, p. 502), "not qualified" (Padron, Waxman, & Rivera, 2002, p. 71), "weak" (Balfanz & Byrnes, 2006, p. 144), and "unqualified" (Barton, 2003, p. 10; Haycock, 1998, p. 14) teachers.

Specifically, Sanders and Rivers (as cited in Hughes, 2003) observed:

… in one Tennessee metropolitan district, about half as many Black students got especially effective teachers as would have been expected if the system was fair, based on

the percentage of the student population they represented. And about 10 percent more Black students were assigned to especially ineffective teachers than would have been expected under equal conditions. (p. 299)

Likewise, the California Center for the Future of Teaching and Learning reports, In schools with the highest percentages of minority students, more than 20 percent of teachers are underqualified as compared with less than 5 percent of teachers in schools serving the lowest percentage of minorities" (Hertert & Teague, 2003, p. 20). And, Scales and colleagues (2006) find, "In elementary, middle, and high schools . . . [disadvantaged] children are twice as likely to attend schools with less-qualified and less-experienced teachers" (p. 401; see also Haycock, 1998).

As we discuss next, "qualified" refers to preparation for the job, including licensure/certification; experience and turnover; and measures of performance, such as college grades and indices of success in the role of teacher (U.S. Commission on Civil Rights, 2004). As an advance organizer here, Kober (2001) confirms:

Minority students are substantially more likely than White students to be taught by teachers without college majors in the subjects they are teaching. Schools with high-poverty and high-minority enrollments have teachers with fewer years of experience, on average, than other schools, and also have higher rates of turnover. Teachers in districts with high percentages of Black or Hispanic students also tend to have lower scores on teacher certification tests than teachers in other districts. (p. 27)

It is also important to remind ourselves that "teachers matter" (Ferguson, 1991, p. 7)— teacher quality is crucial for student learning (U.S. Commission on Civil Rights, 2004). Indeed, "Recent studies have found that differences in teacher quality may represent the single most important school resource differential between minority and white children" (Darling-Hammond & Post, 2000, p. 128). Teacher quality, as we unpack the concept here, is therefore a "contributor to the achievement gap problem" (Spradlin et al., 2005, p. 25) and a keystone plank in the effort to narrow social class and racial learning differentials (Jerald, 2002; Lubienski, 2002, Myers, Kim, & Mandala, 2004).

Preparation

Closely linked to this pattern is the distribution of teacher qualifications with schools serving the greatest concentration of children from low-income families staffed by teachers with the lowest levels of preparation for their work. (Knapp, 2001, p. 178)

The preparation dimension of qualifications attends to the education of teachers to assume teaching responsibilities. The central element here is the depth of knowledge and skills needed to teach effectively (Hughes, 2003). This content knowledge is measured indirectly by courses of study completed, degrees earned, and certificates/licenses secured. On the first item (course of study), analysts generally report on whether teachers have a major or minor in the subjects they teach. Research generally finds that there are important differences in the distribution of teachers here, with disadvantages accruing to low-income and minority youngsters (Darity et al., 2001; Haycock, 1997; Lewis, 2008). For example, Land and Legters

(2002) confirm, "Students in high poverty public secondary schools are less likely to be taught mathematics, biology, chemistry, or physics by a teacher with a major or minor in that subject than students in low poverty public secondary schools" (p. 14); "schools serving disadvantaged children are more likely than others to staff their courses with teachers who lack a major or minor in the subject they are teaching" (Gamoran, 2000, p. 100; see also Peng, Wright, & Hill, 1995). Haycock (2001) reports the following:

- Large numbers of students, especially those who are poor or are members of minority groups are taught by teachers who do not have strong backgrounds in the subjects they teach.
- In every subject area, students in high-poverty schools are more likely than other students to be taught by teachers without even a minor in the subjects they teach.
- The differences are often greater in predominantly minority high schools. In math and science, for example, only about half the teachers in schools with 90 percent or greater minority enrollments meet even their states' minimum requirements to teach those subjects—far fewer than in predominantly white schools ...
- We take the students who most depend on their teachers for subject matter learning and assign them teachers with the weakest academic foundations. (p. 10)

More concretely, Jerald (2002), observes:

Nationally, one out of four secondary classes in core academic subjects (24 percent) are assigned to a teacher lacking even a college minor in the subject being taught. In the nation's high-poverty schools, that rate skyrockets to over one third of classes (34 percent), compared with about one out of every five classes (19 percent) in low-poverty schools. Similarly, 29 percent of classes in high-minority schools are assigned to an out-of-field teacher, compared with 21 percent in low-minority schools. Classes in high-poverty schools are 77 percent more likely to be assigned to an out of field teacher than classes in low-poverty schools. While the gap is not as large between high and low-minority schools, minority students clearly are less likely to get their fair share of qualified teachers as well. Classes in majority non-white schools are over 40 percent more likely to be assigned to an out-of-field teacher than those in mostly-white schools. (p. 4)

And, as an assortment of researchers has concluded, students learn more from teachers with more content-related coursework (Darling-Hammond & Post, 2000; Ferguson, 1991; Wayne & Youngs, 2003).

On the issue of degrees earned, similar patterns are evident. "Students in high-poverty schools are . . . least likely to have teachers with higher levels of education—a master's, specialist, or doctoral degree" (Darling-Hammond & Post, 2000, p. 138). For example, Stiefel and team (2006), using New York City data, reveal that while 80 percent of white eighth graders had teachers with master's degrees in the 2000–01 school year, only 68 percent of African American students did so. And, on this measure of preparation, as was true for in-field majors, there is a positive association between master's degrees and student achievement scores, at least through the middle school grades (Ferguson, 1991).

Finally, when we examine licensure/certification, similar results surface. We discover that low-income and African American children are disproportionately taught by noncertified teachers or "teachers who are not fully credentialed" (Rumberger & Gandara, 2004, p. 2037; see also Bol & Berry, 2005; Land & Legters, 2002; Spradlin et al., 2005)—as are Hispanic youngsters (Hakuta, 2002; Gandara et al., 2003; Velez, 1989). For example, Hertert and Teague (2003), relying on data from the California Center for the Future of Teaching and Learning, show, "In schools where 76 percent–100 percent of students are poor, 19 percent of teachers are not fully credentialed. In contrast, in schools with the lowest percentages of poor students, on average only 8 percent of teachers are not fully credentialed" (p. 20). They also report, "In the lowest-performing schools, as ranked in the Academic Performance Index (API), on average 21 percent of teachers are not fully credentialed" (p. 20). Darling-Hammond and Post (2000), in turn, reveal, "In schools with the highest minority enrollments students had less than a 50 percent chance of getting a science or mathematics teacher who held a license and a degree in the field he or she taught" (p. 138; see also Barton, 2003; Jerald, 2002). Furthermore, Lewis (2008) notes, "In New York State only one of thirty-three teachers is uncertified; in New York City, the figure is one of every seven teachers" (pp. 20–21). While in Baltimore, fully 35 percent of teachers in the highest poverty schools are uncertified (p. xi). And while there is some argument that noncertified teachers may at times "be better in the classroom than credential teachers" (Klein, 2002, p. 163), the bulk of the research arrives at the opposite conclusion (Ferguson, 1991; Wayne & Youngs, 2003).

Experience

The main point, however, is that in almost all cases and for the state as a whole, black students are at a disadvantage relative to white students in terms of their exposure to novice teachers and in most cases the differences are statistically significant. (Clotfelter, Ladd, & Vigdor, 2005, p. 386)

Given everything that we have observed to this point in the area of teacher qualifications, it will come as no surprise to learn that African American and low-income youngsters often receive less-experienced teachers than white and middle-class children (Irvine, 1990; Thompson & O'Quinn, 2001; Uhlenberg & Brown, 2002), what is referred to by Hughes (2003) as "the practice of first-year teacher student assignments" (p. 300).

Scholars help us see that there are there critical aspects of the experience variable, across-school context, within-school context, and within-course context. Murnane and Levy (2004) provide both some history and a portrait of "across-school" differences in teacher experience:

The problem of staffing schools serving poor children with skilled teachers is not new. In 1952 the sociologist Howard Becker described how Chicago teachers tend to start their careers in schools serving poor children but move quickly to schools serving middle-class children (Becker, 1952). This pattern left many central city schools with a succession of beginning teachers. Many subsequent studies have documented the same pattern. (p. 411)

Darling-Hammond and Post (2000) do the same for "in-school" context, discussing the assignment of teachers within schools:

Evidence suggests that teachers themselves are tracked, with those judged to be the most competent and experienced assigned to the top tracks. Within a school the more expert experienced teachers, who are in great demand, are rewarded with opportunities to teach the most enriched curricula to the most advantaged students. Meanwhile, underprepared and inexperienced teachers are often assigned to the students whom others do not care to teach, which leaves them practicing on the students who would benefit most from highly skilled teachers. (pp. 141–142)

On this issue, Clotfelter and team (2005) in their study report: In math the probability of having an inexperienced teacher is 0.127 for remedial courses, 0.098 for standard courses and 0.061 for advanced courses. Hence, even if there were no differences within academic levels by race of the student in the probability of exposure to an inexperienced teacher, black students would be more likely to face an inexperienced teacher by dint of their over-representation in remedial courses and their under-representation in advanced courses. (p. 389)

On the third aspect of experience, "within-course" context, Clotfelter, Ladd, and Vigdor (2005) compile an equally disturbing narrative:

Even within a given academic course level, in most cases black students are disadvantaged relative to white students. Within standard courses, for example, the probability of having an inexperienced teacher is 57 percent higher for a black student than a white student in math and 37 percent higher in English. (p. 389)

Some examples from the research on teacher experience are informative. Jerald (2002) reports that African American youngsters "are about twice as likely as other children to serve as training fodder for inexperienced teachers (21 percent of teachers in high-minority schools versus 10% in low-minority schools)" (p. 9). Barton (2003) confirms this assessment for low-income students, reporting that these children are also twice as likely to have teachers with three or fewer years of experience—20 percent of teachers in high-poverty schools versus 11 percent in low-poverty schools (p. 13). Clotfelter and team (2005) find that "black seventh graders in North Carolina are far more likely to face a novice teacher in math and English than are their white counterparts. The differences are about 54 percent in math and 38 percent in English for the state as a whole, over 50 percent in some of the large urban districts (p. 391). And, Stiefel, Schwartz, and Ellen (2006) report that in New York City during the 2000–01 school year, 57 percent of African American students had teachers who had worked for more than two years in the school, while 68 percent of white students had teachers with the same experience.

At the same time that we are learning that "novice teachers are distributed among schools and among classrooms within schools in a way that disadvantages black students" (Clotfelter, Schwartz, & Ellen, 2005, p. 377) and low-income pupils (Barton, 2003), evidence is being amassed that reveals that "the experience of the teacher does matter" (p. 379) in the student achievement narrative. "While not everyone would agree that more teacher experience makes a higher quality school" (Lee & Burkam, 2002, p. 73), there is a growing consensus (1) that at a minimum, experience "warrants attention as a potentially important contributor to the explanation" (Clotfelter, Schwartz, & Ellen, 2005, p. 391) for patterned achievement differentials by race and income and (2), more likely, that the fact that African American youngsters "are less likely to be taught by teachers with high levels of experience [does] contribute to the achievement gap" (Spradlin et al., 2005, p. 21). Indeed, on this point more generally, Clotfelter and associates (2005) maintain:

> *It seems reasonable to conclude from this previous research that teachers with no prior experience are undoubtedly on average less effective than other teachers. Consequently, students who are exposed to such teachers are likely to receive an inferior education compared to other students. (p. 379)*

More specifically, Ferguson (1991) confirms:

> *Teachers with five or more years of experience produce higher student test scores, lower dropout rates, and higher rates of taking the SAT. Our experiments with other measures show that the percent with five or more years of experience is the best index to capture the effect of teacher experience on test scores. (p. 9)*

Also emerging as one dimension of experience is an understanding of the deleterious impact of teacher turnover on student achievement, and knowledge about the types of students most likely to be effected by this turnover. On the second issue, research confirms that teacher turnover is more pronounced in schools with high concentrations of minority and low-income children (Clotfelter, Schwartz, & Ellen, 2005; Harris & Herrington, 2006; Williams, 2003). Analysts regularly conclude that teachers "tend to transfer out of low-income minority schools as they gain experience. Excessive test pressure tends to accelerate this process, compounding the schools' problems since experienced teachers are a precious resource for schools" (Lee, 2006, p. 7). For example, in his work, Barton (2003) observes, "Fourth-grade students who are Black are much less likely to be in schools where the same teachers who started the year were there when the year ended" (p. 12). He unearths similar findings with students from low-income families as well.

Measures of Performance

> *On average teachers at high-poverty schools . . . come from less selective colleges and fail certification tests more frequently than those who teach at schools with low-poverty and low minority enrollments. (Reynolds, 2002, p. 8)*

> *The most important resource difference between black and white schools seems to be that both black and white teachers in black schools have lower test scores than their counterparts in white schools. (Jencks & Phillips, 1998, p. 47)*

Assessments of teacher qualifications in the domain of performance come in five forms that cluster into three categories: inputs, processes, and outputs. Across all forms and categories, researchers consistently document that teachers working with low-income and

African American youngsters score less well than colleagues teaching more-advanced children (Darling-Hammond & Post, 2000). To begin with, we know that teachers who work in schools with concentrations of minority and poor students, on average, attend less selective colleges and earn lower grades while there (Reynolds, 2002; Wayne & Youngs, 2003). Second, researchers confirm that "teachers with high test scores are . . . quite unequally distributed" (Jencks & Phillips, 1998, p. 49) and that low-income and African American youngsters "are far more likely to be taught by teachers who scored poorly" (Haycock, 1998, p. 16) on end-of-program licensure examinations (Ferguson, 1991; Jerald, 2002). According to Ferguson (1991):

> *Districts with more black students . . . have proportionately more teachers from groups (i.e., black and Hispanic teachers) whose scores are lower. Second, within each race of teachers, the average TECAT [Texas Examination of Current Administrators and Teachers] score is lower for those who teach in districts with more black students. (p. 20)*

Furthermore, "The average scores of white teachers who teach in proportionately more African American districts tend to be lower than the scores of white teachers in white districts" (p. 15). Thus, "Where the percentage of black children in a Texas school district is higher, the average score on the TECAT is typically lower for each race of teachers—black, Hispanic and white" (p. 2).

Third, Borman and Kimball (2005) unearth evidence showing, "Classrooms with high concentrations of minority students [are] taught by teachers with lower evaluation scores than classrooms with low concentrations of minority children" (p. 10). Fourth, teachers who instruct low-income and African American children are more likely to be absent from school than peers teaching other youngsters. For example, Barton (2003) explains, "Black twelfth-grade students are more than twice as likely as White students to be in schools where 6–10 percent of their teachers are absent on an average day" (p. 12). Finally, "There is strong evidence that minority students are assigned to the least effective teachers, as measured by value added [to student achievement]" (Harris & Herrington, 2006, p. 224).

What is important to remember is that these measures of performance have power in the student achievement equation. That is, they are implicated in the achievement gap problem and, as we will see in Chapter 11, linked to its solution. For example, Borman and Kimball (2005) inform us, "Fourth-grade teachers with higher evaluation scores made some progress in closing the achievement gap separating poor and nonpoor children in reading and, to a lesser extent, in math" (p. 16). And perhaps most importantly, researchers confirm, "Students learn more from teachers with higher test scores" (Wayne & Youngs, 2003, p. 100). As Ferguson (1991) notes in general, "the fact that teachers in Texas who instruct children of color tend to have weaker language skills appears, other things equal, to account for more than one quarter of the reading and math score differential between black and white children in Texas" (p. 1), although he acknowledges (1) that "much of the learning that TECAT 'causes' occurs between third and seventh grades" (p. 8) and (2) that "the relationship between teacher scores and student scores appears to show increasing returns at the top end" (p. 27).

Instruction

What ultimately matters, of course, is the quality of teaching practice—what teachers actually do in the classroom. (Thompson & O'Quinn, 2001, p. 9)

Teachers' attitudes and treatment of students impact achievement, and teachers often treat low-income and students of color differently than white middle-class students. (Shannon & Bylsma, 2002, p. 31)

The lower mathematics achievement levels of minority students, particularly Black students, may be indicative of the instruction that these students receive. (Bol & Berry, 2005, p. 33)

In general, black students receive a disproportionate amount of poor teaching. (Singham, 2003, p. 589)

In the previous section, we explored how teacher qualifications influence student learning and how greater exposure to teachers with more limited qualifications disadvantages African American and low-income students, thus impacting achievement gaps. Here, we introduce our discussion of patterns of instructional practices often found in schools and classrooms heavily populated by African American and poor children. We pick up this analysis again in the following section on curriculum courses of study. We will see that, at least to some extent, achievement gaps are instructionally anchored (Ferguson, 1998a; Sloma & Bylsma, 2002). Our aim is to introduce the broad contours of the problem. We return to the topic in Chapter 11 where we outline ways instruction can be harnessed to narrow achievement gaps.

Instructional Design and Focus

If our benchmark is unconditional racial neutrality, there is strong evidence of racial bias in how teachers treat students. (Ferguson, 2003, p. 478)

Data collected on instructional practices indicate differences between how minority and white children are taught. (Bol & Berry, 2005, p. 33)

Low-income youth are more often taught using memorization, drills, and other basic instructional methods that are not conducive to engagement or learning. (Scales et al., 2006, p. 40)

Research in the area of instruction based on race and social class clusters into four categories: anemic instructional designs, inordinate focus on lower-level skills, inappropriate learning contexts, and low teacher expectations for students. On the first two issues (design and focus), analysts suggest that classrooms dominated by low-income and African American pupils are marked by a heavy emphasis on "passive instruction." In some cases, this is defined by an inordinate amount of direct or didactic instruction, or more accurately teacher-centered instruction in which students are passive rather than active participants, a pattern Gamoran (2000) labels "repetitive teaching" (p. 103). Thus, culpability here is linked less to teacher centeredness than to student inaction.

Critics here find that disadvantaged youngsters receive a disproportionate amount of worksheets and drill-based skill work (Bennett et al., 2007; Lubienski, 2002; Strutchens & Silver, 2000); these are often decontextualized assignments with little relevance to either the academic goals of the class or the lives of the students (Bempechat, 1992; Stevenson, Chen, & Uttal, 1990). The focus is often on memorization and low-level skills (Lubienski, 2002), what Irvine (1990) calls "rote learning" (p. 7). Students "work at a low cognitive level of boring tasks that are not connected to the skills they need to learn" (Darling-Hammond & Post, 2000, p. 142). African American and poor children are "typically given more routine highly structured class work focused on low-level intellectual activities" (Shannon & Bylsma, 2002, p. 33). Low-level assessments are commonplace (Entwisle, Alexander, & Olson, 2000; Strutchens & Silver, 2000). The center of gravity is "lecture, drill and practice, and remediation, and student seatwork consisting mainly of worksheets" (Pardon, Waxman, & Rivera, 2002, p. 70). Undifferentiated whole-class instruction dominates (Cooper, 2000; Shannon & Bylsma, 2002). Students are often in classes where "the skills tested on the assessments become the entire curriculum" (Murnane & Levy, 1996, p. 408). The DNA of instruction here becomes behavioral control rather than intellectual engagement and mastery (Cooper, 2000): "Consequently, teachers spend more time controlling students and trying to neutralize potential behavior problems than in [real] teaching" (Shannon & Bylsma, 2002, p. 32). Orderliness displaces the goal of learning (Irvine, 1990; Norman et al., 2001). Students are occupied in "routine busy-work," although they remain "intellectually unengaged" (Shannon & Bylsma, 2002, p. 33).

This "drill and practice as well as other direct teaching methods," it is argued, "may be particularly damaging to minority students" (Learning Point Associates, 2004, p. 9). The focus "retards their learning and their development of higher cognitive skills" (Shannon & Bylsma, 2002, p. 29). Indeed, missing in this framework of "inappropriate teaching practices" (Waxman, Padron, & Garcia, 2007, p. 134), "low level intellectual activity" (Shannon & Bylsma, 2002, p. 33), and "steady diet of worksheets and rote learning" (Darling-Hammond & Post, 2000, p. 142) is any commitment to mastering higher-level skills. Conspicuous by their absence are topics such as "nonroutine problem solving" (Strutchens & Silver, 2000, p. 47) and reasoning (Raudenbush, Fotiu, & Cheong, 1998). Thus, "Low-achieving students continue to fall behind their high-achieving counterparts" (Shannon & Bylsma, 2002, p. 33).

Learning Context

There is also dissonance between the learning preferences of Black learners and the pedagogical style of the predominantly White teaching force in the observed affluent districts. (Hughes, 2003, p. 314)

There is some research that suggests that the context or environment in which learning occurs may be connected to achievement gaps. Specifically, it is maintained that certain contexts hinder efforts to close gaps. Most generally, the problem is traced to a system of education in which African American children are forced to fit into a design developed for white and more affluent youngsters (Seiler & Elmesky, 2007). Scholars expose several dimensions of learning context that are in play. First, they find that a key element of traditional learning environments—competitive individualism (Jagers & Carroll, 2002)—is often inconsistent with, if not oppositional to, the more communal dynamic of African American life (Irvine, 1990). As we will see in Chapter 11, these analysts maintain that teachers of African American youngsters "need to design classroom activities and promote students' intellectual cama-raderie and attitudes toward learning that build a sense of community and responsibility for each other" (Bennett et al., 2007, p. 261): "We believe there is sufficient coherence in the way communalism is expressed and the role it plays in the lives of economically disadvantaged inner-city African American youth to warrant the study of its implications for their academic success" (Seiler & Elmesky, 2007, p. 396).

Second, these analysts assert that classroom "participation structures—the interactional arrangements and rules operating in the learning environment" (Norman et al., 2001, p. 1108)—are often at odds with accepted patterns in the African American community. They find that the well-grooved structures common in most schools are "more problematic for Black students than for White students" (p. 1108). Third, reviewers here condemn schools for the near absence of culturally relevant environments and culturally responsive instruction (Hughes, 2003; Norman et al., 2001; Steele, 1992; 1997), for their failure to "attempt to identify the distinctive cultural retentions of black students and to develop teaching strategies that are compatible with them" (Irvine, 1990, p. 93). According to Hughes (2003), in the instructional domain, "Ineffective teachers tend to use the most common pedagogy in U.S. schools, which assumes that the dominant White middle-class cultural way of schooling is universal, or should be universal and most appropriate for all" (p. 302). According to Norman and team (2001), in the learning environment domain, teachers of children of color are often found to be ill-prepared to "navigate the complexities of cultural interface zones" (p. 1107) that ribbon classrooms, thus dumbing down learning, and missing an opportunity to narrow racial achievement gaps. Finally, analysts of the learning context in classrooms overpopulated by African American students criticize schools for a lack of personalization and a dearth of "caring teacher-student relationships" (Burns, Keyes, & Kusimo, 2005, p. 27).

Expectations

Teachers form different expectations of students as a function of race, gender, and social class. (Bol & Berry, 2005, p. 34)

Minorities and groups of low socioeconomic status experience lower expectations than their counterparts. (Strutchens & Silver, 2000, p. 54)

Teachers set lower expectations for African American than for white or Asian students, and this runs the risk of perpetuating the achievement gap. (Spradlin et al., 2005, p. 3)

Socioeconomic status (SES) is consequential. In general, poor students are expected by teachers to do less well than their middle- and upper-class counterparts regardless of ability. (Roscigno, 1999, p. 161)

The larger context of this chapter posits that "schools often collaborate in the maintenance of poverty, inequality, and the unequal status of black people" (Irvine, 1990, p. 9) and
people from the bottom rungs of the social class ladder. The mechanism engaged is the
unequal treatment of certain children based on biosocial markers such as race and class
(Ferguson, 2003; Miller, 1995). The result then is differential outcomes, especially academic
success, for students in these groups—differences that impact achievement gaps. The particular theme in this larger narrative that occupies us here is teacher expectations.

Differential Expectations and Their Impact. To begin with, there is considerable evidence that
socioeconomic conditions and racial status have bearing on the expectations and beliefs that
teachers form about children (Hertert & Teague, 2003; Miller, 1995): "Socioeconomic class
[and] race affect teachers' expectations for student performance" (Shannon & Bylsma, 2002,
p. 31). Also, "Teachers' expectations of students indeed are often influenced by student characteristics such as social class" (Becker & Luthar, 2002, p. 202). The logic here is "that part of
the reason some students do not excel academically is that schools do not ask them to"
(Reynolds, 2002, p. 12).

More important, these differences in expectations are tilted against African American
children (Burns, Keyes, & Kusimo, 2005; Darity et al., 2001; Ferguson, 2003; Hale-Benson,
1990; Irvine, 1990; Stinson, 2006) and youngsters from poor families (Baron, Tom, & Cooper,
1985; Hallinan, 2001; Haycock, 2001; Lewis, 2008). Also, while it is not our focus in this volume, this conclusion applies to Hispanic students as well (Gandara et al., 2003; Garcia, 1991;
Waxman, Padron, & Garcia, 2007). That is, "Many teachers internalize negative assumptions
about the intellectual competencies of low-income African-American students" (Roscigno,
1998, p. 1035). More specifically, "Teachers expect poor students to do less well than their
middle- and upper-class counterparts regardless of ability" (p. 1035). And, according to
Irvine (1990), teachers expectations for white students are more positive than for African
American students: "Disadvantaged and minority youth are more commonly expected to do
poorly" (Becker & Luthar, 2002, p. 202).

Of particular note here is our earlier discussion of the conclusion that African American
pupils are more school and "teacher dependent" (Irvine, 1990, p. 48) than white students.
What this means in the context of expectations is, "Black students seem to be more sensitive
to their teacher's perceptions than their white classmates are"(Uhlenberg & Brown, 2002,
p. 499), and "The value that black students place on their teachers' approval makes them more
vulnerable to the way teachers view them" (Thompson & O'Quinn, 2001, p. 16). The first corollary here is that African American youngsters are more negatively affected by low expectations—
and, as we will see in Chapter 11, more positively impacted by high expectations—than
are white students (Irvine, 1990). That is, "Teachers' beliefs probably affect Black students
more than Whites" (Ferguson, 2002, p. 495). The second corollary is that teacher expectations "affect subsequent performance more for Blacks than Whites" (p. 473) and "have a
potentially significant influence on . . . Black student performance" (Uhlenberg & Brown,
2002, p. 500).

The essential point here is that expectations are consequential (Ferguson, 2003; Fryer &
Levitt, 2004; Land & Legters, 2002; Peng, Wright, & Hill, 1995). "Teacher expectations are crucial to student performance" (Roscigno, 1998, p. 1039); they "affect how much black youngsters
learn" (Wilson, 1998, p. 504)—they are a "contributing factor in student achievement"
(Spradlin et al., 2005, p. 21) and to the achievement gap problem (Irvine, 1990). At a minimum,

they "sustain differences in student performance levels" (Irvine, 1990, p. 54). In the worst case, they exacerbate the achievement gap problem (Bol & Berry, 2005; Ferguson, 2003; Irvine, 1990), especially as they are cumulated across a school career (Ferguson, 2003). On the other hand, when set more appropriately, i.e., higher, they "can improve learning and reduce inequality" (Gamoran, 2000, p. 114): "High expectations disproportionately lead to high self-efficacy and high subsequent performance among Black students" (Hughes, 2003, pp. 301–302).

Effects Pipeline. It is important to start by reminding ourselves that teacher expectations "are mediated by teacher actions, and student responses to those actions. According to Farkas, Grobe, Sheehan, and Shuan (1990), " [A] teacher's reduced expectations lower students' self-image and effort and lead the teacher to present less-demanding material, resulting in reduced cognitive achievement" (p. 128). Alternatively, low expectations can lead to teacher behaviors that lower motivation and effort thus reinforcing low teacher expectations about the academic potential of low-income and African American students (Reynolds, 2002): "Low expectations that teachers have of poor and minority students . . . affect teachers' determination to help students and also affect students' determination to succeed" (Reynolds, 2002, p. 11). Darity and associates (2001) sum up the expectation hydraulics as follows:

> *The teacher expectations hypothesis places the onus squarely on teacher behavior and practices. Here the argument takes the form of a negative self-fulfilling prophecy. Teachers have beliefs about students' abilities that correlate with ethnicity. If they believe Black students, for example, are generally less able for biological or sociological reasons, they will expect less of them, push them less, and steer them away from tougher courses. Here one can find potential explanations for the mechanisms that lead these students to "disidentify" with schooling and school achievement, as well as a potential explanation for Black students not taking the courses that will enable them to perform better on standardized tests. (p. 17)*

Miller (1995) also exposes the pistons by which teacher expectations are turned into behaviors when he reports, "Variations in teachers' expectations may contribute to decisions that produce differences in the curricula and in the instructional strategies" (p. 231).

We have already highlighted many of the differences in *instructional strategies* for different expectation groups in the earlier discussion of "instructional design and focus." Here we simply reinforce two points. First, low expectations can "affect teachers' determination to help students" (Reynolds, 2002, p. 16) and can lead directly to lessened effort in teaching African American and low-income children (Shannon & Bylsma, 2002). These youngsters are thus often "at risk of being overlooked" (Hale-Benson, 1990, p. 208). That is, low expectations can lead "teachers to ask less of minority students (Miller, 1999, p. 16): "If they expect that Black children have less potential, teachers probably search with less conviction than they should for ways of helping Black children to improve and miss opportunities to reduce the Black-White test score gap" (Ferguson, 2003, p. 494). Second, as we documented, teacher expectations "significantly shape their treatment of students" (Villegas & Lucas, 2002, p. 37). More specifically, they cause teachers to "treat poor and minority students differently" (Biddle, 2001, p. 17). "As a result of their different expectations" (Miller, 1995, p. 228), "these students are treated differently in school than their white and affluent counterparts" (Reynolds, 2002, p. 9). And, as we observed above, different treatments routinely disadvantage African American and low-income students. That is, these children consistently "receive less favorable treatment" (Lee et al., 1990, p. 504).

On the issue of *curriculum,* the key mediating variable between expectations and achievement differentials is student opportunity to learn, and this itself is often mediated by student grouping patterns. We delve deeply into the curriculum variable as well as expand on our narrative on instructional differences in the following section. Here, we simply provide a few introductory notes. First, "Often less is expected of [disadvantaged] students in terms of quantity and quality of work" (Reynolds, 2002, p. 9): "Teachers do treat students differently because of differences in their expectations, and these differences can add up to fewer opportunities to learn for low-expectation students than for high-expectation students" (Miller, 1995, p. 226). These teachers "unwittingly perpetuate the achievement gap by failing to encourage Black and Hispanic students to aim higher or take more demanding courses" (Kober, 2001, p. 27; see also Bol & Berry, 2005). Second, concentrating students who are most likely to be the recipients of low teacher expectations in certain schools exacerbates the expectation effect (Spradlin et al., 2005) and further damages opportunity to learn. Finally, it is important to remind ourselves that students are important actors in the expectation play; they are not passive participants. That is, low teacher expectations and subsequent actions are mediated by student states. For example, Jagers and Carroll (2002) underscore the ways low expectations negatively impact "academic student motivation" (p. 52). Ferguson (2003) and Hale-Benson (1990) make a similar point around the condition of student engagement.

CURRICULAR COURSES OF STUDY

Differences in the content of the education provided to whites and to minorities have historically been among the most important sources of variations in academic achievement. (Miller, 1995, p. 231)

Curricular organization, then, can strengthen the tendency of low-SES students to perform less well than their counterparts rather than weaken it. (Wenglinsky, 1998, p. 271)

We note especially the sorting of students in elementary and secondary schools into ability groups and curricular tracks as a mechanism that can perpetuate or exacerbate educational disadvantages. (Natriello, McDill, & Pallas, 1990, p. 15)

Tracking creates a discriminatory cycle of restricted educational opportunities for minorities that leads to diminished school achievement that exacerbates racial/ethnic and social-class differences in minority and majority school outcomes. (Mickelson & Heath, 1999, p. 570)

In this chapter, we are exploring the relationship between the instructional program in the school and the achievement gap. And, as the structure of the chapter conveys, instructional program comprises two overlapping components, teachers and teaching and curriculum. Our conclusion on the first element presented above (teachers and teaching) is that high teacher qualifications and effective instructional practices are allocated inequitably (less favorably) to African American and low-income students, thus contributing to the achievement gap problem. Our position here on the second element (curriculum) is that poor children and African American students score worse on academic measures of performance "because they have not been exposed to the curriculum that would best prepare them to be successful on tests" (Darity et al., 2001, p. 17); that is, they "encounter a weaker curriculum" (Reynolds, 2002, p. 14) than their more advantaged peers.

We will show that the major engine that produces this condition is ability grouping/tracking, demonstrating that low-SES children and black youngsters are clustered together and "taught a less demanding curriculum" (Farkas, 2003, p. 1123). We will present evidence that this effect unfolds on three levels. First, we will show that these students are disproportionately found in schools where, on average, this weaker curriculum dominates the educational program (Raudenbush, Fotiu, & Cheong, 1998). Second, we will document, "Minority and low-income students are [also] . . . disproportionately placed in lower-ability groups and that these assignments seriously reduce their opportunities for learning" (Farkas, 2003, p. 1126). Third, we will review findings exposing that what transpires in these lower-level classes and groups is of significantly less quality than what takes place in higher-track classes, "that ability group placement or tracking decisions [create] exposure to different instruction" (Reardon, 2003, p. 7)—that "sorting procedures in the school . . . sort students into categories that are treated very differently" (Biddle, 2001, p. 17). The full picture here has been nicely captured by Kober (2001):

> Minority students are more likely to attend schools that do not offer higher math and science courses or AP courses. Even where such courses are offered, access of Black and Hispanic students may be hampered because they were tracked into a less academically challenging curriculum. Research has further found that some schools [and classes] with high-poverty or high-minority enrollments provide a watered down curriculum, meaning that teachers cover less material, give less homework, and award higher grades for lower performance. (p. 27)

It is portrayed by Mickelson and Heath (1999) as well:

> In this way, ability grouping and tracking frequently reinforce the learning problems of disadvantaged students by providing them with less effective instructors who teach the least challenging curricula using the methods least likely to challenge students to learn. (p. 562)

Insights on Tracking Its Impact on the Achievement Gap

> Tracking is another well-documented phenomenon that contributes to unequal access to educational opportunities for low-income and minority students. (Darling-Hammond & Post, 2000, p. 141)

> If there is one educational practice that seems to contribute most to the miseducation and nonachievement of black children, it is the practice of placing students in homogenous ability groups. (Irvine, 1990, p. 9)

Research indicates that grouping/tracking practices continue to contribute to differences in academic achievement among students from different racial/ethnic groups. (Miller, 1995, p. 236)

Student exposure to academic content in schools is influenced by a variety of factors—teacher qualifications, parental expectations, counselor efforts, student motivation and career plans, and so forth. But no factor is more critical, especially for students on the wrong side of the achievement gap, than the way students are sorted into curricular-focused programs of study. The first thing we need to remember about tracking is that it is a direct proxy for one of the two most critical elements in the student learning algorithm, opportunity to learn. On this point, we know, "Tracking functions as a major source of unequal opportunities to learn" (Mickelson & Heath, 1999, p. 569). It is also an indirect proxy for the second critical element, quality of instruction. On this point, we will see that tracking serves as a conduit to differentiated instructional quality, both in terms of teacher qualifications and instructional effectiveness. We explore both of these issues—the curricular and instructional dimensions of tracking—in considerable detail in the following two sections.

The second acknowledgment to be made about tracking is, "Track placements are strongly correlated with students' race and social class" (Mickelson & Heath, 1999, p. 567). The "assignment process . . . favors whites over blacks of equal ability" (Thompson & O'Quinn, 2001, p. 13) and affluent children over poor children of similar abilities (Miller, 1995). On this front, we know that these assignments have deep historical roots, beginning in the early twentieth century with the inculcation of the social efficiency philosophy into education (Murphy, Beck, Crawford, & Hodges, 2001). Under this banner, schools became places in which youngsters were tapped and then educated to fill slots in the larger economy, a process notoriously decoupled from merit and laced with both classism and racism (Kliebard, 1995; Krug, 1964; 1972; Wraga, 1994). Thus, "From the early beginnings of 'tracked' educational programs to contemporary schools, white and more affluent students have had opportunities and access to an education that differs markedly from the education provided for students of color and poverty (Shannon & Bylsma, 2002, p. 29). Alternatively, "Students of low-socioeconomic status are more likely to be placed in academic tracks less conducive to achievement" (Roscigno, 1998, p. 1035). We also know that for all the "research demonstrating the ineffectiveness of low-track classes and of tracking in general, schools continue the practice" (Burris & Welner, 2005, p. 595). Or, as Miller (1995) observes, because of tracking, "Serious inequalities in access to knowledge continue to exist in the nation's schools among students from different social classes and racial groups" (p. 233).

The third point to be made about tracking/ability grouping is that it is highly consequential. It "can reproduce or even exacerbate inequality" (Downey, von Hippel, & Broh, 2004, p. 615) and translate into lower-income and "Black student disadvantage" (Roscigno, 1999, p. 161). Since the focus of our work is the achievement gap, we will concentrate our attention on the link between tracking and learning outcomes. However, it is important to acknowledge that tracking is associated with other outcomes as well (Rosenbaum, 1980). For example, research informs us that track placements "affect students' self concepts" (Irvine, 1990, p. 15) and self-esteem (Alexander & McDill, 1976; Land & Legters, 2002) as well as exposure to "friendship networks" (Lucas & Gamoran, 2002, p. 175) in general and to motivated (or unmotivated) peers in particular (Berends et al., 2005).

Track assignments also shape an especially key variable in the student success story line—"aspirations for the future" (Lucas & Gamoran, 2002, p. 175). There is considerable evidence that track membership has marked consequences for the development of academic orientations and for aspirations for continued education, and particularly post-high school education plans (Alexander & Cook, 1982; Alexander, Cook, & McDill, 1978; Oakes, 1985; Schwartz, 1981). Alexander and Cook (1982) and Heyns (1974) suggest that schools exercise their primary influence over pupil socioeconomic attainment through their role in helping students establish orientations toward educational goals. As Heyns (1974) notes, "It is possible that schools play a more decisive role in the stratification system through encouraging and implementing aspirations than through altering patterns of achievement" (p. 1445). Work on the reproduction of cultural inequalities in American education through differential teaching of both the formal and the "hidden curriculum" at different track levels and at schools with students of varying biosocial backgrounds lends support to this position. Since they cluster students of color, track placements and ability groupings have also been implicated in the resegregation of education, this time within schools, by race and class (Irvine, 1990; Rumberger & Palardy, 2005), what Mickelson and Heath (1999) call "second-generation segregation within schools" (p. 577). As such, it is held, "Tracking policies and practices serve as the major vehicle to institutionalize and perpetuate racial divisions" (Cooper, 2000, p. 620) among school-aged youth and adults (Land & Legters, 2002).

Turning to student learning outcomes, research confirms that sorting students into curricular tracks is associated with high school graduation (Camara & Schmidt, 1999) and degree completion in college (Singham, 2003): "The academic rigor of the courses taken in middle school and high school not only affects students' current achievement, but also is the single most important predictor of college success" (Kober, 2001, p. 27). Studies also reveal the linkage between track assignment and measures of academic achievement (Alexander, Cook, & McDill, 1978; Gamoran, 2000; Hallinan, 1984; Roscigno, 1998; Strutchens & Silver, 2000; Tate, 1997; Weinstein, 1976). Here we find that students in the lower-level track with the "less challenging courses do less well on standardized examinations" (Hall, 2001, p. 22): "Not surprisingly, research shows that academic achievement is closely related to the rigor of the curriculum" (Barton, 2003, p. 8), that the rigor of the curriculum is tightly aligned to track placement (Miller, 1995), and that "ability grouping, on average, has a negative effect on students in the lower tail of the distribution" (Roscigno, 1998, p. 1039). Overall, Gamoran (2000) concludes, "Grouping and tracking not only magnify the differences between high and low achievers, they expand inequality of achievement among students of different social class backgrounds" (p. 104).

Given the narrative just presented, it will come as a surprise to no one to hear that tracking is a central theme in the achievement gap storyline (Cooper, 2002; Darity et al., 2001; Tate, 1997; Uhlenberg & Brown, 2002). For example, based on his research, Gamoran (2000) ascertains, "Grouping and tracking contribute to growing racial and ethnic inequality in student achievement over the high school years" (p. 104). Lubienski (2002) arrives at the same conclusion: "Student course taking appears to be another factor underlying gaps at the secondary level" (p. 283). At the elementary level, Ferguson (1998b) maintains, "Because a larger share of black elementary school children are in lower within-class ability groups and lower ability classrooms, any negative effect of ability groupings on children in slower groups adds to the black-white achievement gap" (pp. 365–366)—an assessment echoed by Gamoran (2000) who finds, "Assignments to different groups [in elementary schools] typically lead to achievement gaps that widen as the school year goes by" (p. 97). Overall then, the research confirms, "To the extent that higher proportions of African-American students are placed in lower tracks, this unequal assignment is bound to widen the gap between what black and white students learn in school" (Thompson & O'Quinn, 2001, p. 12): "The school's tracking system [is] one of the major vehicles that serve[s] to legitimize unequal educational opportunities and perpetrate the persistent achievement gap between the students of color and White students" (Cooper, 2000, pp. 597–98).

We close here with a point that we reinforce throughout the book, the importance of school for children from poor families and for African American children. That is, because these youngsters are more dependent on schooling than their white and more affluent peers, the impact of curricular weakness via tracking "is more pronounced for African-American students" (Camara & Schmidt, 1999, p. 7). Alternatively, as we discuss in Chapter 11, strengthening curricular programs will have "a disproportionately positive effect on students that traditionally underachieve" (Singham, 2003, p. 587).

Curricular Placement and Opportunity to Learn

Different curriculum tracks are associated with different patterns of course taking. (Natriello, McDill, & Pallas, 1990, p. 15)

Curriculum tracking goes beyond simply grouping students of similar ability to offering students in different tracks significantly different sets of courses. (Thompson, 2002, p. 29)

A growing body of work on curriculum differentiation establishes that "lower-track" classrooms (or groupings within classrooms), in which students from low-income backgrounds are disproportionately concentrated, offer a curriculum that is less intellectually stimulating, coherent, and demanding of the learner. (Knapp, 2001, p. 181)

Research also shows that a critical component of the racial gap in achievement is the relative absence of black students in higher-level courses and their disproportionate enrollment in lower-level ones. (Mickelson, 2003, p. 1063)

Four Lines of Findings

The linkages in play in this section are those between tracking decisions and impacts on student learning. The critical issue is that group placements and track assignments provide a direct measure of opportunity to learn, one of the most important causes of student achievement. More specifically, we will see that students at the lower end of these arrangements are often provided with "a substandard education" (Land & Legters, 2002, p. 18). They are "taught less" (Uhlenberg & Brown, 2002, p. 503)—they receive less rigorous and less challenging material (Murnane & Levy, 1996; Spradlin et al., 2005). They are denied the "opportunity to learn the more advanced material available to students in higher groups" (Thompson, 2002, p. 29). The consequence is "a qualitatively different schooling experience" (Cooper, 2000, p. 601), inequality in access to knowledge (Murphy & Hallinger, 1989), and less opportunity to learn (Cooper, 2002; Mickelson & Heath, 1999; Peng, Wright, & Hill, 1995).

The other critical issue in play here is that tracking, at least in terms of raw numbers, is not race and class neutral. Rather, there is stratification by race and social class with African American and poor children much more prevalent on the lower rungs of grouping arrangements (Mickelson & Heath, 1999; Murphy & Hallinger, 1989), although the bulk of the research attends to race. "When tracking is combined with student characteristics of race and class, the result is predictable. Black and poor students are disproportionately enrolled in the lowest ability groups" (Irvine, 1990, pp. 11–12). Four summary findings are of interest here. First, at the broadest level there is some evidence that schools heavily populated with poor children and children of color have access to a less rigorous curricular program, i.e., fewer mathematics and science courses than what is generally found in schools serving more advantaged youngsters (Gamoran, 2000; Raudenbush, Fotiu, & Cheong, 1998). That is, many "higher-minority schools tend to lack rigorous academic coursework" (Spradlin et al., 2005, p. 3); "many of the disadvantaged schools are unable [or unwilling] to offer advanced course-work" (Peng, Wright, & Hill, 1995, p. 73) in academic subjects. A lack of offerings in the area of Advanced Placement for African Americans is often cited in the literature (Mickelson, 2003), and overall, "Schools attended by urban students have fewer courses that can be described as 'advanced' or 'rigorous'" (Norman et al., 2002, p. 1109). And although course enrollment not offerings is the critical issue (Gamoran, 2000), students cannot enroll in courses that are not offered (Norman et al., 2001).

Second, there is evidence that African American youngsters and low-income children enroll in fewer semesters of coursework in the core academic subjects (Haycock, 2001; Strutchens & Silver, 2000), although there has been some significant improvements here over the last quarter century. Barton (2003) reports that while 46 percent of white high school graduates in 1998 completed four years of English, three years of social science and mathematics, and two years of foreign language, only 40 percent of African American students did so (p. 9).

Third, African American and low-income students are much more likely to be found in lower tracks and lower-track classes than are their white and more affluent peers. Children from the wrong side of the achievement gap are dramatically over represented in special education, remedial, compensatory, general, and vocational tracks, or their modern-day equivalents (Cooper, 2000; Miller, 1995; Oakes, 1985)—in the "nonacademic tracks" (Mickelson & Heath, 1999, p. 569) and in the "non-college preparation programs" (Peng, Wright, & Hill, 1995, p. 73). On the special education front, Bingham (1994) reports, "Black students are approximately three times as likely to be in a class for the educable mentally retarded" (p. 5) as whites—and alternatively only "half as likely to be in a class for the gifted and talented" (p. 5). Mickelson and Heath (1999), in a district that they were examining, found that "special education classes are overwhelmingly Black" (p. 572). Researchers also routinely conclude that African American students are over represented in remedial tracks and remedial classes (Clotfelter, Ladd, & Vigdor, 2005). For example, Cooper (2003) in his research found that while African Americans composed only 29 percent of the population, they made up two-thirds of the population in remedial mathematics classes. And, while it is not the focus of attention in this volume, it is worth noting that these findings apply to Hispanic students as well (Gandara et al., 2003; Rumberger & Gandara, 2004). On the vocational track front, Bempechat and Ginsburg (1989) report enrollments of 51 percent for African Americans and 34 percent for whites. Finally, turning to the general track, Peng, Wright, and Hill (1995) find that about 40 percent of African American tenth graders are in general mathematics courses, as compared to about one-fourth of white students (p. 50), a finding echoed by Mickelson and Heath (1999).

Fourth, low-income and "black students are underrepresented in higher track classes" (Land & Legters, 2002, p. 18) and "high-level courses" (Spradlin et al., 2005, p. 3). In particular, researchers document "the underrepresentation of the children of the poor and several minority groups in the college preparatory track in secondary school" (Miller, 1995, p. 330), in "gifted and talented classes [and] enrichment classes" (Shannon & Bylsma, 2002, p. 29), and in more advanced and challenging courses in general, such as Advanced Placement offerings (Mickelson & Heath, 1999).

Starting with the core academic program, we find, "Low SES youth are less likely to find their way to a college-preparatory high school program" (Alexander, Entwisle, & Olson, 2001, p. 175). Evidence also confirms, "Students of higher SES are more likely to be placed into academic tracks conducive to higher achievement" (Roscigno, 1999, p. 161), although, as noted next by Berends et al. (2005), the situation here is improving:

> In 1972 the proportion of black students reporting academic-track placement was 0.28, whereas in 1992, the proportion was 0.41, a 0.13 point increase. About half of all white students in 1972 and 1992 reported academic-track placement. Although the black-white difference in reported track placement was 0.22 in 1972, this difference declined to 0.08 in 1992, a significant reduction suggesting a possible benefit for black students. (p. 57)

Based on their research, Baenen and associates (2002) report that among students who graduated high school in 2001, 79 percent of the white women and 72 percent of the white males completed a chemistry course while 32 percent and 40 percent completed a physics course. The corresponding numbers for African Americans in chemistry are 50 and 40, and in physics 16 and 15. Irvine (1990), in turn, documents in her research review:

> Social class is strongly related to track placement. In her review, she documents that two-thirds or more of high-ability, high-SES (socio-economic status) students were in the academic track, but only one-half of the high ability, low-SES students were enrolled in the academic track" (p. 11). And Burris and Welner (2005) put these numbers in perspective when they note that "a highly proficient student from a low socioeconomic background has only a 50–50 chance of being placed in a high-track class. (p. 595)

Turning to gifted and talented coursework, there is a discernable sense in the research that "one factor that . . . contributes to the Black-White . . . gap is the inequitable selection of students into gifted programs" (Hughes, 2003, p. 301). Mickelson and Heath (1999), in their research, find "Elementary gifted and talented students [are] overwhelmingly white" (p. 576). According to Ford and her colleagues (2008), "Black students are underrepresented by as much as 55 percent nationally in gifted education; although Black students compose 17.2 percent of school districts, they represent 8.4 percent of those identified as gifted" (p. 217). Studies in North Carolina add to the evidence, noting and quantifying underrepresentation: "African-American students are sharply underrepresented in programs for academically and intellectually gifted (AIG) students. During the 1999–2000 school year, black students represented about 30% of the overall student population, but only about 10% of the enrollment in AIG programs" (Thompson & O'Quinn, 2001, p. 12). And, Burns, Keyes, and Kusimo (2005) reveal similar patterns in honor society membership.

Finally, the data on race and social class and Advanced Placement/honors classes are not encouraging. We already reported, as a starting point, that African American youngsters and children from poor families are "likely to attend schools where they have access to fewer advanced placement classes than whites" (Mickelson, 2003, p. 1057). Turning to enrollments, Cooper (2000) confirms, "Although students of color make up more than 50 percent of the student body, they represent less than 10 percent of the students in the . . . advanced-level classes" (p. 598).

Darity and colleagues (2001), in their research in North Carolina, find "underrepresentation of minority students in Honors courses [and] AP courses" (p. 3). They conclude, "The gap between White and Black students in proportional percentages of students enrolled in such programs is significant and widespread" (p. 3). Using data from Indiana, Spradlin and team (2005) document:

> In the 1998–99 school year, the state average for the AHD [Academic Honors Diploma] graduates was 21 percent. A total of 23 percent of white and 7 percent of African American students graduated with an AHD. Over a five-year period, the number of students completing the AHD steadily grew. These improvements were evident when examining the data from the 2003–04 school year. The state average rose to 30 percent, an increase of nine percentage points from the 1998–99 school year. A total of 32 percent of white and 12 percent of African American students graduated with an AHD. . . . With only about one in eight African American students completing the AHD, a significant gap exists, considering that about one in three white students satisfy the requirements for this diploma. (p. 15)

Turning again to data from North Carolina, Darity and colleagues (2001) report that while in 2000 African Americans made up 30 percent of the total school age population, they took only 7 percent of the AP courses completed. Their conclusion is not surprising: "Minority students at the high school level are significantly underrepresented statewide in all four types of AP courses [Biology, English, Calculus, and History] included in the analysis" (p. 20). In examining AP exam data from 2002, Barton (2003) reports that African Americans were 17 percent of the high school population but took only 4 percent of the AP exams that year. Whites, on the other hand, made up 62 percent of the high school population but completed 66 percent of AP exams. And considering both AP enrollments and exams, Baenen and team (2002) ascertain:

> White students were overrepresented in their enrollment in AP courses and in the number of AP exams taken compared to the percent of the eleventh and twelfth grade membership they represent. In contrast, Black students were the most underrepresented. Black students represented 21.4 percent of eleventh and twelfth grade students, yet they represented only 6.2 percent of students enrolled in AP courses and 4.0 percent of students taking AP exams. (p. 35)

These researchers also document hefty disparities in passing grades on AP tests, with 78 percent of white students earning a 3 or higher, while only 55 percent of African American students do so (p. 36).

An Analytic Note on Curricular Tracking and Race

The claim of racial discrimination in group placement by teachers is not supported by research. (Ferguson, 1998b, p. 329)

One important issue highlighted in the research literature on achievement gaps centers on whether disproportionate enrollments equate to discrimination and unfair treatment per se, or whether approaching the issue more scientifically, i.e., with statistical controls, makes more sense—and leads to different conclusions. As we have amply documented above, raw number distributions show quite convincingly that African American and low-income students are overrepresented, sometimes dramatically so, in lower level tracks and less rigorous courses, and undersubscribed, often dramatically so, in higher tracks and more advanced classes in general. Here, as Ferguson (1998b) reminds us, racial imbalance in itself is taken "as prima facie evidence of bias" (p. 327).

However, as scholars are quick to note, this conclusion is "based on gross differences that [do] not take into account students' socioeconomic or cognitive backgrounds" (Lucas & Gamoran, 2002, p.173). When previous achievement is loaded into the achievement algorithm, these disparities often disappear (Hallinan, 2001) or come close to disappearing (Ferguson, 1998b). Hallinan (2001) sums up the storyline here as follows:

> *A number of studies have shown that black students are disproportionately assigned to lower ability groups in middle school and high school. When achievement is taken into account, however, the results are less consistent. (p. 61)*

For example, Mickelson (as cited in Farkas, 2003) finds, "In this district, even after controls for prior achievement, family background, and other characteristics including self-reported effort, Black students are more likely to be found in lower tracks than are White students" (p. 1129). Ferguson (1998b), on the other hand, concludes as follows on race: "In reviewing the evidence on ability groupings and curriculum tracking, I find no evidence for racial bias in placements, once past performance is taken into account" (p. 365)—"that representation in these programs is not racially biased after performance controls" (Bali & Alvarez, 2003, p. 491). Alexander and team (1976; 1978; 1982) and Gamoran (2000) and Lucas and Gamoran (2002) arrive at a similar conclusion: "Access to the academic track is governed almost exclusively by traditional academic criteria, and we see very little indication of appreciable socio-economic, racial or gender bias in curriculum sorting processes" (Alexander & Cook, 1982, p. 637), that is, "no net racial difference in the likelihood of assignment to the college track" (Lucas & Gamoran, 2002, p. 181). Indeed, the research actually shows, Blacks are more likely to be assigned to the college track than are whites, once achievement and social background are controlled" (p. 171). Ferguson (1998b) arrives at a different conclusion when it comes to social class, however. He states:

> *Socioeconomic status does bias placements, such that students from families with more education and income are more likely to be enrolled in challenging tracks, even after*

controlling for test scores. Consequently, racial differences in socioeconomic status account for small racial differences in track placement among students with similar test scores. (p. 336)

In short, "The conclusion of race-linked differences in assignment [is] dependent upon the measure used" (Lucas & Gamoran, 2002, p. 181). Ferguson (1998b) reveals how the answer varies based on the measure employed:

First, are blacks distributed among ability groups, curriculum tracks, and courses in equal proportion to their representation in schools? The answer is clearly no. Second, is there evidence that placements in ability groups or curriculum tracks are racially biased? While there are small racial differences in placement associated with socioeconomic status, most such differences are associated with measurable differences in proficiency (that is, past performance). But there are no consistent racial differences in placements after controlling for these two factors. (p. 326)

He also, however, puts the entire debate in perspective for us here—and in Chapter 11 as well. "Blacks are more heavily represented than whites in less academically challenging tracks. So, if track placement affects test performance, tracking could exacerbate the black-white test score gap even if all track placements were based on race-blind criteria such as past performance" (p. 337).

Instructional Treatment Differentials

There is an extensive literature on the ways in which teachers treat students differently, based on their perceived status as high or low achievers. (Ferguson, 1998b, p. 341)

Schooling creates achievement gaps through more local processes of student-teacher interactions. (Reardon, 2003, p. 8)

Most uses of tracking result in poor instruction for low achievers. (Gamoran, 2000, p. 125)

These results suggest the tendency for some children to get taught and for others with equal entering proficiency who happen to be in different situations to get caught instructionally. The most noteworthy aspect of this tendency is that children generally held to be advantaged are those taught, and children alleged to be disadvantaged are those caught. (Hanson & Schutz, 1978, p. 144)

The major conclusion of the analysis in this chapter is that differences among student outcomes are, to a small but important extent, the result of differences in access to knowledge. The available evidence indicates that curriculum assignment, in addition to its sorting function, is an institutional mechanism for the systematic and selective allocation of important learning resources, systematic in that the allocation occurs in regular patterns and selective in that the resources are distributed in a different manner to various curricular groups. Students in lower-ability groups and nonacademic tracks are systematically discriminated against *vis-à-vis* their peers in more academically oriented groups. Even after controlling for ability and biosocial background factors, students in these less academically oriented groups perform less well than academic-track students. In the last section, we explored how opportunity to learn is unequally allocated under tracking arrangements. In this section we turn the analytic spotlight on instruction.

A number of studies lead to the conclusion that the instruction provided to students in lower-track classes is of a lesser quality than that provided to their peers in more academically oriented groups (Good & Marshall, 1984; Irvine, 1990; Oakes, 1985; Schwartz, 1981). At the secondary level, one of the reasons for this is the implicit assumption that teachers who must teach outside of their areas of expertise can more easily handle lower-level courses. As we reported above, such classes are often assigned to the least well-prepared teachers. Teachers also report less interest in working with lower-track students (Cooper, 2000; Heyns, 1974; Oakes, 1985), and they frequently confess to a lack of knowledge about how to prepare and conduct classes for both general and lower-track students (California State Department of Education, 1984). Also, they spend less time preparing for nonacademic classes (Gamoran, 2000). At the elementary level, students in lower-ability compensatory education classes sometimes receive a large amount of their instruction from aides rather than regular classroom teachers (Brookover, Brady, & Warfield, 1981). Finally, there is evidence that teachers use less demanding standards to judge their own performance with nonacademic-track students and lower-ability groups (Page, 1984; Gamoran, 2000; Schwartz, 1981).

Students in lower-ability classes also seem to be disadvantaged in the type of instruction they receive (Ferguson, 1998b; Irvine, 1990). The following teaching activities have been shown to be associated with student achievement: (1) providing the class with an overview of the lesson, (2) reviewing lesson objectives, (3) spending time actively teaching new content, and (4) maintaining an academic focus (for reviews, see Brophy & Good, 1986; Good, Grouws, & Ebmeier, 1983; Rosenshine, 1983). Evertson (1982) found that objectives were explained and materials introduced more clearly in higher-ability classes. There is also some evidence that, in an effort to get students working, teachers are more likely to skip important introductory learning activities in lower-track classes (Page, 1984; Schwartz, 1981).

Moreover, teachers often engage in less interactive teaching in their lower-track classes (Good & Marshall, 1984; Schwartz, 1981). In lower-track classes, face-to-face interactions within a group context are often threatening to teachers. To avoid these exchanges, teachers use films and worksheets in lieu of direct instruction and dialogues with students (Goodlad, 1984; Irvine, 1990; Shannon & Bylsma, 2002). In addition, other important instructional resources that are associated with student learning, such as teacher clarity, provision of work standards, teacher efforts to hold students accountable for their work, emphasis on higher-order cognitive skills, and teacher enthusiasm and warmth, seem to be disproportionately allocated to higher-ability groups (Cooper, 2000; Oakes, 1985; Page, 1984; Shannon & Bylsma, 2002).

Finally, a number of authors have concluded that lower-track groups are characterized by limited "task orientation" and "academic focus" (Downey, von Hippel, & Broh, 2004; Evertson, 1982; Good & Marshall, 1984; Mickelson, 2003). In her study of lower-track classes at a college-preparatory high school, Page (1984) reported that teachers and students often appear "to go through the motions of teaching and learning" (p. 18). She noted that "genuine academic encounters" (p. 18) are rare in these classes.

Four aspects of academic focus differentiate lower- and higher-ability tracks. First, as Page (1984) has noted, the content of lower-track classes is less academically oriented (Gamoran, 2000; Irvine, 1990). Teachers tend to talk of meeting the personal and social needs of students rather than academic goals; they use more "relevant" subject matter; and they tend to blur academic content by trying to present it in an entertaining manner. Therapeutic goals often displace academic ones. There are also fewer task-related interactions between teachers and students in lower-track classes (Hallinan, 1984; Irvine, 1990; Oakes, 1985; Powell, Farrar, & Cohen, 1985). Second, teachers of lower-track classes and groups, even after controlling for ability, require less academic work of students. Material is covered at a slower pace, lower-level objectives are emphasized, fewer academic standards are specified, fewer reports and projects are assigned, less academic feedback is provided, and fewer tests are given (Gamoran, 2000; Hanson & Schutz, 1978; Powell, Farrar, & Cohen, 1985; Schwartz, 1981; Strutchens & Silver, 2000). Third, work within individual classes in lower-ability tracks is less sequential and integrated than in the academic streams. In addition, because the assorted activities on which lower-track students work are often unrelated, there is a lack of coherence and meaning to their learning (Page, 1984; Powell, Farrar, & Cohen, 1985). Finally, while teachers in higher-track classes stress achievement more than behavior, the situation is often reversed in lower-ability classes. For example, in higher-ability classes teachers use selected teaching functions within lessons to promote academic objectives, while these same functions (e.g., asking questions, providing feedback) are often directed toward the control of student behavior in lower-ability classes (Allington, 1983; Eder, 1981; Schwartz, 1981).

One purpose of ability grouping is to allow students to receive teaching that is most suited to their needs and abilities. Yet, the available studies seem to support the position that there is great homogeneity in instructional approaches across learning groups and curricular tracks in classrooms (Evertson, 1982; Goodlad, 1984). At the elementary level, low ability is no guarantee of placement in a smaller learning group (Hallinan & Sorensen, 1983). At the junior high level, Evertson (1982) found very similar instructional formats across tracks. At the high school level, Page (1984) reported that the "activity format" used in lower-track classes actually further disadvantaged students in these groups. She concluded that students were more likely to receive ersatz individualized instruction in lieu of active teaching. What passed for individualized instruction was often unguided worksheet activity.

Time is another instructional variable that has been correlated with student learning. Students who spend more time on academic tasks and are more actively engaged with these tasks learn more than their nonengaged peers. Yet, it appears that students in nonacademic curricular tracks and lower-ability groups are discriminated against in the distribution of this critical condition of learning (Hallinan, 2001; Meehan et al., 2003; Oakes, 1985; Strutchens & Silver, 2000). Within individual class periods, instruction in low groups tends to start later and end earlier than in high-ability classes. Students in low-ability groups lose more time during transitions and experience more "dead time," or time with no work assignment, than their peers in more academically oriented classes. More time is lost due to student and teacher interruptions in low-ability groups. Homework is also more likely to be assigned as an in-class activity in low groups, thus encroaching upon, rather than extending, learning time (Hall, 2001; Neuman & Celano, 2006). Finally, students in lower-ability groups are generally off task more, or less actively engaged with their work, than pupils in higher-track groups.

Several factors contributing to the poorer use of time in low groups have already been mentioned, including an instructional milieu that lacks an academic focus and the failure to differentiate learning activity formats in an appropriate way. Researchers have noted that students in lower-ability groups can benefit from exposure to a greater variety of learning activities of short duration and fewer sustained periods of seatwork. Yet, students in those groups often receive fewer learning activities and are expected to maintain attention on each one for longer periods of time than pupils in other groups. Periods of uninterrupted seatwork are as long or longer than those experienced by higher-ability students. Page (1984) has attributed the higher rates of off-task activity in low-ability groups to the blurred and confused participation structures that often characterize nonacademic tracks in American schools. Whereas the structures that establish how students in high-ability groups are to participate in classes tend to be clear and stable, students in lower-track classes experience "ambiguous classroom situations, generated by frequently shifting and unclearly marked participation structures" (Eder, 1981, p. 30). In a similar vein, Allington (1983) and Eder (1981) argue that higher rates of off-task activity in elementary reading groups may be due to weaknesses in the instructional environment and inappropriately differentiated instructional treatments. Eder (1981) noted in her study that the higher number of student disruptions in lower-ability groups was due to the fact that the teacher created many more opportunities for disruption in these groups.

As we discussed earlier in our general analysis of quality instruction, positive and appropriate expectations for students are highly correlated with student achievement in both studies of school effectiveness and teacher effects. On the other hand, there is evidence that expectations at both the school (Rutter, Mauhan, Mortimore, & Ouston, 1979) and classroom levels (Brophy, 1982; Good, 1981) often disadvantage students in low groups (Becker & Luthar, 2001; Bol & Berry, 2005; Irvine, 1990). Students in these groups often face negative and inappropriate performance expectations in both the academic and behavioral areas. What makes these differential expectations negative and inappropriate is that they are based upon the beliefs of adults rather than upon diagnosed student needs.

"Established structure," that patterned set of rules and procedures that guide classroom interactions, is also an important variable for which we find inappropriate differences between high- and low-learning groups in classrooms. Where such structure exists and is internalized by students, on-task student behaviors increase, interactions between teacher and students on behavioral matters decrease, and student learning is enhanced. Evidence is beginning to accumulate that "established structure" characterizes more academically oriented groups, while a more chaotic condition is often found in low-ability classes and groups. More important in terms of equity, it appears that this condition is often attributable not to the characteristics of students but to the instructional environment of the classroom, and the specific practices and behaviors of teachers (Allington, 1983; Evertson, 1982; Page, 1984). Thus, a number of studies have found that teachers in low-ability groups invest considerably more time than teachers in high-ability groups in controlling and managing student behavior (Downey, von Hippel, & Broh, 2004; Eder, 1981; Oakes, 1985). This has often been attributed to the characteristics of students in low-ability groups, for example lack of motivation and a short attention span. While there is merit to the argument that students in low groups often make it difficult to develop and maintain "established structure," some recent research suggests that a combination of classroom conditions and teacher behaviors characterize low groups, and make the situation especially problematic: lower teacher expectations for student behavior, greater willingness on the part of teachers to trade structure for student compliance, greater confusion about appropriate modes of student participation, and undifferentiated instructional forms (Evertson, 1982; Page, 1984; Powell, Farrar, & Cohen, 1985; Reeves, 1982; Schwartz, 1981). In addition, there is growing evidence that tracking at all levels of schooling often promotes the formation of lower-stream peer groups that actively resists institutional norms and subvert classroom educational encounters (Good & Marshall, 1984; Oakes, 1985; Page, 1984; Pink, 1984; Rosenbaum, 1980; Schwartz, 1981). Rather than passively accepting the negative messages of schooling, students in lower-ability groups often "act back" on the expectations embedded in the fabric of educational institutions (Weis, n.d., p. 8).

Interpersonal relations comprise a final area in which conditions that are positively related to important student outcomes are inequitably distributed across instructional groups. There is often a lower quality of student-teacher interactions in low tracks (Goodlad, 1984; Oakes, 1985; Page, 1984; Schwartz, 1981). Teachers of lower-track classes tend to distance themselves from their students. Teachers rely heavily upon student feedback, especially evidence of student achievement, as a basis of personal rewards (Lortie, 1975; Rosenholtz, 1985). Since such rewards are generally less evident in low-ability classes, teachers tend not to form close relations with students in these groups. Second, as noted earlier, within low groups, teachers are more likely to trade behavioral and academic performance expectations for student goodwill. Goodwill, however, is not a strong base for forming meaningful relationships. Third, since teaching higher-track classes is often considered more prestigious, teachers tend to invest more time working with students in these classes (Page, 1984). Finally, teachers often find it easier to form relationships with those who share backgrounds and aspirations that are similar to their own.

CONCLUSION

In Chapters 8 and 9, we are examining schooling factors linked to the achievement gap, variables that exacerbate learning differentials or at least fail to help close racial and social class achievement gaps. In this chapter, the spotlight was directed to the instructional program. We saw how the two key elements in the learning equation—instruction and opportunity to learn—are provided in an inequitable manner to students in low-level tracks and classes. We also saw that these allocation patterns are consequential, they depress learning for the African American youngsters and lower-income children who disproportionately occupy places on the lower rungs of the track ladder. In Chapter 9, we turn our attention to school culture and to school structure and support systems.

9

Schooling Causes of the Achievement Gap

School Culture, Structure, and Support

Understanding achievement by blacks may have much to do with the schools black students attend. (Chubb & Loveless, 2002, p. 4)

Differences across schools play some part in driving racial disparities. (Stiefel, Schwartz, & Ellen, 2006, p. 11)

The institutional deficiency theory claims that Black children perform less well academically than White children because the institution of school is organized to favor middle class and upper class, non-minority children. (Stinson, 2006, p. 484)

The education of white children is relatively more successful than that of Black children because the schools were designed for white children. (Hale-Benson, 1990, p. 201)

In this chapter, we continue our analysis of the place of schooling in the achievement gap equation. The last chapter highlighted the instructional program—teaching and curriculum. Here, we investigate the environmental context of schooling, reporting, as Stinson (2006) and others observe, that schools are deficient in the ways that they serve African American and low-income youngsters. In the first section, we begin with a discussion of school culture and review findings that expose how the culture of the school can exacerbate learning differentials by race and social class—although most of the scholarship here is focused on race. We also study research on the learning environment. We close this section with an analysis of the pathway between school culture and depressed student learning, underscoring the importance of student disengagement and oppositional culture. In the second section, we examine school structure and support. We unpack five elements that have been linked to the formation and hardening of achievement gaps.

SCHOOL CULTURE

Another school characteristic that may have a differential influence on black and white students is school climate. (Hallinan, 2001, p. 60)

Children with the lowest achievement seem also to be the most distant—socially and culturally. (Trueba, 1983, p. 411)

Misplaced Culture

The cultural-disjuncture theory argues that impoverished students are handicapped because they come from backgrounds where standards for speech, conduct, and support—as well as cultural histories and ethnic traditions—differ from those commonly stressed in public schools. (Biddle, 2001, p. 13)

Racial/ethnic- and social/class-based cultural differences can produce incompatibilities with the culture of the school. (Miller, 1995, p. 298)

Students from poor and racial/ethnic minority backgrounds experience gaps between home and school, while their middle-class, white peers experience a more seamless connection between the two. (Villegas & Lucas, 2002, p. 44)

In this section, we review analysts' attempts to understand "the persistent failure of many African American students . . . by studying the link between school performance and students' cultural orientations" (Seiler & Elmesky, 2007, p. 397). The essence of the story is found in what Ream and Stanton-Salazar (2007) refer to as "cultural disjuncture" (p. 69), Knapp (2001) calls "cultural discontinuity" (p. 182), Shannon and Bylsma (2002) describe as "family and school disconnect" (p. 28), Miller (1995) refers to as "cultural incompatibilities" (pp. 282–283), and Irvine (1990) talks about as a lack of "cultural synchronization" (p. 22). The starting point is that distinct groups often possess distinct cultures, or at least cultures that have unique elements, and that these cultures are significant: "The basic assumptions, beliefs, and values are shared and held so deeply by a group that they exist in the unconsciousness, and therefore are invisible, even while they affect the individual understanding and view of the world" (Shannon & Bylsma, 2002, pp. 27–28). The next link in the logic chain is that white middle-class families and African American working-class and poor families have different cultures (Irvine, 1990; Miller, 1995). In moving to link three, we discover that schools have their own cultures and that the white middle-class one is the culture that has been hardwired into public education (Miller, 1995). Or, as Shannon and Bylsma (2002) capture it, "The current school system is predominantly characterized by a white middle-class culture" (p. 13).

The corollary, or link four of the logic chain, stresses the fact that "there is often a *discontinuity* between the cultures learners bring to school and the 'culture of the school' as embodied in teachers, other school staff, and those children whose backgrounds fall within the mainstream" (Knapp, 2001, p. 182)—"a disconnect between students who come from different cultures and family conditions and the traditional school structure and expectations" (Shannon & Bylsma, 2002, p. 9). Thus, schools and the families and children that they serve often "lack correspondence or are not synchronized because of differences in culture" (Irvine, 1990, p. 23). According to Irvine (1990), "Data support the supposition that not only do blacks have a culture that is distinct . . . but that the two cultures [black and white] are incongruous and contradictory" (p. 26). Embedded in this disjuncture is the failure on the part of educators "to recognize that black norms and conventions . . . differ from those of whites" (p. 28). The result is that "the educational environment of most black children does not reflect their primary value system" (p. 36).

The fifth link in the logic chain is that schools are not especially adept in dealing with this condition. The softer end of the argument continuum holds that educators "are insensitive to the cultural backgrounds of students . . . in high-poverty settings" (Knapp, 2001, p. 182). Here, it is suggested, school personnel are unable or unwilling to make the effort to understand and respond to the cultures of their students (Trueba, 1983). The harsher end of the argument continuum equates "the white dominance ingrained in the system" (Shannon & Bylsma, 2002, p. 28) with a more active stance of "institutional racism" (p. 28). Whatever end of the continuum one highlights, the end result is the same: schools "generally expect students to change to fit into the molds of the school rather than adapt the school structures to the children" (p. 28). Worse, they "perpetuate the difficulties experienced by minority and poor students as they expect children to behave according to norms of the majority culture without making those norms explicit" (p. 28).

And finally, the last link informs us that this cultural conflict and the resultant school actions dumb down student learning (Irvine, 1990; Norman et al., 2001). More specifically, to the topic of this volume, analysts here "attribute much of the achievement gap to a mismatch between the students' home culture and the dominant culture valued by schools" (Bol & Berry, 2005, p. 42).

Scholars of cultural discontinuity also provide a good deal of illustration—specifics, if you will—in the story narrated above, especially in what it means to say that "the current school system is predominantly characterized by a white middle-class culture" (Shannon & Bylsma, 2002, p. 13). Irvine (1990) and Shannon and Bylsma (2002) remind us on the "personnel" front of the fact that the overwhelming majority of school professionals are white has meaning here, especially in terms of the repertoires of skills needed to change discontinuity into synchronization (Lewis, 2008)—to "construct classrooms that resonate with students' cultural dispositions" (Seiler & Elmesky, 2007, p. 415).

Other researchers illustrate differences in the conventions and the norms of operation in classrooms and schools, what Miller (1995) calls the "social organization" (p. 249) of the system. For example, Shannon and Bylsma (2002) reveal, "Traditional classrooms and schools emphasize individualism, competition, and a future orientation that are generally associated with white middle-class values" (p. 28) and that are, to some extent, out of synch with African American culture (Irvine, 1990; Seiler & Elmesky, 2007). In a similar vein, Wenglinsky (1998) maintains that competitive, opposed to more communal and collaborative, operating rules "reinforce the tendency of low-SES students to lag behind their high-SES counterparts" (p. 272). Irvine (1990) and Uhlenberg and Brown (2002), in turn, provide numerous examples of how white cultural style in terms of the operating norms embedded in schools "interferes significantly in the . . . process" (Irvine, 1990, p.28) of African American students. Three examples from Irvine (1990) help illustrate this conclusion.

- In a heated discussion, African Americans frequently make their points whenever they can enter the discussion. Deference is given to the person who considers his point most urgent. Turn-taking is the style of whites, who usually raise their hands to be recognized. Teachers find African American students impolite, aggressive, and boisterous when they cut off another student or fail to restrain themselves so that every student can have a turn to talk.
- African American students may not maintain constant eye contact with teachers as do white students. Often African American children are accused of not paying attention when they are.
- African American students are more likely than white students to challenge or test school personnel because of beliefs that leadership is derived not from position, credentials, or experience but through personal attributes of strength, forcefulness, persuasiveness, and generosity. (pp. 28–29)

Of special importance here—in the area of social organization—are the sociolinguistic dimensions of classrooms (Miller, 1995). Irvine (1990) underscores this point as follows:

The issue of black students' language in school is a critical variable because school success is largely dependent on competent usage of the language. Like race, language is an obvious characteristic and becomes a method that teachers use to separate and stereotype. Black students who speak standard English are perceived to be of higher ability and more middle-class than black students who speak black English. (p. 30)

And Miller (1995) conveys the larger point when he reports that the cultural fit of the dominant sociolinguistic architecture of classrooms and schools is not an especially favorable one for African American children.

Still other analysts unpack the ways in which the "curriculum" in many schools fails to mesh well with the culture of African American children. Seiler and Elmesky (2007), for example, expose the ways that "school science in many ways opposes central aspects of culture held by many African Americans in communities of economic disadvantage" (p. 396). Indeed, it is sometimes asserted, as Bempechat (1992) states:

Minority groups have been miseducated in that they have not been taught about their own group's contribution to history and culture. The monocultural curriculum used in many schools is seen to foster institutional racism by neglecting the contributions of persons of color to scholarship. (Bempechat, 1992, p. 28)

The absence of culturally adaptive schools and culturally responsive classrooms is regularly surfaced as a problem (Seiler & Elmesky, 2007), and one often linked to achievement gaps.

Nonsupportive Learning Environments

African American students are more likely to report that they feel unsafe in their schools, that their learning is disrupted by other students. (Bankston & Caldas, 1997, p. 715)

Minority students are less likely than White students to attend schools with a favorable disciplinary climate and facilities in good repair. Minority parents are more likely to report concerns about safety in the schools their children attend. (Kober, 2001, p. 281)

Schools in poor neighborhoods generally have higher levels of disorder, disruption, and fear, all of which impede the learning of low-income students. (Barton, 2000, p. 223)

Research over the last thirty years informs us that students are socially and academically advantaged when they attend schools defined by safe and orderly learning environments (Antunez, DiCerbo, & Menken, 2000; Cole-Henderson, 2000). Conversely, they are placed at risk when they attend schools that are characterized by fear, violence, lack of order, and populated by uncaring adults (Baron, 2000; Gandara et al., 2003). On the discipline and order front, two conditions, in particular, can dumb down learning for African American and low-income pupils—discriminatory disciplinary action and unhealthy school climate. And on both factors, even "after controlling for individual characteristics Blacks do appear to be attending much worse schools" (Fryer & Levitt, 2002, p. 6). What makes this conclusion even more troubling is that given the environment confronting many of these children, their "need for a safe and supportive school climate is even more profound" (Bol & Berry, 2000, p. 198).

Safety and Discipline

In the area of "school disciplinary climate" (Raudenbush, Fotiu, & Cheong, 1998, p. 258), researchers maintain, "Discriminatory disciplinary practices that damage black students' educational practices" (Irvine, 1990, p. 19) are in play in many schools. They confirm that African American children in particular receive a disproportionate share of disciplinary attention in schools and are subjected to harsher discipline (Reynolds, 2002). Thus, "One factor related to the nonachievement of black students is the disproportionate use of severe disciplinary practices" (Irvine, 1990, p. 10). Alternatively, researchers find that whites encounter much more favorable disciplinary climates. We know, for example, that a much higher percentage of African Americans than whites are suspended and expelled from school. On this issue, Irvine (1990) reports:

Black students, compared to whites, are two to five times as likely to be suspended at a younger age. In addition, black students are more likely to receive lengthier repeated suspensions. [And] although minority students represent 25 percent of the nationwide school population, they constitute 40 percent of all suspended and expelled students. (pp. 16–17)

Irvine also explains the logic behind discriminatory discipline actions:

A teacher's reaction to disruption is based not solely on the behavior but on the identification of the student who violated the classroom rules. Teachers consider the students' past deportment, social class, and academic achievement when they determine the punishment appropriate for a transgression. High achievers are not punished as severely as low achievers for the same infraction. When a black student is identified as the student who misbehaved, it seems quite possible that the transgression is evaluated with reference not only to the individual child, but to the race, sex, and class groups to which the student belongs. For black males, the outcome can be alarmingly discriminatory. (p. 18)

In the area of "school climate differences and potential effects on achievement" (Roscigno, 2000, p. 269), research confirms that African American and low-income children on average attend schools with environments less conducive to learning. Part of this can be traced to the larger communities in which schools are nested (Land & Legters, 2002), to "neighborhood problems surrounding the school [and] bad conditions near school" (Lee & Burkam, 2002, p. 74), what might best be described as a spillover effect (Fryer & Levitt, 2004). Lee and Burkam (2002) document, for example:

Black children are more likely than their white counterparts to attend public schools located in neighborhoods characterized by problem conditions. The same pattern is evident for children from families living in poverty. . . . The same pattern is even more evident for poor conditions immediately surrounding the elementary schools. Black children are over five times more likely than white children to encounter at least some bad conditions near school. . . . Children from families in poverty (especially in urban areas) are considerably more likely to attend schools located in neighborhoods with problems. (pp. 74, 76)

The logic here suggests that these problem conditions "typically permeate the school wall, making school an unsafe place and creating a climate that is hardly conducive to educational success" (Roscigno, 2000, p. 269).

The other part of the unhealthy climate is generated by actions inside schools, although linkages to the larger community remain significant here also. An assortment of researchers record that gang problems are much more prevalent in schools with large numbers of low-income and African American students than in schools attended by white children and youngsters from more affluent homes (Fryer & Levitt, 2004). Barton (2003) finds that while 29 percent of African American students reported gang activity in their school in the previous six months, only 16 percent of white students did so. A similar pattern emerges in the area of social class. That is, "Students from lower income households were more likely to report the presence of gangs in the school than were those from higher income households" (p. 18).

Likewise, Roscigno (2000) acknowledges significant variations in the amount of crime in schools, with "schools attended by White students experience[ing] the least crime" (p. 275)—so too with violence (Land & Legters, 2002) and fear of violence (Barton, 2000). Other discipline problems also disproportionately mark schools with larger concentrations of low-income and African American students (Luster & McAdoo, 1994): "Minority students are less likely than white students to attend schools with . . . a well-controlled, disciplinary atmosphere" (Spradlin et al., 2005, p. 3). Barton (2000), for example, reports that schools with a minority population of 50 percent or higher "were over twice as likely to report discipline problems as were schools with less than 5 percent minority" (p. 229).

Finally, analysts consistently document that children from poor homes and African American youngsters are more likely than their peers to attend schools with inadequate and substandard facilities (Gandara et al., 2003; Hakuta, 2002; Spradlin et al., 2005). And, to return to the key point here, all of these factors that define unhealthy learning climates are negatively related to student achievement (Barton, 2000).

Caring Environment

For too many black students school is simply the place where, more concertedly, persistently, and authoritatively than anywhere else in society, they learn how little valued they are. (Steele, 1992, p. 78)

As was the case with safety, "Research shows that students who feel their teachers encourage them are more committed to learning and more successful academically" (Becker & Luthar, 2002, p. 202). Studies also reveal, "Achievement benefits . . . accrue through greater emphasis on promoting feelings of school belonging for disadvantaged students" (p. 201): "Effective schools have caring relationships that are a pervasive part of the school culture" (Waxman, Padron, & Garcia, 2007, p. 141). Caring environments are places where students feel valued both for their potential and as persons (Steele, 1992) and where there are opportunities for meaningful involvement in the life of the school (Pardon, Waxman, & Rivera, 2002). They are also spaces where children's parents feel welcome and where they are able to view the school in positive terms (Sanders, Allen-Jones, & Abel, 2002). And again, as with safety, research ascertains, "A supportive academic and social climate may be particularly effective in promoting learning for disadvantaged students" (Hallinan, 2001, p. 61). And, remember, as we have reported consistently throughout this volume: students from African American and working-class and poor homes are especially dependent on schools in general, and their teachers in particular, thus reinforcing the importance of a caring environment (Becker & Luthar, 2002).

Unfortunately, research also records that teachers in schools serving disadvantaged youngsters "have less positive attitudes about students and are less responsive to student needs" (Peng, Wright, & Hill, 1995, p. 36). And, "Because a larger proportion of black students attend disadvantaged schools [they] are more likely than other students to be exposed to such an environment" (p. 36). Lee and Burkam (2002) also confirm that African American and less-affluent youngsters attend schools possessing lesser amounts of two other key elements of a supportive learning environment, collective responsibility and professional community. Remember, again, the DNA of our rationale here: sense of community and caring adults are positively associated with most measures of student achievement.

The Pathway Between School Climate and Achievement Gaps

A substantial body of evidence attests to the association of status characteristics with risk behavior. (Finn & Rock, 1997, p. 221)

One way to better understand low achievement and underachievement within the context of the achievement gap is to examine students' educational attitudes, perceptions, and subsequent behaviors. (Ford, Grantham, & Whiting, 2008, p. 220)

Behavioral and affective disengagement from class and school is a particular problem among minority students from low-income homes. (Finn, 1998, p. 38)

Considerable effort has been channeled to exploring the roadway between institutional deficiency, especially inhospitable school culture, and depressed student achievement. The legs of the trip, it is suggested, unfold as follows: Cultural disconnect and a less than supportive climate lead to conflict on one hand and a sense of distrust on the other. From here, for many African American and low-income children (and their families), the road leads to a sometimes passive, and at other times active disengagement, from the institution of schooling and the education process. This, in turn, leads, sometimes, to efforts to develop one's own culture, often, it is argued, in opposition to the dominant culture of the school.

The starting point is "cultural misunderstanding" (Irvine, 1990, p. 27) and the development, or often reinforcement, of distrust among students. This is, as Learning Point Associates (2004) inform us, the first step down the pathway of failure for many children, as "feelings of trust in the institution and in those who are seen to represent the interests of those institutions [are] a fundamental building block in the affirmative development of high minority achievement" (p. 19).

The roadway to achievement gaps for African Americans is sometimes unfortunately strengthened by what Steele and his colleagues (Steele, 1992; 1997; Steele & Aronson, 1995; 1998) refer to as "stereotype threat." This is a condition that these scholars affirm can interfere with both efforts to perform and subsequent performance in a variety of ways, but most especially for African Americans experiencing success, and particularly as follows: "First, it adds a pressure that may directly undermine performance. Second, if it persists as a chronic feature of the school performance domain, it may force the affected students to disidentify with that domain" (Steele & Aronson, 1998, p. 403). Originally traced to pressures for successful students to do well on performance tests in higher education, Steele's theory is often extended to the K–12 sector, to areas beyond testing situations, and to all African American students—and from Steele's original influence pattern of reduced efficiency in work efforts to reduced efforts to engage work at all.

Steele and Aronson (1998) describe stereotype threat as a "situation," one in which "the existence of a negative stereotype about a group to which one belongs means that in situations where it is potentially applicable, one risks confirming that stereotype, both to oneself and to others" (p. 422). The essence of the theory attends to "the possibility of being judged or treated stereotypically or doing something that would confirm the stereotype" (p. 401). Thus, "Stereotype threat is the awareness that others may judge one's performance in terms of one's racial background, rather than in terms of one's individual background" (Learning Point Associates, 2004, p. 19).

Steele and Aronson (1998) maintain, "Black underachievement derives in part from the stereotype threat that is a chronic feature of African-American students academic environment" (p. 422). They also recount, "Eliminating stereotype threat can dramatically improve blacks' performance" (p. 423). In a real sense then, as Wilson (1998) observes, "The influence of the environment on academic performance is mediated by settings or conditions that involve the relative presence or absence of negative stereotypes" (p. 507). More generally, "Black students have internalized negative perceptions of achievement and intelligence" (Ford, Grantham, & Whiting, 2008, p. 224). Such "devaluation" is described by Steele (1992):

> *[It] sooner or later forces on its victims two partial realizations. The first is that society is preconditioned to see the worst in them. Black students quickly learn that acceptance, if it is to be won at all, will be hard-won. The second is that even if a black student achieves exoneration in one setting—with the teacher and fellow students in one classroom, or at one level of schooling, for example—this approval will have to be rewon in the next classroom, at the next level of schooling. (p. 74)*

The next leg on the trip toward the achievement gap, it is suggested, is the "disidentification" (Miller, 1995, p. 204) with the dominant cultural values of schooling in general, and with the importance of academic achievement in particular (Morgan & Mehta, 2004), with "the systematic rejection of school and academics by African American students" (Stinson, 2006, p. 487). Morgan and Mehta (2004) describe this as "a protective process through which the motivation to achieve declines because conceptions of overall self-worth are gradually separated from performance in school" (p. 83): "Widespread doubt among black students about their ability to do high-quality academic work leads many of them to avoid academic competition" (Miller, 1995, p. 204).

For many, the road between inhospitable culture and depressed learning runs out at withdraw—or "detachment" (Irvine, 1990, p. 42): "Some conclude that their prospects of succeeding in school are small, that academic success is simply not a promising basis for developing or maintaining their self-esteem. So they simply refuse to engage with school, withdrawing into an attitude of indifference" (Thompson & O'Quinn, 2001, p. 16). And, to return to the starting point, it is important to remember that "the process of disengagement" (Becker & Luthar, 2002, p. 201) and "the formation of peer group influence that is less than conducive to educational achievement is not created in a social or perhaps more accurately, an institutional vacuum" (Roscigno, 1998, p. 1047).

For other students, it is held, the pathway between an unhealthy learning climate and depressed achievement continues on one additional step, to the formation of an oppositional culture—a more active response than simple withdraw. In some schools, norms of nonengagement become part of an alternative culture (Steele, 1997; Thompson & O'Quinn, 2001), one scaffolded on student rather than adult values and norms (Roscigno, 1998).

Of particular interest here are theories of cultural inversion that hold that detachment from school can be accompanied by the formation of an alternative African American culture (Ainsworth-Darnell & Downey, 1998; Darity et al., 2001; Ford, Grantham, & Whiting, 2008; Mickelson, 2003; Stinson, 2006), one in which dominant cultural norms are not simply put aside but actively rejected and new "cultural norms oppositional to the norms of White America" (Stinson, 2006, p. 492) are created. Here we find that a peer culture develops that is "oppositional to achievement" (Lee, 2002, p. 7; Mickelson, 2003), a culture of "student oppositionality" (Norman et al., 2001, p. 1106): "Resisting or rejecting school and academic success is often considered part of the Black collective identity because it is perceived to be in opposition to the White identity" (Stinson, 2006, p. 492).

As a consequence, Mickelson (2003) explains:

Activities associated with school success (speaking standard English, carrying books, doing homework, studying for tests) come to be viewed as compromises of black social identity and group solidarity. In this way, the behaviors that lead to academic achievement come to be associated with "acting white." (p. 1068; see also Ford, Grantham, & Whiting, 2008; Wilson, 1998)

Miller (1995) also suggests:

These pressures against academic achievement experienced by black students do not originate exclusively with their peers; they also come from some adults in the African American community, including some parents. This should not be surprising, for many African American adults have had extensive experience with the lack of economic opportunity. Moreover, blacks' stereotypes of whites suggest profound distrust. Survey researchers have repeatedly found that many African Americans are alienated from whites and mistrustful of mainstream institutions. (pp. 207–208)

Acting white, in turn, is "viewed as being bourgeois or arrogant. A Black student who acts white is thought to be uppity, stuck-up, and uptight. He or she is not popular" (Ford, Grantham, &Whiting, 2008, p. 234)—"acting White is viewed as someone who has betrayed his or her racial group, has given up his or her racial or cultural ties, and has adopted the values, attitudes, and behaviors of the oppressor or enemy" (p. 222).

For purposes of addressing achievement gaps linked to cultural conflict, disidentification, and oppositional culture, it is important to remember that conditions here are nested in or mediated by larger environmental forces. Specifically, "Students' academic performance is influenced by their perception of the relationship between academic achievement and access to jobs" (Miller, 1995, p. 210). Here, the scholarship of Mickelson (reviewed in Ford, Grantham, & Whiting, 2008; and Miller, 1995) is especially helpful in understanding reduced expectations for African American youngsters:

Mickelson hypothesized that most black students in her sample would hold an abstract attitude toward education similar to the one generally held by the mainstream (white) population: that education is the key to success. She also hypothesized that many African American students (but relatively few whites) would have a concrete attitude toward education that was much more negative than their abstract attitude: that education frequently does not produce good economic/occupational opportunities for black people such as themselves. Finally, she hypothesized that most black students would have school grades reflecting their concrete, not their abstract, attitude toward education. (Miller, 1995, p. 209)

Mickelson concluded that serious discrepancy exists between their abstract beliefs and concrete beliefs. The model holds that Black students tend to exhibit an attitude-achievement paradox in which there is a discrepancy between beliefs and subsequent behaviors. Mickelson found that the Black high school students supported the belief that hard work plays a major role in one's success (abstract belief); however, they also believed that hard work does not necessarily result in success if one is Black because of such social injustices as prejudice and discrimination (concrete belief). (Ford, Grantham, & Whiting, 2008, p. 220)

These beliefs, in turn, reinforce movement toward withdrawal from schooling and disengagement from learning. Therefore, "Although Black students certainly have the ability to do well in school, too many of them do not exert the effort necessary to achieve at high levels. Some of these students, specifically if discouraged, believe that hard work is a waste of time and energy given the reality of social injustices" (Ford, Grantham, & Whiting, 2008, p. 221). Not surprisingly, motivation is negatively impacted. As Miller (1995) observes:

Over the long term, a crucial factor in determining a racial/ethnic group's motivation to succeed in school is the benefits its members receive from education. If most members of a group believe that education will open the door to good economic and occupational opportunities, children from the group may be more motivated to succeed academically than if they believe that the opposite is true. (p. 257)

Effort is also negatively impacted (Ainsworth-Darnell & Downey, 1998; Farkas, 2003; Peng, Wright, & Hill, 1998).

The line of logic we outlined above, it is held, has a place, perhaps an important one, in the learning gap algorithm: "The disidentification and oppositional-culture explanation identify some proximate causes . . . of the black-white gap in achievement" (Morgan & Mehta, 2004, p. 85). While the robustness of the logic and the theoretical propositions have been called into question in some empirical studies and reviews (see Ainsworth-Darnell & Downey, 1998; Cook & Ludwig, 1998; Darity et al., 1998; Ferguson, 1998b; Morgan & Mehta, 2004), that is, some "researchers contend that Black students are not particularly alienated from schools and are no more likely than Whites to lose peer status for doing well in school . . . [and] others feel that the evidence is inconclusive" (Kober, 2001, p. 281), the roadway sketched above clearly merits attention in the explanation chapters of the achievement gap story, especially the line of work on negative peer pressure (Stinson, 2006), for as Ford and colleagues (2008) conclude, "At whatever level of robustness it contributes to the achievement gap, peer pressure seems to be effective at hindering too many Black students from taking full advantage of certain academic opportunities available to them" (p. 222). Kober (2001) leaves us with a good summary here: "Negative peer pressure can make the achievement gap harder to close even if it is not a dominant factor" (p. 28).

STRUCTURE AND SUPPORT

Black students disproportionately attend lower-resource elementary schools. (Hughes, 2003, p. 312)

In addition to culture, the larger context of schooling is defined by various structures and systems of support that either amplify differences between African American children and low-income youngsters (this chapter), or help narrow those learning differentials (Chapter 11). One point that merits attention here is that there are many strategies proposed to help address the achievement gap problem that are not linked in causal ways to the formation of gaps. For example, remedies such as increased parental choice, heightened accountability measures, additional professional development for teachers, and so forth may contribute to narrowing social class and racial achievement gaps. However, there is little empirical work that connects these ideas to the development of gaps in the first place. Given the causal scaffolding of this chapter, we do not consider these elements here, although we do explore their gap-closing potential in Chapter 11. Our focus here is on variables that have been linked to the formation or reinforcement of achievement gaps: financial resources, school and class size, parental involvement, student mobility, and social class and racial composition of school and classes.

Financial Resources

The way funding [is] allocated can affect student achievement. (Shannon & Bylsma, 2002, p. 30)

It is important to know whether school dollars tend to be invested differently on the basis of the socioeconomic or racial/ethnic status of students because such variations in the deployment of school resources, if they exist, could be a source of differences in group achievement patterns. (Miller, 1995, p. 330)

The Story Line

There is clear evidence that schools with a substantial white presence get more resources of the sort that matter to student achievement. (Thompson & O'Quinn, 2001, pp. 20–21)

High poverty schools tend to have fewer financial and human resources than low poverty schools. (Land & Legters, 2002, p. 14)

While the picture is not completely clear, the bulk of the evidence suggests that there is a connection between the resources available to schools and race and social class, with African American and low-income children "likely to learn in schools with fewer material . . . resources" (Mickelson, 2003, p. 1057): "Specifically, inequality in spending appears to correspond to the racial and class composition of schools. Schools with the highest proportions of poor students are particularly disadvantaged" (Condron & Roscigno, 2003, p. 32). There is also an assessment in the scholarship here that until "poor school funding [as a] real cause of achievement deficits" (Biddle, 1997, p. 10) is addressed in a meaningful way, the gap battle is unlikely to be won. As described by Biddle (2001):

As long as the reluctance to spend more money on the badly underfunded schools in our most impoverished communities persists, it is difficult to believe that the educational problems of impoverished students, or the poor achievement records generated in the underfunded schools they attend for that matter, are likely to go away. (p. 21)

A number of analysts over the last quarter century have thrown the spotlight on funding as a source of learning differentials. Analysis here focuses on the inadequacies of the resources needed to educate disadvantaged children well (Hall, 2001; Rumberger & Gandara, 2004; Strutchens & Silver, 2000). Miller (1999), for example, argues, "One well-known problem for schools serving large numbers of disadvantaged students is that they often simply do not have sufficient resources to meet their students' needs" (p. 14). The major line of work on resource inadequacies stresses inequities in the ways that financial resources are formed and allocated (Lee, 2004; Roscigno, 1998; Shannon & Bylsma, 2002), highlighting the fact that "fewer financial resources are allocated to schools with higher proportions of poor and minority students" (Condron & Roscigno, 2003, p. 29). Researchers regularly discover, "Students who attend resource-poor schools are disproportionately members of minority groups" (Mickelson, 2003, p. 1061) and, "Urban school districts have vastly inferior resources for educating their students" (Villegas & Lucas, 2002, p. 47). Indeed, "Major funding disparities exist between schools with high-minority enrollments and those with low-minority enrollments. Similar disparities exist between schools in high-poverty and low-poverty areas, and between urban or poor rural schools and suburban schools" (Kober, 2001, p. 27). Thus, on average, "Schools serving large concentrations of disadvantaged youth receive inadequate funding" (Becker & Luthar, 2002, p. 201).

In the illumination process revealing that society and its educational institutions "often institutionalize the unequal distribution of resources and serve as instrument[s] by which the powerful maintain the status quo" (Irvine, 1990, p. 4), some scholars create stories and pictures and others amass statistics. Nearly all of them document that there are significant funding differences *between states,* with states with higher percentages of disadvantaged students providing fewer dollars for education. For example, Kober (2001) confirms that there are important resource "disparities in per pupil spending between states that affect the amount of resources available for minority children as much as, and sometimes more than, disparities in spending within state" (p. 27). Biddle (2001) documents a difference of two and one-half times in support for schooling between states. Chubb and Loveless (2002) make the story more concrete, reporting spending in 1995–1996 in New Jersey of $9,090 per pupil versus $4,900 per pupil in Mississippi.

Within state (between districts) data are also provided. For example, Shannon and Bylsma (2002) report, "Disparate funding levels between high- and low-poverty districts [have been] found in 42 states" (p. 30). Reynolds (2002) confirms that there are:

> … *significant differences between dollars spent per pupil in high-poverty districts and dollars spent in low-poverty districts. For example, in Illinois this difference is more than $1,900 and in Michigan the difference is more than $1,200. Such annual differences add up to severe disparity throughout a child's school career. By the end of high school, a student in New York state outside of New York City will have had, on average, $25,975 more spent on his or her education than a student within New York City. (p. 5)*

As Biddle (2000) reminds us:

> *What this means is that a few American students who happen to live in rich suburbs now attend public schools that are funded at $15,000 or more per student per year, while many impoverished students are forced into public schools that receive $3,000 or less in annual per-student funding. (p. 19)*

Darling-Hammond and Post (2002) elaborate further:

The wealthiest 10 percent of school districts in the United States spend nearly ten times more than the poorest 10 percent, and spending ratios of three to one are common within states. Poor and minority students are concentrated in the less well funded schools, most of them located in central cities and funded at levels substantially below those of neighboring suburban districts. (p. 127)

Finally, there is evidence that funding is allocated inequitably *within districts (between schools)* and *within schools (between classrooms)* (Baenen et al., 2002; Roscigno, 1999; Wenglinsky, 1997; 1998). Condron and Roscigno (2003), for example, find local shortfalls to poor schools in districts: "Schools with the lowest proportions of poor students spend $790 more of local instructional funds per pupil than do schools with high proportions of poor students" (p. 27). And Wenglinsky (1998) reports:

Research has shown that there are inequities within schools that are just as significant as inequities between schools. Not only do students of low-SES tend to go to lower quality schools, but within those schools, they can receive a lower quality education than that of high-SES students in the same schools. (p. 271)

Equally important, Wenglinsky concludes that not only does federal (Title I) money not provide a real advantage to children in disadvantaged schools, it does not even "bring the disadvantaged schools up to the level of total per student spending found in disproportionately white and higher-SES schools" (p. 29). In a similar vein, Baenen and colleagues (2002) confirm that supplemental support from parents and community "is more limited in schools with more low income minority students" (p. 43). Their conclusion: "Schools with the lowest percentages of FRL students have more supplemental resources at their disposal than schools with the highest percentages of FRL students" (p. 43).

Importance

Americans impose a huge, additional, unfair burden on impoverished students when they force students to attend underfunded schools. (Biddle, 2001, p. 20)

While we return to the topic of why these inequitable resource patterns exist in Chapter 11, where we address strategies to help close achievement gaps, we note here at a technical level that they result from the way public education is funded in the United States (Biddle, 2001), "to inequities inherent in and perpetuated by current school funding strategies" (Williams, 2003, p. 8). In particular, the heavy reliance on local property taxes to power schooling comes into play: "Disparities exist in per pupil spending because school funding is based on property taxes in most states" (Bol & Berry, 2005, p. 34)—"inequities in resource allocation across districts are related to the tradition of funding public schools through local property tax" (Roscigno, 2000, p. 268). That is, "Because 47.4 percent of all school expenditures are financed by local property taxes, school districts with predominantly low-SES populations tend to have fewer economic resources than those with predominantly high-SES populations" (Wenglinsky, 1997, p. 223).

We also know that while the impact on achievement is not especially robust (Berends et al., 2005; Jencks et al., 1972), that "the relationship between expenditure and achievement scores appears to be relatively weak" (Miller, 1995, p. 297), and financial resources can impact achievement in general and learning gaps in particular (Wenglinsky, 1998). There is also agreement in the research that whatever effect financial resources have on learning is multiplied for African American and low-income children. That is, "The weight of the evidence is shifting toward a hypothesis that resources have their largest and most efficient impact on disadvantaged and minority students" (Flanagan & Grissmer, 2002, p. 201).

Given the points above, answers to the question of just how much financial resource inequities contribute to racial and social class achievement gaps are mixed. Some reviewers, such as Lewis (2008), argue, "By and large current inequality in school-level resources and expenditures appears to be at best a minor explanation for contemporary achievement gaps" (p. 43). Others, however, arrive at a different conclusion (Norman et al., 2001; Spradlin et al., 2005). Villegas and Lucas (2002) conclude, for example, "Fundamental resource inequality between urban and suburban schools contributes in no small way to the achievement gap between urban students and their suburban counterparts" (p. 47). And Mickelson (2003) finds, "The racial discriminatory practices that generate and allocate resources inequitably to schools contribute to the racial gap in outcomes" (pp. 1061–1062).

Perhaps the best points on which to land are as follows: First, given the special significance of financial resources for disadvantaged youth, the limited resources available to be employed in the education of those children probably do "account for some of the achievement" (Norman et al., 2001, p. 1109) gap between majority and minority youngsters and low- and high-income children. Second, the children on the wrong side of the achievement gap need more resources than their peers (Jencks & Phillips, 1998). Third, those resources need to be large enough to make a difference (Condron & Roscigno, 2003). Finally, and perhaps most importantly, "Increasing the amount of money spent on schooling can make a difference for disadvantaged and minority students, but changing how money is spent is often required as well" (Miller, 1999, p. 19). Resources are important to the extent that they follow certain pathways, that is, to the degree that they translate into, or are used to buy, elements of schooling that are themselves associated with student achievement (Condron & Roscigno, 2003; Wenglinsky, 1997). Of particular importance are some of the ingredients of schooling that we examined in Chapter 8, such as opportunity to learn, a quality teaching force, developmentally responsive teaching methods, and so forth.

District, School, and Class Size

Other things equal, larger schools and larger districts do slightly worse. (Ferguson, 1991, p. 10)

Poverty has a negative impact on student achievement, but smaller schools are able to mitigate or even minimize that negative impact. (Johnson, Howley, & Howley, 2002, p. 28)

Large class sizes, especially for inner-city minority students are often cited as exacerbating the achievement gap. (Uhlenberg & Brown, 2002, p. 505)

District, school, and class size, or scale, is a second structural/support element that has been linked to achievement and found to amplify racial and social class learning differentials. In an especially insightful study, Johnson and team (2002) conclude that larger *district size* magnifies inequalities—and equally important, as we will see in Chapter 11, smaller district size can "significantly disrupt" (p. 36) inequities. Johnson and associates also find that *school size* negatively impacts achievement, most noticeably at the lower end of the SES continuum and for African American students (see also Chatterji, 2005a; 2005b). That is, "The influence of size on achievement is not constant but varies with changes in the SES level of the school" (p. 31). Equally important, they provide important insights "about the interactions of school and district size on the equity of performance" (p. 30). Specifically, they confirm, "Inequity is greatest among larger schools in larger districts, somewhat less among smaller schools in larger districts, but inequity is weakest (by far) among smaller schools in smaller districts" (p. 30). And, they conclude, "Smaller district size substantially compounds the positive influence of smaller school size on the equity of achievement—and compounds it well beyond the moderate [influence] provided by changes in school size only" (p. 31).

Research on *class size* also finds that larger is worse for students on the wrong side of the achievement gap. To begin with, evidence suggests that "minority students experience larger classes" (Barton, 2003, p. 14), especially after removing special education classes from calculations (Barton, 2003; Roscigno, 1998)—although the evidence is contested (Boozer & Rouse, 2001; Chatterji, 2005b; Villegas & Lucas, 2002). For example, Lee and Burkam (2002) report:

> *Children with families with more economic need attend schools with larger kindergarten classes…. The strongest associations here refer to location. Compared to the suburbs, children attending schools in urban areas are in much larger kindergarten classes, whereas children in schools in medium cities and rural areas are in smaller classes. (pp. 70, 73)*

Second, the evidence on the benefits of smaller class size is consistent, small but important, and likely applicable only in the elementary grades (Ferguson, 1991). Alternatively, "Large classes lead to lower scores in Grades 1–7" (p. 9). More specifically to the topic at hand in this volume, larger class sizes seem to exacerbate achievement gaps and "pupil-teacher ratio reductions are consistent with explaining part of the large African American score gains" (Flanagan & Grissmer, 2002, p. 201). As Boozer and Rouse (2001) assert based on their studies, "Moving an African-American student into a class the size of an average white student's class would lead to roughly a 0.27 point increase in the test score gain" (p. 186). The important point here for the gap narrative is that larger class size may disproportionately harm disadvantaged youngsters: "Large classes may hinder students' academic achievement, especially those who are poor and racial/ethnic minorities" (Land & Legters, 2002, p. 14). On the flip side, "Small classes may help blacks more than whites" (Jencks & Phillips, 1998, p. 49): "Racial and ethnic minority students and students attending inner-city schools reaped greater benefits from small classes than other students" (Land & Legters, 2002, p. 14), a finding recently confirmed by Ready (as cited in *Education Week*, 2008).

Parental Involvement

> *Family and community involvement in schools is viewed as particularly important and urgent for poor and minority students. (Sanders, Allen-Jones, & Abel, 2002, p. 171)*

The academic achievement gap was partially explained by differences in the levels and effects of parent involvement. (Lee & Bowen, 2006, pp. 209–210)

A central theme of this volume is that schools are not the central causal variable in the achievement gap algorithm. We know that "schools alone cannot adequately provide children and youth with the resources and supports they need to become successful students" (Sanders, Allen-Jones, & Abel, 2002, p. 171). Parents play an especially important role in the student learning narrative. In Chapters 4–7, we made that point in terms of out-of-school activity. Here we report that a dearth of parent involvement with schools can exacerbate learning gaps by race and social class (Reynolds, 2002). That is, "Less involvement at school on the part of some parents may represent a significant disadvantage to their children" (Lee & Bowen, 2006, p. 210). Alternatively, as we discuss in Chapter 11, parents can be a key ingredient in partnership with schools to enhance student learning and to narrow achievement gaps.

To begin with, research reveals that "parents who are poor and of color tend to participate less actively in their children's schooling than white, middle-class parents" (Villegas & Lucas, 2002, p. 41). Lee and Bowen (2006) report:

Involvement at school occurred most frequently for those parents whose culture and lifestyle were most likely to be congruent with the school's culture: parents who were European American, whose children did not take part in the school lunch program, and whose educational attainment was higher and more similar to that of school staff. (Lee & Bowen, 2006, p. 210)

Thus, researchers conclude that "family and community involvement in schools serving large numbers of poor and minority students is still far from what policymakers, researchers, educational leaders, and parents themselves would view as optimal" (Sanders, Allen-Jones, & Abel, 2002, p. 77). Barton (2003), for example, documents that high-income parents are much more likely to attend school events or volunteer at school than are low-income parents. A similar pattern emerges in the area of race as well. Thus, we find, "Parent attendance at school-sponsored events varies by poverty concentration, as defined by the percent of students eligible for free or reduced-price lunch, and minority enrollment in the school" (Sanders, Allen-Jones, & Abel, 2002, p. 177). Equally important, Barton (2003) discloses that teachers at high-poverty schools are twice as likely as their peers at low-poverty schools to report lack of parent involvement as a "moderate or severe problem" (p. 21): "Moreover, the percentage of schools satisfied with the degree of family involvement in different activities decreases as the minority enrollment or the percentage of students eligible for free or reduced-price lunch reaches 50 percent or more" (Sanders, Allen-Jones, & Abel, 2002, p. 177).

There is also a considerable body of scholarship that explores why researchers regularly uncover this pattern of less parental involvement in schools with high concentrations of poor and low-income children. Some of the explanation underscores the problems that poverty creates for developing linkages between home and school. For example, analysts regularly expose the fact that the working arrangements of low-income parents (e.g., both parents working, multiple jobs, less parent-friendly work rules) hinder the development of connections with schools (Lee & Bowen, 2006; Villegas & Lucas, 2002). Other explanations feature cultural differences between home and school that can (1) produce a lack of congruence and even conflict between the two potential partners; (2) lead parents to defer to professional educators (Lareau, 2002); and/or (3) make it difficult for parents to understand the grammar of and to navigate the routines of school (Hughes, 2003; Villegas & Lucas, 2002). Still other explanations stress the failure of school professionals to act proactively to involve parents of disadvantaged pupils as partners in the education of their children (Padron, Waxman, & Rivera, 2002). Here investigators often uncover less-than-inviting environments established by schools and a devaluing of the experiences and potential contributions of nonmajority parents (Hughes, 2003). For example, Barton (2003) confirms that urban and minority parents are more than twice as likely to "feel unwelcome" (p. 20) in their children's schools. Researchers highlight teachers and administrators who are unable or unwilling to work to understand parents who differ from the dominant culture of the school (Lee & Bowen, 2006). And, they unearth a "blame the victim" perspective where "families become viewed as the problems" (Hughes, 2003, p. 319).

Scholars also document the relationship between parent involvement, or lack thereof, and achievement gaps. They argue in the broadest sense, "The failure to bridge the social and cultural gap between home and school may be at the root of the poor academic performance of many, poor minority children" (Comer, as cited in Shannon & Bylsma, 2002, p. 45). They link parent involvement and quality of schooling (Waxman, Padron, & Garcia, 2007) and student learning (Hughes, 2003). More specifically, they conclude that "parents' involvement at school . . . remains of central importance; existing inequalities in the levels of this type of involvement are likely to contribute to the achievement gap" (Lee & Bowen, 2006, p. 214): "Students with parents who are involved in their school tend to have fewer behavioral problems and better academic performance, and are more likely to complete secondary school than students whose parents are not involved in their schools" (Child Trends Data Bank, as cited in Barton, 2003, p. 20).

Family and Student Mobility

Mobility rates . . . vary widely by race and economic status. (Baenen et al., 2002, p. 38)

Student mobility (that is, how frequently children change schools) is related to socioeconomic status and can result in a myriad of problems in school. (Barton, 2003, p. 6)

We found significant negative impacts of mobility on test scores. (Myers, Kim, & Mandala, 2004, p. 94)

The data presented in the present study offer compelling evidence that geographic mobility is an aversive influence on student achievement. (Ingersoll, Scamman, & Eckerling, 1989, p. 148)

In Chapter 5 on the relationship between the family and achievement gaps, we introduced the student mobility variable. We revisit it here with the understanding that while schools cannot control mobility, they can respond to it in ways that either exacerbate or narrow social class and race learning differentials. We begin with a description of the concept from Baenen et al. (2002):

One way of examining mobility is to determine the percentage of students who are "stable" during a school year. Stability, in this case, is defined as the percentage of students at the end of a school year who began school during the first week of the school year and remained in that school for the entire year. Students are identified as 'mobile' if they ended the school year having been enrolled in a school for less than the entire year. (p. 31)

One thing that the research helps us see is that student mobility and the variables in play in this volume—race and social class—are highly correlated (Cole-Henderson, 2000; Myers, Kim, & Mandala, 2004; Ream & Stanton-Salazar, 2007): "There is [a] general correlation between high mobility rates . . . and high student body poverty rates. . . . There is also a high correlation between student mobility and minority status in schools" (Miller, 1995, p. 138). Not surprisingly, we discover, "Mobility is particularly pronounced within large, predominantly minority, urban school districts with high concentrations of students from low socioeconomic backgrounds" (Ream & Stanton-Salazar, 2007, p. 70). More concretely, Barton (2003) informs us, "The percentage of Black . . . students who are frequent changers is double that of White students, and the percent of students from low-income families is triple that of high-income families" (p. 22).

Research also illuminates the pathway between mobility and reduced academic achievement, showing that turnover negatively impacts some of the key elements in the school effects profile. Investigators report that mobility often causes "the curriculum to slow down" (Miller, 1999, p. 14), results in "slower academic pacing" (Barton, 2003, p. 22), and reduces opportunity to learn (Miller, 1995; 1999). Miller (1999) also finds that schools with high student mobility "often have high turnover among teachers and principals, which further undermines the quality of the academic program. Each of these factors can make it more difficult for poor and nonpoor students to do well in school" (pp. 14–15). Ingersoll and team (1989), in turn, document that moves disrupt not only the core technology, but also school culture and accompanying "social support systems" (p. 148).

Finally, from the research, we discern that mobility has a negative influence on student learning and hardens achievement gaps. Indeed, "The bulk of the literature suggests a strong relationship between mobility and achievement" (Myers, Kim, & Mandala, 2004, p. 92). One theme here is that mobility impacts all students in negative ways, not just the frequent movers (Miller, 1999), and, "High mobility rates reduce a school's ability to meet the educational needs of both groups of students" (Miller, 1995, p. 137). Rothstein (2004) makes the point as follows: "When children move in and out of schools, not only does their own achievement suffer but so too does the achievement of their classmates whose learning is also disrupted" (p. 135). According to Ream and Stanton-Salazar (2007):

Mobile students are not the only ones who suffer the consequences of student mobility: students with stable attendance records may also be academically impaired if they attend schools with highly mobile populations. To illustrate, students who attended high schools with overall mobility rates of 40 percent scored significantly lower on tenth grade standardized mathematics tests than students who attended high schools with mobility rates of 10 percent. (pp. 74–75)

For the movers themselves, researchers confirm lower achievement scores (Barton, 2003; Miller, 1995; Myers, Kim, & Mandala, 2004): "The clearest interpretation of our data remains that geographic mobility, particularly mobility within the school year, has a disruptive influence on achievement" (Ingersoll, Scamman, & Eckerling, 1989, p. 148). For example, Barton (2003) cites a Government Accountability Office (GAO) study that found "that 41 percent of these frequent school changers were below grade level in reading and 33 percent in math, compared with 26 percent and 17 percent respectively of students who had never changed schools" (p. 22). He also documents "reduced likelihood of high school completion" (Barton, 2003, p. 22; see also Velez, 1989). One useful caveat here has been provided by Ream and Stanton-Salazar (2007). That is, "The impact of student mobility may have something to do with its timing, and timing might be associated with the reasons students change schools" (p. 74).

Composition of Schools and Classes

Researchers have long recognized that the compositional characteristics of their school's student body can affect individual student achievement. (Rumberger & Palardy, 2005, p. 2003)

The school factor most correlated with variations in standardized test scores was the composition of the study body. The characteristics of students' peers were more closely associated with variations in students' test scores than differences in teacher characteristics, school facilities, or the curriculum. (Miller, 1995, p. 86)

Racial context of the school may be important for the academic socialization and achievement of young children. (Entwisle & Alexander, 1992, p. 73)

The family structure prevailing in school appears to make more of a difference for students than their own family backgrounds. (Caldas & Bankston, 1999, p. 98)

The lead question here has been nicely framed up by Caldas and Bankston (1999): How much does the socioeconomic composition of a school determine its effectiveness? The answer, as we explain as follows, is a good deal. Both racial and class segregation have "dampening effect[s] on achievement" (Roscigno, 1998, p. 1035; Fryer & Levitt, 2002; Land & Legters, 2002), although, as we have reported throughout this volume, class trumps race: "Family economic factors far outweigh the influence of the racial mix of the school" (Berends et al., 2005, p. 28). According to Caldas and Bankston (1999) then, "The family structure of school populations [is] the critical variable in predicting individual test scores" (p. 97).

Concentration

To begin with, analysts document what many of us see on a daily basis; that is, there is considerable concentration by race and social class in America's schools (Armor, 2008; Hale-Benson, 1990; Roscigno, 2000)—"considerable racial and socioeconomic segregation among schools" (Reardon, 2003, p. 19). According to Villegas and Lucas (2002), "The United States has created two racially segregated and economically unequal systems of education—one urban, mostly for children who are poor and of color; the other suburban, largely for white, middle-class children" (p. 48). Mickelson (2003) expands on this concentration phenomenon:

> *Even though a majority of black students do not live in inner city ghettos, the majority of these students live in urban areas and are increasingly likely to attend segregated minority schools. At the same time, the suburbanization of middle class Americans, particularly whites—facilitated by tax and transportation policies—results in more privileged students attending newer, better resourced schools with few peers from low-income, poorly educated families. (p. 1072)*

On the topic of race, Fryer and Levitt (2002) document:

> *In our data which samples roughly twenty children each from approximately 1,000 schools, in 35 percent of those schools there is not a single Black child in the sample. The mean Black student in our sample attends a school that is 59 percent Black and 8 percent Hispanic. In contrast, the typical White student goes to a school that is only 6 percent Black and 5 percent Hispanic. (p. 21)*

Bankston and Caldas (1998) report that in 1990, "About two-thirds of African American school children were attending segregated schools" (p. 715): "The percentage of Black students in predominantly minority schools (50–100 percent minority) was 70 percent in 1999" (Lee, 2004, p. 65). Similar patterns emerge when we turn to social class (Lee & Burkam, 2002): "Particularly poor children are likely to be concentrated in low-SES schools" (Lee et al., 1990, p. 504).

Impact

Another message that scholars convey is that the act of segregating students by race and class is consequential: "Schools with larger poor or Black student bodies have lower achievement levels than others" (Caldas & Bankston, 1999, p. 99)—"variations in the composition of the student bodies of schools [are] more strongly associated with variations in students' standardized test scores than any other school-based factor" (Miller, 1995, p. 135). Indeed, Caldas and Bankston (1999) suggest, "Success in applying the tenets of effective schools—including strong leadership, high expectations, stable climate, positive faculty-student relations—may be held hostage to the prevailing family-type principally found in the school" (p. 98).

On one front, we discover, "The racial composition of the schools is important for blacks" (Hanushek & Raymond, 2005, p. 312). Scholars routinely affirm, "The concentration of African American young people in schools has a negative effect on achievement independent of socioeconomic status" (Bankston & Caldas, 1998, p. 716; see also Berends et al., 2005; Uhlenberg & Brown, 2002). More forcefully, "Black students are hurt by greater concentration in the schools" (Hanushek & Raymond, 2005, p. 321) and, "Segregation harms the academic achievement of African American students (Armor, 1992, p. 71). Segregation constitutes a disadvantage over and above that of individual students' own racial status (Bankston & Caldas, 1996; 1998). Reardon (2003), for example, documents, "Students in schools with more black students have much lower reading learning rates than those in predominantly white schools"

(p. 24). Roscigno (1998) finds, "On average there is a 3.9 point penalty associated with attending a black segregated school" (p. 1046). Overall, the data reveal, "One of the most salient characteristics of schools attended by minority students, their racial concentration, is one of the greatest barriers to educational accomplishment" (Bankston & Caldas, 1998, p. 532), and "that an increased Black concentration in schools has a detrimental effect on Black achievement" (Hanushek & Raymond, 2008, p. 299). These conclusions are especially salient for African American children in elementary schools and for the subject area of reading (Jencks & Phillips, 1998; Reardon, 2003) and for African-American pupils "in the top half of the performance distribution" (Farkas, 2003, p. 1130). Results are small but consistent (Bali & Alvarez, 2003; Mickelson, 2003).

The flip side of this analysis helps us see not only "that students in predominantly minority schools have average learning rates lower than students of the same race/ethnicity and SES in predominantly white schools" (Reardon, 2003, p. 25), but that African American students in integrated schools have "greater academic gains" (Rumberger & Palardy, 2005, p. 2007). Researchers consistently document that "African-American children are helped by integrated school settings, while white children do as well in integrated as in segregated settings" (Entwisle & Alexander, 1992, p. 73): "The proportion of Blacks in the school negatively affected Blacks, but Whites . . . were unaffected by student body composition" (Hanushek & Raymond, 2008, p. 312). Alternatively, Mickelson (2003) finds "that the longer blacks and whites learn in desegregated schools and classrooms the better are their academic outcomes" (p. 1062). More fully, he explains that five decades of research lead to the conclusion that "there is little argument about the positive long-term effects of desegregation on minority students' status attainment, racial attitudes, and other life course indicators" (p. 1062).

Analysts also document linkages between segregation by social class and learning. Here, "The explicit variable of concern is concentration of poverty within the school" (Myers, Kim, & Mandala, 2004, p. 83). And, researchers conclude, "The poverty status of the students attending the school significantly affects the performance level of the students in the school" (Beckford & Cooley, 1993, pp. 12–13)—"schools with higher proportions of students from high socioeconomic backgrounds have higher achievement, higher graduation rates, and more college-bound graduates" (Berends et al., 2005, p. 27). Thus, there is an "inverse relationship between school poverty and test scores" (p. 83). Rumberger and Palardy (2005) report on the importance of this association, noting "that effect sizes for school are almost as large overall and even larger in certain areas than the effect sizes for student SES" (p. 2014), a point Caldas and Bankston (1999) make as follows: "The SES of the student body is almost as strong a predictor of academic achievement as an individual's own family SES" (p. 92).

We learn from the research, not surprisingly, that segregating students by social class is especially harmful to poor children: "For those impoverished children who attend school with other impoverished children, the odds of attaining normal levels of academic accomplishment grow even worse" (Johnson, Howley, & Howley, 2002, p. 7). But we also find that the downward spiral of academic achievement is not confined to children from low-income homes: "High levels of poverty within a school tend to depress achievement for all the children in that school, whether or not they are poor themselves" (Kober, 2000, p. 27). And finally, we discover, "There is a sizable benefit from attending a high-SES school" (Rumberger & Palardy, 2005, p. 2015).

In addition to poverty, we learn, "Variations in academic performance among schools are connected closely to family situations that prevail in schools" (Caldas & Bankston, 1999,

p. 97). Specifically, "[A] concentration of students from single-parent families has been shown to lower achievement" (Goldsmith, 2004, p. 124): "The percentage of students from single-parent families in schools has a strong negative relation to standardized test scores" (Bankston & Caldas, 1998, p. 721). And as we reported above with income, the effect is not confined to the targeted group, children from single-parent homes in this case: "Regardless of their own family structure, students tend to do worse in schools that contain large proportions of one parent families" (Caldas & Bankston, 1999, p. 99). In slightly different form, "Being in a school dominated by students from single-parent families can have a negative influence on a student's academic performance even if that student comes from a two-parent family" (p. 98). On the other side of the ledger, "The concentration of students from two parent families does seem to boost individual academic achievement" (p. 99).

Pathways

The ground that is highlighted here is the space between concentration and segregation of students at one point in time and the differential outcomes at some later point in time. What explains the reduced learning and the achievement gaps for low-SES and African American children? Scholars stress three explanatory pathways. They maintain first that much of the problem can be traced to the lower-quality educational experiences found, on average, in schools with high concentrations of children of color and students from low-income homes (Beckford & Cooley, 1993; Peng, Wright, & Hill, 1995; Steele, 1992). As Cook and Evans (2000) inform us, "The divergence in reading [and math] scores appears due entirely to a worsening in the relative quality of schools located in poor, inner-city areas and in schools that are less than 20% white" (p. 747). In particular, analysts confirm that segregation "translates into disparities in educational resource allocation[s]" (Roscigno, 2000, p. 268) and the opportunities these resources afford, such as the chance to hire higher quality teachers (Roscigno, 1998). The logic here has been nicely laid out by Reardon (2003):

> School characteristics influence students' learning rates, and if minority students and students of lower-socioeconomic status are disproportionately concentrated in schools less equipped to promote learning, such students will fall behind their white and more advantaged counterparts as a direct result of features of their schools. (p. 6)

Here, as Rumberger and Palardy (2005) report, "The effects of social composition are indirect, operating through their association with resources and the organizational and structural features of schools" (p. 2007). One particular argument holds, "Concentrations of poverty reduce the effectiveness of teacher resources. The concentration of poverty within a school strains existing resources causing a displacement of teaching activities to other funds—such as discipline, maintaining order, and attention to home and family problems" (Myers, Kim, & Mandala, 2004, p. 83).

A second line of explanation for reduced achievement and the solidification of achievement gaps attends to the influence of peers, especially racial peers. It is argued, "Social composition matters in terms of student achievement [because of] the influence of peers" (Rumberger & Palardy, 2005, p. 2007). Inequity arises from the segregation itself (Gandara et al., 2003). Caldas and Bankston (1999) report:

The backgrounds for inputs that students bring to school, moreover, may raise or lower the quality of education by the mere concentration of the student peer group that has certain levels of preparation, standards of performance, or attitudes for learning in general—all of which are associated with family socioeconomic status. (p. 91)

We explored much of this line of analysis earlier when we examined school culture. We saw that in some cases African American youth respond to discrimination and inhospitable school environments in ways that promote disengagement from schooling and learning, and, "A poor opportunity structure may produce a range of responses that can have a negative impact on academic performance" (Miller, 1995, p. 210).

One message in the research is that peers can exercise considerable influence over many of the conditions that can promote or inhibit learning. Indeed, "Research has shown a significant association between academic failure among disadvantaged youth and the presence of antiacademic norms in their peer groups" (Becker & Luthar, 2002, p. 203). Research suggests that student achievement is directly impacted by the schools' racial and socioeconomic composition of schools directly affects student achievement. According to Rumberger and Palardy (2005):

[This occurs] through three peer mechanisms: "the influence of peers on learning through in-class and out-of-class interactions (e.g., cooperative work groups, study groups), the influence of peers on the motivation and aspirations of fellow students, and the influence of peers on the social behavior of other students. (p. 2007)

A second message is that in segregated schools, "It is often extremely difficult for black students to become members of peer groups that are supportive of academic achievement" (Miller, 1995, p. 210). The position underscored in the literature is that "in-group peers disparage [colleagues] who conform to those values, abilities, and behaviors that raise achievement" (Goldsmith, 2004, p. 124), that "peer pressure may cause students to scorn academic success" (Spradlin et al., 2005, p. 3), and that in highly segregated settings, these perspectives can dominate the school culture: "Influence is exacerbated in predominantly minority schools because in-group peers surround blacks" (Goldsmith, 2004, p. 124). Thus, "Few blacks profess [achievement-oriented] attitudes and optimism in minority-segregated schools" (p. 124). African Americans are "hurt by segregation because they are less likely than other students to be surrounded by peers who excel in schools" (Gandara et al., 2003, p. 34), or who view high achievement as a worthy goal. The larger theme has been portrayed by Bankston and Caldas (1996):

If students create the social environment of schools from the advantages or disadvantages they bring to educational institutions, it would seem to follow that minority concentration schools exercise a negative influence on students, beyond the influence of any student's own race. (p. 535)

The DNA in the above line of analysis is "aspirations," the formation of positive aspirations about learning and aspirations for a productive future. Schools, it is suggested, strongly influence aspirations. Indeed, such action might be the most important thing that schools do to promote success for disadvantaged youngsters. Concentrating children in schools where there is "lack of models of children who are achieving at high or even moderate levels" report Rumberger and Gandara (2004), "inhibits academic achievement" (p. 2049). Likewise, placing youngsters in schools where there are clusters of families whose aspirations for their children are not especially high has a dampening effect on the motivation and efficacy of children: "Other factors related strongly to achievement are the education background and aspirations of the students in the school" (Shannon & Bylsma, 2002, p. 20) and segregating African American and low-income families oftentimes helps foster an environment where students are not exposed to high aspirations, although at least on the racial front of the argument counter hypotheses have been surfaced (see Goldsmith, 2004). Thus, "The concentration of blacks from poor neighborhoods in segregated-minority schools may create a normative climate of low expectations" (Goldsmith, 2004, p. 124), i.e., aspirations.

Finally, and closely related to the issues of peers and aspirations, is the argument that separating low-income and African American children in schools hinders development of social capital (Coleman et al., 1966). In particular, such actions "limit access to important social networks" (Gandara et al., 2003, p. 34), networks that hold considerable power over educational opportunities and life chances of children.

CONCLUSION

In this chapter, we continued our analysis of causes of achievement gaps that reside inside schools. In the last chapter, we examined ways in which teaching and curriculum (the instructional program) exacerbate gaps. Here, we unpacked ways in which school culture, and the structures and support systems in schools (the school environment), amplify, or at least fail to reduce, patterned learning differentials by race and social class.

PART III

OPENING THE DOORS OF POSSIBILITY

Strategies for Closing Achievement Gaps

The hourglass long ago upended.

—Erik Larson

INTRODUCTION

The crux of the discussion on the achievement gap is to answer the question of what can be done to reduce and ultimately eliminate the achievement gap. (Shannon & Bylsma, 2002, p. 34)

Thus far researchers have been more effective at identifying a plethora of causes than recommending programs and policies to close the gap. (McGee, 2003, p. 9)

Improving student performance and narrowing racial gaps are not beyond the reach of public policy. (Ferguson, 1991, p. 29)

Closing the gap is a complex task that will require multiple, simultaneous, and long-term efforts that target school, home, community, and social factors. (Kober, 2001, p. 29)

In Part I (Chapters 1 and 2), we examined the form and the scope of achievement gaps in the United States. Part II attended to the causes of those gaps, exploring factors external to schooling (Chapters 3–7) and conditions under the control of the formal educational system (Chapters 8 and 9). While insights can be found in those chapters about actions that could help narrow achievement gaps, here we provide a much more explicit framework for overcoming deep-rooted learning differentials between children from lower- and higher-income families and between African American and white youngsters. Paralleling the structure of Part II, Chapter 10 is dedicated to strategies that tackle causes external to schooling, while Chapter 11 considers solutions that can be undertaken inside schools. Before we commence, however, we offer three general notes on the topic of solutions to achievement gaps—a word about the sense of possibilities, a note on the need for a commitment to a broad-based social and educational attack on the problem, and a reminder about the complexity of the work ahead. A rereading of the last section of Chapter 1, "Cautions for the Voyage," would be helpful at this point as well.

A Sense of Possibility

We begin with the message in the title to this part of the book, hope (Cook & Evans, 2000; Lee, 2006; Rouse, Brooks-Gunn, & McLanahan, 2005). Although there are studies that directly or indirectly suggest that little can be done to close gaps in performance between African American and white students (Cook & Evans, 2000), the bulk of the research confirms that "gaps in achievement levels can be narrowed" (Bainbridge & Lasley, 2002, p. 433), and "that these gaps are not immutable . . . that appropriately designed public policies can reduce educational disparities between black and white children" (U.S. Department of Education, 2001a, p. 42). Equally important, we know "that schools can and do affect test scores and the black-white test score gap" (Ferguson, 1998b, p. 368). As McGee (2003) reveals, on the schooling issue, "There are schools with a high percentage of low-income students and high percentages of minority children who have excellent records of achievement" (p. 7; see also Rumberger & Palardy, 2005). Further, "Research clearly points to some commonalities of what can and in some cases does close the achievement gap" (McGee, 2003, p. 18). Indeed, "The research and professional literature reveal many strategies for reducing and ultimately eliminating the achievement gap" (Shannon & Bylsma, 2002, p. 9). Thus, according to Barton (2003), "Gains in student achievement can most likely be realized wherever along the development continuum the effort is made" (p. 36).

Concomitantly, there is abundant evidence that the work here is not easy and that results are not guaranteed (Stiefel, Schwartz, & Ellen, 2006), "that closing the achievement gap between white children and children of color is much more difficult than many policy-makers anticipated" (Murnane & Levy, 2004, p. 412) and that "education theories and classroom practices to combat the continuing problem of the achievement gap . . . continue to elude educators" (Stinson, 2006, p. 498). At times even, "Because the roots of the problem are far-reaching and deep and the solutions require major efforts on many different fronts, closing the gap may seem like an insurmountable policy agenda" (Kober, 2001, p. 12; see also McGee, 2003).

Earlier, we reported that important research has been amassed in the service of understanding the causes of achievement gaps in the United States. At the same time, research about the path forward in closing gaps is considerably less abundant (Rothstein, 2006). For example, in their hallmark work in this area Jencks and Phillips (1998) discovered, "The available research raises as many questions as it answers" (p. 53). They explain that this is the case "partly because psychologists, sociologists, and educational researchers have devoted far less attention to the test score gap over the past quarter century than its political and social consequences warranted" (p. 53). Miller (1995) arrived at a parallel conclusion, holding, "Limitations of the knowledge base represent an important constraint on the educational progress that we can expect minorities to make in the short to medium term" (p. 341).

In addition, as outlined in Chapter 1, "Wise policy decisions require an understanding of both causal mechanisms *and* cost-effective interventions that produce desired changes" (Magnuson & Duncan, 2006, p. 387). Yet our sense of comfort in knowing what gap-reduction actions to follow is reduced by the knowledge that very little work has been undertaken to date to determine the benefits and costs of the various reform ideas (Miller, 1995; Rothstein, 2004). Finally, staying with the cost stream of analysis, there is considerable support for the claim that closing achievement gaps has been hampered by the reality (1) that many of the interventions that are needed are quite expensive (Bainbridge & Lasley, 2002; Rothstein, 2006)—"to overcome the huge resource gaps between minorities and majority, much more of society's resources must be committed to the educational and other needs of minorities than is now the case" (Miller, 1995, p. 341)—and (2) that society has either failed to "grasp the very large-scale and long-term dimensions of these challenges" (p. 380) or, less charitably, has been unwilling to pursue the more expensive solutions (Rothstein, 2004).

An Environmental and Educational Attack

There is considerable evidence that not only are the causes of the gap located in schools, in the larger social and economic environments, and in family context, but so too are the solutions (Alexander, Entwisle, & Olson, 2001; Grissmer et al., 1998; Hoerander & Lemke, 2006; Learning Points, 2004)—"All children can learn, but how much they learn depends on socioeconomic conditions as well as school effectiveness" (Rothstein, 2004, p. 82). That is, "Access to education-relevant forms of capital, combined with research-based educational interventions, may be necessary in closing the achievement gaps that exist between black, Hispanic, Native American, and low-income children and their European American, Asian American, and more economically advantaged peers" (Bennett et al., 2007, p. 266). To help eliminate patterned differences in student performance, it is necessary to both "reduce differences in socioeconomic status between blacks and whites [and] to con-sider educational policies that would make children's test scores less dependent on their parent's education and income" (Hedges & Nowell, 1998, p. 167): "Schools are not the only segments of society that can close the achievement gap. What happens at home and in com-munities is also critical" (Kober, 2001, p. 9). Or, as Miller (1995) captures the theme here, "The educational advancement of poor minority youngsters requires the aggressive use of a broad range of government policies to address their economic, social, health, and school-ing needs" (p. 342).

In short, the recommendation in this volume is consistent with the scholarship of Miller (1995), Rothstein (2004), and a host of other social scientists who have examined the gap issue deeply. The approach to the gap "should invest in several institutions, not simply the school" (Miller, 1995, p. 341).

A Reminder About the Complexity of the Task

So far, we have treated two issues in this introduction, the sense of hope, tempered with an understanding of the difficulty of the assignment, and an acknowledgment that the solution pathway needs to feature actions aimed at schools and at the larger environment in which schools are nested. We close with a few notes that, in conjunction with those that we surfaced in Chapter 1, help illuminate the work that must be engaged to close gaps in student performance, some additional guiding principles if you will.

Perhaps most important, since "basing the response on an analysis of the reason for a lack of progress is more likely to result in improvement than automatic sanctions not tailored to the source of the low achievement . . . the choice of response should depend on the source of the problem" (Murnane & Levy, 2004, p. 410). Or, as Fryer and Levitt (2004) assert, since the list of potential solution steps is nearly unlimited (Miller, 1995), "The appropriate public policy choice (if any) to address the test score gap depends critically on the underlying source of the gap" (Fryer & Levitt, 2004, p. 447).

A number of analysts maintain that reform activities on the margins of the problem are unlikely to be of much assistance; they call instead for bold and large-scale action (Kober, 2001; Miller, 1995). These same reviewers hold that since the gap problem is so complex (Braun et al., 2006; U.S. Commission, 2004) and the factors causing it so numerous (U.S. Commission, 2004) that single-strategy designs will be ineffectual (Braun et al., 2006), that "there need[s] to be efforts on several fronts simultaneously" (North Carolina, 2000, p. 11); "a combination of approaches" (Miller, 1995, p. 342) is required. There is no silver bullet or any "dramatic 'breakthrough' intervention" (Thompson & O'Quinn, 2001, p. 5); a series of actions is needed to gain purchase on gap problems in the United States. "A complex combination of conditions for success is required" (McGee, 2003, p. 65), and a comprehensive approach is necessary (Becker & Luther, 2002; Shannon & Bylsma, 2002).

Scholars of the gap also provide insight into the ingredients of the reform cocktail. While there is some difference of thinking here, the collective scientific wisdom is that some improvement strategies should focus specifically on the needs of African American and low-income children, while others should attend to conditions of learning more generally (Ferguson, 1991; Miller, 1995). As we discussed above, there is also consensus that "neither in-school nor out-of-school factors can be tackled in isolation" (Reynolds, 2002, p. 11). These same scholars confirm that a "linear approach may not be the best strategy" (Singham, 2003, p. 587) for addressing racial and income-based learning differentials, that a simultaneous attack on multiple fronts will be more effective: "To successfully close the achievement gap, action on several fronts must occur simultaneously. Some changes necessary to eliminate the achievement gap need to be made at the broader system level; others need to be made by individuals, schools, and communities" (Shannon & Bylsma, 2002, p. 48). They assert that a long-term focus is generally needed (Gamoran, 2000; Kober, 2001; Miller, 1995).

Finally, analysts inform us that these multiple and simultaneous efforts, over time, need to be integrated or coordinated if they are to garner maximum leverage on narrowing achievement gaps (Peng, Wright, & Hill, 1995; Shannon & Bylsma, 2002). As expressed by Reynolds (2002), "Just as the causes of achievement gaps are interrelated, so must be the attempts to close them" (p. 15). One particularly useful type of integration is what Miller (1995) calls "institutional complementarity" (p. 342), both within-institution complementarity (e.g., within the school) and between institution complementarity (e.g., between the school and community agencies). A second coordinating mechanism is "institutional redundancy" (p. 342), that is, the development of backup systems that provide duplicate capacity.

10

Closing Achievement Gaps

Focusing on the Social and Economic Environment

Clearly, the achievement gap is not only a school and classroom issue, but a societal issue that must be addressed by a broad array of stakeholders that extends beyond educators, state officials, and policymakers. (Spradlin et al., 2005, p. 24)

More effective use of available school resources alone cannot be expected to close more than a fraction of the academic achievement gap between advantaged and disadvantaged students. If the nation is to accelerate the educational advancement of minorities more resources will be required. And since much of the educational resource gap between advantaged and disadvantaged students is located outside the school, one must look carefully at where and how these additional investments should be made in minority youngsters. (Miller, 1995, p. 336)

We can make big strides in narrowing the student achievement gap, but only by directing greater attention to economic and social reforms that narrow the differences in background characteristics with which children come to school. (Rothstein, 2004, p. 131)

And denying the role of these outside happenings—or the impact of a student's home circumstances—will not help to endow teachers and schools with the capacity to reduce achievement gaps. Also, insistence that it can all be done in the school may be taken to provide excuses for public policy, ignoring what is necessary to prevent learning gaps from opening. Schools are where we institutionalize learning; they are also places where we tend to institutionalize blame. (Barton, 2003, p. 36)

In Chapters 3–7, we documented that much of the achievement gap that we find in schools in the United States can be connected to larger social and economic conditions in society, and also to the family environment in which children are reared. Therefore, it should come as no surprise to discover that conquering the achievement gap problem will require a connected attack on the inequities found in these forces external to schools.

The starting point here is that school-based efforts alone are unlikely to be sufficient to close gaps (Downey, von Hippel, & Broh, 2004; Hedges & Nowell, 1999; Payne & Biddle, 1999). Then, because "school reform alone is unlikely to eliminate the gap" (Braun et al., 2006, p. 9), we need "more than school-based solutions" (Bali & Alvarez, 2003, p. 486). More specifically, Miller (1995) argues, "Good educational practices applied within the confines of existing . . . family resource variations are not sufficient to produce the needed improvement in minority student achievement" (p. 305). While more effective school practices can help reduce the gap, "School reform . . . is not enough" (Rothstein, 2004, p. 9): "Educators and educational reformers who focus on systematic reform or teacher quality without giving attention to social-environmental factors will continue to be frustrated by more failure than success" (Bainbridge & Lasley, 2002, p. 430). In short, there is a "limit to how much inequality in student outcomes can be eliminated through school reforms versus social policies that address inequalities in student and family circumstances that affect student learning" (Rumberger & Palardy, 2004, p. 2012) and, as Stiefel and associates (2006) conclude, "Meaningful reductions [in achievement gaps] ultimately call for strategies that are beyond the scope of schools and school policies" (p. 27). Miller (1995) identifies school capacities more specifically, stating:

Another major issue is how much of the variation in resources among racial/ethnic groups can be addressed directly through the schools. Although the school can be a vehicle for investing several types of education-relevant resources in children, it has been designed to provide particular kinds of human capital. Schools are staffed by professional educators who are expected to provide instructional services. Ordinarily teachers can also provide a modest amount of social capital to most students, but the number of children with whom they can develop relatively close relationships is usually limited. Schools can also provide some health services, although few currently have the ability to meet more than a fraction of the health needs of students. Similarly, schools have an extremely limited capacity to provide financial capital to students. (p. 94)

If school action alone is unlikely to carry the day, then what is called for is direct action on the environmental factors linked to student learning and to the formation of achievement gaps by race and social class (Kober, 2001), that "home factors and wider societal issues also must be addressed" (Williams, 2003, p. 6), "that eliminating environmental influences between black and white families could go a long way toward eliminating the test score gap" (Phillips et al.,

1998a, p. 38), and that "eliminating the social class differences in student outcomes requires eliminating the impact of social class in American society" (Rothstein, 2004, p. 149).

The story line here is the attack on the structure of inequality, for here is, as Wilson (1998) informs us, the most productive pathway to "drastically reduce and eventually eliminate environmental differences that create the present gap in black and white achievement" (p. 510). More specifically, Rumberger and Palardy (2005) help us see that the key issue in this structure of inequity is to "address the pervasive inequalities in family and community resources" (p. 2033; see also Miller, 1995). The conclusion to the narrative is that we need to reweave the political tapestry and the policy fabric in the United States (Jencks et al., 1972). "Policies aimed at preventing either economic deprivation itself or its effects" (Duncan & Brooks-Gunn, 2000, p. 194) provide the path forward at the societal level for attacking the gap problem, as described by Miller (1995):

> *The differences in academic achievement patterns between high- and low-SES children are due in large measure to the fact that the differences in education-relevant family resources between these groups are too large for schools to overcome under existing arrangements. Until the nation can find a way to increase markedly the education-relevant family resources available to low-SES children, similar educational results are unlikely to be produced for high- and low-SES youngsters. (p. 337)*

In the balance of this chapter, we investigate policy solutions to the structure of inequality in the larger society in which the educational enterprise is located. We explore policies in the two areas suggested by Duncan and Brooks-Gunn (2000) above: improving the economic conditions of the poor directly (income-transfer strategies) and compensating for the conditions of poverty (service-delivery strategies)—"raising families out of poverty and providing the care and experiences presumed to be missing in the lives of poor children" (Hertert & Teague, 2003, p. 10). We begin with a caveat and a comment on the potential for success.

First, the caveat: because "from a public policy perspective it is more difficult to improve student achievement through student background factors than by influencing school policies" (Bali & Alvarez, 2003, p. 487) and "because government has more control over schooling than over home environment, public policy has emphasized the former" (Entwisle, Alexander, & Olson, 2000, p. 9). That is, policy strategies in the area of the achievement gap have been directed almost exclusively at schools (Rothstein, 2004). Equally noteworthy, the moral commitment to address achievement gaps by influencing public policy outside the school sector has been lacking (Hall, 2001; Jencks et al., 1972; Payne & Biddle, 1999; Wilson, 1998). To date, the implications of the narrative presented throughout this volume about the essential location of socioeconomic and family factors in the gap-closure algorithm have been too readily overlooked. Inadequate effort and insufficient resources have been directed to a comprehensive attack on the problem (Rothstein, 2004).

And now, to the sense of hope: although, as discussed above, environmentally grounded solutions will be costly and a good deal of work needs to be done to assess these costs vis-à-vis the benefits (Duncan & Brooks-Gunn, 2001; Rothstein, 2004), Miller (1995) reminds us:

> *What a negative opportunity structure has wrought, a positive opportunity structure can undo. These problems did not develop in a day and will not disappear overnight.*

But real change can occur if the larger society chooses to provide genuine economic and educational opportunity . . . on a sustained basis. (p. 280)

IMPROVING THE ECONOMIC AND SOCIAL CONDITIONS OF LOW-INCOME FAMILIES

If poor children suffer real disadvantages in life that depress their chances in education, the obvious way to help them out is to reduce the rate of childhood poverty. (Biddle, 2001, p. 15)

The best way to reduce the gap in educational performance is to implement policies that reduce economic inequality. (Ainsworth-Darnell & Downey, 1998, p. 551)

To moderate the achievement gap, the most compelling need is to reduce family and youth poverty. (Alexander, Entwisle, & Olson, 2001, p. 176)

By increasing significantly direct financial support for families with children, with emphasis on the poor, the nation can expand the effectiveness range of working-poor families and support greater intergenerational educational advancement. (Miller, 1995, p. 347)

As we stated above, the focus here is on policies designed to reduce poverty. For, as we have consistently argued, because "the gap in achievement can probably not be narrowed substantially as long as the United States maintains vast differences in socioeconomic conditions" (Rothstein, 2004, p. 129), "a policy of reducing social-class differences may be needed to reduce differences in test scores" (Hedges & Nowell, 1999, p. 131). And, as Rothstein (2004) affirms, there are a variety of public policies that can be engaged to "narrow racial and economic gaps between lower- and middle-class children" (p. 9).

Earlier in this book, we allocated considerable space to examining poverty in the United States. We will not repeat that analysis here. Rather, we simply reinforce the central themes from that narrative. First, poverty in the United States is a huge problem (Payne & Biddle, 1999), especially child poverty (Biddle, 1997): "The child poverty rate in America is not only much higher than the rate among the elderly, but also higher than the rate among children in most other industrialized nations" (Miller, 1995, p. 345). Second, the changing structure of the U.S. economy is exacerbating rather than reducing poverty: "Thus, the last few decades have seen a widening income gap between those in the bottom and those in the middle" (Rothstein, 2004, p. 133). Third, initiatives to date to reduce poverty among children have been inadequate at best (Miller, 1995). All of this, of course, bodes ill for efforts to overcome achievement gaps between lower- and higher-income families.

At the same time, scholars have also provided support for income-enhancement policies in the service of narrowing achievement gaps, although the storyline is less than crystal clear (Duncan & Brooks-Gunn, 2000; Duncan & Magnuson, 2005; Phillips et al., 1997; Rouse, Brooks-Gunn, & McLanahan, 2005). Duncan and Magnuson (2005) conclude, "For young children, family income gains of roughly $1000 per year translate into achievement gains of about 0.07 standard deviations" (p. 40). They assert, therefore, "Reducing the racial and ethnic differences in family income by several thousand dollars would reduce achievement gaps" (p. 47). Kober (2001) and Grissmer and colleagues (reviewed in Berends et al., 2005) connect the War on Poverty programs of the 1960s and 1970s with reductions in the achievement gap between African American and white youngsters. Likewise, based on his analysis, Rothstein (2006) maintains that a wage increase for low-income families "could well have an impact on student performance comparable to that of within school educational reforms" (p. 2). He counsels, "Doing something about the wide income gap between lower- and middle-class parents could be one of the most important educational reforms we could consider" (Rothstein, 2004, p. 133).

These analysts also furnish useful insights about the appropriate focus of income-enhancement policy initiatives. They remind us that the cardinal rule is, "Priority should be given to policies that expand the family resources available to poor youngsters" (Miller, 1995, p. 343). Miller also cautions, "Only if this is done can the nation expect increases in school resources to pay large dividends" (p. 343). Scholars conclude that targeting "families fac[ing] deep and persistent poverty" (Duncan & Magnuson, 2005, p. 401) makes considerable sense, and children in these families "would gain the most from added income" (p. 40). They also counsel that policies aimed at avoiding the harmful consequences of poverty in early childhood are preferable (Hall, 2001; Magnuson & Duncan, 2006). Collectively, "[The] research on the impact of poverty on children suggests that avoiding the adverse consequences of deep poverty in early childhood is key for the healthy cognitive development of children" (Duncan & Brooks-Gunn, 2000, p. 65).

Finally, scholars who promulgate ideas about how to improve the economic conditions of the poor illuminate a variety of policy strategies that can be put into action to create more racially balanced social classes, to enhance student performance, and to narrow achievement gaps. We cluster these policy strategies into four categories: welfare, job training, taxes, and employment. In the first domain, Grissmer (1998) underscores the importance of "expanded welfare programs for poor families" (p. 183). Duncan and Brooks-Gunn (2001) assert that an obvious recommendation is to "exempt families with young children from the adverse effects of [welfare] time limits, sanctions, and categorical restrictions" (p. 68). And Miller (1995) maintains that policies directly increasing financial capital to poor families will help offset economic inequalities and provide purchase on reducing learning differentials by race and social class.

Job training is a second policy domain that can be leveraged to improve the economic and social conditions of low-income families (Duncan & Magnuson, 2005; Hertert & Teague, 2003). According to Duncan and Brooks-Gunn (2001), policy actions here work "to liberate long-term recipients from welfare" (p. 69) by providing participants with the skills needed to break into the job market and "to move into higher skilled positions" (Brooks-Gunn, Klebanov, & Duncan, 1996, p. 405)—and out of poverty. While to date, policy interventions to provide "access to favorable labor markets" (Miller, 1995, p. 115) have not proven as effective as envisioned (Duncan & Magnuson, 2005; Magnuson & Duncan, 2006), reformers remain guardedly optimistic that policy tools here can advantage low-income families and enhance the academic performance of youngsters in those families.

A third set of interventions for helping move families out of poverty reside in the tax-structure toolbox. One approach here is to "eliminate the tax burden on low-income families" (Hertert & Teague, 2003, p. 3). Another is "to change the tax structure to narrow the gap between wealth and poverty" (p. 3). Policy can be enacted to establish a high-tax threshold.

Another tool is to offer generous income-tax credits for low-income families (Magnuson & Duncan, 2006; Rothstein, 2004), to augment the resources of poor working families via the earned income tax credit (Duncan & Magnuson, 2005).

Lastly, employment policies open another avenue of attack on the economic disadvantages confronting many low-income families, and African American families in particular (Miller, 1995). A policy commitment to low unemployment would, according to Rothstein (2004), be "particularly helpful to low-income families and minorities" (p. 134). In addition, more aggressive action in the area of minimum-wage law would be helpful in offsetting the impact of poverty (Brooks-Gunn et al., 1996; Hertert & Teague, 2003). Rothstein (2004), in particular, counsels that "an increase in the minimum wage could well have an impact on student performance" (p. 134) equal to the effect of school-based reforms. In a related vein, Rothstein (2004) also holds that low-income wage earners would benefit from policies that make it easier for them to participate in collective bargaining. And, of course, any policies that help generate more high-paying, low-skill jobs would disproportionately advantage low-income families and the children in those families (Miller, 1995).

COMPENSATING FOR THE CONDITIONS OF POVERTY AND DISCRIMINATION

> *It is important to recognize, moreover, that it has not been possible for governments to meet all the needs of poor families for living productive lives simply through financial transfer programs. Investments in such key institutions as the health care and education system have also been crucial. (Miller, 1995, p. 343)*

> *If the goal is promote the healthy development of children, it is important to go beyond cash transfers and consider service delivery programs such as those providing nutrition supplements and education; medical care; early childhood education; and housing. (Duncan & Brooks-Gunn, 2000, p. 193)*

> *Going beyond SES interventions, child and parenting interventions may prove to be the most cost-effective ways of addressing disparities in achievement. (Magnuson & Duncan, 2006, p. 393)*

> *Two types of programs seem most promising—those that help parents learn the behaviors that promote child development and school readiness and those that directly teach poor and low-income children school readiness skills, both intellectual and behavioral. (Haskins & Rouse, 2005, p. 2)*

In addition to direct efforts to strengthen the economic foundations of low-income families, polices can also address achievement gaps by working to offset the impact of poverty and discrimination (Karoly et al., 1998). While the earlier discussion featured income transfer as the engine of equalization, here the spotlight is on service delivery; the provision of "tax supported services" (Payne & Biddle, 1999, p. 7) is highlighted. The theory of action here, as Neuman and Celano (2006) explain, is that policies for low-income children and their families are expected "to compensate for the material resources that are lacking in economically disadvantaged neighborhoods and homes" (pp. 180–181), "that approaches that directly address child and parental behaviors that contribute to school readiness will prove more effective than programs that . . . increase the socioeconomic state of families" (Rouse et al., 2005, p. 11).

The most essential of these service-delivery domains, in terms of addressing learning differentials by race and social class, are programs to assist parents with young children; preschool services; extended schooling opportunities, including summer school programs; and health and welfare services (e.g., housing, transportation). And, as Hertert and Teague (2003) remind us, we have abundant research on the effectiveness of actions in these service-delivery domains, although data on the cost effectiveness of many of these programs and information on the best ways to bundle them are less available (Miller, 1995). Next, we examine each of these four areas. We want to be clear from the start, however, that it is not our intention to provide a comprehensive review of the research in each domain. Rather, our objective is to illuminate key policy interventions that have promise for closing achievement gaps between more-advantaged and less-advantaged youngsters.

Parenting Programs

Changing the way parents deal with their children may be the single most important thing we can do to improve children's cognitive skills. (Jencks & Phillips, 1998, p. 53)

The literature on home influences in African American families suggests that that the importance of parental educational socialization practices—both cognitive and academic—cannot be overstated. (Bempechat, 1992, p. 45)

Parenting programs, if implemented, could reduce the racial gap in school readiness. (Brooks-Gunn & Magnuson, 2005, p. 154)

Educational programs for parents and preschool education programs for children have potential to narrow these disparities by at least half. (Haskins & Rouse, 2005, p. 1)

In Chapter 4, we explored, in considerable detail, the critical role of parents in the educational-attainment equation of children. We confirmed, "Parents are their child's first and most important teachers. The public, policymakers, and research all point to the quality—or competence and confidence—of parenting as the single most important determinant of healthy growth and development" (Child and Family Policy Center, 2005, p. 7). We also documented that patterns of parenting are linked to achievement gaps. Here, we review the other side of the ledger. We examine policies that can encourage parenting practices associated with more productive academic and social development of youngsters. The overarching goal is to increase access to parenting programs for low-income families (Miller, 1995). The more immediate aim, as Spradlin and colleagues (2005) so nicely frame it, is "to ensure that [these] parents acquire the knowledge, skills, and resources needed to be successful as their child's first teacher" (p. 24).

There are two broad categories of reform action here: efforts to enhance the formal education of parents, especially mothers, and programs to improve parental provision of learning experiences to children (Brooks-Gunn & Markman, 2005; Brooks-Gunn et al., 1995). The first dimension is more indirect, operating under the assumption that additional education will equip parents with a larger stock of effective parenting practices that, in turn, will positively impact student academic achievement. The second dimension is more direct, operating primarily to develop more productive parenting practices (Karoly et al., 1998).

We have woven the discussion of policies to promote parental education throughout this chapter. Here we only wish to make three integrative comments. First, as Magnuson and Duncan (2006) affirm, "It is critical to identify policies to improve mothers' educational attainment" (p. 388). Second, increasing the level of formal education for low-income parents can make a dent in achievement gaps (Cook & Evans, 2000; Duncan & Magnuson, 2005). For example, Rouse and associates (2005) maintain, "Increasing the schooling of all black mothers by one or two years . . . would significantly narrow the school readiness gap of their children" (p. 11). In particular, Duncan and Magnuson (2005) reveal, "Interventions that increase rates of high school completion may have a large payoff for future generations" (p. 42). They explain further:

> *With the achievement gain between whites and blacks at one half to three quarters of a standard deviation, a policy that could increase maternal schooling for all black mothers by an average of one or two years, without also changing the schooling of white mothers, would go a long way toward eliminating the achievement gaps. (p. 387)*

Third, policy actions to date have not been especially effective in reaching the goal of increased formal education for the parents of at-risk students, nor older at-risk students themselves (Duncan & Magnuson, 2005; Rouse et al., 2005). Thus, we need fresh perspectives about how to craft more productive policies to extend formal education for low-income youngsters and their parents (Magnuson & Duncan, 2006).

The second "intervention approach [here] is to promote educational activities among parents" (Duncan & Magnuson, 2005, p. 42), to tackle the task of helping parents improve their parenting skills directly (Hertert & Teague, 2003) and to assist them to become more involved in the education of their children (Magnuson et al., 2004). Duncan and Brooks-Gunn (2001) capture the logic-in-action here as follows: "Since about one-half of the effect of family income on tests of cognitive ability is mediated by the home environment, including learning experiences in the home, interventions might profitably focus on working with parents" (p. 69). Schwartz (2001) and Williamson (2005) provide us with frameworks for addressing the assignment. They highlight the following goals of parenting programs: "to help families learn how to make a concrete commitment to their children's success while they are still very young, to teach families to promote a child's cognitive and social development through creation of homes as learning environments, and to encourage families to take advantage of school and community resources that support achievement" (Williamson, 2005, p. 36). Of special importance here is helping parents "learn how to organize their homes around learning, and, in particular, how to engage children to better meet the demands of the school" (Bempechat, 1992, p. 45), themes we dissected in some detail in Chapter 4. Another important insight in this area flows from the research of Newman and Celano (2006) on neighborhood effects on gap closures. These analysts reinforce the position that while providing resource to families to strengthen the learning of children is important, it is the ways that parents mediate those resources that is critical. Policy in the area of parenting programs needs to be somewhat prescriptive about how parents should orchestrate, guide, and direct their children's learning.

Scholars in this area also disclose the three policy pathways that have been employed to strengthen parental teaching skills. First, they report that policy can be used to establish communication channels through which information about strategies to help children learn at home can be broadcast (Kober, 2001). As we will see in Chapter 12, schools can make a significant contribution here. Second, home-visiting programs can be crafted to teach adults effective parenting skills. While these programs have not proven especially efficacious to date (Brooks-Gunn, Klebanov, & Duncan, 1996; Brooks-Gunn & Markman, 2005; Child and Family Policy Center, 2005; Haskins & Rouse, 2005), and suffer from insufficient intensity and lacking in well-trained supervisors (Brooks-Gunn & Markman, 2005), there is reason to believe that they can be strengthened and thus be made more productive "if the programs are linked to other supports, truly build relationships with the families they serve, and are staffed by trained and competent and passionate workers" (Child and Family Policy Center, 2005, p. 7). Third, parenting programs can be integrated into prekindergarten and other center-based programs for children (Brooks-Gunn & Markman, 2005). These programs, in addition to directly focusing on students, "target the parent for intervention to improve outcomes for the child" (Karoly, Kilburn, & Cannon, 2005, p. 23).

What does research convey about parenting programs and the achievement gap? To begin with, they are more effective in meeting the goal of reducing gaps when structured to disproportionately serve minority, low-income, young, and single parents (Brooks-Gunn & Markman, 2005). When they do, as was the case with providing more formal education, there is evidence that these programs can help in the attack on the gap problem, "They can produce some of the greatest gains for children" (Child and Family Policy Center, 2005, p. 7). The logic is as follows: We know that there are parenting-related factors that can impact student learning (Duncan & Brooks-Gunn, 2001; Haskins & Rouse, 2005; Miller, 1995): "Families are America's smallest schools" (Barton, 2003, p. 36). Those "linked with school readiness are lower for black mothers than for white mothers" (Brooks-Gunn & Markman, 2005, p. 157; see also Haskins & Rouse, 2005). Interventions to assist African American and low-income parents to develop those parenting skills can work (Brooks-Gunn & Markman, 2005). And, when they do, they improve the achievement of youngsters in these targeted families and reduce gaps in performance.

Finally, policy makers and educational leaders need to attend to the elements that explain the effectiveness of these programs. As stated by the Child and Family Policy Center (2005):

> Different researchers have provided different "take away" messages from the existing research, but it is clear that effective programs require skilled workers who can establish relationships with families, connect families to sources of support, and offer modeling and guidance that enables families to strengthen their parenting capacities. (p. 7)

Preschool

> Efforts to remove disparities cannot wait until high school and, we would argue, cannot even wait until kindergarten. (Davidson et al., 2004, p. 761)

> It seems quite obvious that a major way to reduce social inequalities in children's cognitive status (and social competence) as they begin kindergarten is through

*disadvantaged children's participation in well-designed preschool preparation pro-
grams with at least some academic content. (Lee & Burkam, 2002, p. 82)*

*The most dramatic way to address those justice issues is to ensure quality preschool
programming in high-poverty areas. (Bainbridge & Lasley, 2002, p.430)*

*From a high achievement perspective, the evidence suggests that our society should be
rapidly expanding access to high-quality preschool for all underrepresented minority
children. (Miller, 1999, p. 20)*

Setting the Stage

Over the last forty years, considerable conceptual, moral, and empirical support has been
mustered about the hallmark place of quality preschool programs in the struggle to improve
the life chances of low-income children and minority youngsters. More recently, the seminal
role of preschool programs in reducing racial and social-class achievement gaps has moved
onto the center stage of school reform. The embedded logic runs as follows. First, by kindergarten, low-income and African American youngsters "are on average already far behind their
more advantaged peers in reading and math readiness" (Haskins & Rouse, 2005, p. 1; see also
Phillips et al., 1998a). Indeed, as Rothstein (2004) confirms, "The achievement gap is already
huge at three years of age" (p. 10). By kindergarten, disadvantaged students, on average, are
"one year behind their middle-class peers in reading and vocabulary" (Spradlin et al., 2005,
p. 3). Second, the longer discrepancies exist the more difficult they are to close (Beckford &
Cooley, 1993; Natriello, McDill, & Pallas, 1990). For example, Neuman and Celano (2006) confirm that even "small early deficits in intellectual capital can build into extraordinary gaps
after just a few years of schooling" (p. 198). Third, youngsters will be able to "take best advantage of [future] educational opportunities only if they have been prepared in their earlier
years" (Child and Family Policy Center, 2005, p. 9). According to Bainbridge and Lasley (2002),
it is imperative, therefore, that children be equipped at the start of school with the intellectual
capital required for school success. Or, as Rothstein (2004) frames up the position, "Low-
income and minority children can benefit fully from good schools only if they enter these
schools ready to learn" (p. 139). Fourth, organized preschool programs are an essential element in providing students with that needed intellectual capital (Fuchs & Reklis, 1994;
Chatterji, 2006; Spradlin et al., 2005): "State and federal governments should invest in developing early childhood programs to assist more minority students to start schooling at an
early age" (Beckford & Cooley, 1993, p. 13)—"the most important focus of investment should
probably be on early childhood programs" (Rothstein, 2004, p. 10), funds should "be targeted
to promote the enrollment of racial and minority children in center care or preschool"
(Magnuson & Waldfogel, 2005, p. 182).

While we explore the impact of these programs a bit later, it is important to note that the
reasoning outlined above, especially the final link in the chain, draws support from scholarship that finds that the provision of quality preschool programs can positively influence the
intellectual development of low-income and African American children (Child and Family
Policy Center, 2005; Haskins & Rouse, 2005; Thompson & O'Quinn, 2005). For example, based
on their research, Magnuson and Waldfogel (2005) maintain, "Initiatives that substantially
raise both enrollment in and the quality of center care for low-income children could narrow

racial and ethnic school readiness gaps considerably, reducing black-white gaps by up to 24 percent" (p. 187). And, according to Rouse and associates (2005), "The best research confirms that high-quality early childhood programs make great headway in closing racial gaps in school readiness" (pp. 12–13).

The central point here, as Myers, Kim, and Mandala (2004) reveal, is that these early childhood programs help offset the damaging effects of poverty, and expanding the supply of preschool opportunities for African American students can have a powerful and positive impact on the achievement gap between them and their white peers. In the way of summary here, Miller (1995) informs us, "Three decades of research have established that high-quality preschool programs for disadvantaged three- and four-year olds increase their preparedness for elementary school and are associated with long-term improvements in their academic and social success" (p. 353): "Students in these early childhood programs have increased cognitive performance during early childhood, higher high school graduation rates and higher enrollment in post secondary programs than children who do not participate in these programs" (Beckford & Cooley, 1993, pp. 11–12).

The logic train, especially the final leg of the argument, also draws power from analyses that portray work on preschool to date as inadequate (Lee & Burkam, 2002). While the preschool idea has received considerable attention over the last four decades and there has been some enthusiasm in the policy world for devoting additional resources to preschool programs (Currie & Thomas, 1995; Hallinan, 2001; Karoly, Kilburn, & Cannon, 2005), if the first key "to using preschool programs to reduce the achievement gap is to enroll all children from low-income families in a preschool program," as Haskins and Rouse (2005, pp. 4–5) suggest, then the flow of energy can best be characterized as limited and insufficient (Haskins & Rouse, 2005; Rothstein, 2005), or, in the words of the Child and Family Center (2005), there is a significant "investment gap" (p. 1) here. For example, research reveals, "For every $1.00 invested in a school-aged child, 52.1 cents is invested in a college-aged youth, but only 21.3 cents is invested in a pre-school aged child and 8.9 cents in an infant or toddler" (p. 1). More specifically, researchers document, "High-quality early childhood programs reach only a small portion of low-income children" (Rouse et al., 2005, pp. 12–13). Magnuson and Waldfogel (as cited in Haskins & Rouse, 2005) document that more than 800,000 low-income four-year-olds are not enrolled in center-based education programs (p. 5). Miller (1995) reports that in the early 1990s, Head Start only had funding sufficient to serve 30 percent of eligible youngsters (p. 353). While by 2002, that number had risen to 65 percent of eligible three- and four-year-olds (Magnuson & Waldfogel, 2005, p. 171), one in three youngsters is still not being served. And, what is true for low-income and minority students applies to children in single-parent families as well (Spradlin et al., 2005).

Quality Elements

What is abundantly clear in the research on preschool, and its impact on school readiness and more delayed measures of performance for low-income and African American children, is that program quality is key. The magnitude of the effect of preschool depends not only on the number of children affected but on "how much quality is improved" (Magnuson & Waldfogel, 2005, p. 183): "Comparing racial enrollments tells only part of the story. Other important pieces of evidence are the time spent in preschool and the quality of the program attended" (p. 181). In total then, "Early interventions to keep the achievement gap from opening wide in the first place should be a high priority; and the earlier the better, with the kinds of preschool compensatory education initiatives that have proven effective" (Alexander et al., 2001, p. 176).

While this is not the appropriate venue to compile a compendium of the elements of high-quality preschool programs, it is important to provide a brief description of those elements as they surface in discussions centered on achievement gaps. We also remind the reader of Ronald Ferguson's (1991) and Richard Rothstein's (2004) cogent caveats here: In general, African American and low-income children do not require something different in the nature of education; what they need is more of the ingredients found in high-quality programs for more advantaged youngsters. That is, "Lower-class children's preschool experiences should provide an intellectual environment comparable to what middle-class children experience" (Rothstein, 2004, pp. 139–140).

To begin with, the weight of the evidence suggests that what is required here is not universal preschool but a more targeted focus, more preschool opportunities for low-income youngsters (Karoly et al., 1998; Magnuson et al., 2004). That is, "Only preschool programs directed exclusively at poor children will help close the gap" (Entwisle et al., 2000, p. 26). Alternatively, from Magnuson and Waldfogel (2005), "Initiatives to boost preschool enrollment without regard to racial or ethnic background [will] be less effective at closing racial and ethnic school readiness gaps than more targeted initiatives" (pp. 183–184). The goal here, then, as explained by Rouse and colleagues (2005), "is to increase access to high-quality center-based early childhood education for all low-income three- and four-year olds" (p. 12). Such a step, they hold, will go far in reducing achievement gaps as students enter kindergarten. Absent the will to focus (limit) resources in this way, a more universal system can be created with a design "so that the types and amounts of services can be varied to meet the needs of different population segments" (Miller, 1995, p. 35).

On the topic of program type, one form seems more important than others: center-based care (Lee & Burkam, 2002). Relatedly, there is evidence to suggest that venue can be important. Specifically, placing preschool programs for low-income youngsters in public schools is a wise strategy (Magnuson et al., 2004). This is the case because programs located in regular schools are often richer in terms of the other quality elements of preschools that we examine next (Magnuson & Waldfogel, 2005).

In terms of structure, studies disclose that structured formats are more effective in closing gaps than are less formal designs (Davidson et al., 2004). Intensity also matters (Neuman & Celano, 2006). High-intensity programs start early (Rothstein, 2004), much earlier than many programs that have proven ineffective (Spradlin et al., 2005). They also operate for longer periods of time, ideally year-round (Rothstein, 2004). They offer full-day care (Magnuson & Waldfogel, 2005), especially for three- and four-year-olds. They are "resource intensive" (Miller, 1999, p. 20) as well. They have more money to achieve goals than what is found in the typical program (Miller, 1995), including resources for transportation (Thompson, 2002).

Finally, preschools are most effective in narrowing learning gaps when they carefully coordinate their activities with the kindergarten program in the public school (Haskins & Rouse, 2005; Rouse et al., 2005). That is, "to bring young children to school ready to learn" (Davidson et al., 2004, p. 759), preschools must display "a determination to align early childhood programs with the goals of K–12 education" (p. 759). On the coordination front, Davidson and associates (2004) affirm that in addition to organizational overlap, common leadership is a desirable element. So too is tight curriculum alignment between the preschool and the kindergarten (Lewis & Palk, 2001).

In terms of educational components, "[The] content focus of early childhood programs is crucial" (Thompson, 2002, p. 10). Insights about appropriate content focus are ribboned throughout the research. First and foremost is an explicit focus on cognitive development (Flanagan & Grissmer, 2002; Jencks & Phillips, 1998; Schwartz, 2001), especially in building cognitive skills in literacy and numeracy (Slavin & Madden, 2006). Emphasis is also crucial. Preschool "programs that [make] a deliberate effort to familiarize children with letters, sound-letter correspondence, numbers, and other content important to success in the early grades [give] at-risk children an advantage when they start school" (Thompson & O'Quinn, 2001, p. 8).

Quality preschool programs that advantage low-income youngsters are defined by the presence of professional staff, personnel often absent in many child-care activities (Magnuson & Waldfogel, 2005) where "typical staff for lower-class children are poorly paid and often have educations that are no greater than the children's parents" (Rothstein, 2006, p. 5). Staff in high-quality programs, on the other hand, have at least "bachelor degrees and training in early childhood education" (Rouse et al., 2005, p. 12). Quality programs also have more staff than is the norm; i.e., they have lower child-staff ratios (Child and Family Policy Center, 2005; Rothstein, 2004; Thompson, 2002).

In addition, quality preschool programs for low-income students generally incorporate a component that attends to the role of parents in the education process (Sanders, Allen-Jones, & Abel, 2002). They include a "parent-training component" (Rouse et al., 2005, p. 12). This is important because there is evidence that center-based programs with parenting activities appear more successful at closing readiness gaps than programs without them (Brooks-Gunn & Markman, 2005): "There is widespread agreement that high-quality programs that emphasize . . . parent involvement can reduce the achievement gap" (Haskins & Rouse, 2005, p. 4).

Finally, programs effective in offsetting the harmful effects of poverty and in bringing low-income youngsters closer to their more-advantaged peers, in terms of academic readiness, include a rich array of activities and services for youngsters (Magnuson & Waldfogel, 2005). In addition to the academic focus discussed previously, these programs emphasize activities that promote social development and physical well-being (Magnuson et al., 2004; Rothstein, 2004; Rouse et al., 2005).

Effects

Key to policymakers' decisions is an accounting of whether the programs represent a worthwhile investment of limited public funds. (Magnuson et al., 2004, p. 144)

Most policymakers and advocates for the poor believe that preschools can compensate for factors that place children from disadvantaged backgrounds behind their peers in academic terms before they even enter kindergarten. In reviewing the evidence, two questions are of concern. First, does attending compensatory preschool raise test scores in kindergarten? The best research on this question finds that the answer is yes. Second, do the effects of attending preschool persist into adulthood? The evidence on this question is, at best, mixed. (Ferguson, 1998b, p. 319)

While useful research on the effects of preschool programs has been undertaken, much of the landscape remains to be explored. From the gap perspective, the key questions that have been investigated are in line with the ones noted above in the Ferguson quote: (1) Does preschool help youngsters to be more successful when they start school (the readiness issue)? (2) Does preschool produce cognitive effects that carry over into the elementary and secondary years of school (the sustainability issue)? (3) Does preschool provide noncognitive benefits (the other outcomes issue)? And (4) Across all of these questions, does preschool disproportionately benefit lower-income students and African American children, i.e., does it help close achievement gaps (the target-group issue)? On the first question, the weight of the empirical evidence is affirmative. There is support for the position that the presence of public funding for preschool programs moves more families to participate. More to the point, Ferguson's (1998b) research reveals that preschool can positively impact IQ. "Taken as a whole for the nation, center-based programs are helping prepare children for school" (Haskins & Rouse, 2005, p. 4; see also Beckford & Cooley, 1993; Magnuson & Waldfogel, 2005; Magnuson et al., 2004). That is, "Preschool programs have demonstrated some success in preparing children to enter public school more equipped to achieve" (Reynolds, 2002, p. 15).

Turning to the fourth question, at this point, requires us to investigate whether consistent positive findings on preschool's impact in general on school readiness also help reduce achievement gaps. The answer here is mixed. On the one hand, as just noted, quality preschool programs seem to benefit all youngsters regardless of race or social class (Bali & Alvarez, 2003). And, as we discussed earlier, there is even some evidence that white children may gain more from quality preschool programs than African American youngsters (Alexander et al., 2001; Entwisle & Alexander, 1992), thus "actually add[ing] to the black-white test score gap" (Ferguson, 1998b, p. 365). On the other hand, research on preschool programs that target low-income and African American students—where the comparison is with nonparticipating white and middle class youngsters—affirms, "Providing high-quality preschool education programs to poor children is a strategy that has been shown to enhance children's developmental outcomes" (Brooks-Gunn et al., 1996, p. 405). This latter body of work documents "positive short-term effects for minority academic achievement" (Armor, 1992, p. 76) and "confirms that quality early childhood programs make great headway in closing racial gaps in school readiness" (Rouse et al., 2005, pp. 12–13). Of particular importance here is the finding that the most socially and cognitively disadvantaged African American students appear to gain the most from preschool, at least in the form of Head Start (Lee, Brooks-Gunn, Schnur, & Liaw, 1990). For example, Brooks-Gunn and Markman (2005) found, "Early childhood education programs seem to have more benefits for children of mothers with a high school education (or less)" (p. 156). Campbell and Ramsey (1995) also conclude, "Early failure among African-American children can be significantly reduced with an intensive preschool program" (p. 764).

Turning to the second question, the sustainability issue, we conclude, as did Ferguson (1998b) previously, that the evidence is mixed. The research consensus based on the best studies is that early academic benefits are not sustained (Armor, 1992; 2008). Using Head Start as a proxy for preschool programs more generally, questions remain about the extent to which preschool policies sustain cognitive gain for youngsters, particularly of differing ethnic and racial backgrounds, making conclusions about their role in reducing test-score gaps less than firm (Brooks-Gunn & Markman, 2005; Duncan & Brooks-Gunn, 2000; 2001). While there is some support for readiness carrying over into the early primary years (Grade 1)

(Chatterji, 2006; Duncan & Brooks-Gunn, 2001; Le, Kirby, Barney, Setodji, & Gershwin, 2006), by the end of the third grade, at the latest, effects for African Americans have faded out (Ferguson, 1998b). Currie and Thomas (1995) explain:

> *When we focus on only young African-American children, we find clear benefits of Head Start. However, in a sample of African-American children of all ages, there is no effect of Head Start. This is because the benefits die out very quickly. In contrast, white children experience the same initial gains from Head Start, but they retain these benefits for a much longer period. . . . Thus, for example, by age 10, African-American children have lost any benefits they gained from Head Start, while ten-year-old white children retain a gain of 5 percentile points. (p. 358)*

While no one has crafted a conclusive rationale for this phenomenon, common explanations point to issues of quality in the preschool programs themselves, or more accurately, the absence of widespread high-quality programs (Rouse et al., 2005), and to issues of quality in the K–12 educational system, or more specifically the failure of the K–12 system to build on preschool readiness benefits (Ferguson, 1998b).

On the third question, noncognitive benefits of preschool, we are able to craft a more positive narrative (Karoly et al., 1998; Lee et al., 1990). Studies confirm a variety of benefits that materialize before kindergarten and after formal schooling begins (Haskins & Rouse, 2005), what Bingham (1994) calls "lifelong dividends" (p. 38). For example, Magnuson and colleagues (2004; 2005) find that children who attend center-based programs are less likely to be retained in kindergarten. There is also evidence that youngsters who participate in preschool programs have fewer grade retentions in later years and are assigned to special education services less frequently than nonparticipating peers (Campbell & Ramey, 1995; Thompson & O'Quinn, 2001). These programs also appear to "decrease behavior problems and increase persistence and enthusiasm for learning" (Duncan & Brooks-Gunn, 2001, p. 64). They can "reduce the risks of school problems, . . . delinquency, dropout, and early parenting" (Child & Family Policy Center, 2005, p. 7). Duncan and Brooks-Gunn (2001) also affirm "Early childhood programs . . . influence maternal outcomes, including mental health, coping skills, knowledge about child-rearing, and mother-child interactions" (p. 64; see also Karoly et al., 1998). On the back end of the benefit chain, Miller (1999) reports, "High-quality preschools may indirectly help many more children in the next generation perform at high levels, because more of the current generation of disadvantaged youngsters will be better educated parents" (p. 20).

Perhaps what is most appropriate, in the way of summary, is that high- quality preschool programs, especially in conjunction with efforts to strengthen parenting skills and initiatives to make afterschool and summer school more productive—as part of a "comprehensive approach to service delivery" (Magnuson et al., 2004, p. 120)—can help low-income and African American children be better prepared for and more successful in school. Yet while preschool is a powerful tool in the gap-closure toolbox, it is not a magic one (Lee et al., 1990). According to the Child Family and Policy Center (2005):

> *High quality preschool programs can benefit all children, but particularly low-income children, although they are not a silver bullet that alone will eliminate the disparities in "what children know and can do" at the time of school entry. (p. 7)*

Indeed, Lee and associates (1990) remind us:

> *Inducing sustained and successful academic experiences for children of poverty throughout their educational careers, rather than focusing on efforts to "fix" the problem with one-year preschool programs (however successful they may be), is absolutely essential. (p. 505)*

In particular, "Given the nature of the evidence [on] . . . whether benefits persist" (Ferguson, 1998b, p. 325), there is a need to ratchet up enrollment in and the quality of preschool programs, especially those that target low-income and African American students.

Extended Learning Opportunities

> *The most disadvantaged children may need to experience an array of intellectual and social development opportunities equivalent to the combined home and school experiences of advantaged children during the primary school years. (Miller, 1995, p. 351)*

> *Providing afterschool and summer experiences to lower-class children that are similar to those middle-class children take for granted would also likely be an essential part of narrowing the achievement gap. (Rothstein, 2004, pp. 10–11)*

> *The next logical step after improving preschooling is to develop summer school programs for poor children. Preschools can reduce the achievement gap when children start first grade, but then we need to keep the faucet open and provide the extra resources for poor children when school is closed that middle-class parents provide for their children. (Entwisle et al., 2000, p. 27)*

As Miller (1995) explains in the preceding quote, students who begin school with cognitive deficits need additional time if they are ultimately to catch up with their peers. In addition to the expanded education provided in well-organized preschool programs, they will require "more extended time and assistance during the early years of school" (Shannon & Bylsma, 2002, p. 18). "Remediation efforts cannot be confined to the school alone" (Natriello, McDill, & Pallas, 1990, p. 13). Rather, "Once in school, disadvantaged children need year-round supplemental programming to counter the continuing press of family and community conditions that hold them back" (Alexander et al., 2001, p. 176).

Full-Day Kindergarten

> *Full-day kindergarten is seen as a way to help level the playing field for disadvantaged children with much lower levels of school readiness. (Le et al., 2006, p. 5)*

Researchers generally examine three types of extended learning opportunities: full-day kindergarten, summer school, and additional time before or after school. While the full-day kindergarten solution takes us into school-based attacks on the achievement gap, it also provides a useful link between in-school and out-of-school policy initiatives to depress learning differentials between lower- and higher-income youngsters. One line of analysis here argues, "Disadvantaged children need to attend high quality, full-day kindergarten programs" (Alexander et al., 2001, p. 183). Researchers justify this policy thrust by noting:

> *The benefits of full-day as compared to half-day kindergartens for children are considerable. With family background and many other variables allowed for, first graders who attended full-day kindergarten were absent fewer days in first grade, were less often retained, and earned higher marks and test scores in first grade than half-day attendees. (p. 184)*

Other work, however, holds that there is insufficient evidence to extract firm assessments about the power of full-day kindergarten in closing achievement gaps. For example, some researchers assert that the expected benefits for low-income and African American students may fail to materialize (Le et al., 2006). We elect to keep full-day kindergarten in the achievement gap policy toolbox awaiting further study.

Summer Programs

Given the role that summer periods between the grades play in exacerbating racial and social-class achievement differentials (Entwisle et al., 2000), a logical approach to help close achievement gaps "would be to provide summer school programs for poor youngsters" (Entwisle & Alexander, 1992, p. 82). More forcefully, the logic dictates "that public policies should be aimed at . . . summer interventions" (Fryer & Levitt, 2004, p. 458): "An education that hopes to narrow the achievement gap significantly, therefore, should provide comparable summer experiences" (Rothstein, 2004, p. 143), comparable to the experiences enjoyed by middle- and high-SES youngsters during summer months (Miller, 1995).

Unfortunately, research on this policy lever shows that this "one seemingly obvious method for reducing the achievement gap has turned out to be highly ineffective" (Entwisle et al., 2000, p. 10). Summer programs "do not help students who are behind catch up" (Entwisle & Alexander, 1992, p. 82). Rather, as Heyns (1978) first discovered, summer programs may "reinforce rather than overcome the effect of family background" (p. 195), and "gains accrue disproportionately to the relatively affluent" (p. 190). The overall conclusion from the research, then, is "Summer school can widen the achievement gap when programs are offered for all children" (Borman & Dowling, 2006, p. 27).

In attempting to understand this somewhat paradoxical finding, some researchers assign blame to the "content and focus" of programs (Borman & Dowling, 2006, p. 27), especially to summer programs that are "unrelated to academic curricula" (Burkam et al., 2004, p. 4). Other scholars such as Entwisle and his team (2000) remind us that it is "critical to understand the distinction between summer school in general and summer school as means to close the gap in cognitive skills between rich and poor students" (p. 24). They find that, for a variety of reasons, providing add-on services, such as summer school across the board, will not close gaps. They also criticize most empirical work in this area for failing to account for expected summer loss in determining impacts. Specifically, they claim, "Unless the likelihood of a summer loss is taken into account, programs that produce no gains look ineffective, yet a summer program that kept poor children from losing ground could be exceedingly valuable" (Entwisle & Alexander, 1992, p. 83).

The question at hand for leaders and policy makers, then, is, what can be done to improve the usefulness of this seemingly powerful but often ineffective tool? First, as just explained, designs that account for expected summer loss in learning are needed. This might prevent the failure label being attached to summer school programs that are, in reality, "successful in helping disadvantaged students" (Entwisle & Alexander, 1992, p. 83). Second, and most importantly, Entwisle, Alexander, and Olson (2000) conclude that for summer school programs to be effective in closing gaps, "they have to be designed especially for poor children and provided only for them" (p. 250; see also Alexander et al., 2001).

Third, more needs to be done to ensure that summer school programs include the right elements. On a basic level, for example, Borman and Dowling (2006) argue that student attendance is a key program ingredient. Students need to be in attendance to garner benefits from the program. They also affirm that participation across multiple years is a good idea: "Simple assignment of the students to the program is not likely to make a difference. Encouraging and sustaining students' long-term participation in the program" (p. 45) is essential. Chin and Phillips (2004), in turn, discuss the importance of establishing summer programs that align with the work schedules of parents. In addition, Borman and Dowling (2006) maintain that while many summer programs are reactionary, good programs feature designs that are "proactive and preventative" (p. 26). Along these lines, Entwisle and team (2000) assert that it is very important that "summer programs not be scheduled as 'make-up' or billed as being for children who have failed" (p. 28). These scholars also hold that programs that bracket first grade can be especially helpful. They remind us that program location is also important, stating, "Programs need to be located near pupils' homes so children can get to them easily and so parents can become involved" (p. 28).

Finally, a number of scholars propose that more attention be given to the activities that define summer programs, to the program content. Here we know that getting the right teachers is important (Entwisle et al., 2000). A cardinal conclusion is that "activities related to reading" (p. 27) need to predominate (Heyns, 1978; Rothstein, 2004). As Alexander, Entwisle, and Olson (2001) advise:

> A strong curriculum comes first, focused on reading, it being the foundation for all that follows. Heyns (1978) found that the single summer activity most strongly and consistently related to summer learning is reading, whether measured by the number of books read, by the time spent reading, or by the regularity of library usage. (p. 184)

Aligning program content with the scope and sequence of learning in the school is also a wise strategy (Borman & Dowling, 2006). At the same time, a range of activities that supplement work found in the school during the regular year should be available (Chin & Phillips, 2004; Rothstein, 2004).

In the face of the less-than-overwhelming empirical evidence accumulated to date, perhaps the best summative conclusion is that if summer programs are done well, and if they are "targeted specifically at disadvantaged students they [can] serve to close the achievement gap" (Borman & Dowling, 2006, p. 27; see also Entwisle et al., 2000).

Extended-Day Programs

A strategy to close the achievement gap between lower-class and middle-class children cannot ignore these non-school hours. (Rothstein, 2004, p. 59)

Employing logic similar to that visible in the previous discussion on summer school, analysts hold that well-planned and well-structured afterschool and weekend programs can make a dent in achievement gaps between more- and less-advantaged youngsters (Rothstein, 2004). Indeed, many reviewers find that the logic for these "after-school programs is compelling" (Thompson, 2002, p. 30). Rothstein (2006) frames that logic as follows: "It is foolish to think that lower-class children can achieve, on average, at middle-class levels without similar opportunities" (p. 7). Without repeating the analysis above, it is important to note that the literature here holds that the design elements and the content focus outlined in the discussion of summer school programs apply to extended-day programs as well. In particular, we learn that funds should be used to "support after school programs which are closely linked to state standards and the local curriculum, which are staffed by qualified teachers and other staff, and which provide one-on-one tutoring to at-risk students" (Thompson, 2002, p. 31; see also Gandara & Fish, 1994; North Carolina State Department of Public Instruction, 2000).

Two conclusions hold across all of these additional learning opportunities—full-day kindergarten, summer programs, and extended-day programs. First, the services need to be directed at the target students, not youngsters more generally. Second, the structural intervention is just the start. Only by scaffolding the intervention on quality designs and loading the programs with effective elements will these additional learning opportunities help close achievement gaps.

Health and Welfare Actions

Without adequate health care for lower-class children and their parents, there is little hope of fully closing the achievement gap. (Rothstein, 2006, p. 4)

Because black infants are more likely than white to fall into the lowest weight ranges, preventing low birth weight is likely to be more effective than remedial intervention at narrowing racial gaps in school readiness. (Reichman, 2005, p. 107)

Analysts who chronicle the critical role of out-of-school factors in explaining achievement gaps argue persuasively that concerted attacks on these conditions will be required if the battle for equality in learning outcomes is ever to be won (see especially Rothstein, 2004). They underscore social conditions that will "improve the quality of life for disadvantaged minority families through housing, nutrition, health care, crime reduction, and other social policies" (Kober, 2001, p. 30). Across social policy, they emphasize five domains where reform work is required "to offset the negative effects of poverty on children's physical and cognitive development" (Hertert & Teague, 2003, p. 12): children and family health, family housing, job training, family structure, and family income. The last three of these domains were explored in detail in the first half of this chapter, where strategies for improving the economic and social environments of families at risk were described. We concentrate here, therefore, on issues of health and housing.

Health

Increasingly, scholars are proposing that the "provision of health care services to lower-class children and their families is needed to narrow the achievement gap" (Rothstein, 2004, p. 11), that "improving the health of mothers and infants may help to close racial and ethnic gaps in school readiness" (Rouse et al., 2005, p. 9)—and that appropriate health services may well "play an important role in improving the cognitive functioning and future school attainments of impoverished children" (Currie, 2005, p. 131). They point to the importance of "understanding the education equality component in things like dealing with environmental hazards . . . and assuring adequate nutrition" (Barton, 2003, p. 36). Rothstein (2004) concludes:

> *Because many lower-class children have health problems that impede learning, an adequate education cannot be delivered to these children unless they have adequate medical care. Because parents in poor health cannot properly nurture children, an adequate education also requires that lower-class parents get the means to achieve good health for themselves. (p. 138)*

The objective of these scholars is to narrow achievement gaps by improving "health capital" for low-income families (Miller, 1995, p. 343) and by "improving access to health care" (Hertert & Teague, 2003, p. 3). And again, the logic is that the payoffs for actions on the health front may be more pronounced than are school-based efforts to address achievement gaps (Rothstein, 2004).

In the health domain, analysts feature reform efforts across a number of interconnected areas. One strategy is to ensure that children from low-income families have adequate health insurance (Miller, 1995), an area where we have seen some real progress over the last twenty years (Currie, 2005; Rouse et al., 2005). However, because "the development of effective responses to these [health] problems entails more than increasing the availability of health insurance" (Miller, 1995, p. 347), another strategy is to make health care services more accessible to poor families by bringing services to their neighborhoods (Miller, 1995; Rothstein, 2004), "preferably in a central location" (Schwartz, 2001, p. 5). Schools are often a featured venue for locating these health services (Rothstein, 2004). Activists here argue for a wide range of coordinated health services in these school-based health centers (Schwartz, 2001). Rothstein (2004) recommends, specifically:

> *To narrow the achievement gap, a school-community clinic should include services that middle-class families take for granted and that ensure children can thrive in school. Clinics associated with schools in lower-class communities should include obstetric and gynecological services for pregnant and postpartum women, pediatric services for children through their high school years, physicians to serve parents of all school-age children, nurses to support these medical services, dentists and hygienists to see both parents and children semi-annually, optometrists and vision therapists to*

serve those who require treatment for their sight, social workers to refer families to other services, community health educators, and psychologists or therapists to assist families and children who are experiencing excessive stress and other emotional difficulties. (pp. 138–139)

Particular stress in the health domain is often placed on the importance of children receiving appropriate immunizations (McGee, 2003) and adequate nutritional support (Rothstein, 2004). Scholars in this area also emphasize health issues related to teen parenthood, advocating for more extensive and higher quality services for pregnant women and mothers with newborn children (Natriello, McDill, & Pallas, 1990; Rothstein, 2004) and for pregnancy prevention programs (Magnuson & Duncan, 2006). Within this realm, much reform attention is directed to the implementation of "programs both to prevent low-birth weight babies and to improve the life chances of low-birth weight babies" (Reichman, 2005, p. 103). Finally, analysts maintain that programs that tackle the issue of substance abuse can increase the stock of health capital in families, improve the cognitive functioning of children, and help narrow achievement gaps (Miller, 1995).

Housing

Rothstein (2004) provides support for the belief that policy in the area of housing can have an impact on the social and cognitive development of children, and subsequently on the development and closure of achievement gaps. He argues, "A serious commitment to narrowing the academic achievement gap should include a plan to stabilize the housing of working families with children who cannot afford adequate shelter" (p. 135). He goes on to assert that a national housing policy "that reduced the mobility of low-income working families with children might also do more to boost test scores of their children than many commonly advocated instructional reforms" (p. 135).

Bempechat (1992), Rothstein (2004), and other analysts whose work touches this area, believe that housing policy impacts student learning in general and achievement gaps in particular via the integration of social cases. Helpful policies "permit families of different classes to live in close proximity so their children can attend the same school" (Rothstein, 2004, p. 130). And, it is this mixing of social classes that is most critical, "since it is the presence of middle-class students, regardless of ethnicity, [that] appears to raise achievement" (Bempechat, 1992, p. 41). We return to this issue in Chapter 11.

Overall, the health and welfare approach to help close achievement gaps in the United States appears to be quite promising, especially in the area of family health (Currie, 2005; Miller, 1995; Reichman, 2004; Rothstein, 2004). The data on housing policy are less definitive (Magnuson & Duncan, 2006). Perhaps the best summary here has been provided by Duncan and Magnuson (2005) who conclude:

Residential mobility programs, then, will not by themselves remedy the achievement problems of children in public housing and high-poverty neighborhoods. Interventions focused exclusively on neighborhoods rather than on influences directly related to the child, family, and school cannot solve the myriad problems of children growing up in high-poverty urban neighborhoods. (p. 45)

CONCLUSION

In Chapters 3–7, we explored factors external to schooling that contribute to achievement gaps between high-income and low-income students and African American and white youngsters. In this chapter, we turned the table and addressed policy and leadership solutions to the structure of inequality reflected in these external conditions. We examined policies in two broad areas: strategies designed to improve the economic status of the poor directly and interventions crafted to compensate for the conditions of poverty.

On the first front, income-transfer strategies, we discussed income-enhancement ideas under the topics of welfare, job training, taxes, and employment. On the second front, service-delivery strategies, we investigated the role that parenting programs, preschool experiences, extended learning opportunities, and health and welfare actions can play in narrowing achievement gaps among children from different social classes and races. We now turn to an exploration of what schools can do to reduce these patterned learning differentials.

11

Closing Achievement Gaps

A Focus on Schooling

Still, it is the schools we turn to for a solution. But we would do well to remember that we are asking schools to solve a problem not of their own making. (Porter, 2007, p. 8)

If it is possible to do so, it is essential to intervene directly in the quality of education provided to African American children while we are waiting for social and economic equity to arrive. (Slavin & Madden, 2001, p. 6)

Equity-minded educators are choosing to shift the framing of this inquiry from explaining the academic failure of students of color to exploring alternative structures, organizations, and practices that lead to greater academic success for all students. (Cooper, 2003, p. 599)

No matter what policies are passed, what laws are enacted and what best practices are replicated, it is the teachers and principals working with individual children and their families who ultimately make the difference. (McGee, 2003, p. 45)

INTRODUCTION

The question at hand at this point in our narrative is, what can schools contribute to closing racial and social class achievement gaps? "What mix of . . . school arrangements and educator practices would consistently produce a distribution of achievement for poor and/or culturally different minority children" (Miller, 1995, pp. 369-370). On the one side of the ledger, there is reason to be less than sanguine, especially when considering "school only" solution designs. For example, in their classic work on inequality, Jencks and colleagues (1972) report, "There is no evidence that school reform can substantially reduce the extent of cognitive inequality, as measured by tests of verbal fluency, reading comprehension, or mathematical skill" (p. 8). Nearly a quarter of a century later, in his hallmark volume on the achievement gap, Rothstein (2004) argues, "The influence of social class characteristics is probably so powerful that schools cannot overcome it, no matter how well trained are their teachers and no matter how well designed are their instructional programs and climates" (p. 5). As we saw in Chapter 2, while at certain times across history gaps narrowed, the overall trend lines show little improvement (Lee, 2002; 2004). And, Ferguson (1998a) reminds us, "National data show that, at best, the black-white test score gap is roughly constant (in standard deviations) from the primary through the secondary grades" (p. 273).

> As Hertert and Teague (2003) confirm, "Taken as a whole research findings are inconclusive and have yet to reveal 'what works' to narrow the achievement gap" (p. 6). Unfortunately, this silence reflects an absence of knowledge; relatively little research exists that examines within-school disparities in performance and assesses the prospects for school-level policies and programs to change them. (Stiefel, Schwartz, & Ellen, 2006, p. 8)

> The extent to which particular school practices and policies ... increase reading achievement levels in high-risk groups is still unknown. (Chatterji, 2006, p. 491)

> Education research over the last thirty years has included extensive investigations of the factors influencing student achievement. The results of much of this research—especially as it pertains to public schooling—are inconclusive, if not contradictory, and provide few definitive answers on how best to improve learning for all students, in particular the lowest-performing students. (Hertert & Teague, 2003, p. 17)

Efforts to reduce gaps, in turn, have not routinely been successful, even when solution strategies are relatively clear (e.g., summer school programs). Becker and Luthar (2002) summarize the storyline as follows: "Thus, despite more than three decades of urban school research and reform aimed at improving disadvantaged student achievement performance, current data on urban achievement reveal that these programs have not met the task" (p. 198). Davison and colleagues (2004) weigh in here as well: "While individual students may make up lost ground, data suggest that groups of students seldom make up even small amounts of lost ground" (p. 753).

Worse still, as Cook and Evans (2000) document, the quality of schools for African American students is on a downward not upward trajectory: "There have been substantial changes in relative school quality across different types of schools. In particular, there has been a decline in the relative quality of disadvantaged urban schools and in the relative quality of predominantly minority schools" (p. 749). Overall then, "While the push for higher levels of achievement may have increased, the tools needed to make it happen on a broad scale in high-poverty schools ... have not followed in sufficient scope and magnitude" (Balfanz & Byrnes, 2006, p. 145).

On the other side of the ledger, however, there are some positive entries to record as well. Some strong theoretical work links "factors over which schools have control" (Caldas & Bankston, 1999, p. 92) and academic outcomes. There is also considerable evidence that, in general, schools can impact the achievement scores of youngsters. That is, "School policies can have an impact on test scores" (Bali & Alvarez, 2003, p. 487). We also know that "schools are most beneficial for those [students] who need them most" (Entwisle & Alexander, 1992, p. 83). There are also numerous existence proofs of schools successfully educating low-income children and African American students (Burns, Keyes, & Kusimo, 2005).

Turning to the gap issue directly, as we portrayed on the deficit side of the ledger, the analysis is mixed. Much of the research concludes that "once achievement gaps between student groups emerge, they tend to persist over time" (Davison et al., 2004, p. 758), and that "school factors can have an impact on test scores but they cannot close the race gap" (Bali & Alvarez, 2003, p. 501). Still other scholars arrive at an alternative position, holding, "In addition to the contributions of families and communities, schools can make a difference in closing the achievement gap" (Braun et al., 2006, p. 9). Thus, according to analysts such as Stiefel and associates (2006), "Evidence exists to suggest that school policies . . . can help reduce gaps" (p. 11).

The takeaway messages here for educators and policy makers are as follows: First, while much of the heavy lifting to address the achievement gap problem must be done by those outside of education, schools have a part to play. Second, when that part is played well, schools advantage historically disadvantaged youngsters. Third, any specific school-based intervention can account for only a small part of any change in the distribution of achievement scores. Fourth, therefore, a significant package of actions across the reform landscape is needed to tackle the knotty problem of achievement gaps. We turn to an analysis of helpful school-based interventions in a proceeding section. Our goal is "to identify individual and school processes that lead to and foster success among students of color [and poor children] and close the achievement gap" (Cooper, 2000, p. 600). Before we do so, however, we provide ten more general rules of engagement to guide gap reduction work.

GENERAL RULES OF ENGAGEMENT

Coherent and intentional actions need to be taken to create and improve the conditions needed to close the gap. (Shannon & Bylsma, 2002, p. 47)

Research indicates that from a long-term perspective, most of the solution lies in reducing the number of high-school-age students who did poorly in elementary school. (Miller, 1995, p. 57)

We begin our discussion of school-based, gap closing strategies by expanding upon some of the strategic rules of action introduced in Chapter 1. In a real sense, these are the key framing ideas that need to be followed in selecting more specific interventions for working to narrow achievement gaps.

1. There is no silver bullet that will solve the achievement gap problem (Balfanz & Byrnes, 2006)—and "no magic laundry list" (Baenen et al., 2002, p. 48) either. There are no

"dramatic 'breakthrough' interventions" (Thompson & O'Quinn, 2001, p. 5). Neither is there a "detailed blueprint" (Jencks & Phillips, 1998) for educators. As Stiefel and colleagues (2006) remind us, there are no easy answers laying about to this exceedingly complex problem (Braun et al., 2006). And, as Thompson and O'Quinn (2001) astutely observe, "important complexities and pitfalls" (p. 5) are associated with all gap closing reform strategies, and "none is easy to carry out" (p. 5). It is also "difficult to know precisely how much an intervention will narrow the gap" (Rothstein, 2004, p. 6).

What this tells us is that "since there is little evidence that any existing strategy can close much more than a fraction of the overall achievement gap between high- and low-SES children" (Miller, 1995, p. 334), only comprehensive, multifaceted, integrated, and coherent designs offer hope of success (Chatterji, 2005a; Shannon & Bylsma, 2002; Thomson & O'Quinn, 2001). In short, an integrated, cohesive design that thoughtfully arrays multiple strategies is desirable; isolated ad hoc actions are of more limited value. A cohesive design to close achievement gaps would be characterized by the following critical elements. It would be comprehensive (Kober, 2001), and a "complex combination of conditions for success" (McGee, 2003, p. 65) would be highlighted (Miller, 1995; U.S. Commission on Civil Rights, 2004). It would provide "major efforts on many different fronts" (Kober, 2001, p. 12). It would attack problems "on several fronts simultaneously" (North Carolina, 2001, p. 11), not in linear fashion (Singham, 2003). It would afford a multi-layered and "multitiered" (Roscigno, 1998, p. 1033) approach, focusing on what actions at all levels of the educational system can accomplish (Miller, 1995; U.S. Commission on Civil Rights, 2004): "Strong sustained leadership from many quarters is the answer" (McGee, 2003, p. 49). The design would include an "interconnected" (Roscigno, 1998, p. 1033), "coordinated" (Shannon & Bylsma, 2002, p. 48), and integrated (Reynolds, 2002) "mix of strategies" (Thompson, 2002, p. 5). It would feature what Miller (1995) calls the principle of "complementarity" (p. 376) at both the strategy and institutional levels. It would attend to both the short and the long term (Kober, 2001). It would offer "redundancy" and "backup capacity" (Miller, 1995, p. 42). A comprehensive blueprint would feature both support and pressure (Hertert & Teague, 2003).

2. If we underscore the dominant understanding of closing the achievement gap as an increase in equity—or improving the rate of learning for targeted students at a faster rate than for other pupils (Davison et al., 2004; Kober, 2001), then it is apparent that closure requires actions that disproportionately advantage these students (Braun et al., 2006; Harris & Harrington, 2006; Myers, Kim, & Mandala, 2004; Spradlin et al., 2005): "Disadvantaged students cannot catch up to their initially higher scoring peers by making the same progress as those peers" (Ding & Davison, 2005, p. 94); "as long as the same level of improvement occurs, the gap will not close" (Shannon & Bylsma, 2002, p. 48).

Equity can only be achieved if reform design features strategies that disproportionately advantage children on the wrong side of the achievement gap. That is, to narrow gaps, "[the] gains required of initially low achieving students will [need to be] greater than the gain required of initially higher achieving students" (Ding & Davison, 2005, p. 83): Low-income and "minority students need to accelerate achievement at a faster rate" (Shannon & Bylsma, 2002, p. 8).

The advantaging process can occur in two ways. First, as Alexander, Entwisle, and Olson (2001) remind us, "To address the achievement gap specifically, programs will need to target disadvantaged students specifically" (pp. 176–177). Interventions made available to all youngsters are likely to help minority and low-income students (Hedges & Nowell, 1998). However, they may also maintain or even exacerbate learning differentials (e.g., universal preschool). This logic throws into question the gap-reduction approach of closing gaps by improving the education and the learning outcomes of all students, regardless of race or social class (Becker & Luthar, 2002).

Second, policy makers and educators can underscore interventions that "influence the test scores of groups differentially" (Bali & Alvarez, 2003, p. 486). That is, they can spotlight strategies that provide greater gains to targeted students. Because low-income and minority youngsters, on average, are more school dependent (Haycock, 1998; Shannon & Bylsma, 2002), or more accurately, "the impact of school is more determinate" (Heyns, 1978, p. 188)—that is, "within-school factors have a greater impact on the achievement of students of color than they do on white students' achievement" (Symonds, 2004, p. 7)—many quality educational interventions applied generally (e.g., small class size) have the potential to accelerate their learning vis-à-vis more advantaged youngsters (Slavin & Madden, 2001). "We need to realize that implementing remedies that are good for all can be even better for those who are currently falling behind" (Singham, 2003, p. 591).

The key guidelines for educators and policy makers here are as follows: (1) raising student achievement generally and reducing the achievement gap are not the same thing; (2) if equity is the goal, focusing on reform strategies that power higher achievement for all youngsters along similar trajectories will not ameliorate the gap problem; and (3) different policies are required for different goals (Hanushek & Raymond, 2005).

3. At the same time, while there is some support for the belief that strategies to reduce achievement gaps should be different, the bulk of the evidence suggests that these youngsters do not need different types of interventions (Ferguson, 1991; Rothstein, 2004; Singham, 2003). Rather, they require "much more intensive support" (Thompson, 2002, p. 19) and much more of the quality educational factors (e.g., rigorous curriculum) that promote higher levels of student achievement whenever they are found (Haycock, 1998; Rothstein, 2004).

4. When the portfolio of school-based, gap narrowing strategies is filled, both academic (e.g., student grouping practices) and environment or cultural (e.g., clubs for African American students) factors need to be emphasized (Balfanz & Byrnes, 2006; Rothstein, 2004). Indeed, "a combined emphasis [is] especially important for disadvantaged students' achievement" (Becker & Luthar, 2002, p. 209). Becker and Luthar (2002) explain:

> *Methods that demand higher educational standards without a similar emphasis on the social-emotional needs of early adolescents will not result in much success, efforts to improve the social-emotional needs of disadvantaged students without a comparable application of instructional and curricular methods to attain academic excellence will be similarly ineffective. (pp. 204–209)*

Also, as Rothstein (2004) argues, "A serious effort to narrow the black-white gap should find ways to help schools narrow the gap in non-cognitive as well as cognitive skills" (p. 127).

5. Lee (2002) reports, "Past studies of racial and ethnic achievement gap trends tended to assume implicitly that the effects of certain factors on student achievement are constant

across time periods and racial and ethnic groups" (p. 10). Important recent work has caused analysts to challenge this conclusion. Thus, as work unfolds on addressing the needs of students of color and low-income youngsters, it is important to pay attention to differences between groups and within groups (Carpenter, Ramirez, & Severn, 2006). This is true in particular "if indicators of low student achievement are associated with students' particular cultural groups" (Burns et al., 2005, p. 18).

To begin with, evidence suggests that some gap solution strategies work better with one group (say Hispanic youngsters) than others (say African American students) (Bali & Alvarez, 2003; Downey, von Hippel, & Broh, 2004). That is, "School factors [may] influence the test scores of racial groups differently" (Bali & Alvarez, 2003, p. 486). Also, the commonly accepted assumption that factors contributing to gaps and their reductions "are the same or sufficiently similar for all minority groups" (Carpenter, Ramirez, & Severn, 2006, p. 113) may not be accurate (Bali & Alvarez, 2003). For example, Ferguson (1991) found that while greater teaching experience and the possession of a master's degree had a small positive impact on African American students relative to white students (i.e., helped close the African American-white achievement gap), these factors where negative for Hispanic students relative to white youngsters (i.e., increased the Hispanic-white achievement gap).

Second, there are differences within groups of students that have real implications for how schools address learning gaps (Knapp, 2001). All African American students are not the same, nor are all low-income youngsters. For example, while it is true that the average twelfth-grade African American pupil performs significantly below the average white student, in the neighborhood or four years below, some African American students perform very well relative to other African Americans and relative to whites. The caution is that grouping masks individual differences, differences to which educators need to attend.

6. Some gap interventions carry more weight in certain periods of a student's career. The mechanisms through which families and schools exert influence are, to some extent at least, "a function of the age of the individual" (Brooks-Gunn et al., 1997, p. 280). For example, in the double-barreled approach emphasized in this volume (e.g., in-school and out-of-school interventions), we know that "the relative importance of non-school factors decreases over time" (Fryer & Levitt, 2002, p. 25)—"family background matters more for the test scores of primary-school-age- children than it does for older children" (Entwisle, Alexander, & Olson, 2000, p. 11). Within each category, timing matters as well. For example, in the out-of-school area, poverty's effects are worse for younger children than adolescents. The same conclusion holds for living in a single-parent family. In the in-school domain, small class size is more valuable in the early grades.

7. Not all factors are equal; some carry more weight than others. For example, while there are numerous in-school factors that can help narrow achievement gaps, quality instruction and curricular rigor are especially powerful interventions.

8. Local context matters a good deal. Indeed, "There is considerable evidence that different strategies . . . work best in different settings" (Thompson, 2002, p. 4).

9. Since closing achievement gaps once they have developed is difficult work, prevention always trumps remediation (Alexander, Entwisle, & Olson, 2001; Heckman, 1995). It is easier to solve the ninth-grade problem in preschool than in the ninth grade. At the broadest

level, this means that "interventions are most likely to be effective when they are applied to the young" (Heckman, 1995, p. 1117; see also Rathburn & West, 2004). Because the rate of cognitive growth declines as one progresses through school (Entwisle, Alexander, & Olson, 2000), because young students seem to catch up more than older students, and "given the stubborn persistence of achievement gaps, preventing the disparities from emerging in the first place would seem to be the wisest course" (Davison et al., 2004, p. 753).

Thus, all the data from all sources "suggest that if the nation wishes to use schools to reduce achievement differences among groups, it must maximize its efforts in the early years. By the third grade, the problem appears to be less a matter of preventing large achievement gaps from developing than of finding ways to recover lost ground" (Miller, 1995, p. 136). More specifically, at any age, it means that early interventions to address difficulties are more likely to be effective "than attempts to intervene after maladjustment has become well entrenched" (Becker & Luthar, 2002, p. 209; Ding & Davison, 2004; Knapp, 2001): "Policy and practice designed to remove wide gaps in achievement ... need to nip inequality in the bud" (Barton, 2003, p. 36).

10.   Time issues are critical in three ways. First, there is considerable evidence that there are no short terms solutions (Gamoran, 2000). For society, "Sustained intergenerational educational advancement requires an enormous investment over time, especially for groups that have had little previous experience with such education or that have been systematically denied educational opportunity" (Miller, 1995, p. 380). Second, length of time in treatment is important. For many gap interventions (e.g., small class size, quality instruction), benefits escalate the longer the intervention unfolds. Third, one rarely arrives. Care should be taken in withdrawing supports even when gaps are closed. Continued work is likely to be needed to hold gains.

In short, "sustained effort" (Hertert & Teague, 2003, p. 27) over a long period of time in an intensive fashion is called for, both when states and districts design and/or select gap reduction initiatives and for districts and schools when they engage the work (Balfanz & Byrnes, 2006; Miller, 1995): "Time is a critical element in allowing changes to be fully implemented and in determining their ultimate impact" (Darity et al., 2001, p. 65), and "support for efforts for a sufficient period of time [is] in order" (p. 66).

GAP CLOSING STRATEGIES

Policy strategies that target teachers' work and careers ... may be a viable category of intervention in the education offered to children of poverty. (Knapp, 2001, pp. 199–200)

Disadvantaged students should benefit greatly from access to supportive teachers within the context of a rich and challenging curriculum. (Becker & Luthar, 2002, p. 202)

In the last section, we presented general school-based guidelines that would be wise to attend to in efforts to narrow achievement gaps. Here, we examine more specific gap closing actions. These initiatives mirror the discussion in Chapters 8 and 9 on the ways schools exacerbate learning gaps between African American and low-income students and their majority and more affluent peers. We describe actions in three domains: the instructional program, school culture, and structure and support.

The Instructional Program

According to much of the research, the single most important school resource linked to academic success is the teacher. (Hertert & Teague, 2003, p. 19)

Both intuition and empirical research tell us that the achievement of school children depends substantially on the teachers they are assigned. (Wayne & Youngs, 2003, p. 89)

Improving teacher quality is an essential element of closing the achievement gap. (U.S. Commission on Civil Rights, 2004, p. 31)

The impact of the teacher is far greater for minority students. (Singham, 2003, p. 589)

At the heart of the instructional program are teachers. The starting point, as Ferguson (1998a) reminds us, is that "no matter what material resources are available, no matter what strategies school districts use to allocate children to schools, and no matter how children are grouped for instruction, schoolchildren spend their days in social interaction with teachers" (p. 274). The second point is that these social interactions are consequential for learning and achievement. According to Lewis (2008), "Teacher expertise account[s] for more variation in student achievement than any other factor (about 40 percent of the total)" (p. 20). Equally important for our purposes here, these interactions are relevant in the achievement gap narrative (Borman & Kimball, 2005). Other essential elements in the instructional program are curriculum and assessment, both of which also can play a role in narrowing achievement gaps.

> *1. Ensure that youngsters on the wrong side of the achievement gap have excellent teachers.*
>
> *Another strategy for closing achievement gaps is to ensure that traditionally under-served populations have access to high-quality teaching. (Reynolds, 2002, p.14)*

While there is some debate over the value of the various indices of quality (Grissmer, 1998), there is unqualified support in the research that better qualified teachers promote student learning and that poorly qualified teachers harm student achievement (Darling-Hammond & Post, 2000)—"that teachers' measured skills are important determinants of students' scores" (Ferguson, 1998b, p. 356). According to Thompson and O'Quinn (2001):

> *Analysis of TVAAS [Tennessee Value-Added Assessment System] data has shown differences in the effectiveness of teachers to be the single most important factor accounting for differences in students' academic growth from year to year, far more important than the size of classes, the homogeneity or heterogeneity of the achievement levels of students in a class, or students' prior level of achievement. A string of particularly effective or ineffective teachers can have either a huge positive effect or a disastrously negative effect on students' learning. Students who get three very effective teachers in a row in Grades 3–5 score fifty percentile points above students who are unlucky enough to get three ineffective teachers in a row. The effects of even a single ineffective teacher are enduring enough to be measurable at least four years later. (p. 9)*

Equally important, researchers connect quality of teachers and gap reductions. More generally, Ferguson (1998b) concludes, "Attracting and retaining talented people with strong skills to teach in the districts where black students are heavily represented is part of the unfinished business of equalizing educational opportunity" (p. 354). More specifically, Harris and Herrington (2006) find, "Attracting and retaining effective teachers in low-performing schools is critical to reducing the achievement gap" (p. 224). For example, Thompson and O'Quinn (2001) and Haycock (1998) argue as follows:

> If we but took the simple step of assuring that poor and minority children had teachers of the same quality as other children, about half of the achievement gap would disappear. If we went further and assigned our best teachers to the students who most need them, there is persuasive evidence to suggest that we could entirely close the gap. (Thompson & O'Quinn, 2001, p. 3)

Also, Haycock (1998) explains:

> Equalizing teacher assignment patterns could eliminate nearly all of the gap not attributable to poverty and its correlates. (p. 6)

Thus, our first initiative requires schools to ensure that low-income and African American youngsters are "assigned teachers who are just as able and well-prepared as those assigned to teach their well-to-do-white counterparts" (Thompson & O'Quinn, 2001, p. 8), to ensure that they "are taught by competent, authentically caring, well-prepared, [and] experienced teachers" (Hughes, 2003, p. 315), a condition that we saw in Chapter 8 is not the norm; i.e., "it is often minority students who have the least qualified teachers teaching them" (U.S. Commission on Civil Rights, 2004, p. 38). Here we reinforce a point threaded throughout this volume. Specifically, quality instruction is critical because poor and African American children are school dependent; they "depend on their teachers like no others" (Haycock, 1998, p. 20). Our recommendation for action has two parts: moving highly qualified teachers into, and less qualified teachers out of, contact with children of color and youngsters from low-income families (Hughes, 2003; Jerald, 2002), with the overall aim of "ensuring an adequate supply of well-qualified teachers in high-minority and high-poverty schools" (Kober, 2001, p. 13).

Research identifies a small bundle of variables that make up the teacher quality construct, some of which add small amounts to student achievement and others of which are more powerful. The following "indirect" measures of teacher quality all seem important, although the question of how important remains contested and unsettled: test scores, race, job performance evaluation ratings, personal characteristics, experience, credentials, and degrees.

To begin with, because (1) "teachers' test scores have been more consistently linked to achievement scores than any other characteristics" (Grissmer, 1998, p. 218) and (2) "evidence exists for raising the quality of teachers by hiring those with higher test scores" (Flanagan & Grissmer, 2002, p. 200), the search for higher-quality teachers should start here. In particular, on average, higher verbal ability test scores mean higher quality (Thompson & O'Quinn, 2001).

Data on the power of race in quality education (Ferguson, 2001; Wayne & Youngs, 2003) are mixed, although the picture on minority representation in schools is much clearer. The U.S. Commission on Civil Rights (2004) reports:

> *Teachers of color account for approximately 13.5 percent of all K–12 teachers, while minority students compose about one-third of the student population. In urban school districts, teachers of color account for approximately 36 percent of the teaching force, while minority students compose 69 percent of the total enrollment in these schools. A full 42 percent of public schools report having no minority teachers at all. (p. 32)*

One part of the storyline here features the race of the teacher who instructs children. In particular, the "cultural congruence hypothesis [holds] that black children should learn more in classes taught by black teachers" (Ferguson, 1998b, p. 347). While the data on this hypothesis are less than firm (Ferguson, 1998b), Porter (2007) reports in his review that "most results show that when black teachers teach black students, black students achieve more than when taught by white teachers" (p. 6), that students' achievement will increase "by simply having a same-race teacher" (Goldsmith, 2004, p. 127). Relatedly, research also shows that "gap-closing schools are more likely to have people of color in positions of leadership" (Symonds, 2004, p. 32).

The second part of the storyline on race attends to teacher diversity across the faculty, as measured by the percent of minority teachers (Bali & Alvarez, 2003). Overall, the diversity contribution to the assignment of reducing gaps is positive but small.

> *Larger percentages of minority teachers (both Hispanic and African America) in a school correspond to higher scores for minority students. (Bali & Alvarez, 2003, p. 486)*

> *The percentage of teachers of color has a positive impact on the academic achievement of students of color. (Symonds, 2004, p. 7)*

Indeed, "Findings suggest that segregated minority schools are better able to serve minority students when they employ many minority teachers" (Goldsmith, 2004, p. 142). One point we need to remember is that it is a series of small gains rather than any major impact that will lead to gap closures. We also need to remember that we are talking about indirect measures of teacher quality. Therefore, "What surely matters most is that teachers of any race have the skills they need to be effective in the classroom" (Ferguson, 1998b, p. 367). Nonetheless, the strategy of hiring and retaining African American teachers seems appropriate in the quest to narrow achievement gaps.

Related to the issue of race is the variable of socioeconomic status, especially "working class background." While far from settled in the research, there is a sense in the gap literature that teachers "who themselves [come] from inner-city, low socioeconomic backgrounds tend to positively influence students' performance" (Uhlenberg & Brown, 2002, p. 501). That is, "working-class background benefits black students" (Goldsmith, 2004, p. 127) academically.

Teacher quality is also defined at times as "scores on the teacher performance evaluation system" (Borman & Kimball, 2005, p. 6). While the research here is quite limited, one major study that examined this variable in depth suggests that using these scores as an indicator of teacher quality is not a wise idea. Borman and Kimball illustrate:

> *The evaluation composite accounted for no classroom-to-classroom variability in mean achievement or in closing the gap between higher and lower achievers. (Borman & Kimball, 2005, p. 14)*

> *Teachers rated higher on the teacher evaluation system do not appear to be reducing gaps in achievement between low and high achieving students and students from low-income or minority backgrounds. (p. 18)*

Teacher quality is also defined in terms of subject matter knowledge as reflected in degrees earned and credentials accumulated and experience on the job. Here, as elsewhere in the teacher quality narrative, studies arrive at varying conclusions; the results are mixed and the evidence is sometimes weak (Grissmer, 1998; Wayne & Youngs, 2003). And again, as Hertert and Teague (2003) remind us, "Teacher quality no matter how it is defined is most often associated with only modest gains in student performance" (pp. 19–20; see also Armor, 2008).

On the teacher knowledge front, Thompson and O'Quinn (2001) maintain that subject matter knowledge is correlated with higher student achievement (see also Stiefel, Schwartz, & Ellen, 2006). They find that while possession of a master's degree is "only weakly related to effectiveness, the evidence is stronger that advanced education in the subject that the teacher actually teaches does increase teacher effectiveness" (p. 9), especially in the area of mathematics (Armor, 2008), although again gains to students are small.

The same conclusion appears to hold for credentials and in-field teaching as well—positive but small to moderate effects. Chatterji (2006) explains:

> *Some schooling factors emphasized in reforms did seem to make a difference. More certified teachers yielded significant additive effects on reading school means in first grade.... Higher teacher certification rates in elementary education was the main statistically significant and positive correlate, affecting school outcomes in a positive direction. (pp. 503–504)*

However, in both of these areas, degrees and credentials, gains accrue in roughly equal measure to all youngsters. According to Bali and Alvarez (2003):

> *Beginning with the teacher credentials, we find it has a statistically significant effect on students' test scores: a 10 percent increase in full credentials increases reading scores by close to 1 point and math scores by over 1 point. The benefits of full credentialing generally work equally for all students without helping reduce the race gap, and without helping one racial group at the cost of another. (p. 494)*

> *Full credentials has a significant though small impact on all students' test scores, but it does not strongly benefit only minorities and thus it is not a likely candidate to decrease the "race gaps." (p. 499)*

The message here is clear: underqualified teachers, as defined by absence of degrees and credentials, can exacerbate learning problems for youngsters on the wrong side of the achievement gap. These students benefit from having teachers with advanced degrees and credentials. In high minority classrooms and schools, these educators can reverse learning declines. In more racially mixed classrooms and schools, they will benefit minority children and majority children about equally.

On the question of experience, Hughes (2003) concludes, "Effective teaching of Black students means being experienced" (p. 299). Darling-Hammond and Post (2000), in their review of this topic, arrive at a similar conclusion, finding, "Experience is associated with increases in student achievement" (p. 131). Grissmer (1998), however, reaches a different end point, reporting, "Production-function studies show no consistent effects of teachers' experience on student achievement" (p. 217). Here, as with many of the indicators of teacher quality, we find mixed results. The benefits teacher experience bring to student learning in general, and to the closing of achievement gaps in particular, are small, at best.

The overall conclusion in the area of teacher quality might best be summed up as follows. First, "the qualifications and training of students' teachers is important in the achievement narrative" (Darling-Hammond & Post, 2000, p. 132), although in what ways and how much is part of an ongoing debate in the academic community. Second, placing low-quality teachers as defined above in classrooms with high concentrations of low-income and African American students "serve[s] only to exacerbate the inequalities low-income and minority children experience" (p. 133). Third, today, "too many school[s] assign teachers without thinking about the ramifications for their students" (Jerald, 2002, p. 10). Fourth, more thoughtful and equitable teacher assignments can help in the quest to narrow achievement gaps (Thompson & O'Quinn, 2002, p. 23). Finally, educators and other policy makers need to be more proactive in "work[ing] toward a fair distribution of teacher talent" (Jerald, 2002, p. 13). In particular, more attention needs to be given to thinking through the types of incentives that must be developed to encourage high-quality teachers to teach in high-poverty and low-income schools in general, and to work with students below water on the gap issue in particular (Hertert & Teague, 2003; Kober, 2001). Or, as Thompson and O'Quinn (2001) capture it, "proposals to offer incentives to attract good teachers to low-performing schools may be essential" (p. 18) to address the gap problem. "Programs to attract high-quality teachers to high-poverty, high-minority schools can help to close the gap in teaching quality" (Reynolds, 2002, p. 14) and this can contribute to narrowing race and social class gaps in student achievement.

2. Provide additional instructional support to those in need.

There are some children, and in high poverty settings perhaps many, whose academic problems are not redressed by our current repertoire of well-crafted programs, and to help them probably will require even more far-reaching reforms. (Alexander, Entwisle, & Olson, 2001, p. 185)

As advocates for at-risk students have argued forcefully, it is unreasonable to expect and demand success without providing at-risk students with effective assistance to meet the expectations and standards. (Thompson & O'Quinn, 2001, p. 18)

A key message here is that one way to increase the number of high academic achievers from underrepresented groups may be to promote much wider use of out-of-school strategies used by the most educationally sophisticated or savvy parents and groups. Extensive supplementary education systems that support the use of these strategies could be a central element in such an effort. (Miller, 1999, p. 18)

Some approaches to closing achievement disparities involve additional instructional time outside the regular school day. (Davison et al., 2004, p. 760)

Throughout our analysis of the causes of achievement gaps, we saw that, on average, deficits build up for low-income and African American children in the preschool and early elementary years. Data from Chapter 2 also reveal that efforts to close gaps have not been especially productive. The same problem that has confronted us for the last forty years is staring us in the eye today. We also know that if schools are to be effective in this realm, they must "play a compensatory role to counteract the external forces that exist in the home and community" (Shannon & Bylsma, 2002, p. 21): "Schools may in fact play a compensatory role for children who do not receive adequate scholastic support through their family environments" (Chatterji, 2006, p. 504).

Where this storyline leads is to the following conclusion: schools (and parents and communities) need to find ways to add instructional time and other instructional resources—to "provide extended learning time and intensive supports" (Kober, 2001, p. 6)—to the educational package low-income and African American children receive (Alexander et al., 2001). What is important here is that these augmented resources (1) be of high quality (Miller 1999); (2) flow primarily to students on the wrong side of the achievement gap (Armor, 1992); (3) supplement not supplant current instructional resources (Ding & Davison, 2005; Schwartz, 2001; Spradlin et al., 2005), e.g., they add time; and (4) be a part of a comprehensive system of supports (Child and Family Policy Center, 2005).

What is called for is "a significant expansion and strengthening of supplementary education opportunities available to underrepresented minority students, from preschool through high school. High-quality after-school, summer, and other supplementary programs should be available for many more underrepresented minority students" (Miller, 1999, p. 3): "Academic support and enriched activities for students before and after regular school hours" (Hertert & Teague, 2003, p. 21) are especially important.

An academically rich summer program is an important piece of the support structure (Kober, 2001; Stinson, 2006). Because "full-day kindergarten appears to be effective in reducing achievement gaps" (Spradlin et al., 2005, p. 24), this too should be a key ingredient in the package of additional instructional support. So also should be a program of afterschool individual tutoring by highly trained tutors, preferably certified teachers (Schwartz, 2001; Thompson, 2002). The overarching goal is in thoughtful ways "to extend academic learning time to operate beyond the normal school day and to educate students longer than the current school year" (McGee, 2003, p. 491), to "create a network of supplemental opportunities for [disadvantaged] children that may best be described as a parallel education system" (Miller, 1999, p. 20).

3. Feature balanced instruction emphasizing basic skills,
teaching for understanding, and culturally responsive pedagogy.

When all is said and done, the main concern is quality of teaching. (Ferguson, 1998b, p. 366)

Better teaching appears to be related to better learning outcomes. (Borman & Kimball, 2005, p. 17)

Researchers have noted that achievement gap differences may be due to the kinds of teaching that occurs in classrooms. (Meehan et al., 2003, p. 7)

Racial differences in performance can be reduced through high quality instruction. (Shannon & Bylsma, 2002, p. 43)

To begin with, as we have reported throughout this volume, "teachers matter" (Ferguson, 1991, p. 7): "The role that teachers play in the school performance of black children is central and critical. Teachers' personal and cultural attributes as well as their attitudes and behaviors are important" (Irvine, 1990, p. 46). Indeed, "Instruction matters more than standards" (McGee, 2003, p. 35). Thus, on the one hand, research informs us, "Researchers' perceptions, expectations, and behaviors probably do help to sustain, and perhaps even to expand, the black-white test score gap" (Ferguson, 1998a, p. 313). On the other hand, this same research helps us see that instruction can help narrow achievement gaps (Shannon & Bylsma, 2002). All of this in turn is prelude to the argument that the data "urge us to question what can be done differently in classrooms" (Seiler & Elmesky, 2007, p. 393): "The research on learning requires rethinking about how students of color and poverty are taught" (Shannon & Bylsma, 2002, p. 49). For example, based on his research, Ferguson (1998a) concludes that "reducing the amount of unresponsive and ineffective teaching is almost surely an important response to the black-white test score gap" (p. 301), although he cautions that "whether particular teaching strategies can change rank order of performance among students" (p. 311) is an underinvestigated question.

Starting with Ferguson's caveat, research does shed some empirical light on instructional actions that may help students on the wrong side of the achievement gap. We highlight seven of these in this section. To begin with, (1) because "the way students are grouped for instruction can narrow or widen achievement gaps" (Thompson, 2002, p. 29), (2) because "ability grouping as commonly practiced widens rather than reduc[es] achievement gaps" (Thompson & O'Quinn, 2001, p. 6), and (3) because "sounder and more equitable grouping practices can do the reverse—narrow the gaps" (p. 6), there is a need to employ more equitable grouping arrangements in schools and to establish groups "only if it is done in a way that maximizes the positive effects and minimizes the negative ones" (Thompson, 2002, p. 29; see also Ferguson, 1998b). When students are clustered for instruction, it is important that the practice "places students of color in proportion to their numbers in high ability classes in the early grades and in higher tracks and college preparatory classes in high school" (Schwartz, 2001, p. 4). Research also helps us see that student grouping is more likely to result in positive outcomes for low-income and African American youngsters when students are grouped "for only one or two subjects, if students are grouped strictly on the basis of their skills in each specific subject to be taught, the teacher actually does pitch instruction to the right skill level and pace for each group, [and if] students [are] also reassessed often and reassigned to groups as appropriate" (Thompson & O'Quinn, 2001, p. 11; see also Slavin & Madden, 2001).

Second, instructional designs that "improve student-teacher interactions" (Balfanz & Byrnes, 2006, p. 156) help students catch up, thus narrowing achievement gaps (Balfanz & Byrnes, 2006).

On this front, Ferguson (2002) finds that positive "teacher-student relationships may be an especially important resource for motivating black students" (p. 1). He posits, "When teachers have strong content knowledge and are willing to adapt their pedagogies to meet student needs, adding good teacher-student relationships and strong encouragement to the mix may be key" (p. 1). In short, adding "high personalization" to "academic press" is especially effective for children who are currently disadvantaged.

Third, "theor[ies] of racial differences in response to instruction" (Slavin & Oickle, 1981, p. 180) suggest that healthy doses of cooperative learning strategies can narrow gaps (Irvine, 1990; Thompson & O'Quinn, 2001) and lead to "positive social outcomes as well" (Irvine, 1990, p. 100). Specifically, "Without holding back the achievement of whites, cooperative learning strategies apparently have the capability to significantly reduce achievement disparities between blacks and whites" (Slavin & Oickle, 1981, p. 179). Seiler and Elmesky (2007) refer to this more deeply as the prevalence of pedagogy that underscores social connectedness. They conclude that there is "a strong positive relationship between the academic performance of African American students and learning contexts that are communally oriented rather than contexts promoting competition and individualism" (p. 393).

Fourth, high expectations for student performance is an important instrument in the pedagogical gap reduction toolbox, one that is especially relevant in light of the research we reviewed in Chapter 8 that showed that teachers often hold different and lower expectations for African American and low-income children than they do for white and middle-class youngsters. The research is extensive and consistent, showing that teacher expectations matter in small but important ways (Magnuson & Duncan, 2006; Shannon & Bylsma, 2002): "The average effect of teacher expectancy is small in absolute terms [but] it can loom large for the academic fortunes of many students" (Miller, 1995, p. 227).

According to scholars in this area, higher expectations "increase both teacher and student perception of student capacity to learn" (Shannon & Bylsma, 2002, p. 35). They cause teachers to "reject deficit assumptions about children" (Burns et al., 2005, p. 23). Expectations and accompanying teacher efficacy "influence the choices that teachers make in their classrooms, in the activities, instructional materials, and disciplinary methods they use" (Shannon & Bylsma, 2002, p. 36). High expectations cause teachers to behave differently, and in ways that foster academic achievement (McGee, 2003).

Thus, teacher expectations are implicated in student learning. That is, "teacher expectations of themselves and their students also play a large role in how well students perform" (Shannon & Bylsma, 2002, p. 9): "Teachers' expectations do appear to influence their students' academic performance. Research indicates that low teacher expectations tend to lower students' academic performance and high expectations tend to raise it" (Miller, 1995, p. 227). In particular, "Those who are viewed negatively are disadvantaged" (Shannon & Bylsma, 2000, p. 36). Equally important for our purposes here, expectations are consequential in the achievement gap chronicle (Hughes, 2003; Meehan et al., 2003). Thus on the one hand, "The evidence . . . suggests that teachers' expectations and behaviors do contribute to the achievement gap between black and white students" (Hallinan, 2001, p. 63). On the other hand, these expectations can help reduce patterned learning differentials by race and social class. Hughes (2003), for example, concludes, "High expectations can disproportionately lead to . . . high subsequent performance among Black students" (p. 319). And, Meehan and colleagues (2003) report that teachers in minimum gap schools are more likely to communicate high expectations to their students. Bainbridge and Lasley (2002) provide a nice summary of the evidence here:

> *One of the elements appears especially critical to closing the gap—the teacher believes all students can succeed. Emerging evidence suggests that in schools where teachers evidence a real belief in students' abilities and are also able to communicate those beliefs in explicit ways, students do achieve better, and the gap does close. (p. 431)*

High expectations is an appealing if often an exhortatory and poorly illustrated concept (Thompson, 2002). Nonetheless, research on gap closing schools reveals that it is defined in action by the following: setting and maintaining high standards for low-income and African American youngsters—the same standards as for more advantaged children (Cole-Henderson, 2000); the refusal to accept excuses for limited effort and/or poor quality work (McGee, 2003); "nonjudgmental responsiveness" (Steele, 1997, p. 625); fierce persistence in ensuring that African American and low-income students reach targets (Shannon & Bylsma, 2002); and assuming individual and collective responsibility for student performance (Burns et al., 2005).

Fifth, research reveals that "culturally responsive teaching" (Burns et al., 2005, p. 28)—and the bundle of elements that make up "culturally relevant" (Uhlenberg & Brown, 2002, p. 28) or "culturally sensitive" (Norman et al., 2001, p. 1111) pedagogy—can help offset initial deficits and thus reduce racial gaps in achievement (Burns et al., 2005; Meehan et al., 2003). Indeed, "culturally consistent instruction can be beneficial to African American students" (Slavin & Madden, 2006, p. 390)—cultural theory alerts educators "to the fundamental role of cultural phenomena in explaining the origins of the achievement gap and its persistence and given these understandings, potentially promising avenues of intervention" (Norman et al., 2001, p. 1111).

Culturally responsive teaching, according to Gay (as cited in Shannon & Bylsma, 2002), uses "the cultural knowledge, prior experiences, frames of reference, and performance styles of ethnically diverse students to make learning encounters more relevant to and effective for them. It teaches to and through the strengths of these students" (p. 38). In culturally sensitive teaching, "principles of learning reinforce the importance of using a child's background as a foundation for teaching her or him" (p. 37): "One of the major attributes of culturally responsive instruction is that teachers build on the strengths and knowledge students bring to school" (Burns et al., 2005, p. 9) and see "students' home cultures and experiences as sources of learning" (p. 23; see also Steele, 1992; 1997). They "incorporate students' ways of being and doing" (Seiler & Elmesky, 2007, p. 413). As Knapp (2001) reminds us here, "The extent to which teachers can treat learners' backgrounds as a resource and proactively draw upon that resource in teaching distinguishes capable teaching of non-mainstream youngsters from less effective forms of teaching" (p. 195).

More concretely, Burns, Keyes, and Kusimo (2005) reveal:

> When educators exhibit cultural competence, they contextualize instruction in the experiences and skills of students' homes and communities. They also maintain ongoing dialogue with students, parents, and community, and they include parents and community members in school and classroom activities. Thus, they recognize a

variety of knowledge, skills, and values of the cultures and ethnicities represented in the classroom and incorporate them into the curriculum. Furthermore, educators extend their relationships with students and families beyond the classroom and school and into the community. Perhaps most important, they help students learn to be bicultural: that is, they help students learn to honor and embrace the best of their community's culture, language, and values. (pp. 29–30)

In culturally responsive pedagogy, teachers highlight culturally anchored sources of material (Meehan et al., 2003; Miller, 1999) and activities that "capitalize on cultural learning styles" (Irvine, 1990, p. 89): "In the minimum-gap schools, classrooms . . . relate topics to students' lives more than their counterparts" (Meehan et al., 2003, p. 29).

Sixth, effective instruction for African American and low-income students features both direct instruction on the basics and teaching for understanding for higher-order skills (Burns et al., 2005; Lewis, 2008; Shannon & Bylsma, 2002). Successful teachers use explicit instructional designs and teach for understanding inside an "open, risk-free environment" (Meehan, 2003, p. 21). On the teaching for understanding side of the ledger, we find the use of "cognitively demanding instructional strategies" (Knapp, 2001, p. 195) embedded in an understanding "that learners in high-poverty settings deserve, and can benefit from, challenging forms of instruction that are more prevalent (though still infrequent) in other settings" (p. 195). We also learn that a focus on "learning for understanding has been shown to dramatically improve the performance of traditionally under-achieving students" (Shannon & Bylsma, 2002, p. 9) inside the storyline of higher achievement for all. Although the issue of an equally good effect vs. a differential impact for disadvantaged students remains open, evidence leans to the conclusion that "more 'meaning-centered' teaching and learning approaches appear to have greater educational impact among minority and low-income students than among more advantaged students" (Scales et al., 2006, p. 44).

Finally, researchers have unearthed a small set of discrete teaching behaviors that advantage youngsters who are lagging academically. Most of these are found in the routines of teaching and classroom management—questioning, assessing, providing feedback, and so forth—that compose the grammar of the classroom. For example, questions that promote a high success rate benefit low-SES students more than high-SES youngsters (Bempechat, 1992). Extending wait time after questions also privileges low-income youngsters (Ferguson, 1998b; Shannon & Bylsma, 2002). Tailoring or differentiating instruction for pupils who are behind is beneficial as well (Ferguson, 1998b; McGee, 2003). So too is "diversify[ing] the assessment of Black students and mov[ing] away from strict multiple-choice tests as the only form of assessment" (Hughes, 2003, p. 319). Reducing time on classroom management and administrative routines also advantages African American students (Meehan et al., 2003): "Classroom time [is] used more effectively in minimum-gap schools" (Meehan et al., 2003, p. 27).

4. Ensure that all low-income and African American children complete a rigorous curriculum.

Our data support the conclusion that level of curriculum is a major concomitant of achievement. (Payne & Biddle, 1999, p. 10)

If black students are not challenged, there is little hope of decreasing the discrepant performance between blacks and whites in school achievement. (Beckford & Cooley, 1993, p. 16)

Because of the essential role of knowledge acquisition in all other aspects of learning, focusing on improving African-American knowledge acquisition is the first step in bridging the achievement gaps. (Learning Point Associates, 2004, p. 11)

The gains from taking a more demanding mathematics curriculum are even greater for African-American students than for white students. (Thompson & O'Quinn, 2001, p. 14)

While we know from earlier analysis that tracking and related actions in the domain of curricular rigor do not "cause" achievement gaps (Bali & Alvarez, 2003; Braun et al., 2006), a "challenging curriculum" (Hallinan, 2001, p. 60) has the power to help reduce patterned learning differentials between low-income and high-income students and African American and white pupils (Balfanz & Byrnes, 2006). Shannon and Bylsma (2002) maintain, for example, "To reduce the achievement gap, students of color and poverty must have access to cognitively rich, relevant curriculum content that is appropriate for their grade level" (p. 40). Other scholars also conclude that by "addressing disparities in curriculum" (Kober, 2001) "by dismantling tracking and providing the high-track curriculum to all, we can succeed in closing the achievement gap on important measures of learning" (Burris & Welner, 2005, p. 595).

The starting point here is that curriculum rigor is closely linked to learning: "High school and college outcomes seem to be strongly related to high school curricula" (Darity et al., 2001, p. 11).

Regardless of their prior grades and scores, students in college prep mathematics learned the most, "transition mathematics" students the next most; and low-track mathematics, the least. In other words, the higher level of mathematics curriculum students were exposed to, the more they learned, regardless of prior performance. (Thompson & O'Quinn, 2001, p. 13, noting the work of Porter)

American SIMS [Second International Mathematics Study] scores vary sharply depending on the level of curricular demand to which students are exposed. (Payne & Biddle, 1999, p. 9)

Adelman's work demonstrates that students who take more mathematics in high school are much more likely to complete a bachelor's degree than students who take less. On Adelman's five step "ladder" of mathematics coursework—with Pre-Algebra and Algebra at the bottom and Pre-Calculus and Calculus at the top—each step up the ladder increases a student's chances of graduating from college by more than two and one half times. (Thompson & O'Quinn, 2001, p. 14)

The connection between curricular rigor and learning for those on the wrong side of the achievement gap has been laid out by Shannon and Bylsma (2002): "Achievement differences among students of different racial and ethnic groups in such areas as mathematics, science, and foreign language are strongly related to differences in course taking" (p. 40). After addressing relevant controls, we learn, "Track placement maintains or exacerbates race-linked differences in measured achievement" (Lucas & Gamoran, 2002, p. 189). Most importantly, policies that have increased capacity and exposure to rigorous content have helped reduce the achievement gap (Balfanz & Byrnes, 2006; Harris & Herrington, 2006). That is, "for students who have the opportunity to take similar courses, achievement test scores differences by race narrow substantially" (Shannon & Bylsma, 2002, p. 40): "Thus, educational polices and reforms that require students to take college preparatory courses like mathematics are likely to further narrow the achievement gap, or at least keep it from widening" (Berends, 2005, p. 79). Indeed, "Minority and low-income students seem to benefit more than others from stronger course requirements" (Thompson, 2002, p. 30).

While curriculum rigor is the central component of our narrative at this point, it is important to place action here in context. This means that curriculum is connected to the three important elements of standards, alignment, and assessment. The standards "form the basis for curriculum development" (Schwartz, 2001, p. 2); they are the engine that powers curriculum (Spradlin et al., 2005). A key issue here is to ensure that curriculum development be informed by common content standards for all youngsters, regardless of race or social class (Meehan et al., 2003). Reynolds (2002) explains:

> There is a budding research agenda that points to some promising strategies for tackling achievement gaps. One common theme among them is the need for clear and public standards to guide teachers, students, administrators, and parents on what is expected from students at various benchmarks. Implicit in standards-based reform is that the standards apply to all students, precluding the notion that differing levels of success should be expected from different kinds of students. (p. 12)

When developers follow this prescription, historically disadvantaged youngsters benefit (Harris & Herrington, 2006). Alignment, in turn, ensures that what is valued in terms of curricular content is what actually unfolds in classrooms, is what is taught regardless of "program" or "conditions of children," and "alignment includes making sure that teachers know what is required by the state curriculum standards and that they use the standards to guide what they actually teach on a day to day basis" (Thompson, 2002, p. 20). Also, assessment means that the DNA in tests of all varieties is the standard that form the architecture of the curriculum (Kober, 2001; Thompson & O'Quinn, 2001).

Additionally, rigorous curriculum content rests on two supporting pillars. The first is the presence of "appropriate supports" (Shannon & Bylsma, 2002, p. 49), of "social and emotional support mechanisms for students" (Darity et al., 2001, p. 9). Ratcheting up academic press without the establishment of supports to help students succeed will not be maximally effective (Hertert & Teague, 2003): "Ultimately, programs that rely entirely on increasing academic standards without parallel attention to social-emotional factors associated with achievement motivation and performance will be less likely to improve student achievement outcomes" (Becker & Luthar, 2002, p. 200). In fact, it could "be both unsuccessful and destructive" (p. 199). Therefore, "Appropriate and persistent instruction and personal encouragement by 'warm demanders,' couched in caring and supportive classroom environments, must accompany the increase in challenging curriculum for students of color and poverty to thrive" (Shannon & Bylsma, 2002, p. 40).

The other supporting pillar is extra time for students to master challenging curricular content. This means first changing current practice to capture more time in the school day, recovering time being lost or poorly used, and privileging new uses of time (McGee, 2003; Shannon & Bylsma, 2002). It also entails the addition of time to master content (Haycock, 2001; North Carolina, 2000; Symonds, 2004), creating "extended learning time" (Shannon & Bylsma, 2002, p. 39). And, as Chatterji (2005a) reminds us, "For poor versus well-to-do children, more instructional time per day to mathematics and reading ha[s] a positive and significant effect on school achievement means" (p. 24).

Turning the spotlight more fully on the issue of ensuring that low-income and African American students learn in a rigorous curricular program, we already reported that, in general, these youngsters are on the wrong side of the opportunity divide, that "in too many schools some students are taught with a high-level curriculum, whereas other students continue to be taught with a low-level curriculum" (Spradlin et al., 2005, p. 21). We also revealed that while the situation is much less of a problem today than it was a generation ago (Berends et al., 2005), children from African American and low-income homes remain underrepresented in the top tracks in schools (Thompson & O'Quinn, 2001). In an even more balanced classes, these children are "taught less well" (Ferguson, 1998b, p. 366) than their peers. The result is that "opportunity to learn," one of the two critical variables in the learning algorithm, is unequally distributed, African American and low-income youngsters are held back, and gaps cannot be bridged (Lucas & Gamoran, 2002): "Students in advanced mathematics programs are exposed to material not available to others. Unless Black students are recommended for advanced courses in a school, to be privy to such material, gaps will persist" (Hughes, 2003, p. 317). Tracks, or curricular pathways are, therefore, implicated in African American-white and social class test score gaps (Lucas & Gamoran, 2002; Rumberger & Palardy, 2005), and in ways that harm children from black and poor homes.

Since "closing the racial gap in participation in challenging curricula may constitute an important mechanism for closing the gap on achievement test scores" (Darity et al., 2001, p. 11), educators need to see that each child takes rigorous coursework. As Mickelson and Heath (1999) affirm, " [A] secondary school's overall racial composition [is] less important for academic outcomes than the racial composition of the track in which a student [is] placed" (pp. 579–580). Thompson and O'Quinn (2001) further recommend:

> *What does seem necessary is for districts and schools to monitor the proportions of African-American and European-American students in the tracks they offer, and to take steps to assure that black and white students are distributed across tracks in roughly the same proportions as they are found in the schools' total population. (p. 13)*

One line of attack is on curricular programs themselves. Here, the guidance from the literature is to drop inadequately challenging courses and to strengthen the rigor of the remaining classes (Darity et al., 2001). Since "achievement follows from opportunities— opportunities that tracking denies" (Burris & Welner, 2005, p. 598), there are also recommendations that tracking procedures be dismantled and arbitrary barriers to participation in higher-level courses be removed (Darity et al., 2001). It is also suggested that schedules be established so that demanding gateway classes be completed by all students in the middle grades (Kober, 2001; Shannon & Bylsma, 2002). The rationale here is as follows: "In general, a more demanding curriculum that is successfully completed in middle school will more likely lead to the confidences and competency to take more demanding courses in high school" (Darity et al., 2001, p. 60). That is, "Exposure to a more challenging curriculum in the early grades better prepares students to meet the requirements (e.g., heavy work load, in-depth material, etc.) of advanced courses as they progress through school" (p. 46).

5. Develop a cohesive system for collecting, analyzing, and using data to understand, address, and close achievement gaps.

Making informed decisions about how to narrow the achievement gap requires consistent, reliable, and pertinent data and the skills to analyze it. (Hertert & Teague, 2003, p. 26)

Data alone doesn't improve schools, but data used effectively can lead schools to narrow and ultimately close the achievement gaps. (Symonds, 2004, p. 56)

Research increasingly exposes the importance of assessment as a tool in gap reduction work (Bennett et al., 2007; Shannon & Bylsma, 2002): "What does it take to close the achievement gap? Our findings suggest that what matters most is how schools use data" (Symonds, 2004, p. 15). The same studies also reveal three key dimensions of assessment: system elements, effectiveness criteria, and support. On the system front, scholars highlight two frameworks. The first features systematic methods of collecting, analyzing, and using data in decision making. The second underscores using data to understand, address, and impact patterned learning differentials. Across the system dimension, investigators confirm that educators who are successful in reducing achievement gaps are often quite proficient in analyzing data and using that information to improve conditions (e.g., instruction, school culture) that benefit African American and low-income youngsters (McGee, 2003). Teachers and school leaders are adept at "us[ing] data to understand skills gaps of low achieving students" (Symonds, 2004, p. 1). They are skilled at connecting data to gaps. They also systematically use data to monitor the impact of their decisions (Burns et al., 2005; North Carolina, 2000; Spradlin, et al., 2005). Overall, "They use test results wisely" (McGee, 2003, p. 28). Collectively, work around these two system frameworks produces "a continual improvement process [in which] those closing gaps are constantly examining strengths and weaknesses, trying new strategies, and evaluating progress" (Symonds, 2004, p. 51).

Data analysis linked to success in narrowing gaps is defined by certain elements or criteria. Systematic methods for gathering and employing data are in place (McGee, 2003). The work features multiple data gathering strategies across an assortment of the key domains of schooling (Symonds, 2004); it is not narrow in scope. Data work is frequent and ongoing (Schwartz, 2001; Slavin & Madden, 2001). For example, in the achievement domain, "Teachers at gap-closing schools are more likely to administer frequent assessments of students" (Symonds, 2004, p. 1). Data work that helps address gaps tends to be "fine-grained" (North Carolina, 2000, p. 7). There is a "real-time" (Symonds, 2004, p. 48) feature to data work; the turnaround from collection to analysis to use is short.

Schools that use data effectively in the service of narrowing achievement gaps tend to buttress those efforts with a comprehensive system of supports, that is, they support the data work in a variety of ways (Symonds, 2004). Time for the work is provided. For example, "In gap-closing schools teachers are more likely to have structured time during the school day to talk about results and next steps" (Symonds, 2004, p. 16). Collaborative work is stressed (Burns et al., 2005). Training on how to analyze and use data is provided. Key figures in the school are identified to lead and support data work (Darity et al., 2001). Policies to facilitate the work are crafted and put in place (Symonds, 2004). In short, gap reducing schools have "an infrastructure to support the consistent use of data with staff resources and time" (Symonds, 2004, p. 36).

Culture

School social environment positively influences achievement. (Wenglinsky, 1997, p. 225)

If school reforms are to close the achievement gap, they must recognize the role of culture in schooling. (Burns et al., 2005, p. 10)

Resolving the problem of the gap in achievement between African American students and other populations in U.S. urban schools may require a more sustained and systematic consideration of the wider issues of culture than previously has been the case. (Norman et al., 2001, p. 1111)

6. Develop a culture of high academic press and high personalization.

The more difficult it is for disadvantaged students to see positive things in the economic opportunity structure, the more important a genuinely engaging learning environment becomes for their academic success. (Miller, 1995, p. 258)

An academic climate, supported by a strong, school-oriented social network, promotes students' learning. (Hallinan, 2001, p. 60)

Research informs us that positive culture is an essential dimension of high performing schools. It also exposes the linkages between culture and achievement gaps. Finally, it tells us that "culture should be incorporated as a positive asset in the education of African American children" (Jagers & Carroll, 2002, p. 61) and low-income students. The two central extractions from all this research are as follows: A culture marked by high academic press and high personalization is key to helping ensure greater equity in learning. And the harmonies between the two—"caring in combination with high expectations" (Shannon & Bylsma, 2002, p. 35)—are critical. To be effective, "High expectations and warm personal relationships must both be present" (Thompson & O'Quinn, 2001, p. 16). To push academic press without attention to personalization "is not only unwise but unjust" (Becker & Luthar, 2002, p. 202). Synthetic work here also underscores the central role of school-based educators, for, as Raudenbush and colleagues (1998) inform us, "Effective adult leadership in a school setting is arguably the primary ingredient in creating such a climate" (p. 265). Reviews also tell us that the ability of these adults to model among themselves what they seek to create among students is especially important (McGee, 2003).

We begin with two notes that place boundaries around the analysis here. First, we have already spent considerable time exploring the first element in the organizing frame in this recommendation—high academic press or a "culture of achievement" (North Carolina, 2000,

p. 10). In the process, we described an "achievement ethic" (Ford, Grantham, & Whiting, 2008, p. 235) marked by "high learning standards, high expectations, and a culture of success for all" (McGee, 2003, p. 36). We do not repeat that analysis here. Second, our focus here is the culture of schooling as it relates to students. A comprehensive investigation of culture also needs to target teachers and parents. We address these other players in the school narrative later in this chapter.

Turning our attention, then, to the second element of the organizing frame—high personalization—we note that the goal is quite simple, if nonetheless complex: "A school environment that supports learning [where] every student is a valued member of the community" (Lewis, 2008, p. 43)—a place where every student is well known and cared for. On the one hand, this means developing a culture that offsets the negative aspects of climate found in many schools, e.g., anonymity, isolation, especially overcoming the forces (1) pushing students to "oppositionality," "resistance," and "disengagement" (Norman et al., 2001, p. 1103); (2) reinforcing "cultural stereotypes . . . that [are] linked to the underperformance of minority children" (Magnuson & Duncan, 2006, p. 391); and (3) fomenting alienation (Becker & Luthar, 2002; Miller, 1995). On the other hand, it means fostering a climate permeated by trust (Bennett et al., 2007). "Based on the belief that students' greater attachment to the school community should in turn promote greater commitment to school norms and values as reflected in student behavior" (Becker & Luthar, 2002, p. 200), it means developing strategies to bond youngsters to important school values (Burns et al., 2005). And, to presage our conclusion, Becker and Luthar (2002) help us see that these "feelings of school belonging . . . consistently show positive associations with achievement outcomes" (p. 202).

Elements. More concretely, research enables us to unpack the concept of high personalization into defining characteristics. One element is caring (Shannon & Bylsma, 2002). As noted, in schools characterized by highly personalized climates, each student is well known and cared for: "The entire school exudes a zealous commitment to reaching each and every child" (McGee, 2003, p. 29). According to Shannon and Bylsma (2002):

> *Genuine caring values the individual and conveys belief in [his/her] capacity to learn. Caring entails listening sincerely to students, knowing something about the students and their lives, and developing positive relationships with them. Explicit caring creates the relationships, the "bonds" necessary to ensure learning. (p. 34)*

A second characteristic is trust—trust in the school and the educators who work there (Bennett et al., 2007). Miller expands on this as follows:

> *In order to be successful in school, children must trust their teachers and the school as an institution. They must also eventually trust society's commitment to provide them with real economic opportunity. To the degree that students trust both the school and the society, they will put forth effort to learn; to the degree that they lack trust, they will resist becoming educated. (Miller, 1995, p. 283)*

A third element is affiliation inside community. Indeed, "Evidence shows that better outcomes are achieved by 'personal-communal' school models that foster common learning experiences [and] opportunities for cooperative work and continual relationships" (Darling-Hammond

& Post, 2000, p. 163): "Research suggests that teaching philosophies and practices that are consistent with the notion of school as community can help to create fertile social contexts for African American children" (Jagers & Carroll, 2002, p. 61). That is, high personalization via community can help narrow achievement gaps. The hydraulics of this phenomenon are as follows:

> *[Because] motivation in African-American children from low socioeconomic groups is more influenced by the need for affiliation than for achievement (Delpit, as cited in Shannon & Bylsma, 2002, p. 34), social support and belonging in the classroom may be one of the most important factors involved in disadvantaged students' achievement motivation and engagement . . . community [is] positively associated with most measures of academic attitudes and motives, with results especially pronounced among the most disadvantaged student populations. (Becker & Luthar, 2002, p. 201)*

For teachers, these personalized communities are defined (1) by a willingness to really know students as individuals; (2) by shared goals, shared work, and shared accountability for student outcomes (McGee, 2003; Thernstrom & Thernstrom, 2002); and (3) by a commitment to help each student succeed (Thompson & O'Quinn, 2001).

A fourth essential element of personalization is the prevalence of nurturing and supportive relationships between educators and students (Becker & Luthar, 2002). Personalization is the antidote to the anonymity so common in the culture of many schools, especially those serving predominantly low-income and African American youngsters.

Given our focus here on African American children, a fifth element of personalization that has received considerable attention in the literature is the crafting of school culture that is reflective of the culture of students' homes and communities (Burns et al., 2005; Schwartz, 2001). And, as is the case with other elements of personalization (e.g., community), research reveals, "Efforts to adapt school practices to the cultural attributes of a particular group of children can be educationally very rewarding" (Miller, 1995, p. 265). The goal is to replace the cultural clash that many African American children experience in school, what Miller calls "the cultural incompatibility between the home and the school" (p. 286), with a climate that acknowledges, respects, and builds from the experiences of the students' environment (Thompson & O'Quinn, 2001). Culturally responsive cultures "offer an important basis for establishing trust in the school by respecting the culture of the children and providing the bridges required for them to develop the capacities to succeed in the mainstream" (Miller, 1995, p. 283): "Learning begins with the learners' frame of reference, so culture cannot be separated from schooling" (Shannon & Bylsma, 2002, p. 37) and "understanding how the student's culture influences his or her learning and social needs can help teachers and administrators create a learning environment that is welcoming to all students and fully engages each in learning" (Williamson, 2005, p. 25).

According to Hale-Benson (1990), educational change in the service of better outcomes for African American children "will not occur until we root the . . . practice of education . . . in the context of their culture" (p. 202). Hale-Benson maintains, therefore, that "interrelated learning environments must be created in which African-American culture in all its diversity is integrated comprehensively" (p. 202) into the classroom and school (see the earlier discussion of culturally responsive classrooms in the section on the "Instructional Program"). Biddle (2001) concurs, arguing "Schools can increase chances for impoverished students if only they will modify their programs so as to grant greater status to the subcultural traditions those students represent" (p. 13). Indeed, it is generally held that "the absence of such culturally attuned practices increase the likelihood of school failure and isolation" (Miller, 1995, p. 283). Such a culture recognizes "the impact of poverty on the lives and learning of children" (Shannon & Bylsma, 2002, p. 38) and "explicitly honors students and their heritage" (p. 39). A culturally responsive culture acknowledges that "race matters" (Symonds, 2004, p. 53) and promotes conversations about race. As Symonds asserts, it is not color blind:

> *Talking about race and taking action with particular groups of students in mind may seem controversial or counterintuitive to many people raised to think color blindness is the goal, but the findings of this study strongly suggest that addressing race is what it will take to narrow the achievement gaps in our nation's schools. (p. 53)*

Strategies. Research does more than unearth the elements of a personalized learning environment, however. It also highlights strategies that educators can employ to create personalized learning climates, as well as some barriers that stand in the way of this work. On the obstacle side of the ledger, Miller (1995) reports:

> *The capacity of educators to meet the needs of a culturally different group of students may be limited or compromised by one or more of the following conditions: (1) incongruities between the culture of the school and that of the group of students, (2) teachers' failure to recognize these cultural differences, (3) the lack of proven strategies for altering school practices to accommodate certain cultural differences, (4) the lack of consensus that specific practices should be implemented in the school to address cultural differences, (5) the lack of training for teachers and administrators in the relevant knowledge base for addressing cultural differences, (6) insufficient financial resources to implement available strategies, and (7) the absence of humane social and economic conditions and associated public policies that are crucial to the academic success of the children. (pp. 284–285)*

On the positive side of the ledger, scholars outline productive initiatives. Hiring more African American teachers and school leaders is a productive strategy (Miller, 1995), so too is offering culturally relevant services. At the school level, culturally anchored clubs have been found to be effective in bonding African American youngsters to valued school norms and in promoting student achievement (Goldsmith, 2004; Symonds, 2004). Providing structured opportunities for faculty to discuss race has also been found to be a strategy characterizing gap closing schools (Symonds, 2004). Creating opportunities for students to become meaningfully involved in school activities and to assume leadership roles in the school is a proven way to increase personalization (Murphy, Beck, Crawford, & Hodges, 2001). In a similar fashion, creating a rich array of extra or cocurricular activities and working to ensure that students partake of these opportunities builds connections to the school and nurtures academic success (Burns et al., 2005; Lewis, 2008). As Banks and colleagues (as cited in Shannon & Bylsma, 2002) inform us:

> *Significant research supports the proposition that participation in afterschool programs, academic associations like language clubs, and school-sponsored social*

activities contributes to academic performance, reduces high school drop-out rates and discipline problems, and enhances interpersonal skills among students from different ethnic backgrounds. (p. 41)

Thompson (2002) reinforces this conclusion, reporting, "Active efforts to involve at-risk students in extracurricular activities where they have more opportunity to form personal bonds with adults, appear to have surprisingly strong effects" (p. 24).

Personalization is also deepened by building up programs that provide guidance and counseling to targeted students (Darity et al., 2001). These include formal counseling programs, student support teams, and mentoring programs (e.g., adult-student advisory groupings) that allow students to be known well by adults, and adults to serve as advocates for youngsters (Darling-Hammond & Post, 2000; Schmid, 2001; Symonds, 2004). Elsewhere in this chapter, we report on the academic benefits that flow to African American youngsters from cooperative approaches to learning and small classes/schools. Here we add that these interventions, when done well, contribute to the creation of personalized learning environments (Darling-Hammond & Post, 2000). In a related vein, offering comprehensive services at the school for young people deepens connections between them and the school (Becker & Luthar, 2002; Symonds, 2004).

Because "differential risk and protection factors . . . profoundly influence students' achievement motivation and performance" (Becker & Luthar, 2002, p. 201), youngsters are more likely to become part of the school community when they are enmeshed in a safe and orderly learning climate (McGee, 2003), "where staff and students demonstrate respect for each other . . . and where the code of conduct is well-publicized, fair, and uniformly enforced" (Schwartz, 2001, p. 4)—where students do not feel singled out for disciplinary action (Burns et al., 2005; Williams, 2003). Students are also more likely to connect to the school, and to perceive the culture as personalized, when the school commits time and resources "to celebrate achievement and to highlight the accomplishments of students" (North Carolina, 2000, p. 10), where there is a culture of "shared pride and success" (McGee, 2003, p. 27).

7. Mix students by race and class.

Who sits next to whom does matter. (Rothstein, 2004, p. 130)

It will be recalled that the Coleman report concluded that a student's school peers were the most important school factor in predicting his or her academic achievement. (Miller, 1995, p. 208)

Researchers who have focused on the impact of school peers on academic achievement have found a close relationship between the two factors. (Caldas & Bankston, 1997, p. 271)

There is a growing research literature showing that student performance is determined as much by the characteristics of students' peers as the characteristics and performance of their teachers and administrators. (Harris & Herrington, 2006, p. 222)

For most students, school culture is shaped by the peers with whom they interact: "Schoolmates create their own social context, independent of any individual's own background, which has a strong influence on individual academic achievement" (Caldas & Bankston, 1997, p. 271). We revealed, in our earlier causal analysis of achievement gaps, how peers can pull students into a culture that is oppositional to core school values and norms. We argue here that schools can shape peer influence on school culture. They can permit "peer group effects" (Lee, 2004, p. 64) to damage the achievement of youngsters or they can influence peer interactions in ways that help ensure a more equitable distribution of learning.

The starting point is the current state of affairs in which we often find similar types of students in terms of race and social class clustered together in classrooms and schools. The second link in the chain is the findings from the more rigorous studies that "support the view that [this] race and class segregation matter[s]" (Roscigno, 2000, p. 269): "Who sits next to whom is not trivial. It makes a difference in student learning" (Thompson & O'Quinn, 2000, p. 20):

> *Because of the paramount role of the peer group in adolescent lives, educational outcomes usually attributed to students' own family traits may be a result of the general climate established by the traits of schoolmates. (Caldas & Bankston, 1997, p. 272)*

> *Racial segregation can affect relative educational achievement through several mechanisms. One of the most widely discussed channels is a peer exposure effect, arising from the fact that students' outcomes depend on the expectations and achievement of their peers and from a presumed correlation between these characteristics and the racial composition of the peer group. (Card & Rothstein, 2007, p. 2160)*

The third point is that reversing segregation matters: "The benefits of integration are clear, especially for the most disadvantaged students" (Entwisle & Alexander, 1992, p. 83). As Cook and Evans (2000) reveal, a recent study "by the National Academy of Science identified desegregation as one of the two contributing factors to the convergence in white and black test scores" (p. 732). The final step in our logic chain was introduced above; that is, schools need to be more aggressive on the policy and practice fronts to create "more equitable distribution[s] of children" (Lee & Burkam, 2002, p. 85) across classrooms and schools. They need to actively manage the "peer influence effect" (Card & Rothstein, 2007, p. 2160). The appropriate intermediate goal is "reciprocity among racial groups" (Lee, 2004, p. 64) and social groups, with the end result of narrowed gaps in student achievement.

Segregation and School Culture. Embedded in the above narrative are two storylines: (1) segregation and its impact on achievement (and, by relation, desegregation and its impact on learning) and (2) the theory of action about these influences and impacts. In the first storyline, the question is "how much of the academic achievement of students from one group affects the achievement of students from the other groups and how this peer group effect has any bearing on equity" (Lee, 2004, p. 64). Here, the research informs us that segregation in schools and classrooms imposes real costs on low-income and African American students. That is, "Accounting for disparities in school composition is important in examining relationships to the continuing inequalities in black-white test score differences" (Berends et al., 2005, p. 65).

Let us begin with race. While there is not complete agreement among researchers (see Armor, 1992; Card & Rothstein, 2007; Hallinan, 2001), and while the massive community segregation in many locations places considerable constraints on the use of desegregation as a tool for change (Goldsmith, 2004), i.e., "the possibilities for mixing students are limited" (Entwisle & Alexander, 1992, p. 83), the bulk of the evidence holds, as explained by Bankston and Caldas (1998):

> Not only does the proportion of African American students have a negative correlation with test scores, but also that a small amount of the achievement gap between African Americans and Whites is associated with the fact that African Americans are, by definition, more likely to be found in schools with large numbers of minority students. (p. 720).

Thus, "Minority concentration in school has a powerful effect on the academic achievement of Black . . . students" (Mickelson & Heath, 1999, p. 568). African American students learn less in segregated schools, "significantly less than whites who attend segregated schools" (Entwisle & Alexander, 1992, p. 80): "The greater the percentage of African American students, the lower students' test scores, controlling for minority race" (Bankston & Caldas, 1998, p. 720).

On the flip side of the page, we discover that integration advantages African American youngsters (Coleman et al., 1966; Entwisle & Alexander, 1992; Gordon, 1976; Mickelson & Heath, 1999), that "desegregation is an important tool for closing minority achievement gaps" (Thompson, 2002, p. 34): "studies of the long-term effects consistently show that desegregation is related to positive outcomes" (Berends et al., 2005, p. 28) in terms of "minority students' achievement scores" (p. 28). More specifically for the purposes of this volume, "Progress in desegregation [has] contributed to narrowing the Black-White achievement gap" (Lee, 2002, p. 10).

Moving the spotlight from racial composition to socioeconomic composition does not change the picture, for, as we have reported throughout this volume, race is a marker for SES and family structure; that is, "racial segregation is strongly related to socioeconomic segregation" (Rumberger & Palardy, 2005, p. 2001). And while race matters, socioeconomic status matters even more (Rumberger & Palardy, 2005). "The combination of school and individual SES, apart from race and other factors, has a powerful influence on academic achievement" (Caldas & Bankston, 1997, pp. 279–280):

> The social composition of the student body is more highly related to achievement, independent of the student's own social background, than is any school factor. (Coleman et al., 1968, p. 325)

> Going to school with classmates from relatively high family social status backgrounds does make a strong and significant contribution to academic achievement, independent of one's own family SES or race. (Caldas & Bankston, 1997, p. 281)

The Cultural Pathway. The key question for our second storyline is "why does the SES [and race] of a school's student body matter" (Rumberger & Palardy, 2005, p. 2016). There is a considerable body of work that addresses this question, illuminating the pathways between segregation (and desegregation) by class and race and student learning. That research also informs us "that the mechanisms by which peer groups effect the academic achievement of individuals are complex" (Caldas & Bankston, 1997, p. 272). Some of these pathways have already been explored in detail. For example, we examined the association between segregation by social class and race, and the provision of important school resources that explain student learning. In so doing, we reported, "The social composition affects student achievement largely because of its relationship to other, seemingly alterable characteristics of schools, such as school resources, structures, or practices" (Rumberger & Palardy, 2005, p. 2002). That is, "There is clear evidence that schools with a substantial white presence get more resources of the sort that matter to school achievement, such as good teachers and access to instructional materials" (Thompson, 2002, p. 33). We also investigated the connections between class and race segregation and the allocation of expectations and demands for excellence by educators. In both of these earlier analyses (resources and expectations), we saw that African American and low-income children are disadvantaged by attending schools and sitting in classrooms that are segregated by race and social class.

Here, in our discussion of school climate, we throw the spotlight on a third pathway, peer effects and peer culture. We argue, along with others, that "the peer effects of segregation itself may be the problem" (Rumberger & Palardy, 2005, p. 2002), or at least a central part of the problem. The essence of the position is twofold. First, concentrating low-income and African American students helps produce a culture in which negative school attitudes, poor behavior, low motivation, limited effort, and poor self-concept blankets students (Ainsworth-Darnell & Downey, 1998; Balfanz & Byrnes, 2006; DuBois, 2001). Consistent with our use of a cultural frame, we find, "Shared beliefs, habits, and peer pressure . . . [act] as important mechanisms by which peer groups affect individual academic achievement" (Caldas & Bankston, 1997, p. 271). Second, segregation helps create a culture in which students have limited exposure to high aspirations for school success and for post-school opportunities, the reverse of the so-called "middle-class peer effect" (Rumberger & Palardy, 2005, p. 2001). To return to the central point here, researchers have established a "consistent relationship between peer influence and students' standardized test scores, course grades, educational aspirations, and occupational aspirations" (Miller, 1995, pp. 208–209).

Strategies. Unraveling the peer effects of segregation and desegregation by race and social class, on the formation of school culture and on valued student learning outcomes, is important. But, taking action to counteract peer effects is still required if gaps are to be closed. Thus, we arrive back at our guideline: mix students by race and class. We know that African American and low-income students often have "difficulty becoming members of peer group[s] in which academic achievement [is] encouraged" (Miller, 1995, p. 209). Concomitantly, these students are often pulled into peer groups with decidedly non-pro achievement norms (Caldas & Bankston, 1997). If who sits next to whom in our classrooms is important, then educators need to be much more proactive in working through ways to get students on the wrong side of the achievement gap into meaningful contact with peers with proachievement norms, strong academic performance, and high aspirations for school and postschool success. In particular, these youngsters need to spend time (1) with high-ability and high-SES peers (Rumberger & Palardy, 2005) and (2) in high achievement-gain classrooms (Balfanz & Byrnes, 2006). Stiefel and associates (2006) provide a concrete example of action as follows:

> *If the students in these [restructuring] schools were placed in schools that performed at the average of their borough, our estimates suggest that the black-white gap would decline by .03 standard deviations in both fifth and eighth grades. While these are small reductions, if these relationships held ever year from fifth to twelfth grade, and such changes were made each year, the overall black-white gap would decline by .24 standard deviations by high school graduation. (p. 26)*

Structure and Support

> *Structural aspects of schooling ... can influence school performance, and more particularly, structural manipulation of the educational system might be used in the service of improving achievement and equity outcomes. (Johnson, Howley, & Howley, 2002, p. 7)*

So far, we have provided guidelines for closing achievement gaps focusing on the instructional program and the school culture. Here, we offer gap closing strategies that address school structure and support. We highlight three areas: linkages between school and home, professional development, and class and school size.

> *8. Build linkages between home and school that focus on student learning.*

> *Countless studies have demonstrated the importance of parental support and school involvement on the educational achievement of disadvantaged students. (Becker & Luthar, 2002, p. 200)*

> *The recognition of the power of schools to make a difference in the lives of poor students needs to be coupled with efforts to involve parents and communities in the schooling process so that all parents, not just middle-class parents, are active collaborators in the education of their children. (Entwisle et al., 2000, p. 30)*

> *Increasing parent involvement has been identified as a possible strategy for reducing the achievement gap. (Lee & Bowen, 2006, p. 194)*

> *The achievement gap will be eliminated only through partnerships that involve families and communities in the education of students of color and poverty. (Shannon & Bylsma, 2002, p. 50)*

There is an extensive body of evidence that "parent education and involvement have a direct and strong impact on student achievement" (McGee, 2003, p. 47); that is, "parent involvement is known to be an important predictor of students' success in school" (Gandara et al., 2003, p. 37). There is also a growing body of research that suggests, "Close cooperation between schools, parents, and the community is one of the keys to closing the achievement gap" (Shannon & Bylsma, 2002, p. 10). To be more specific, reviews of research conclude,

"When families and schools cooperate, students achieve higher grades and test scores" (Shannon & Bylsma, 2002, p. 44). Students also experience the following benefits:

- Better attendance and more homework done
- Fewer placements in special education
- More positive attitudes and behavior
- Higher graduation rates
- Greater enrollment in postsecondary education. (p. 45)

Scholars of home-school linkages provide a variety of frames for "build[ing] an ethos of achievement from the classroom to the home" (Chubb & Loveless, 2002, p. 8). For example, Kosters and Mast (2003), present a three part framework, featuring "policies that carve out a bigger role for families, that create incentives for parents to be better informed about their children's progress, and that afford families more choice about their children's education (p. 97). Lee and Bowen (2006), in turn, provide a two-pronged framework highlighting parent involvement at the school and parent involvement at home, "both of which may be related to the achievement gap" (p. 196). They maintain, "Parent involvement at school promotes connections between adults in two of the child's primary microsystems, the home and the school, while parent educational involvement at home conveys congruence in the attitudes and behaviors governing these two microsystems" (p. 196).

On the first element of Lee and Bowen's (2006) framework, parental involvement in the school, research informs us that schools that reduce gaps are "deliberate in recruiting parent involvement in school activities" (Burns et al., 2005, p. 9). Educators "extend themselves to make school a comforting, welcoming place" (McGee, 2003, p. 32). Because they understand that "the fit between home and school environments is important" (Bainbridge & Lasley, 2002, p. 431), they are especially adept at bridging home and school cultures (Burns et al., 2005; Hughes, 2003). Additionally, they design interventions that "build on each family's unique strengths" (Lee & Bowen, 2006, p. 215). While Sanders et al. (2002) acknowledge that "schools with high concentrations of poor and minority students, unlike their more affluent counterparts, must . . . plan partnership programs that are meaningful and focus on important goals for student learning" (p. 179), they also advise these schools to "address challenges that might impede the participation of poor and minority families" (p. 179). That is, institutions successful with gap closing are also active in removing barriers that hinder parental involvement (Schwartz, 2001). They employ "creative strategies to overcome barriers related to work schedules, transportation, negative interpretations of cultural differences on the part of school staff, and discomfort in the school setting on the part of the parents" (Lee & Bowen, 2006, p. 14; see also Sanders et al., 2002). They do not force a single model of connections on parents (Miller, 1995). They are sincere about parent engagement.

In their quest to create "congruence between family habitus and the educational field" (Lee & Bowen, 2006, p. 212), gap-reducing schools "offer multiple opportunities for parents to be involved and informed" (Lewis, 2008, p. 14). They create venues for parents to volunteer at the school. They "organiz[e] leisure activities with an academic focus" (Schwartz, 2001, p. 6). They provide numerous parent-teacher conferences and "programs featuring students" (Lee & Bowen, 2006, p. 194).

"Just as it is important to provide children with the appropriate educational opportunities, it is also necessary to ensure that parents have the necessary skills to assist their children"

(Beckford & Cooley, 1993, p. 16). As Meyers and colleagues (2004) remind us, "If parents must bear greater burdens to improve minority students' test scores, then we must determine what resources and knowledge they need to do the job and do it effectively. It is of little use to say that parents must ultimately be responsible for their children's math and reading readiness without providing parents with the instruction or assistance necessary to fulfill this responsibility" (p. 94). It is not surprising, therefore, that many schools that experience success in narrowing achievement gaps are proactive and skilled in "teaching parents how to parent" (McGee, 2003, p. 32), and in "offering parent outreach and education programs" (Uhlenberg & Brown, 2002, p. 497; see also Slavin & Madden, 2001).

In the second category, parental support of the education of children at home, researchers confirm, "The more time parents spend in educationally supportive ways with their children, the better their children are likely to do in school" (Miller, 1995, p. 97). They also delineate lines of action and strategies that help damp down learning differentials between high- and low-income youngsters and white and African American children (Jarrett, 1997; McGee, 2003; Rumberger & Gandara, 2004). On the "line of action" front, for example, Lee and Bowen (2006) hold, "Parent educational involvement at home may include providing help with homework, discussing the children's schoolwork and experiences at school, and structuring home activities" (p. 194).

On the "strategies" front, scholars reveal a number of specific parental actions that can support the education of children at home. One critical action that is linked to achievement in general, and gap reduction in particular, is ensuring that children attend school on a regular basis (Barton, 2003; Chatterji, 2006). A second action is to promote high expectations at home for school success (Schwartz, 2001; Shannon & Bylsma, 2002). A third behavioral pathway for families to pursue is to "create a home environment that encourages learning" (Shannon & Bylsma, 2002, p. 45), including "providing a specific, quiet place" (Thompson, 2002, p. 32) for schoolwork. Another activity that may carry extra weight in the gap reduction toolbox is to work with children on their homework (Lee & Bowen, 2006). This often includes encouragement to complete homework (Barton, 2003), "insisting on a time for homework, checking that homework is complete" (Thompson, 2002, p. 32), and working directly with children at home on school assignments (Chatterji, 2006). A fifth step is to link children with enhanced learning opportunities outside of school, i.e., in the larger community (Ferguson, 2002; Shannon & Bylsma, 2002). Reading to and with children is also an especially powerful strategy that parents can pursue to support learning at home, especially in the early grades (Chatterji, 2006; Gandara et al., 2003). We note, again, the special place that shared reading plays in helping to narrow achievement gaps:

Reading deficits tend to decline for African American children at schools in which the average reading time given to children at home is higher. (Chatterji, 2006, p. 504)

[In addition] more reading time given by parents, on average, had a large positive effect on school mathematics achievement means, controlling for children's background characteristics. Although the study did not establish causal links, the association of mathematics achievement with increased reading activities at home is encouraging. (Chatterji, 2005a, p. 24)

We close our discussion on parent involvement at home with two notes. First, this valuable resource can be developed and nurtured by school staff. Indeed, if it is to materialize in any systematic way for low-income and African American families, such support is essential (Hughes, 2003; McGee, 2003). Second, "Many educators lack the organizational skills required to develop and implement schoolwide partnership programs within their given time and resource constraints. This fact is especially salient in schools with high concentrations of poor and minority students" (Sanders et al., 2002, p. 179). Professional development to help educators learn to assist parents in their home education role is, therefore, probably essential (Sanders et al., 2002).

9. Provide high-quality professional development to help teachers close achievement gaps.

The persistence of the achievement gap calls for sustained teacher professional development that will help teachers to implement effective strategies that will enable all students to learn in that culturally complex environment. (Norman et al., 2001, p. 1111)

Investing in teachers really does pay dividends. (Haycock, 1998, p. 27)

Simply cajoling teachers to raise their expectations for Black children, using phrases such as "all children can learn," is probably a waste of time. However, good professional development programs can make a difference. (Ferguson, 2003, p. 494)

Gap-closing schools give their teachers more frequent professional development. (Symonds, 2004, p. 42)

Earlier in our analysis of the instructional program, we documented that quality instruction is a particularly important strategy in the gap reduction portfolio. Here, we argue that the ongoing education of teachers is key to enhancing instructional quality (Trueba, 1983), and given an almost unlimited call on school resources, "funds for professional development are especially important" (Gamoran, 2000, p. 113). We start with a review of key findings. First, there is a "link between professional development and student learning as measured by standardized tests" (Thompson, 2002, p. 13; see also Cole-Henderson, 2000; Gandara et al., 2003). Second, professional development in general, and the education of teachers of poor and African American children in particular, leaves a good deal to be desired (Hertert & Teague, 2003). Too often, teachers in the latter group "are left to fend for themselves with inadequate . . . training" (Hakuta, 2002, p. 28). Third, because a "critical part of capacity building is increasing the skills of teachers on the job [and] because incentives for agents to do something that they do not know how to do are likely to lead to dysfunctional responses" (Murnane & Levy, 2004, p. 412), much more professional development is needed (Hughes, 2003; Singham, 2003). If gaps are ever to be closed, "teachers need to be able to know what to do and how to do it" (Symonds, 2004, p. 52). And fourth:

Increased or redirected spending toward professional development for teachers aimed at improving (a) teacher-student relationships, (b) quality instruction, and (c) methods of handling student misbehavior in ways that do not detract from the quality of teacher-student relationships or from learning opportunities should assist teachers in producing the major achievement improvements demanded by accountability policies. (Becker & Luthar, 2003, p. 200)

Process Issues. Learning experiences for teachers that will enhance achievement need to scaffold on the principles of high quality professional development. Researchers who have examined the reasons why professional development serves to enhance teacher performance and student outcomes, and analysts who have traced the characteristics of professional development programs that are the most effective, have amassed a fruitful body of wisdom for those interested in closing achievement gaps. To begin with, professional development is most efficacious when it is highly valued at the school by the teachers and especially by the principal (Fisher & Adler, 1999). Adult learning also works best when educators at the site have a "positive attitude toward staff growth and development" (Hoffman & Rutherford, 1984, p. 87) and a commitment to improvement (Mattson, 1994).

Thinking about professional development from the perspective of structure or organization, we know that most staff development is freestanding, short-term, nonsystematic, and infrequent. We also understand that these characteristics make implementation of change problematic and do little to enhance teacher performance (Richardson, 1998). On the other hand, professional development is most effective in garnering improvements when it is part of a thoughtful plan, is long-term in nature, and employs frequent learning sessions for teachers (Hiebert & Pearson, 1999; Morris et al., 1990; Samuels, 1981). Inservice tends to be most influential when the "education programs involve teachers who choose to participate" (Anders et al., 2000, p. 730). Furthermore, because "achieving and sustaining . . . gains is often difficult when improvements are introduced on a classroom-by-classroom basis" (Snow et al., 1998, p. 11), schoolwide professional development often leads to more favorable results (Richardson, 1998; Taylor et al., 1999). Inservice is carefully joined to other aspects and dimensions of the organization (Au & Asam, 1996; Phi Delta Kappa, 1980) and "the aspects of school change" (Askew & Gaffney, 1999, p. 87). The provision of sufficient time for learning is also a distinguishing characteristic of quality professional development (Anders et al., 2000; Taylor & Taxis, n.d.). Finally, professional development in successful schools is defined by high levels of administrative support (Anderson et al., 1985; Dungan, 1994; Hiebert & Pearson, 1999) and involvement, especially "principal participation in training" (Samuels, 1981, p. 268). Indeed, "Staff development programs are most meaningful when principals and other administrators participate directly in them at the classroom level" (Manning, 1995, p. 656).

Continuous and intensive support over time is an essential ingredient of inservice programs that promote high levels of student achievement (Askew & Gaffney, 1999; Hiebert et al., 1992). Another critical point is "that teacher change needs support in the context of practice" (Anders et al., 2000, p. 730). Effective professional development grows from "child-driven data gathering" (Askew & Gaffney, 1999, p. 85) and from student needs. It builds from student performance data and school results (Briggs & Thomas, 1997).

The programs that are successful are practice-anchored and job-embedded; that is, they are context sensitive. "Context specificity" (Hiebert & Pearson, 1999, p. 13) contains a number of key ideas, but primarily it means "building from analysis of [one's] own setting" (p. 13).

Sensitivity to context implies that "teachers learn in the classrooms and schools in which they teach" (Stigler & Hiebert, 1999, p. 135). They "learn how to teach more effectively while teaching" (Lyons & Pinnell, 1999, p. 205), rather than in traditional out-of-class and school activities. Growth is "connected to and derived from teachers' work with children" (Askew & Gaffney, 1999, p. 87) and effectiveness comes to be defined in terms of "what works with the children [one is] teaching" (Duffy-Hester, 1999, p. 489; see also Pinnell et al., 1994). The center of gravity is real challenges in the classroom (Au & Asam, 1996), that is, "resolving instructional problems" (Manning, 1995, p. 656). "All theory building is then checked against practice" (Askew & Gaffney, 1999, p. 85) and "application is direct and obvious" (Stigler & Hiebert, 1999, p. 165).

Concomitantly, professional learning is not insular. Effective programs are adept at bringing outside help to bear on local issues as appropriate (Rowe, 1995). Schools with quality inservice programs are also likely to be part of a network of support of others engaged in learning efforts (Allington, 1997; Hiebert et al., 1992; Pinnell et al., 1994) and to be part of "collaborative arrangements" (Fisher & Adler, 1999, p. 19) formed "among different role groups" (Anders et al., 2000, p. 730).

A trusting context for learning, especially the freedom to try out ideas in a safe environment is also a key element of effective professional development (Lyons & Pinnell, 1999; Neuman, 1999). Another is the tendency to focus on growth rather than deficits. Finally, there is abundant support for the claim that reflection is a critical variable in the effective training equation (Askew & Gaffney, 1999; Duffy-Hester, 1999). Lyons and Pinnell (1999) phrase this idea nicely when they explain, "Teacher development is effective when there is a balance between demonstration of specific teaching approaches and the reflection and analysis needed to build the process of thinking about teaching" (p. 210). The "teacher as inquirer" (Richardson, 1998, p. 307) and teacher as researcher metaphors hold center stage in effective professional development (Richardson, 1998).

Content Issues. While Ferguson (2003) reminds us that "we need more research on how professional development programs affect both test score levels and the Black-White test score gap" (p. 495), we do know enough to get started on the improvement work. Working with increasingly diverse students represents a new challenge to many educators and a unique set of challenges to nearly everyone. To do so successfully, most teachers require considerably more knowledge and a much larger portfolio of skills than they currently possess (Ferguson, 1998a; Spradlin et al., 2005). One area of skill development centers on helping teachers become culturally adept (Burns et al., 2005), on becoming "familiar with racial identity and its impact on achievement" (Ford et al., 2008, p. 236)—that is, "professional development to help them gain the knowledge, skills, attitudes, and dispositions necessary to explore how ethnicity and culture impact teaching and learning" (Burns et al., 2005, p. 3). Darity and associates (2001) conclude, for example, that to address gaps, teachers require much more professional development in "the area of multicultural education and meeting the diverse needs of under-served populations" (p. 61). An even more critical set of tools are those that "enable staff to meet the instructional requirements of an increasingly diverse student body" (Spradlin et al., 2005, p. 20), the development of "teaching strategies . . . effective in diverse classrooms" (Schwartz, 2001, p. 5) and instructional techniques that help educators teach common "context to a diverse range of learners" (Thompson, 2002, p. 14).

Professional development must directly address those skills and behaviors that are most likely to narrow achievement gaps. Given the other guidelines presented herein, readers already have familiarity with some of these skills. The general rule is, "The content focus of professional development is crucial" (Thompson, 2002, p. 13). Deep subject knowledge is critical if a "robust curricular program" is to take root and grow in schools. Skill development in the area of literacy in general, and writing in particular, is especially important in the gap closing battle (North Carolina, 2000; Symonds, 2004). Professional development on understanding and using achievement data to plan the instructional program (Thompson, 2002) is also crucial. Training on "new instructional strategies [and] . . . on how to tailor instruction to student needs" (Symonds, 2004, p. 3) is essential if quality teaching is to work its magic on overcoming learning differentials by race and class (Symonds, 2004; Spradlin, 2005). For example, Meehan and colleagues (2003) suggest "that some consideration be given to professional development sessions for teachers in schools with large achievement gaps on many of the basic principles of effective instruction" (p. 29).

To be effective, it is likely that professional development will need to be more community focused than is the norm in the profession. While professional development in general "is most effective when it engages teachers collectively" (Thompson, 2002, p. 15), this rule holds a special place in the achievement gap handbook (McGee, 2003). Professional development needs to be designed to get teachers in contact with other learners. Teachers need opportunities to see effective instruction for low-income and African American students (Symonds, 2004). Educators require "time to help one another with challenges and [for] sharing strategies that work" (Symonds, 2004, p. 52). In short, "they need to observe and learn from other teachers" (Shannon & Bylsma, 2002, p. 36), and be part of professional communities of learners.

10. Reduce class size in the early primary grades, especially in schools with high concentrations of low-income and African American students.

Results suggest that differences in class size are key to understanding racial and ethnic differences in student achievement. (Boozer & Rouse, 2001, p. 187)

The effect of assignment to a small class on the racial test score gap is sizable. (Krueger & Whitmore, 2001, p. 27)

On the basis of the cumulative correlational evidence, a policy implication may be for schools to consider resource allocations toward smaller classes in early grades. (Chatterji, 2006, p. 504)

11. Reduce school size in communities with high concentrations of low-income and African American students.

If the school is to have a chance of becoming a learning community for disadvantaged children and youth, it must have a small student enrollment. (Miller, 1995, p. 348)

The negative effects of poverty on student achievement are considerably stronger in larger schools and districts than in smaller ones (or viewed another way, that smaller schools and districts are considerably more successful in disrupting or mitigating the relationship between poverty and student achievement). (Johnson, Howley, & Howley, 2002, p. 4)

Although "it is not a silver bullet" (Hertert & Teague, 2003, p. 25) and other cautions apply, because "smaller classes are clearly a viable candidate for explaining some part of the black NAEP gains and some part of the reduction in the black-white gap" (Grissmer, 1998, p. 216), research suggests that reducing class size at the primary level in high-minority and high-poverty schools is a good way to help narrow race and class gaps in learning (Bingham, 1994; Lewis, 2008; U.S. Commission on Civil Rights, 2004). That is, because "research confirms that reducing the size of classes in Grades K–3 can produce large and lasting gains in student learning, and that small classes improve achievement for all students, but help minority and low-income students the most" (Thompson, 2001, p. 11), "federal, state, and local education agencies should purposefully target class size reduction for the highest minority and poverty schools in order to help reduce the achievement gap" (U.S. Commission on Civil Rights, 2004, p. 6).

In general, but not always (Armor, 2008), researchers find "that class size negatively affect[s] achievement" (Chatterji, 2005a, p. 23; see also Finn & Achilles, 1990; Krueger & Whitmore, 2002) and that "sharply reducing the size of classes in the early grades can produce large . . . gains in student learning" (Thompson & O'Quinn, 2001, p. 10; see also Finn & Achilles, 1990, p. 368). The evidence of the lasting benefits of being in smaller classes is mixed (Bingham, Krueger, & Whitmore, 2002).

Especially relevant for our purpose in this volume are findings on the equity effects of class size reductions. Researchers consistently find, "Reduced class size does not have the same impact on white and minority students" (Finn & Achilles, 1990, p. 567). More specifically, they conclude that the benefits of smaller classes flow disproportionately to schools with higher concentrations of low-income youngsters and African American students (Finn & Achilles, 1990; Grissmer, 1998; Krueger & Whitmore, 2002; Miller, 1995), and "smaller classes help students from all backgrounds, but they give the greater boost to minority and low-income students" (Thompson & O'Quinn, 2000, p. 10)—benefits are "largest for disadvantaged students" (Grissmer, 1998, p. 214): "Black students tend to advance further up the distribution of tests scores from attending a small class than do white students, both while they are in a small class and afterward" (Krueger & Whitmore, 2001, pp. 39–40). What this means, of course, is that "effect size diminishes as . . . SES increases" (Krueger & Whitmore, 2002, p. 22) and that there is a "considerably reduced achievement gap" (Finn, 1998, p. 18).

Research helps us conceptualize class size reductions, i.e., provide a more nuanced understanding about how policy makers and educators can use this tool. Analysts confirm that the "size of the reduction—the difference between the size of classes before and after class size reduction—affects the size of the gains that may be reported" (Thompson, 2002, p. 11), with greater gains associated with larger differentials. While "there is no consensus on how small classes should be" (Ferguson, 1998b, p. 368), the literature in this area suggests that class sizes below eighteen are more effective (Finn & Achilles, 1990; Hertert & Teague, 2003; Miller, 1995; Schwartz, 2001). Researchers are also clear that the real benefits of class size reduction are manifest in primary classrooms (Finn, 1998; Reynolds, 2002): "The evidence that smaller classes promote increased learning is stronger for grades K–3. The evidence favoring smaller classes is weaker at other grade levels" (Thompson & O'Quinn, 2001, p. 10).

Length of treatment is also relevant (Kober, 2001; Krueger & Whitmore, 2001). That is, "For students to get substantial long-term gains from smaller classes, they need to be in smaller classes for at least two years. The longer students are in smaller classes, the more they benefit" (Thompson & O'Quinn, 2001, p. 10): "Differences between minority and white achievement for all years and class sizes tended to be largest for the 3 years time in treatment" (Bingham, 1994, p. 3). Scholars also conclude that effects are similar in urban and rural areas and that "small classes are most beneficial in reading and mathematics" (Finn, 1998, p. 12).

These same studies also offer some clues about why students in general, and more particularly why low-income and African American students, benefit from attending smaller classes in the primary grades. All suggestions highlight the fact that "reduced class sizes opens opportunities for schools and teachers to actually do things differently with children in classrooms" (Chatterji, 2006, p. 491). They confirm, "It is not just smallness but what smallness allows that is the key" (Hertert & Teague, 2003, p. 25). One line of explanation centers on the behavioral domain of classrooms (Thompson, 2002). It is suggested that smaller classes permit teachers to practice more effective classroom management practices, practices that result in less disruptive behavior, more student engagement, and higher levels of achievement (Finn, 1998; Krueger & Whitmore, 2002; Thompson & O'Quinn, 2001). Focusing on the equity benefit to African American children, Ferguson (1998b) hypothesizes, "If black children have less effective work habits and pose more behavioral challenges, the greater opportunities for individual attention afforded by small classes may be especially important for them" (p. 359).

A second line of explanation spotlights the instructional domain of classrooms (Chatterji, 2006). Scholars maintain, "Teaching in small classes also affords more individual attention through one-on-one tutoring and brief on-the-fly help from teachers" (Thompson & O'Quinn, 2001, p. 10). They conclude, "With smaller classes teachers are able to individualize their instruction more and use a range of instructional practices that may be more developmentally appropriate" (Chatterji, 2006, p. 504). This, they suggest, leads to the formation of "an environment in which students' early academic difficulties can be tackled" (p. 491) more effectively. For example, Finn (1998) suggests, "A small class setting may make it difficult for a youngster to withdraw from participating and make it difficult for a teacher to overlook the needs of particular students" (p. 27).

A third line of explanation underscores relations with parents. Here, investigators assert, "Teachers with smaller classes spend more time communicating with parents than do teachers with larger classes" (Thompson, 2002, p. 11). They also remind us of a finding we reported above: stronger parent-school connections are linked to higher student achievement.

Analysts of the class size intervention do provide a number of cautions to which educators should attend. Most critically, as noted above, they inform us that small size is just a vehicle that allows good things to happen for children. In itself, it ensures nothing (Hertert & Teague, 2003; Thompson, 2002). Second, context matters. This intervention appears to be much more effective when used in the early grades. Third, class size reductions alone cannot win the gap reduction battle. This strategy needs to be combined with other reforms (Thernstrom & Thernstrom, 2002). Fourth, unintended consequences need to be surfaced for analysis. For example, facilities problems can derail expected benefits. The unintended consequence caveat is especially true when the class size intervention is targeted on particular schools or classes (Finn, 1998). And finally, there are real costs to dramatically reducing class size. Such costs need to be weighed against the costs and benefits of other gap reduction strategies (McGee, 2003; Thompson, 2002).

In closing, we add a note on the related topic of small school size. While "the evidence in favor of small schools is far from conclusive" (McGee, 2003, p. 24) and all the cautions we outlined above apply to small school size as well as small class size, there is evidence that smaller schools can help educators effectively narrow achievement gaps (Darity et al., 2001; Stiefel, Schwartz, & Ellen, 2006; Williams, 2003), "that small schools are better at raising student achievement . . . for minority and low-income students" (Chatterji, 2006, p. 491): "School size appears to have an impact on student achievement, particularly that of the lowest-performing high school students" (Hertert & Teague, 2002, p. 25). In this area, the longitudinal work of Howley and colleagues is especially important. These investigators find that the equity effects of small school size are quite robust, "that in smaller schools, the relationship between achievement and SES is substantially weaker in the smaller schools than in larger schools" (Howley, Strange, & Bickel, 2000, p. 4). Or, in another form, "smaller school size mitigates the negative effects of poverty on achievement" (Johnson, Howley, & Howley, 2002, p. 8): "Small schools help to thwart threats that poverty imposes on school performance" (Howley et al., 2000, p. 4). As Bainbridge and Lasley (2002) report, "Significantly, however, if school size is important, the effects may be more pronounced for poor children than for those from affluent backgrounds: Students from poverty environments tend to do better in small schools" (p. 429). "Benefits to the equity of school performance seem to be maximized most consistently among smaller schools in smaller districts" (Johnson et al., 2002, p. 39). And, what is true for children from working-class and poor homes is true for African American youngsters as well (Johnson et al., 2002).

District size occupies a central place in this narrative as well. Howley and colleagues conclude that positive effects on achievement for disadvantaged youngsters are greatest in small schools that are nested in small districts (Johnson et al., 2002). Indeed, they conclude that small size really only works well inside smaller districts. Their guidance for policy makers and educators here is quite unequivocal:

> *If school reformers are serious about making systemic reforms that would be predicted to diminish the inequity of school outcomes in . . . the United States, keeping schools and districts small would seem to be a most productive policy. Widespread consolidations of either districts or schools, by contrast, would be predicted to increase inequity and to degrade academic accomplishment in most . . . schools and districts. (p. 37)*

Additionally, they argue, "The poorer the community, the smaller the school should be" (Howley et al., 2000, p. 2): "The consensus clearly suggests that schools in impoverished communities should be smaller, much smaller" (p. 4).

CONCLUSION

In this final chapter, we reviewed what the research tells us schools can do to help meet the goal of closing African American-white and social class achievement gaps. We began by outlining ten general rules of engagement for the gap reduction work. We then discussed, in considerable detail, eleven gap closing strategies. We organized these strategies into the major categories of instructional program, culture, and structure and support.

References

ACT (1997–2008). *ACT national scores, composite scores* [data file]. Available from http://www.act.org/news/data.html.

Ainsworth-Darnell, J. W., & Downey, D. B. (1998). Assessing the oppositional culture explanation for racial/ethnic differences in school performance. *American Sociological Review, 63* (4), 536–553.

Alexander, K. L., & Cook, M. A. (1982). Curricula and coursework: A surprise ending to a familiar story. *American Sociological Review, 47* (5), 626–640.

Alexander, K. L., Cook, M., & McDill, E. L. (1978). Curriculum tracking and educational stratification: Some further evidence. *American Sociological Review, 43,* 47–66.

Alexander, K. L., Entwisle, D. R., & Bedinger, S. D. (1994). When expectations work: Race and socioeconomic differences in school performance. *Social Psychology Quarterly, 57* (4), 283–299.

Alexander, K. L., Entwisle, D. R., & Olson, L. S. (2001). Schools, achievement, and inequality: A seasonal perspective. *Educational Evaluation and Policy Analysis, 23* (2), 171–191.

Alexander, K. L., & McDill, E. L. (1976). Selection and allocation within schools: Some causes and consequences of curriculum placement. *American Sociological Review, 41,* 936–980.

Alexander, K. L., Olson, L. S., & Entwisle, D. R. (2007). Lasting consequences of the summer learning gap. *American Sociological Review, 2* (72), 167–180.

Allington, R. (1983). The reading instruction provided readers of differing reading ability. *Elementary School Journal, 83* (5), 548–559.

Allington, R. (1997). Why does literacy research so often ignore what really matters? In C. K. Kinzer, K. A. Hinchman, & D. J. Leu (Eds.), *Inquiries in literacy: Theory and practice* (pp. 1–12). Chicago: National Reading Conference.

Alvermann, D. E. (2005). Literacy on the edge: How close are we to closing the literacy achievement gap? *Voices From the Middle, 31* (1), 8–14.

Anders, P. L., Hoffman, J. V., & Duffy, G. G. (2000). Teaching teachers to teach reading: Paradigm shifts, persistent problems, and challenges. In M. L. Kamil, P. B. Mosenthal, P. D. Pearson, & R. Barr (Eds.), *Handbook of reading research* (Vol. 3) (pp. 719–742). Mahwah, NJ: Lawrence Erlbaum.

Anderson, R. C., Hiebert, E. H., Scott, J. A., & Wilkinson, I. A. G. (1985). *Becoming a nation of readers: The report of the Commission on Reading.* Washington, DC: The National Institute of Education. U.S. Department of Education.

Antunez, B., DiCerbo, P. A., & Menken, K. (2000). *Framing effective practice: Topics and issues in educating English language learners. A technical assistance synthesis.* Washington, DC: The George Washington University, National Clearinghouse for Bilingual Education. Center for the Study of Language and Education.

Armor, G. (1992). Why is black educational achievement rising? *The Public Interest, 108* (3), 65–80.

Armor, G. (2008). Can NCLB close achievement gaps?! In A. R. Sadovnik, J. A. O'Day, G. W. Bohrnstedt, & K. M. Borman (Eds.), *No Child Left Behind and the reduction of the achievement gap* (pp. 323–342). New York: Routledge.

Askew, B. J., & Gaffney, J. S. (1999). Reading recovery: Waves of influence on literacy education. In J. S. Gaffney & B. J. Askew (Eds.), *Stirring the waters: The influence of Marie Clay* (pp. 75–98). Portsmouth, NH: Heinemann.

Au, K. H., & Asam, C. L. (1996). Improving the literacy achievement of low-income students of diverse backgrounds. In M. F. Graves, P. van den Broek, & B. M. Taylor (Eds.), *The first R: Every child's right to read* (pp. 199–223). New York: Teachers College Press.

Bacharach, V. R., Baumeister, A. A., & Farr, R. M. (2003). Racial and gender science achievement gaps in secondary education. *The Journal of Genetic Psychology, 164* (1), 115–126.

Baenen, N., Dulaney, C., Yamen, K., & Banks, K. (2002). *Gaps in academic achievement: WCPSS status, 2001–02.* Raleigh, NC: Wake County Public Schools, Department of Evaluation and Research.

Bainbridge, W. L., & Lasley, T. J. (2002). Demographics, diversity, and K–12 accountability. *Education and Urban Society, 34* (4), 422–437.

Baker, D., & Stevenson, D. L. (1986). Mothers' strategies for children's school achievement: Managing the transition to high school. *Sociology of Education, 59* (3), 156–166.

Baldi, S., Jin, Y., Skemer, M., Green, P. J., & Herget, D. (2007). *Highlights from PISA 2006: Performance of U.S. 15-year-old students in science and mathematics literacy in an international context* (NCES 2008–016). Washington, DC: National Center for Education Statistics, Institute of Education Sciences, U.S. Department of Education.

Balfanz, R., & Byrnes, V. (2006). Closing the mathematics achievement gap in high-poverty middle schools: Enablers and constraints. *Journal of Education for Students Placed at Risk, 11* (2), 143–159.

Bali, V. A., & Alvarez, R. M. (2003). Schools and educational outcomes: What causes the 'race gap' in student test scores? *Social Science Quarterly, 84* (3), 485–507.

Bankston, C., & Caldas, S. J. (1998). Family structure, schoolmates, and racial inequalities in school achievement. *Journal of Marriage and the Family, 60* (3), 715–723.

Baron, R., Tom, D., & Cooper, H. (1985). Social class, race, and teacher expectations. In J. Dusek (Ed.), *Teacher expectancies* (pp. 251–269). Hillsdale, NJ: Lawrence Erlbaum.

Barton, P. E. (2000). Unequal learning environments: Discipline that works. In R. D. Kahlenberg (Ed.), *A notion at risk: Preserving public education as an engine for social mobility* (pp. 223–250). New York: The Century Foundation Press.

Barton, P. E. (2003). *Parsing the achievement gap.* (Policy Information Report). Princeton, NJ: Educational Testing Service.

Becker, B. E., & Luthar, S. S. (2002). Social-emotional factors affecting achievement outcomes among disadvantaged students: Closing the achievement gap. *Educational Psychologist, 37* (4), 197–214.

Beckford, I. A., & Cooley, W. W. (1993). *The racial achievement gap in Pennsylvania.* Pittsburgh, PA: Pennsylvania Educational Policy Studies, University of Pittsburgh.

Bempechat, J. (1992). *Fostering high achievement in African American children: Home, school, and public policy influences* (Contract No. R188062013). New York: Teachers College, Columbia University. (ERIC Document Reproduction Service No. ED 348 464).

Bempechat, J., & Ginsburg, H. (1989). *Underachievement and educational disadvantage: The home and school experiences of at-risk youth* (Urban Diversity Series No. 99). New York: Teachers College, Columbia University. (ERIC Document Reproduction Service No. ED 315 485).

Bennett, A., Bridglall, B. L., Cauce, A. M., Everson, H. T., Gordon, E. W., Lee, C. D., Mendoza-Denton, R., Renzulli, J. S., & Stewart, J. K. (2007). Task force report on the affirmative development of academic ability: All students reaching the top: Strategies for closing academic achievement gaps. In E. W. Gordon & B. L. Bridglall (Eds.), *Affirmative development: Cultivating academicability* (pp. 239–275). Lanham, MD: Rowman & Littlefield.

Berends, M., Lucas, S. R., Sullivan, T., & Briggs, R. J. (2005). *Examining gaps in mathematics achievement among racial-ethnic groups, 1972–1992.* Santa Monica, CA: RAND.

Biddle, B. J. (1997). Foolishness, dangerous nonsense, and real correlates of state differences in achievement. *Phi Delta Kappan, 78* (1), 9–13.

Biddle, B. J. (2001). Poverty, ethnicity, and achievement in American schools. In B. J. Biddle (Ed.), *Social class, poverty, and education: Policy and practice* (pp. 1–30). New York: Routledge.

Bingham, C. S. (1994, February). *Class size as an early intervention strategy in white-minority achievement gap reduction.* Paper presented at the annual meeting of the American Association of School Administrators, San Francisco.

Bol, L., & Berry, R. O. (2005). Secondary mathematics teachers' perceptions of the achievement gap. *The High School Journal, 88* (4), 32–45.

Boozer, M., & Rouse, C. (2001). Intraschool variation in class school: Patterns and implications. *Journal of Urban Economics, 50* (1), 163–189.

Borman, G. D., & Dowling, N. M. (2006). The longitudinal achievement effects of multi-year summer school: Evidence from the teach Baltimore randomized field trial. *Educational Evaluation and Policy Analysis, 28* (1), 25–48.

Borman, G. D., & Kimball, S. M. (2005). Teacher quality and educational equality: Do teachers with higher standards-based evaluation ratings close student achievement gaps? *The Elementary School Journal, 106* (1), 3–20.

Braun, H. I., Wang, A., Jenkins, F., & Weinbaum, E. (2006). The black-white achievement gap: Do state policies matter? *Education Policy AnalysisArchive, 14* (8), 1–109.

Briggs, K. L. & Thomas, K. (1997). *Patterns of success: Successful pathways in elementary literacy in Texas Spotlight Schools.* Austin: Texas Center for Educational Research.

Brookover, W. B. (1985). Can we make schools effective for minority students? *Journal of Negro Education, 54* (3), 257–268.

Brookover, W. B., Brady, N. V., & Warfield, M. (1981). *Educational policies and equitable education: A report of studies of two desegregated school systems.* East Lansing: Center for Urban Affairs, Michigan State University.

Brooks-Gunn, J., Duncan, G. J., Leventhal, T., & Aber, J. L. (1997). Lessons learned and future directions for research on the neighborhoods in which children live. In J. Brooks-Gunn, G. J. Duncan, & J. L. Aber (Eds.), *Neighborhood poverty: Context and consequences for children* (Vol. 1) (pp. 279–326). New York: Russell Sage Foundation.

Brooks-Gunn, J., Klebanov, P. K., & Duncan, G. J. (1996). Ethnic differences in children's intelligence test scores: Role of economic deprivation, home environment, and maternal characteristics. *Child Development, 67* (2), 396–408.

Brooks-Gunn, J., Klebanov, P. K., & Liaw, F. R. (1995). The learning, physical, and emotional environment of the home in the context of poverty: The infant health and development program. *Child and Youth Services Review, 17* (1/2), 251–276.

Brooks-Gunn, J., Klebanov, P. K., Smith, J., Duncan, C. J., & Lee, L. (2003). The black-white test score gap in young children: Contributions of test and family characteristics. *Applied Developmental Science, 7* (4), 239–252.

Brooks-Gunn, J., & Markman, L. (2005). The contribution of parenting to ethnic and racial gaps in school readiness. *The Future of Children, 15* (1), 139–168.

Brophy, J. (1982). Successful teaching strategies for the inner-city child. *Phi Delta Kappan, 63* (8), 527–530.

Brophy, J., & Good, T. L. (1986). Teacher behavior and student achievement. In M. Wittrock (Ed.), *Handbook of Research on Teaching* (3rd ed.) (pp. 328–375). New York: Macmillan.

Burkam, D. T., Ready, D. D., Lee, V. E., & LoGerfo, L. F. (2004). Social-class differences in summer learning between kindergarten and first grade: Model specification and estimation. *Sociology of Education, 77* (1), 1–31.

Burns, R., Keyes, M., & Kusimo, P. (2005). *Closing achievement gaps by creating culturally responsive schools*. Charleston, WV: Appalachia Educational Lab.

Burris, C. C., & Welner, K. G. (2005). Closing the achievement gap by detracking. *Phi Delta Kappan, 86* (6), 594–598.

Burton, N. W., & Jones, L. V. (1982). Recent trends in achievement levels of black and white youth. *Educational Researcher, 11* (4), 10–14, 17.

Caldas, S. J., & Bankston, C. (1997). The effect of school population socioeconomic status on individual academic achievement. *The Journal of Education Research, 90* (5), 269–286.

Caldas, S. J., & Bankston, C. L. (1999). Multilevel examination of student, school, and district-level effects on academic achievement. *Journal of Educational Research, 93* (2), 91–99.

California State Department of Education (1984). *Time and learning in California Public Schools*. Sacramento: California State Department of Education.

Camara, W. J., & Schmidt, A. E. (1999). *Group differences in standardized testing and social stratification*. (College Board Report No. 99–5). New York: The College Board.

Campbell, F. A., & Ramey, C. T. (1995). Cognitive and school outcomes for high-risk African American students at middle adolescence: Positive effects of early intervention. *American Educational Research Journal, 32* (4), 743–772.

Card, D., & Rothstein, J. (2007). Racial segregation and the black-white test score gap. *Journal of Public Economics, 91*, 2158–2184.

Carpenter, D. M. II, Ramirez, A., & Severn, L. (2006). "Gap" or "gaps": Challenging the singular definition of the achievement gap. *Education and Urban Society, 39* (1), 113–127.

Ceci, S. J., & Papierno, P. B. (2005). The rhetoric and reality of gap closing: When the 'have-nots' gain but the 'haves' gain even more. *American Psychologist, 60* (2), 149–160.

Chase-Lansdale, P. L., Gordon, R. A., Brooks-Gunn, J., & Klebanov, P. K. (1997). Neighborhood and family influences on the intellectual and behavioral competence of preschool and early school-age children. In J. Brooks-Gunn, G. J. Duncan, & J. L. Aber (Eds.), *Neighborhood poverty: Context and consequences for children* (Vol. 1) (pp. 79–118). New York: Russell Sage Foundation.

Chatterji, M. (2005a). Achievement gaps and correlates of early mathematics achievement: Evidence from the ECLS K-First grade sample. *Education Policy Analysis Archives, 13* (46), 1–35.

Chatterji, M. (2005b, June). Closing Florida's achievement gaps (FIE Policy Brief No. 4). Jacksonville: Florida Institute of Education at the University of North Florida.

Chatterji, M. (2006). Reading achievement gaps, correlates, and moderators of early reading achievement: Evidence from the Early Childhood Longitudinal Study (ECLS) kindergarten to first grade sample. *Journal of Educational Psychology, 98* (3), 489–507.

Child and Family Policy Center (2005). *Early learning left out: Closing the investment gap in America's youngest children* (2nd ed.). Washington, DC: Author.

Chin, T., & Phillips, M. (2004). Social reproduction and child-rearing practices: Social class, children's agency, and the summer activity gap. *Sociology of Education, 77* (3), 185–210.

Chubb, J. E., & Loveless, T. (2002). Bridging the achievement gap. In J. E. Chubb & T. Loveless (Eds.), *Bridging the achievement gap* (pp. 1–10). Washington, DC: Brookings Institution Press.

Clotfelter, C. T., Ladd, H. F., & Vigdor, J. (2005). Who teaches whom? Race and the distribution of novice teachers. *Economics of Education Review, 24* (4), 377–392.

Cole-Henderson, B. (2000). Organizational characteristics of schools that successfully serve low-income urban African American students. *Journal of Education for Students Placed at Risk, 5* (1/2), 77–91.

Coleman, J. S., Campbell, E. Q., Hobson, C. F., McPartland, J., Mood, A. M., Weinfield, F. D., & York, R. L. (1966). *Equality of Educational Opportunity*. Washington, DC: Department of Health, Education, and Welfare.

College Board (1996–2008). *SAT data and reports* [data file]. Available from http://professionals. collegeboard.com/data-reports-research/sat/archived.

College Board (1997–2007). *Advanced Placement program: National summary reports* [data file]. Available from http://professionals.collegeboard.com/data-reports-research/ap/archived.

College Board (2009a). *Calculus: Calculus AB Calculus BC: Course description*. New York: Author.

College Board (2009b). *English: English Language and Composition, English Literature and Composition: Course description*. New York: Author.

Condron, D. J., & Roscigno, V. J. (2003). Disparities within: Unequal spending and achievement in an urban school district. *Sociology of Education, 76* (1), 18–36.

Cook, M., & Evans, W. N. (2000). Families or schools? Explaining the convergence in white and black academic performance. *Journal of Labor Economics, 18*, 729–754.

Cook, P. J., & Ludwig, J. (1998). The burden of "acting white": Do black adolescents disparage academic achievement? In C. Jencks and M. Phillips (Eds.), *The black-white test score gap* (pp. 375–400). Washington, DC: Brookings Institution Press.

Cooper, R. (2000). Urban school reform from a student-of-color perspective. *Urban Education, 34* (5), 597–622.

Currie, J. (2005). Health disparities and gaps in school readiness. *The Future of Children, 15* (1), 117–138.

Currie, J., & Thomas, D. (1995). Does Head Start make a difference? *American Economic Review, 85* (3), 341–364.

Dabady, M. (2003). Measuring racial disparities and discrimination in elementary and secondary education: An introduction. *Teachers College Record, 105* (6), 1048–1051.

Darity, W., Jr., Castellino, D., Tyson, K., Cobb, C., & McMillen, B. (2001). *Increasing opportunity to learn via access to rigorous courses and programs: One strategy for closing the achievement gap for at-risk and ethnic minority students*. Raleigh: North Carolina State Department of Public Instruction, Raleigh Division of Accountability.

Darling-Hammond, L., & Post, L. (2000). Inequality in teaching and schooling: Supporting high-quality teaching and leadership in low-income schools. In R. D. Kahlenberg (Ed.), *A notion at risk: Preserving public education as an engine of social mobility* (pp. 127–167). New York: The Century Foundation Press.

Davison, M. L., Young, S. S., Davenport, E. C., Butterbaugh, D., & Davison, L. J. (2004). When do children fall behind? What can be done? *Phi Delta Kappan, 85* (10), 752–761.

Dickens, W. T. (2005). Genetic differences and school readiness. *The Future of Children, 15* (1), 55–69.

Ding, C. S., & Davison, M. L. (2005). A longitudinal study of math achievement gains for initially low achieving students. *Educational Psychology, 30* (1), 81–95.

Downey, D. B., von Hippel, P. T., & Broh, B. A. (2004). Are schools the great equalizer? Cognitive inequality during the summer months and the school year. *American Sociological Review, 69*, 613–635.

DuBois, D. L. (2001). Family disadvantage, the self, and academic achievement. In B. J. Biddle (Ed.), *Social class, poverty, and education: Policy and practice* (pp. 133–174). New York: Routledge.

Duffy-Hester, A. M. (1999). Teaching struggling readers in elementary school classrooms: A review of classroom reading programs and principles for instruction. *The Reading Teacher, 52* (5), 480–495.

Duncan, G. J., & Aber, J. L. (1997). Neighborhood models and measures. In J. Brooks-Gunn, G. J. Duncan, & J. L. Aber (Eds.), *Neighborhood poverty: Context and consequences for children* (Vol. 1) (pp. 62–78). New York: Russell Sage Foundation.

Duncan, G. J., & Brooks-Gunn, J. (2000). Family poverty, welfare reform, and child development. *Child Development, 71* (1), 188–196.

Duncan, G. J., & Brooks-Gunn, J. (2001). Poverty, welfare, and children's achievement. In B. J. Biddle (Ed.), *Social class, poverty, and education: Policy and practice* (pp. 49–76). New York: Routledge.

Duncan, G. J., & Magnuson, K. A. (2005). Can family socioeconomic resources account for racial and ethnic test score gaps? *The Future of Children, 15* (1), 35–54.

Dungan, F. (1994). Teachers say administrators can make a difference in the school's reading program. *State of Reading, 1* (1), 46–48.

Eder, D. (1981). Ability grouping as a self-fulfilling prophecy: A micro-analysis of teacher-student interaction. *Sociology of Education, 54* (3), 151–161.

Education Week (2008). *Report roundup: Smaller classes seen as no silver bullet, 28* (25), 5.

Egan, T. (2006). *The worst hard time.* Boston: Houghton Mifflin.

Entwisle, D. R., & Alexander, K. L. (1992). Summer setback: Race, poverty, school composition, and mathematical achievement in the first two years of school. *American Sociological Review, 57,* 72–84.

Entwisle, D. R., Alexander, K. L., & Olson, L.S. (2000). Summer learning and home environment. In R. D. Kahlenberg (Ed.), *A notion at risk: Preserving public education as an engine for social mobility* (pp. 9–30). New York: The Century Foundation Press.

Everson, H. T. (2007). The problem of transfer and adaptability: Applying the learning sciences to the challenge of the achievement gap. In E. W. Gordon & B. L. Bridglall (Eds.), *Affirmative development: Cultivating academicability* (pp. 221–237). Lanham, MD: Rowman & Littlefield.

Evertson, C. (1982). Differences in instructional activities in higher- and lower-achieving junior high English and math classes. *Elementary School Journal, 82* (4), 329–350.

Farkas, G. (2003). Racial disparities and discrimination in education: What do we know, how do we know it, and what do we need to know? *Teachers College Record, 105* (6), 1119–1146.

Farkas, G., Grobe, R. P., Sheehan, D., & Shuan, Y. (1990). Cultural resources and school success: Gender, ethnicity, and poverty groups within an urban school district. *American Sociological Review, 55* (1), 127–142.

Farley, R. (1984). *Blacks and whites: Narrowing the gap?* Cambridge, MA: Harvard University Press.

Ferguson, R. F. (1991). Racial patterns in how school and teacher quality affect achievement and earnings. *Challenge: A Journal of Research on Black Males, 2* (1), 1–35.

Ferguson, R. F. (1998a). Teachers' perceptions and expectations and the black-white test score gap. In C. Jencks & M. Phillips (Eds.), *The black-white test score gap* (pp. 273–317). Washington, DC: Brookings Institution Press.

Ferguson, R. F. (1998b). Can schools narrow the black-white test score gap? In C. Jencks and M. Phillips (Eds.), *The black-white test score gap* (pp. 318–374). Washington, DC: Brookings Institution Press.

Ferguson, R. F. (2002). *Addressing racial disparities in high-achieving suburban schools* (Policy Issues 13). Napierville, IL: North Central Regional Educational Lab. Retrieved October 20, 2007, from http://ncrel.org/policy/pubs/html/piv0113/dec2002b.htm

Ferguson, R. F. (2003). Teachers' perceptions and expectations and the black-white test score gap. *Urban Education, 38* (4), 460–507.

Finn, J. D. (1998). *Class size and students at risk. What is known? What is next?* Washington, DC: National Institute on the Education of At-Risk Students.

Finn, J. D., & Achilles, C. M. (1990). Answers and questions about class size: A statewide experiment. *American Educational Research Journal, 27* (3), 557–577.

Finn, J. D., & Rock, D. A. (1997). Academic success among students at risk for schoolfailure. *Journal of Applied Psychology, 82* (2), 221–234.

Fisher, C., & Adler, M. A. (1999). *Early reading programs in high-poverty schools: Emerald Elementary beats the odds.* Ann Arbor: University of Michigan, Center for the Improvement of Early Reading Achievement.

Flanagan, A., & Grissmer, D. (2002). The role of federal resources in closing the achievement gap. In J. E. Chubb & T. Loveless (Eds.), *Bridging the achievement gap* (pp. 199–225). Washington, DC: Brookings Institution Press.

Ford, D. Y., Grantham, T. C., & Whiting, G. W. (2008). Another look at the achievement gap: Learning from the experiences of gifted black students. *Urban Education, 43* (2), 216–239.

Fryer, R. G., & Levitt, S. D. (2002). *Understanding the black-white test score gap in the first two years of school* (Working Paper No. 8975). Cambridge, MA: National Bureau of Economic Research.

Fryer, R., & Levitt, S. D. (2004). The black-white test score gap in the first two years of school. *Review of Economics and Statistics, 86* (2), 447–464.

Fuchs, V., & Reklis, D. (1994). *Mathematical achievement in eighth grade: Interstate and racial differences* (Working Paper No. 4784). Cambridge, MA: National Bureau of Economic Research.

Fuller, E. J., & Johnson, J. F., Jr. (2001). Can state accountability systems drive improvements in school performance for children of color and children from low-income homes? *Education and Urban Society, 33* (3), 260–283.

Gamoran, A. (2000). High standards: A strategy for equalizing opportunities to learn. In R. D. Kahlenberg (Ed.), *A notion at risk: Preserving public education as an engine for social mobility* (pp. 93–126). New York: The Century Foundation Press.

Gandara, P., Rumberger, R., Maxwell-Jolly, J., & Callahan, R. (2003). English learners in California schools: Unequal resources, unequal outcomes. *Educational Policy Analysis Archives, 11.* Retrieved October 19, 2007, from http://epaa.asu.edu/epaa/v11n36/

Garcia, G. E. (1991). Factors influencing the English reading test performance of Spanish-speaking Hispanic children. *Reading Research Quarterly, 26* (4), 371–392.

Goldsmith, P. A. (2004). Schools' racial mix, students' optimism, and the black-white and Latino-white achievement gaps. *Sociology of Education, 77* (2), 121–147.

Good, T. L. (1981). Teacher expectations and student perceptions: A decade of research. *Educational Leadership, 38* (5), 415–422.

Good, T. L., Grouws, D., & Ebmeier, H. (1983). *Active mathematics teaching.* New York: Longman.

Good, T. L., & Marshall, S. (1984). Do students learn more in heterogeneous or homogeneous groups? In P. L. Peterson, L. C. Wilkinson, & M. Hallinan (Eds.), *The social context of instruction: Group organization and group processes* (pp. 15–38). Orlando, FL: Academic Press.

Goodlad, J. I. (1984). *A place called school: Prospects for the future.* New York: McGraw-Hill.

Gordon, E. W., & Bridglall, B. L. (2007). *Affirmative development: Cultivating academic ability.* Lanham, MD: Rowman & Littlefield.

Gordon, E. W., Frede, E., & Irvine, J. J. (2004). Affirmative student development: Closing the achievement gap by developing human capital. *ETS Policy Notes, 12* (2), 1–12.

Gordon, M. T. (1976). A different view of the IQ-achievement gap. *Sociology of Education, 49* (1), 4–11.

Grissmer, D., Flanagan, A., & Williamson, S. (1998). Why did the black-white score gap narrow in the 1970s and 1980s? In C. Jencks & M. Phillips (Eds.), *The black-white test score gap* (pp. 182–226). Washington, DC: Brookings Institution Press.

Hakuta, K. (2002). *English language learner access to basic educational necessities in California: An analysis of inequities.* Retrieved October 19, 2007, from http://www.mofo.com/decentschools/expert_reports/hakuta_report.pdf

Hale-Benson, J. (1990). Achieving equal educational outcomes for black children. In A. Barona & E. E. Garcia (Eds.), *Children at risk: Poverty, minority status, and other issues in educational equity* (pp. 201–215). Washington, DC: National Association of School Psychologists.

Hall, P. M. (2001). Social class, poverty, and schooling: Social contexts, educational practices and policy options. In B. J. Biddle (Ed.), *Social class, poverty, and education: Policy and practice* (pp. 213–242). New York: Routledge.

Hallinan, M. T. (1984). *A place called school: Prospects for the future.* New York: McGraw-Hill.

Hallinan, M. T. (2001). Sociological perspectives on black-white inequalities in American schooling. *Sociology of Education, 74* (0), 50–70.

Hallinan, M. T., & Sorensen, A. B. (1983). The formation and stability of instructional groups. *American Sociological Review, 48* (6), 838–851.

Halpern-Felsher, B. L., Connell, J. P., Spencer, M. B., Aber, J. L., Duncan, G. J., Clifford, E., Crichlow, W. E., Usinger, P. A., Cole, S. P., Allen, L., & Seidman, E. (1997). Neighborhood and family factors predicting educational risk and attainment in African American and White children and adolescents. In J. Brooks-Gunn, G. J., Duncan, & J. L. Aber (Eds.), *Neighborhood poverty: Context and consequences* (Vol. 1) (pp. 79–118). New York: Russell Sage Foundation.

Hanson, R. A., & Schutz, R. E. (1978). A new look at schooling effects from programmatic research and development. In D. Mann (Ed.), *Making change happen?* (pp. 120–149). New York: Teachers College Press.

Hanushek, E. A., & Raymond, M. E. (2005). Does school accountability lead to improved student performance? *Journal of Policy Analysis and Management, 24* (2), 297–327.

Harris, D. N., & Herrington, C. D. (2006). Accountability, standards, and the growing achievement gap: Lessons from the past half-century. *American Journal of Education, 112* (2), 209–238.

Hart, B., & Risley, T. R. (1995). *Meaningful differences in the everyday experience of young children.* Baltimore: Paul H. Brookes.

Haskins, R., & Rouse, C. (2005). Closing achievement gaps (Policy Brief). *The Future of Children, 16* (1), 1–7.

Haycock, K. (1998). Good teaching matters: How well-qualified teachers can close the gap. Washington, DC: The Education Trust.

Haycock, K. (2001). Closing the achievement gap. *Educational Leadership, 58* (6), 6–11.

Heckman, J. J. (1995) Review: Lessons from the *Bell Curve. The Journal of Political Economy, 103* (5), 1091–1120.

Hedges, L. V., & Nowell, A. (1998). Black-white test score convergence since 1965. In C. Jencks and M. Phillips (Eds.), *The black-white test score gap* (pp. 149–181). Washington, DC: Brookings Institution Press.

Hedges, L. V., & Nowell, A. (1999). Changes in the black-white gap in achievement test scores. *Sociology of Education, 72* (2), 111–135.

Hiebert, E. H., Colt, J. M., Catto, S. L., & Gury, E. C. (1992). Reading and writing of first grade students in a restructured Chapter 1 program. *American Educational Research Journal, 29* (3), 545–572.

Hiebert, E. H., & Pearson, P. D. (1999). *Building on the past, bridging to the future: A research agenda for the Center for the Improvement of Early Reading Achievement.* Ann Arbor: University of Michigan, Center for the Improvement of Early Reading Achievement.

Hertert, L., & Teague, J. (2003). *Narrowing the achievement gap: A review of research, policies, and issues.* Palo Alto, CA: EdSource, Inc. (ERIC Document Reproduction Service No. ED 473 724).

Heyns, B. (1974). Social selection and stratification within schools. *American Journal of Sociology, 79* (6), 1434–1451.

Heyns, B. (1978). *Summer learning and the effects of schooling.* New York: Academic Press.

Hoerandner, C. M., & Lemke, R. J. (2006). Can No Child Left Behind close the gaps in pass rates on standardized tests? *Contemporary Economic Policy, 24* (1), 1–17.

Hoffman, J. V., & Rutherford, W. L. (1984). Effective reading programs: A critical review of outlier studies. *Reading Research Quarterly, 20* (1), 79–92.

Howley, C., Strange, M., & Bickel, R. (2000). *Research about school size and school performance in impoverished communities.* Charleston, WV: Clearinghouse on Rural Education and Small Schools. (ERIC Document Reproduction Service No. ED 448968).

Hughes, S. (2003). An early gap in black-white mathematics achievement: Holding school and home accountable in an affluent city school district. *The Urban Review, 35* (4), 297–322.

Ingersoll, G. M., Scamman, J. P., & Eckerling, W. D. (1989). Geographic mobility and student achievement in an urban setting. *Educational Evaluation and Policy Analysis, 11* (2), 143–149.

Irvine, J. J. (1990). *Black students and school failure: Policies, practices, and prescriptions.* New York: Greenwood.

Jagers, R. J., & Carroll, G. (2002). Issues in educating African American children and youth. In S. Stringfield & D. Land (Eds.), *Educating at-risk students. 101ˢᵗ yearbook of the National Society for the Study of Education. Part II* (pp. 49–65). Chicago: University of Chicago Press.

Jarrett, R. L. (1997). Bringing families back in: Neighborhood effects on children development. In J. Brooks-Gunn, G. J. Duncan, & J. L. Aber (Eds.), *Neighborhood poverty: Policy implications in studying neighborhoods* (Vol. 2) (pp. 48–64). New York: Russell Sage Foundation.

Jencks, C., & Phillips, M. (1998). America's next achievement test. *The American Prospect, 40,* 44–53.

Jencks, C., Smith, M., Acland, H., Bane, M. J., Cohen, D., Gintis, H., Heyns B., & Michelson, S. (1972). *Inequality: A reassessment of the effect of family and schooling in America.* New York: Basic Books.

Jerald, C. D., data analysis by Ingersoll, R. M. (2002). *All talk, no action: Putting an end to out-of-field teaching.* The Education Trust [On-line]. Available from http://www.edtrust.org/main/documents/AllTalk.pdf

Johnson, J. D., Howley, C. B., & Howley, A. A. (2002). *Size, excellence and equity: A report on Arkansas schools and districts.* Athens: College of Education, Ohio University. (ERIC Document Reproduction Service No. ED 459 987).

Johnson, W. R., & Neal, D. (1998). Basic skills and the black-white earnings gap. In C. Jencks & M. Phillips (Eds.), *The black-white test score gap* (pp. 480–497). Washington, DC: Brookings Institution Press.

Karoly, L. A., Greenwood, P. W., Everingham, S. S., Houbé, J., Kilburn, M. R., Rydell, C. P., Sanders, M., & Chiesa, J. (1998). *Investing in our children. What we know and don't know about the costs and benefits of early childhood interventions.* Santa Monica, CA: RAND.

Karoly, L. A., Kilburn, M. R., & Cannon, J. S. (2005). *Early childhood interventions: Proven results, future promise.* Santa Monica, CA: RAND.

Klein, D. (2002). High achievement in mathematics: Lessons from three Los Angeles elementary schools. In J. E. Chubb & T. Loveless (Eds.), *Bridging the achievement gap* (pp. 157–170). Washington, DC: Brookings Institution Press.

Klein, S. P., Josavnoic, J., Stecher, B. M., McCaffrey, D., Shavelson, R. J., Haertel, E., Solano-Flores, G., & Comfort, K. (1997). Gender and racial/ethnic differences on performance assessments in science. *Educational Evaluation and Policy Analysis, 19* (2), 83–97.

Kliebard, H. M. (1995). *The struggle for the American curriculum 1893–1958* (2nd ed.). New York: Routledge.

Knapp, M. S. (2001). Policy, poverty, and capable teaching: Assumptions and issues in policy design. In B. J. Biddle (Ed.), *Social class, poverty, and education. Policy and practice* (pp. 175–212). New York: Routledge.

Kober, N. (2001, April). *It takes more than testing: Closing the achievement.* A report of the Center on Education Policy. Washington, DC: Center on Education Policy.

Kosters, M. H., & Mast, B. D. (2003). *Closing the education achievement gap. Is Title I working?* Washington, DC: The AEI Press.

Krueger, A. B., & Whitmore, D. M. (2001). The effect of attending a small class in the early grades on college-test taking and middle school test results: Evidence from project STAR. *Economic Journal, 111* (468), 1–28.

Krueger, A. B., & Whitmore, D. M. (2002). Would smaller classes help close the black-white achievement gap? In J. E. Chubb & T. Loveless (Eds.), *Bridging the achievement gap* (pp. 11–46). Washington, DC: Brookings Institution Press.

Krug, E. A. (1964). *The shaping of the American high school.* New York: Harper & Row.

Krug, E. A. (1972). *The shaping of the American high school, 1920–1941.* Madison: University of Wisconsin Press.

Land, D., & Legters, N. (2002). The extent and consequences of risk in U.S. education. In S. Stringfield & D. Land (Eds.), *Educating at-risk students. 101st yearbook of the National Society for the Study of Education. Part II* (pp. 1–28). Chicago: University of Chicago Press.

Lara-Cinisomo, S., Pebley, A. R., Vaiana, M. E., & Maggio, E. (2004). Are L.A.'s children ready for school? Santa Monica, CA: RAND.

Lareau, A. (2002). Invisible inequality: Social class and childrearing in black families and white families. *American Sociological Review, 67* (5), 747–776.

Le, V., Kirby, S. N., Barney, H., Setodji, C. M., & Gershwin, D. (2006). *School readiness, full-day kindergarten, and student achievement: An empirical investigation.* Santa Monica, CA: RAND.

Learning Point Associates (2004). *All students reaching the top: Strategies for closing academic achievement gaps.* Naperville, IL: Learning Point Associates.

Lee, J. (2002). Racial and ethnic achievement gap trends: Reversing the progress toward equity. *Educational Researcher, 31* (1), 3–12.

Lee, J. (2004). Multiple facets of inequity in racial and ethnic achievement gaps. *Peabody Journal of Education, 79* (2), 51–73.

Lee, J. (2006). *Tracking achievement gaps and assessing the impact of NCLB on the gaps: An in-depth look into national and state reading and math outcome trends.* Cambridge, MA: The Civil Rights Project at Harvard University.

Lee, J. S., & Bowen, N. K. (2006). Parent involvement, cultural capital, and the achievement gap among elementary school children. *American Educational Research Journal, 43* (2), 193–218.

Lee, V. E., Brooks-Gunn, J., Schnur, E., & Liaw, F. (1990). Are Head Start effects sustained? A longitudinal follow-up of disadvantaged children attending Head Start, no preschool, and other preschool programs. *Child Development, 61* (2), 495–507.

Lee, V. E., & Burkam, D. T. (2002). *Inequality at the starting gate. Social background differences in achievement as children begin schools.* Washington, DC: Economic Policy Institute.

Lemke, M., Sen, A., Pahlke, E., Partelow, L., Miller, D., Williams, T., Kastberg, D., & Jocelyn, L. (2004). *International Outcomes of Learning Mathematics Literacy and Problem Solving: PISA 2003 Results From the U.S. Perspective.* (NCES 2005–003). Washington, DC: U.S. Department of Education, National Center for Education Statistics.

Levin, H., Belfield, C., Muenning, P., & Rouse, C. (2007). *The costs and benefits of excellent education for all of America's children.* New York: Teachers College, Columbia University.

Lewis, A. (2008). *Add it up. Using research to improve education for low-Income and minority students.* Washington, DC: Poverty and Race Research Action Council. Available from http://www.prrac.org/pubs_aiu.pdf.

Lortie, D. (1975). *Schoolteacher: A sociological study.* Chicago: University of Chicago Press.

Lubienski, S. T. (2002). A closer look at black-white mathematics gaps: Intersection of race and SES in NAEP achievement and instructional practices data. *The Journal of Negro Education, 71* (4), 269–287.

Lucas, S. R., & Gamoran, A. (2002). Tracking and the achievement gap. In J. E. Chubb & T. Loveless (Eds.), *Bridging the achievement gap* (pp. 171–198). Washington, DC: Brookings Institution Press.

Luster, T., & McAdoo, H. P. (1994). Factors related to the achievement and adjustment of young African American children. *Child Development, 65* (4), 1080–1094.

Lyons, C. A., & Pinnell, G. S. (1999). Teacher development: The best investment in literacy education. In J. S. Gaffney & B. J. Askew (Eds.), *Stirring the waters: The influence of Marie Clay* (pp. 197–220). Portsmouth, NH: Heinemann.

Magnuson, K. A., & Duncan, G. J. (2006). The role of family socioeconomic resources in the black-white test score gap among young children. *Developmental Review, 26* (4), 365–399.

Magnuson, K. A., Meyers, M. K., Ruhme, C. J., & Waldfogel, J. (2004). Inequality in preschool education and school readiness. *American Educational Research Journal, 41* (1), 115–157.

Magnuson, K. A., & Waldfogel, J. (2005). Early childhood care and education: Effects on ethnic and racial gaps in school readiness. *The Future of Children, 15* (1), 169–196.

Manning, J. C. (1995). "Ariston metron." *The Reading Teacher, 48* (8), 650–659.

Marshall, R., & Tucker, M. (1992). *Thinking for a living: Work, skills, and the future of the American economy.* New York: Basic Books.

Maruyama, G. (2003). Disparities in educational opportunities and outcomes. What do we know and what can we do? *Journal of Social Issues, 59* (3), 653–676.

Mattson, P. A. (1994). Baltimore Highlands Elementary School. *The Reading Teacher, 48* (1), 60–61.

McGee, G. W. (2003, April). *Closing Illinois' achievement gap: Lessons from the 'Golden Spike' high poverty high performing schools.* Paper presented at the Annual Meeting of the American Educational Research Association, Chicago.

Meehan, M. L., Cowley, K. S., Schumacher, D., Hauser, B., & Croom, N. D. M. (2003). *Classroom environment, instructional resources, and teaching differences in high-performing Kentucky schools with achievement gaps.* Charleston, WV: AEL, Inc.

Mickelson, R. A. (2003). When are racial disparities in education the result of racial discrimination? A social science perspective. *Teachers College Record, 105* (6), 1052–1086.

Mickelson, R. A., & Heath, D. (1999). The effects of segregation and tracking on African American high school seniors' academic achievement. *Journal of Negro Education, 68* (4), 566–586.

Miller, L. S. (1995). *An American imperative: Accelerating minority educational advancement.* New Haven, CT: Yale University Press.

Miller, L. S. (1999). *Reaching the top: A report of the National Task Force on minority high achievement.* New York: The College Board.

Milne, A. M., Myers, D. E., Rosenthal, A. S., & Ginsburg, A. (1986). Single parents, working mothers, and the educational achievement of school children. *Sociology of Education, 59* (3), 125–139.

Morgan, S. L., & Mehta, J. D. (2004). Beyond the laboratory: Evaluating the survey evidence for the disidentification explanation of black-white differences in achievement. *Sociology of Education, 77* (1), 82–101.

Morris, D., Shaw, B., & Perney, J. (1990). Helping low readers in Grades 2 and 3: An after-school volunteer tutoring program. *The Elementary School Journal, 91* (2), 133–150.

Murnane, R. J., & Levy, F. (1996). *Teaching the new basic skills: Principles for educating children to thrive in a changing economy.* New York: The Free Press.

Murnane, R. J., & Levy, F. (2004). Will standards-based reforms improve the education of children of color? *National Tax Journal, 54* (2), 401–415.

Murphy, J. (2006). The evolving nature of the American high school: A punctuated equilibrium model of institutional change. *Leadership and Policy in Schools, 5* (4), 1–39, 285–324.

Murphy, J., Beck, L. G., Crawford, M., & Hodges, A. (2001). *The productive high school: Creating personalized academic communities.* Thousand Oaks, CA: Corwin.

Murphy, J., & Hallinger, P. (1989). Equity as access to learning: Curricular and instructional treatment differences. *Journal of Curriculum Studies, 21* (2), 129–149.

Murphy, J., Hallinger, P., & Peterson, K. D. (1986). The administrative control of principals in effective school districts: The supervision and evaluation functions. *The Urban Review, 18* (3), 149–175.

Murphy, J., Hull, T., & Walker, A. (1987). Academic drift and curricular debris: An analysis of high school course-taking patterns with implications for local policy makers. *Journal of Curriculum Studies, 19* (4), 341–360.

Myers, S. L., Jr., Kim, H., & Mandala, C. (2004). The effect of school poverty on racial groups in test scores: The case of the Minnesota Basic Standards Tests. *The Journal of Negro Education, 73* (1), 82–98.

Natriello, G., McDill, E. L., & Pallas, A. M. (1990). *Schooling disadvantaged children: Racing against catastrophe.* New York: Teachers College Press.

Neuman, S. B. (1999). Books make a difference: A study of access to literacy. *Reading Research Quarterly, 34* (3), 286–311.

Neuman, S. B., & Celano, D. (2006). The knowledge gap: Implications of leveling the playing field for low-income and middle-income children. *Reading Research Quarterly, 41* (2), 176–201.

Nisbett, R. E. (1998). Race, genetics, and IQ. In C. Jencks and M. Phillips (Eds.), *The black-white test score gap* (pp. 86–102). Washington, DC: Brookings Institution Press.

Norman, O., Ault, C. R., Jr., Bentz, B., & Meskimen, L. (2001). The black-white "achievement gap" as a perennial challenge for urban science education: A sociocultural and historical overview with implications for research and practice. *Journal of Research in Science Teaching, 38* (10), 1101–1114.

North Carolina State Department of Public Instruction (2000). *Closing the achievement gap: Views from nine schools.* Raleigh, NC: Author.

Oakes, J. (1985). *Keeping track: How schools structure inequality.* New Haven, CT: Yale University Press.

Orr, A. J. (2003). Black-white differences in achievement: The implications of wealth. *Sociology of Education, 76* (4), 281–304.

Page, R. N. (1984). *Lower-track classes at a college-preparatory high school: A caricature of educational encounters.* Paper presented at the annual meeting of the American Educational Research Association, New Orleans, LA.

Padron, Y. N., Waxman, H. C., & Rivera, H. H. (2002). Issues in educating Hispanic students. In S. Stringfield & D. Land (Eds.), *Educating at-risk students. 101st yearbook of the National Society for the Study of Education. Part II* (pp. 66–88). Chicago: University of Chicago Press.

Payne, K. J., & Biddle, B. J. (1999). Poor school funding, child poverty, and mathematics achievement. *Educational Researcher, 28* (6), 4–13.

Peng, S. S., Wright, D., & Hill, S. T. (1995). *Understanding racial-ethnic differences in secondary school science and mathematics achievement.* (NCES 95–710). Washington, DC: U.S. Department of Education.

Phi Delta Kappa (1980). *Why do some urban schools succeed? The Phi Delta Kappa study of exceptional urban elementary schools.* Bloomington, IN: Author.

Phillips, M., Brooks-Gunn, J., Duncan, G. J., Klebanov, P., & Crane, J. (1998a). Family background, parenting practices, and the black-white test score gap. In C. Jencks and M. Phillips (Eds.), *The black-white test score gap* (pp. 103–145). Washington, DC: Brookings Institution Press.

Phillips, M., Crouse, J., & Ralph, J. (1998b). Does the black-white test score gap widen after children enter school? In C. Jencks & M. Phillips (Eds.), *The black-white test score gap* (pp. 229–272). Washington, DC: Brookings Institution Press.

Pink, W. (1984). Creating effective schools. *Educational Forum, 49* (1), 91–107.

Pinnell, G. S., Lyons, C. A., DeFord, D. E., Bryk, A. S., & Seltzer, M. (1994). Comparing instructional models for the literacy education of high-risk first graders. *Reading Research Quarterly, 29* (1), 9–39.

Porter, A. (2007). Rethinking the achievement gap. *Penn GSE: A Review of the Research, 5* (1), 1–8.

Powell, A. G., Farrar, E., & Cohen, D. K. (1985). *The shopping mall high school: Winners and losers in the educational marketplace.* Boston: Houghton Mifflin.

Rathbun, A., & West, J. (2004). *From kindergarten through third grade: Children's beginning school experiences* (NCES-007). U.S. Department of Education, National Center for Educational Statistics. Washington, DC: U.S. Government Printing Office.

Raudenbush, S. W., Fotiu, R. P., & Cheong, Y. F. (1998). Inequality of access to educational opportunity: A national report card for eighth-grade math. *Educational Evaluation and Policy Analysis, 20* (4), 253–267.

Ream, R. K., & Stanton-Salazar, R. D. (2007). The mobility/social capital dynamic: Understanding Mexican American families and students. In S. J. Paik & H. J. Walberg's (Eds.), *Narrowing the achievement gap: Strategies for educating Latino, Black, and Asian students* (pp. 67–89). New York: Springer Science+Business Media.

Reardon, S. F. (2003). *Sources of inequality: The growth of racial/ethnic and socioeconomic test score gaps in kindergarten and first grade.* Working Paper No. 03005, Population Research Institute, University Park, PA, Pennsylvania State University.

Reeves, J. K. (1982). *Loose-coupling and elementary school social composition: The organizational copout in ghetto education.* Unpublished manuscript.

Reichman, N. (2005). Low birth weight and school readiness. *The Future of Children, 15* (1), 91–116.

Reynolds, G. M. (2002). *Identifying and eliminating the achievement gaps and in-school and out-of-school factors that contribute to the gaps.* Naperville, IL: North Central Regional Educational Laboratory.

Richardson, V. (1998). Professional development in the instruction of reading. In J. Osborn & F. Lehr (Eds.), *Literacy for all: Issues in teaching and learning* (pp. 303–318). New York: Guilford Press.

Rock, D. A., & Stenner, A. J. (2005). Assessment issues in the testing of children at school entry. *The Future of Children, 15* (1), 15–34.

Roscigno, V. J. (1998). Race and the reproduction of educational disadvantage. *Social Forces, 76* (3), 1033–1061.

Roscigno, V. J. (1999). The black-white achievement gap, family-school links, and the importance of place. *Sociological Inquiry, 69* (2), 159–186.

Roscigno, V. J. (2000). Family/school inequality and African-American/Hispanic achievement. *Social Problems, 47* (2), 266–290.

Rosenbaum, J. E. (1980). Social implications of educational grouping. In D.C. Berliner (Ed.), *Review of research in education* (Vol. 8) (pp. 361–401). Washington, DC: American Educational Research Association.

Rosenholz, S. J. (1985). Effective schools: Interpreting the evidence. *American Journal of Education, 93* (2), 352–389.

Rosenshine, B. (1983). Teaching functions in instructional programs. *Elementary School Journal, 83* (4), 335–351.

Rothstein, R. (2004). *Class and schools: Using social, economic, and educational reform to close the black-white achievement gap.* Washington, DC: Economic Policy Institute.

Rothstein, R. (2006). *Reforms that could help narrow the achievement gap.* San Francisco: WestEd.

Rothstein, R. (2008, January/February). Leaving "No Child Left Behind" behind. *The American Prospect,* 50–54.

Rouse, C., Brooks-Gunn, J., & McLanahan, S. (2005). Introducing the issue. *The Future of Children, 15* (1), 5–14.

Rowe, K. J. (1995). Factors affecting students' progress in reading: Key findings from a longitudinal study. *Literacy, Teaching and Learning, 1* (2), 57–110.

Rumberger, R. W., & Gandara, P. (2004). Seeking equity in the education of California's English learners. *Teachers College Record, 106* (10), 2032–2056.

Rumberger, R. W., & Palardy, G. J. (2005). Does segregation still matter? The impact of student composition on academic achievement in high school. *Teachers College Record, 107* (9), 1999–2043.

Rutter, M., Maughan, B., Mortimore, P., & Ouston, J. (1979). *Fifteen thousand hours: Secondary schools and their effects on children.* Cambridge, MA: Harvard University Press.

Samuels. S. J. (1981). Characteristics of exemplary reading programs. In J.T. Guthrie (Ed.), *Comprehension and teaching: Research review* (pp. 255–273). Newark, DE: International Reading Association.

Sanders, M., Allen-Jones, G. L., & Abel, Y. (2002). Involving families and communities in the education of children and youth placed at risk. In S. Stringfield & D. Land (Eds.), *Educating at-risk students. 101st yearbook of the National Society for the Study of Education. Part II* (pp. 171–188). Chicago: University of Chicago Press.

Scales, P. C., Roehlkepartain, M. N., Keilsmeier, J. C., & Benson, P. L. (2006). Reducing academic achievement gaps: The role of community service and service-learning. *Journal of Experimental Education, 29* (1), 38–60.

Scarr, S., & Weinberg, R. A. (1976). IQ test performance of black children adopted by white families. *American Psychologist, 31* (10), 726–739.

Scarr, S., & Weinberg, R. A. (1983). The Minnesota adoption studies: Genetic differences and malleability. *Child Development, 54* (2), 260–267.

Schmid, C. L. (2001). Educational achievement, language-minority students, and the new second generation. *Sociology of Education, 74* (0), 71–87.

Schwartz. F. (1981). Supporting or subverting learning: Peer group patterns in four tracked schools. *Anthropology and Education Quarterly, 12* (2), 99–121.

Schwartz, W. (2001). *Closing the achievement gap: Principles for improving the educational success of all students* (No. 169. UDO-UD-01-8). New York: Teachers College, Columbia University. (ERIC Document Reproduction Service No. ED 460 190).

Seiler, G., & Elmesky, R. (2007). The role of communal practices in the generation of capital and emotional energy among urban African American students in science classrooms. *Teachers College Record, 100* (2), 391–419.

Shannon, S. G., & Bylsma, P. (2002, November). *Addressing the achievement gap: A challenge for Washington state educators.* Olympia, WA: Washington Office of the State Superintendent of Public Instruction. (ERIC Document Reproduction Service No. ED 474 392).

Singham, M. (2003). The achievement gap: Myths and reality. *Phi Delta Kappan, 84* (8), 586–591.

Slavin, R. E., & Madden, N. A. (2001). *Reducing the gap: Success for All and the achievement of African-American and Latino students.* Washington, DC: Office of Educational Research and Improvement.

Slavin, R. E., & Madden, N. A. (2006). Reducing the gap: "Success for All" and the achievement of African American students. *The Journal of Negro Education, 75* (3), 389–400.

Slavin, R. E., & Oickle, E. (1981). Effects of cooperative learning teams on student achievement and race relations: Treatment by race interactions. *Sociology of Education, 54* (3), 174–180.

Snow, C. E., Burns, M. S., & Griffin, P. (Eds.). (1998). *Preventing reading difficulties in young children.* Washington, DC: National Academy Press.

Spradlin, T. E., Kirk, R., Walcott, C., Kloosterman, P., Zaman, K., McNabb, S., & Zapf, J. (2005). *Is the achievement gap in Indiana narrowing? Special report.* Bloomington, IN: Center for Evaluation and Education Policy.

Steele, C. M. (1992). Race and the schooling of black Americans. *Atlantic Monthly, 269* (4), 68–78.

Steele, C. M. (1997). A threat in the air: How stereotypes shape the intellectual identities and performances of women and African Americans. *American Psychologist, 52* (6), 613–629.

Steele, C. M., & Aronson, J. (1995). Stereotype threat and the intellectual test performance of African Americans. *Journal of Personality and Social Psychology, 69* (5), 797–811.

Steele, C. M., & Aronson, J. (1998). Stereotype threat and the test performance of academically successful African Americans. In C. Jencks & M. Phillips (Eds.), *The black-white test score gap* (pp. 401–427). Washington, DC: Brookings Institution Press.

Stevenson, H. W., Chen, C., & Uttal, D. H. (1990). Beliefs and achievement: A study of black, white, and Hispanic children. *Child Development, 61* (2), 508–523.

Stiefel, L., Schwartz, A. E., & Ellen, I. G. (2006). Disentangling the racial test score gap:Probing the evidence in a large urban school district. *Journal of Policy Analysis and Management, 26* (1), 7–30.

Stigler, J. W., & Hiebert, J. (1999). *The teaching gap: Best ideas from the world's teachers for improving education in the classroom.* New York: Free Press.

Stinson, D. W. (2006). African American male adolescents, schooling (and mathematics): Deficiency, rejection, and achievement. *Review of Educational Research, 76* (4), 477–506.

Strutchens, M. E., & Silver, E. A. (2000). NAEP findings regarding race/ethnicity: Students' performance, school experiences, and attitudes and beliefs. In E. A., Silver & P. A. Kenney (Eds.), *Results from the seventh mathematics assessment of the National Assessment of Educational Progress* (pp. 45–72). Reston, VA: National Council of Teachers of Mathematics.

Symonds, K. W. (2004). *After the test: Closing the achievement gaps with data.* Naperville, IL: Learning Point Associates.

Tate, W. F. (1997). Race-ethnicity, SES, gender, and language proficiency trends in mathematics achievement: An update. *Journal for Research in Mathematics Education, 28* (6), 652–679.

Taylor, B. M., Pearson, P. D., Clark, K. F., & Walpole, S. (1999). *Beating the odds in teaching all children to read.* Ann Arbor: University of Michigan, Center for the improvement of Early Reading Achievement.

Taylor, B. M., & Taxis, H. (n. d.). *Translating characteristics of effective school reading programs into practice.* Handout.

Thernstrom, A., & Thernstrom, S. (2002). Schools that work. In J.E. Chubb & T. Loveless (Eds.), *Bridging the achievement gap* (pp. 131–156). Washington, DC: Brookings Institution Press.

Thompson, C. L. (2002). *Research-based review of reports on closing achievement gaps: Report to the education cabinet and the joint legislative oversight committee.* Chapel Hill: North Carolina Education Research Council.

Thompson, C. L., & O'Quinn, S. D., III. (2001). *Eliminating the black-white achievement gap: A summary of research.* Chapel Hill, NC: North Carolina Education Research Council. (ERIC Document Reproduction Service No. ED 457 250).

Toenjes, L. A., Dworkin, A. G., Lorence, J., & Hill, A. N. (2002). High-stakes testing, accountability, and student achievement in Texas and Houston. In J. E. Chubb & T. Loveless (Eds.), *Bridging the achievement gap* (pp. 109–130). Washington, DC: Brookings Institution Press.

Trueba, H. T. (1983). Adjustment problems of Mexican and Mexican-American students: An anthropological study. *Learning Disability Quarterly, 6* (4), 395–404.

Turley, R. N. L. (2003). When do neighborhoods matter: The role of race and neighborhood peers. *Social Science Research, 32* (1), 61–79.

Uhlenberg, J., & Brown, K. M. (2002). Racial gap in teachers' perceptions of the achievement gap. *Education and Urban Society, 34* (4), 493–530.

U.S. Commission on Civil Rights (2004). Closing the achievement gap: The impact of standards-based education reform on student performance. (Draft report for commissioners' review). Author.

U.S. Department of Education, Institute of Education Sciences (n.d.) *The condition of education: Student effort and educational progress, 1971 through 2007.* Retrieved from http://nces.ed.gov/programs/coe/2008/section3/table.asp?tableID=907

U.S. Department of Education, National Center for Education Statistics (2001a). *Educational achievement and black-white inequality,* NCES 2001–061, by Jonathan Jacobson, Cara Olsen, Jennifer King Rice, Stephen Sweetland, & John Ralph. Washington, DC: U.S. Government Printing Office.

U.S. Department of Education, National Center for Education Statistics (2001b). *Outcomes of learning: Results from the 2000 Program for International Student Assessment of 15-Year-Olds in Reading, Mathematics, and Science Literacy,* NCES 2002–115, by Mariann Lemke, Christopher Calsyn, Laura Lippman, Leslie Jocelyn, David Kastberg, Yan Yun Liu, Stephen Roey, Trevor Williams, Thea Kruger, and Ghedam Bairu. Washington, DC: U.S. Government Printing Office.

U.S. Department of Education, Institute of Education Sciences, National Center for Education Statistics (2009a). *Long-term trend (LLT) National Assessment of Educational Progress (NAEP) data explorer* [data file]. Available from http://nces.ed.gov/nationsreportcard/lttdata/.

U.S. Department of Education, National Center for Education Statistics (2009b). *Main National Assessment of Educational Progress (NAEP) data explorer* [data file]. Available from http://nces.ed.gov/nationsreportcard/naepdata/dataset.aspx.

Velez, W. (1989). High school attrition among Hispanic and non-Hispanic white youths. *Sociology of Education, 62* (2), 119–133.

Villegas, A. M., & Lucas, T. (2002). *Educating culturally responsive teachers: A coherent approach.* Albany: State University of New York Press.

Wayne, A. J., & Youngs, P. (2003). Teacher characteristics and student achievement gains: A review. *Review of Educational Research, 73* (1), 89–122.

Waxman, H. C., Padron, Y. N., & Garcia, A. (2007). Educational issues and effective practices for Hispanic students. In S. J. Paik & H. J. Walberg (Eds.), *Narrowing the achievement gap: Strategies for educating Latino, Black, and Asian students* (pp. 131–151). New York: Springer Science+Business Media.

Weinstein, R. (1976). Reading group membership in first-grade: Teacher behaviors and pupil experience over time. *Journal of Educational Psychology, 68* (1), 103–116.

Weis, L. (n.d.). *Issues in education: Schooling and the reproduction of class and gender inequalities* (Occasional paper no. 10). Buffalo: State University of New York, Buffalo, Department of Educational Organization.

Wenglinsky, H. (1997). How money matters: The effect of school district spending on academic achievement. *Sociology of Education, 70* (3), 221–237.

Wenglinsky, H. (1998). Finance equalization and within-school equity: The relationship between education spending and the social distribution of achievement. *Educational Evaluation and Policy Analysis, 20* (4), 269–283.

Williams, D. T. (2003, spring). Closing the achievement gap: Rural schools. *CSR connection.* Washington, DC: National Clearinghouse for Comprehensive School Reform.

Williamson, S. (2005, March). *RAC Northwest: For educational needs assessment: A report to the U.S. Department of Education on educational challenges and technical assistance needs for the Northwest region.* Northwest Regional Advisory Committee.

Wilson, W. J. (1998). The role of the environment in the black-white test score gap. In C. Jencks & M. Phillips (Eds.), *The black-white test score gap* (pp. 501–510). Washington, DC: Brookings Institution Press.

Wraga, W. G. (1994). *Democracy's high school: The comprehensive high school and educational reform in the United States.* Lanham, MD: University Press of America.

Zill, N., & West, J. (2001). *Entering kindergarten: Findings from the condition of education, 2000.* Washington, DC: National Center for Educational Statistics, U.S. Department of Education.

Zimmer, R., & Buddin, R. (2005). *Charter school performance in urban districts: Are they closing the achievement gap?* Working Paper (WR-282-EDU). Santa Monica, CA: RAND.

Index

Absolute improvement, 16, 17 (figure)
Academic expectations:
  parents, 116–117
  teachers, 161–164, 176
Achievement equity, 10, 14, 15 (figure), 16, 18
Achievement gap:
  absolute improvement, 16, 17 (figure)
  at-risk students, 18–19
  cautionary guidelines, 10–21
  curriculum impact, 164–177
  data comprehension, 11–12
  data interpretation, 12–17
  defined, 3–49–10
  economic causation, 8–9
  family structural characteristics,
    101, 102, 103–104
  genetic differences, 131–133
  home environment impact, 105–121
  individual costs, 5–6
  intervention outcomes, 20–21
  learning measures, 14–16
  problem importance, 5–9
  racism impact, 127–131
  reduction limitations, 17–20
  reduction strategies, 19–20
  relative improvement, 16, 17 (figure)
  research literature, 77–82
  school composition impact, 198–203, 256–260
  school culture impact, 185–189
  school readiness impact, 136–140
  school structure/support, 189–203
  social causation, 8–9
  social class impact, 87–91, 94–98
  social costs, 7–8
  subgroup differences, 13–14, 19
  summer school impact, 140–144
  teacher qualifications, 152–158
  teaching practices, 159–164

Achievement gap strategies, 205–208
  educational context, 207
  environmental context, 207
  possibility for, 206–207
  task complexity, 207–208
  See also School reforms ; Socioeconomic reforms
Achievement level, 10, 14–15, 16
ACT college exam, 51–52
  African Americans, 54–55
  Hispanics, 54–55
Advanced Placement Program (AP):
  African Americans, 49–51, 52 (figure), 171–172
  Calculus AB exam, 49, 50 (figure), 51
  Calculus BC exam, 49, 50 (figure), 51
  English Language exam, 49, 51
  English Literature exam, 49, 51, 52 (figure)
  Hispanics, 49–51, 52 (figure)
African Americans:
  ACT college exam, 54–55
  Advanced Placement Program (AP), 49–51,
    52 (figure), 171–172
  college advanced degrees, 64–67
  college completion, 63, 64 (figure), 74
  college entrance exams, 51–55
  college matriculation, 61–63
  collegiate measures, 61–67, 74
  community characteristics, 124–127
  discrimination, 128–131, 172–173
  elementary school, 68–70
  family composition, 103
  family size, 101–102
  gang activity, 184
  genetic differences, 131–133
  grade-level assessment, 67–74
  grade point average, 56
  health conditions, 119–121
  high school completion rates, 56–57
  high school dropout rates, 58–60, 61 (figure)

home resources, 107–108
instructional reforms, 238–252
international assessments, 48–49
learning measures, 15–16
maternal employment, 102
mobility, 104
national assessments, 14, 24, 25–45
oppositional culture, 130–131, 187–189
parental education, 89–91
parental occupation, 89
parenting practices, 111–114
poverty dimensions, 93–95
poverty rate, 92–93
qualified teachers, 152–158
racial segregation, 198–203, 252–260
racism, 127–131
residence, 104
SAT college exam, 51–54, 74
school-age population, 9
school composition, 198–203, 252–260
school culture, 180–189
school culture reforms, 252–260
school readiness, 136–139
school structure/support, 189–190, 194, 198–203
school structure/support reforms, 266–269
state assessments, 45–48
subgroup differences, 13–14, 19
summer school, 140–141
teaching practices, 159–164
teen motherhood, 102
tracking impact, 165–173, 247–251
Alaska, 46
Asian Americans, 13–14
Assessments:
    absolute improvement, 16, 17 (figure)
    achievement equity, 10, 14, 15 (figure), 16, 18
    achievement gap trends, 23–25
    achievement level, 10, 14–15, 16
    Advanced Placement Program (AP), 49–51,
        52 (figure)
    college entrance exams, 51–55
    collegiate measures, 61–67, 74
    combining assessments, 45
    data comprehension, 11–12
    data interpretation, 12–17, 251–252
    elementary school, 68–70
    focus limitations, 18
    grade levels, 67–74
    grade point average, 56
    grade retention rates, 56
    high school, 71–74
    high school completion rates, 56–57
    high school dropout rates, 58–60, 61 (figure)

instructional reforms, 251–252
international level, 48–49
learning measures, 14–16
middle school, 70–71
national level, 25–45
postsecondary education, 74
preK education, 68
relative improvement, 16, 17 (figure)
standardized test scores, 9–10, 12, 18
state level, 45–48
subgroup differences, 13–14, 19
value-added learning, 10, 14, 15, 16
Asthma, 120
At-risk students, 18–19
Authoritarian parenting, 109
Authoritative parenting, 109

Bachelor's degree (BA), 64 (figure)

Calculus AB exam (AP), 49, 50 (figure), 51
Calculus BC exam (AP), 49, 50 (figure), 51
California, 70
California High School Exit Exam (CAHSEE), 47, 73
California Standards Test (CST), 47
Class size, 193–194
    reduction strategies, 266–269
College advanced degrees:
    African Americans, 64–67
    doctoral degree, 66 (figure), 67
    graduate enrollment, 64, 65 (figure)
    Hispanics, 64–67
    master's degree, 64, 66 (figure)
    professional enrollment, 64, 65 (figure)
College completion:
    African Americans, 63, 64 (figure), 74
    Hispanics, 63, 64 (figure), 74
College entrance exams:
    ACT, 51–52, 54–55
    African Americans, 51–55
    Hispanics, 51–55
    SAT, 51–54
College matriculation:
    African Americans, 61–63
    Hispanics, 62–63
    socioeconomic status (SES), 63
Community characteristics:
    achievement gap impact, 125–127
    African Americans, 124–127
    collective socialization, 125, 126
    defined, 124
    peer influences, 125–126
    resources, 115, 125
    socioeconomic status (SES), 124–127

Crime, 184–185
Culture:
 discontinuity of, 180, 181, 186
 disidentification, 187–189
 disjuncture, 180
 incompatibilities, 180
 misunderstanding of, 186
 oppositional, 130–131, 187–189
 synchronization, 180
 See also School culture; School culture reforms
Curriculum:
 achievement gap impact, 164–177
 African Americans, 165–173
 gifted programs, 170–171
 instructional reforms, 247–251
 instructional treatment differentials, 173–177
 learning opportunities, 168–173
 social class impact, 165–173
 tracking, 165–177, 247–251

Data:
 comprehension of, 11–12
 instructional reforms, 251–252
 interpretation of, 12–17, 251–252
Disciplinary practices:
 parents, 111–112
 school culture, 183–185
District size, 193–194
Doctoral degree, 66 (figure), 67

Early Childhood Longitudinal Study, Kindergarten
  Class of 1998–99 (ECLS-K), 14, 43–44, 68–69
 African Americans, 14, 43–44, 68–69
 Hispanics, 43–44, 68–69
 math assessment, 44, 68–69
 reading assessment, 44, 68–69
 science assessment, 44
 socioeconomic status (SES), 44
Earnings. *See* Income
Elementary and Secondary Education Act (ESEA)
  (2001), 8–9
Elementary school assessments, 68–70
Employment:
 job training programs, 213
 maternal employment, 102
 opportunities, 6
 parental occupation, 89, 213, 214
 policies, 214
 See also Income
English Language exam (AP), 49, 51
English Literature exam (AP), 49, 51, 52 (figure)
Equality of Educational Opportunity (EEO), 45
Extended-day programs, 227

Family composition, 102–104, 111, 201
Family home environment, 104–121
 achievement gap impact, 105–121
 community resources, 115, 125
 defined, 101
 environmental stimulation, 110–114
 health conditions, 118–121
 home resources, 107–108
 language acquisition, 113–114
 nurturance, 111
 parenting practices, 108–121, 216–217
 physical environment, 111
 reading to children, 112–113
 schooling management, 115–118, 216–217
 socioeconomic status (SES), 105–121
 time management, 112, 117
Family size, 101–102
Family structural characteristics, 101–104
 achievement gap impact, 101, 102, 103–104
 composition, 102–104
 defined, 100
 maternal employment, 102
 mobility, 104, 196–198
 residence, 104
 size, 101–102
 socioeconomic status (SES), 101–102, 103–104
 teen motherhood, 102
Florida, 47
Full-day kindergarten, 224–225

Gang activity, 184
Genetic differences, 131–133
Gifted programs, 170–171
Grade-level assessment:
 African Americans, 67–74
 elementary school, 68–70
 high school, 71–74
 Hispanics, 67–74
 middle school, 70–71
 postsecondary education, 74
 preK education, 68
 socioeconomic status (SES), 69–70, 71
Grade point average, 56
Grade retention rates, 56

Head Start, 68, 222
Health care:
 immunizations, 229
 services, 228–229
Health conditions:
 African Americans, 119–121
 low birth weight (LBW), 119, 229
 socioeconomic status (SES), 119–121

Health insurance, 228
High School and Beyond (HSB), 45
High school assessments, 71–74
High school completion rates:
 African Americans, 56–57
 Hispanics, 56–57
 tracking impact, 167
High school dropout rates:
 African Americans, 58–60, 61 (figure)
 event rate, 59, 60, 61 (figure)
 Hispanics, 58–60, 61 (figure)
 socioeconomic status (SES), 59–60, 61 (figure)
 status rate, 58, 60 (figure)
Hispanics:
 ACT college exam, 54–55
 Advanced Placement Program (AP), 49–51,
  52 (figure)
 college advanced degrees, 64–67
 college completion, 63, 64 (figure), 74
 college entrance exams, 51–55
 college matriculation, 62–63
 collegiate measures, 61–67, 74
 grade-level assessment, 67–74
 high school completion rates, 56–57
 high school dropout rates, 58–60, 61 (figure)
 international assessments, 48–49
 national assessments, 24, 25–45
 reading to children, 112–113
 SAT college exam, 51–54, 74
 school-age population, 9
 state assessments, 45–48
 subgroup differences, 13–14, 19
Home environment. *See* Family home environment
Home resources, 107–108
Housing policy, 229

Idaho, 46
Illinois, 69–70, 191
Illinois Standards Achievement Test (ISAT), 46, 48
Immunizations, 229
Income, 6, 91–97
Income-transfer strategies, 211, 212–214
Indiana, 48, 70
Indiana Statewide Testing for Educational Progress-
 Plus (ISTEP+), 46
Indifferent parenting, 109
Indulgent parenting, 109
Instructional program, 147–151
 curriculum, 164–177
 teacher qualifications, 152–158
 teaching practices, 159–164
Instructional reforms:
 additional instructional support, 242–243
 African Americans, 238–252

 curriculum, 247–251
 data assessment, 251–252
 socioeconomic status (SES), 238–252
 summer school, 243
 teacher qualifications, 238–242
 teaching practices, 243–247
Intelligence, 94, 131–133
International assessments:
 African Americans, 48–49
 Hispanics, 48–49
 math, 48, 49
 reading, 48–49
 science, 48, 49

Job training programs, 213

Kentucky, 48
Kindergarten, full-day, 224–225

Language:
 acquisition environment, 113–114
 school culture, 182
Learning measures:
 achievement equity, 10, 14, 15 (figure), 16, 18
 achievement level, 10, 14–15, 16
 value-added learning, 10, 14, 15, 16
Louisiana Graduation Exit Examination, 47
Low birth weight (LBW), 119, 229

Master's degree (MA), 64, 66 (figure)
Maternal employment, 102
Math assessment:
 Early Childhood Longitudinal Study, Kindergarten
  Class of 1998–99 (ECLS-K), 44, 68–69
 international level, 48, 49
 SAT college exam, 53, 54 (figure)
 state level, 46–48
 See also National Assessment of Educational
  Progress (NAEP)
Michigan, 48, 191
Middle class, 88
Middle school assessments, 70–71
Minnesota, 46, 71
Mississippi, 191
Mobility, 104, 196–198
Montana, 46

National Assessment of Educational Progress
 (NAEP), 14, 24, 25–43, 52
 African Americans, 25–43, 70, 72–73
 Hispanics, 25–43, 70, 72
 long-term math gap (age 9), 26, 27 (table), 33, 34
 long-term math gap (age 13), 26, 28 (table), 34
 long-term math gap (age 17), 26, 29 (table), 33, 34

long-term math trends (age 9), 26, 27 (figure), 33
long-term math trends (age 13), 26, 28 (figure)
long-term math trends (age 17), 26, 29 (figure), 33
long-term reading gap (age 9), 26, 30 (table), 33, 34
long-term reading gap (age 13), 26, 31 (table), 34
long-term reading gap (age 17), 26, 32 (table), 33, 34
long-term reading trends (age 9), 26, 30 (figure), 33
long-term reading trends (age 13), 26, 31 (figure)
long-term reading trends (age 17), 26, 32 (figure), 33
long-term trends, 25–34
main assessment, 34–43
main math gap (grade 4), 35, 36 (table), 42, 70
main math gap (grade 8), 35, 37 (table), 42, 70
main math gap (grade 12), 35, 38 (table), 42, 72
main math trends (grade 4), 35, 36 (figure)
main math trends (grade 8), 35, 37 (figure)
main math trends (grade 12), 35, 38 (figure)
main reading gap (grade 4), 35, 39 (table), 42, 70
main reading gap (grade 8), 35, 40 (table), 42, 70
main reading gap (grade 12), 35, 41 (table), 42, 72
main reading trends (grade 4), 35, 39 (figure)
main reading trends (grade 8), 35, 40 (figure)
main reading trends (grade 12), 35, 41 (figure)
science assessment, 35, 42, 70, 73
socioeconomic status (SES), 35, 42–43
state-level assessment, 48
writing assessment, 42
National Center for Education Statistics (NCES), 43, 68–69
National Education Longitudinal Study of 1988 (NELS:88), 44–45
    African Americans, 44–45, 71
    math assessment, 44, 71
    reading assessment, 44–45, 71
    socioeconomic status (SES), 44–45, 71
National Longitudinal Study of the High School Class of 1972 (NLS:72), 45
National Longitudinal Study of Youth (NLSY), 45, 68
New Jersey, 191
New York, 48, 191
No Child Left Behind (NCLB) (2001), 8–9, 46
North Carolina, 171–172
North Carolina Competency Test, 47

Oppositional culture, 130–131, 187–189
Oregon, 46
Organisation for Economic Co-operation and Development (OECD), 48–49
Out-of-school learning experiences. See Extended-day programs; School readiness; Summer school

Parental education, 89–91, 216
Parental occupation, 89, 213, 214
Parenting:
    academic expectations, 116–117
    African Americans, 111–114
    discipline, 111–112
    nurturance, 111
    reading to children, 112–113, 262
    schooling management, 115–118, 216–217
    school involvement, 194–196, 260–263
    school reforms, 260–263
    socioeconomic reforms, 215–217
    socioeconomic status (SES), 108–121
    See also Family home environment; Family structural characteristics
Parenting style, 109
Peer influences:
    community characteristics, 125–126
    oppositional culture, 131
    school composition, 201
    school culture reforms, 256–260
Postsecondary education, 74, 167
Poverty:
    dimensions of, 93–95
    federal level, 88, 93
    rates, 92–93
Prairie State Achievement Examination (PSAE), 46, 47
Pregnancy:
    low birth weight (LBW), 119, 229
    prevention programs, 229
    teen motherhood, 102
Preschool programs, 217–224
    See also School readiness
Program for International Student Assessment (PISA), 48–49

Racial discrimination, 128–131, 172–173
Racial segregation, 198–203, 252–260
Racism, 127–131
    oppositional culture, 130–131, 187–189
Reading assessment:
    Early Childhood Longitudinal Study, Kindergarten Class of 1998–99 (ECLS-K), 44, 68–69
    international level, 48–49
    SAT college exam, 53
    state level, 46–48
    See also National Assessment of Educational Progress (NAEP)
Reading to children, 112–113, 262
Relative improvement, 16, 17 (figure)
Residence, 104

Resources:
    community, 115, 125
    home environment, 107–108
    school funding, 190–193

SAT college exam:
    African Americans, 51–54, 74
    Hispanics, 51–54, 74
    math assessment, 53, 54 (figure)
    reading assessment, 53
    socioeconomic status (SES), 54
School composition, 198–203, 252–260
School culture:
    achievement gap impact, 185–189
    African Americans, 180–189
    caring environment, 185
    discipline, 183–185
    misplaced culture, 180–183
    nonsupportive learning environment, 183–185
    safety, 184–185
    social organization system, 181–182
    socioeconomic status (SES), 180–185
School culture reforms:
    achievement ethic, 252–253
    African Americans, 252–260
    high personalization climate, 253–256
    school composition, 256–260
School funding, 190–193
Schooling management, 115–118, 217–217
School readiness:
    achievement gap impact, 136–140
    African Americans, 136–139
    dimensions, 137–139
    importance, 140
    pathways, 139
    preschool programs, 217–224
    socioeconomic status (SES), 136–139, 217–224
School reforms:
    instructional program, 238–252
    rules of engagement, 233–237
    school culture, 252–260
    school structure/support, 260–269
    See also Socioeconomic reforms
School safety, 184–185
School size, 193–194
School structure/support:
    achievement gap, 189–203
    African Americans, 189–190, 194, 198–203
    class size, 193–194
    district size, 193–194
    family mobility, 196–198
    financial resources, 190–193
    parental involvement, 194–196

school composition, 198–203
school size, 193–194
socioeconomic status (SES), 189–203
School structure/support reforms, 260–269
    African Americans, 266–269
    class size reduction, 266–269
    parental involvement, 260–263
    professional development, 263–266
    socioeconomic status (SES), 266–269
Science assessment:
    Early Childhood Longitudinal Study, Kindergarten
        Class of 1998–99 (ECLS-K), 44
    international level, 48, 49
    National Assessment of Educational Progress
        (NAEP), 35, 42, 70, 73
Service-delivery strategies, 211, 214–229
Single-parent families, 102–104, 111, 201
Social class, 87, 88
Social organization system, 181–182
Socioeconomic reforms:
    employment policies, 214
    extended-day programs, 227
    full-day kindergarten, 224–225
    health care policy, 228–229
    housing policy, 229
    income-transfer strategies, 211, 212–214
    job training programs, 213
    parenting programs, 215–217
    preschool programs, 217–224
    service-delivery strategies, 211, 214–229
    summer school, 225–226
    taxation policy, 213–214
    welfare programs, 213
    See also School reforms
Socioeconomic status (SES):
    achievement gap impact, 87–91, 94–98
    college matriculation, 63
    community characteristics, 124–127
    defined, 87–88
    Early Childhood Longitudinal Study, Kindergarten
        Class of 1998–99 (ECLS-K), 44
    educational outcomes, 95–96
    environmental stimulation, 110–114
    family composition, 102, 103–104
    family mobility, 104, 196–198
    family residence, 104
    family size, 101–102
    family structure, 101–102, 103–104
    grade-level assessment, 69–70, 71
    grade retention rates, 54
    high school dropout rates, 59–60, 61 (figure)
    home environment impact, 105–121
    home resources, 107–108

income, 91–97
instructional reforms, 238–252
maternal employment, 102
middle class, 88
National Assessment of Educational Progress
     (NAEP), 35, 42–43
parental education, 89–91, 216
parental occupation, 89, 213, 214
parenting practices, 108–121, 216–217
poverty dimensions, 93–95
poverty level, 88, 93
poverty rates, 92–93
racial intersection, 98
SAT college exam, 54
school composition, 198–203, 256–260
school culture, 180–185
school readiness, 136–139, 217–224
school structure/support, 189–203
school structure/support reforms, 266–269
social class, 87, 88
state-level assessments, 47–48
summer school attendance, 140–144
teacher qualifications, 152–158
teaching practices, 159–164
teen motherhood, 102
tracking impact, 165–173, 247–251
wealth, 97–98
working class, 88
Standardized test scores:
     assessments, 9–10, 12, 18
     criterion-referenced, 9
     norm-referenced, 9
State-level assessments:
     African Americans, 45–48
     Hispanics, 45–48
     math, 46–48
     reading, 46–48
     socioeconomic status (SES), 47–48
     writing, 46
Stereotype threat, 186–187
Substance abuse, 229
Summer school:
     achievement gap impact, 140–144
     African Americans, 140–141

instructional reforms, 243
socioeconomic reforms, 225–226
socioeconomic status (SES), 140–144

Taxation policy, 213–214
Teacher qualifications:
     achievement gap impact, 152–158
     experience, 155–157
     licensure/certification, 155
     low-income schools, 152–158
     minority schools, 152–158
     performance measures, 157–158
     preparation, 153–155
     professional development, 263–266
     school reforms, 238–242, 263–266
Teaching practices:
     achievement gap impact, 159–164
     expectations, 161–164, 176
     instructional design, 159–160, 163–164
     instructional reforms, 243–247
     learning context, 160–161
     low-income schools, 159–164
     minority schools, 159–164
     passive instruction, 159–160
     See also Curriculum
Teen motherhood, 102
Tennessee Value-Added Assessment
     System (TVAAS), 238
Texas Assessment of Academic Skills (TAAS), 47
Time management, 112, 117
Tracking, 165–177
     instructional reforms, 247–251

Value-added learning, 10, 14, 15, 16

Washington Assessment of Student Learning
     (WASL), 46
Wealth, 97–98
Welfare programs, 213
West Virginia, 48
Working class, 88
Writing assessment:
     national level, 42
     state level, 46

CORWIN
A SAGE Company

The Corwin logo—a raven striding across an open book—represents the union of courage and learning. Corwin is committed to improving education for all learners by publishing books and other professional development resources for those serving the field of PreK–12 education. By providing practical, hands-on materials, Corwin continues to carry out the promise of its motto: **"Helping Educators Do Their Work Better."**